LOCAL AREA NETWORKS

SECOND EDITION

Gerd Keiser

PhotonicsComm Solutions, Inc.

Boston   Burr Ridge, IL   Dubuque, IA   Madison, WI   New York   San Francisco   St. Louis
Bangkok   Bogotá   Caracas   Kuala Lumpur   Lisbon   London   Madrid   Mexico City
Milan   Montreal   New Delhi   Santiago   Seoul   Singapore   Sydney   Taipei   Toronto

McGraw-Hill Higher Education

*A Division of The **McGraw-Hill** Companies*

LOCAL AREA NETWORKS, SECOND EDITION

Published by McGraw-Hill, a business unit of The McGraw-Hill Companies, Inc., 1221 Avenue of the Americas, New York, NY 10020. Copyright © 2002, 1999 (custom product), 1989 by The McGraw-Hill Companies, Inc. All rights reserved. No part of this publication may be reproduced or distributed in any form or by any means, or stored in a database or retrieval system, without the prior written consent of The McGraw-Hill Companies, Inc., including, but not limited to, in any network or other electronic storage or transmission, or broadcast for distance learning.

Some ancillaries, including electronic and print components, may not be available to customers outside the United States.

This book is printed on acid-free paper.

International   1 2 3 4 5 6 7 8 9 0 QPF/QPF 0 9 8 7 6 5 4 3 2 1
Domestic   1 2 3 4 5 6 7 8 9 0 QPF/QPF 0 9 8 7 6 5 4 3 2 1

ISBN 0–07–239343–2
ISBN 0–07–112238–9 (ISE)

General manager: *Thomas E. Casson*
Publisher: *Elizabeth A. Jones*
Sponsoring editor: *Catherine Fields Shultz*
Developmental editor: *Michelle L. Flomenhoft*
Executive marketing manager: *John Wannemacher*
Project manager: *Jane Mohr*
Senior production supervisor: *Sandy Ludovissy*
Designer: *K. Wayne Harms*
Cover/interior designer: *Rokusek Design*
Cover images: *Rokusek Design, Inc., and PhotoDisc (Vol. 4 Science and Tech.)* The wires and tower ghosted in are from PhotoDisc. The remaining photos, artwork, and manipulation are Rokusek Design.
Senior supplement producer: *Tammy Juran*
Media technology senior producer: *Phillip Meek*
Composition and Art: *Techsetters, Inc.*
Typeface: *10/12 Times Roman*
Printer: *Quebecor World Fairfield, PA*

Library of Congress Cataloging-in-Publication Data

Keiser, Gerd.
    Local area networks/Gerd E. Keiser.—2nd ed.
        p.   cm.
    ISBN 0–07–239343–2 — ISBN 0–07–112238–9 (ISE)
    1. Local area networks (Computer networks). I. Title.

TK5105.7 .K39   2002   2001042752
004.6′8—dc21   CIP

INTERNATIONAL EDITION ISBN 0–07–112238–9
Copyright ©2002. Exclusive rights by The McGraw-Hill Companies, Inc., for manufacture and export. This book cannot be re-exported from the country to which it is sold by McGraw-Hill. The International Edition is not available in North America.

www.mhhe.com

TO CHING-YUN AND NISHLA

ABOUT THE AUTHOR

Gerd Keiser is the founder and president of PhotonicsComm Solutions, Inc., a firm specializing in consulting and education for the optical communications industry. The web address of the firm is http://www.photonicscomm.com. Previously his experience has included 25 years at Honeywell, GTE, and General Dynamics in research, development, and application of optical networking technology and digital switch development for telecommunication applications.

Dr. Keiser has served as an Adjunct Professor of Electrical Engineering at Northeastern University and Tufts University, has been an Industrial Advisor to the Wentworth Institute of Technology, and is currently an Associate Editor of the technical journal *Optical Fiber Technology*. He is a Fellow of the IEEE and is also the author of the book *Optical Fiber Communications,* published by McGraw-Hill.

Dr. Keiser received his B.A. and M.S. degrees in mathematics and physics from the University of Wisconsin in Milwaukee and a Ph.D. degree in solid-state physics from Northeastern University in Boston.

CONTENTS

PREFACE

Local area networks (LANs) originated in the 1970s from the idea to interconnect relatively inexpensive but powerful desktop workstations since they provided low-cost computing capabilities. The basic drive for developing LANs was to link these computers with each other and with more expensive resources, such as high-quality printers, disk storage systems, central files, and databases. Today LANs are playing a major role in our lives both at work and at home. They have found applications in every conceivable area where humans work and interact, including businesses, educational institutes, research organizations, medical facilities, government buildings, warehouses, and stock exchanges. In addition, wireless LANs are used in homes, office areas, stores, restaurants, and other environments for voice and data transfer among computing and communication devices, such as personal computers, cordless telephones, a personal digital assistant, computer games, and other portable devices.

Developers proposed a variety of technologies over the years, but only several contenders managed to gain support. For example, an evolution of Ethernet, which was the first LAN concept, has become a dominant LAN architecture. It not only offers reliable service, but, owing to its widespread installations, users feel comfortable with its new technology extensions to higher speeds and greater versatility. Ethernet evolved significantly from the time of its inception. Having started as a contention-based system operating at 10 Mbps with stiff coaxial cable, Ethernet now offers several options ranging from a 10-Mbps hub-based architecture to a 10-Gbps switched technology using high-performance twisted-pair wires and optical fiber cables. In addition, it is migrating from pure LAN use to transport of information within a metropolitan area network (MAN).

This book presents the fundamental concepts needed to understand, design, and implement a local area network. The sequence of topics systematically takes the reader from the underlying theory of LAN architectures, through descriptions of fundamental LAN types and applications, to the internetworking of a LAN with other networks, and finally to the management and security issues of LANs. Key features of the text for accomplishing this are:

- A discussion of how standard network-architecture models and their associated protocols apply to LAN concepts.
- A basic overview of communication theory techniques that are useful for understanding the principles and operations of different categories of LANs.

xvii

- Detailed discussions of LAN technologies, including Ethernet, token rings, ATM-based LANs, wireless LANs, storage area networks, personal area networks, and LAN offerings for use in homes and in small offices.
- A presentation of internetworking concepts that effectively create a single large, loosely coupled network from many different local, metropolitan, and wide area networks, thereby allowing LAN users to gain access to resources on other networks.
- Descriptions of network management services, which use a variety of hardware and software tools, applications, and devices to assist human network managers in monitoring and maintaining LANs in the areas of performance, configuration, accounting, fault, and security management.
- An overview of network security issues. The topics covered include the formulation of security policies, the application of data encryption techniques, the use of firewalls to protect LANs from external intrusions, the implementation of access control methods, the application of IP security, and the concepts of virtual private networks (VPNs).
- A Windows-based CD-ROM from VPIsystems, Inc packaged with the book contains a network capacity planning tool, which can help to design networks of any size.

Local Area Networks, second edition, provides the basic material for an introductory senior-level or graduate course in the understanding, design, and implementation of local area networks and their interaction with other networks. It also will serve well as a working reference for practicing engineers dealing with LAN applications. The background required to study this book is that of typical senior-level engineering students. To help those readers with little background in data communications, Chapter 3 gives an introductory overview of basic communication theory concepts and their applications to LANs. Since modern networking makes extensive use of acronyms, a list of the most common ones and their meanings is given at the end of the book. To assist readers in learning the material and in applying it to practical designs, a selection of examples is given throughout the book. In addition, a collection of 211 homework problems is included to help test the reader's comprehension of the material covered and to extend and elucidate the text.

In preparing this book and its previous edition, a great deal of thanks go to the manuscript reviewers whose comments enhanced and clarified the content and organization of the book. They include Robert J. Borns, Purdue University; Earl T. Farley, Texas Tech University; Frank Whetten, Embry Riddle University; Gregory B. Brewster, Depaul University; Gertrude Levine, Fairleigh Dickinson University; Jeffrey Carruthers, Boston University; and Berk Sunar, Worcester Polytechnic University. In addition, I am greatly indebted to the many people with whom I had numerous discussions and who supplied me with various material. Among them are Doug Forster and Jack Kretovics, General Dynamics; Tri Ha, Naval Postgraduate School; Nishla Keiser, MIT; Steve Leiden and Jay Luck, Verizon; Bruce McDonald, Northeastern University; Arnie Michelson, Raytheon; and Kurt Leszek Reiss, Crossbeam Systems. Special thanks go to Kay Iversen, Markus Buchner, Elizabeth Parsons Morgan, and Dirk Seewald from VPIsystems, Inc. for various aspects related to supplying the modeling tool on the CD-ROM. Particularly encouraging for doing the second edition were the many positive comments on the previous edition received from users and adapters at numerous institutions worldwide. This edition especially benefited from the expert guidance of the McGraw-Hill personnel: Sponsoring Editor Catherine Fields Shultz who provided decisive support for various concepts of the book, Developmental Editor Michelle Flomenhoft who was truly wonderful and amazing in providing immediate responses to all my questions and requests, and Project Manager Jane Mohr who saw the book through the publication cycle. As a final personal note, I am grateful to my wife Ching-yun and my daughter Nishla for their patience, help, and encouragement during the time I devoted to writing and revising this book.

Further information on new developments and reference material related to the text can be found on the following McGraw-Hill website for this book: http://www.mhhe.com/engcs/electrical/keiser2.

Gerd Keiser

CHAPTER

1

OVERVIEW OF
LOCAL
AREA
NETWORKS

E ver since ancient times people have continuously devised new techniques for communicating their ideas, needs, and desires to others. Thus many forms of increasingly
sophisticated and, in general, more complex communication systems have appeared over
the years. The basic motivations behind each new system were either to improve the transmission fidelity, to increase the data rate so that more information could be sent, or to
increase the transmission distance between relay stations.

Along with the development of faster and higher-capacity transmission systems,
the past several decades have witnessed a phenomenal growth in the computer industry.
As advances in integrated-circuit technology have allowed computers to become smaller,
less expensive, more powerful, and widely available, people have become increasingly
interested in connecting them together to form networks. Today communication networks
have become an essential worldwide infrastructure, particularly for services such as
e-mail and Internet access.

Networks are traditionally divided into the following three broad categories, as
Fig. 1.1 illustrates:

1. *Local area networks* (LANs) interconnect users in a localized area, such as a room,
   a department, a building, an office or factory complex, or a campus. Here the word
   campus refers to any group of buildings that are within reasonable walking distance
   of each other. For example, it could be the buildings of a research and development
   organization or of a university complex. LANs usually are owned, used, and operated
   by a single organization.

2. *Metropolitan area networks* (MANs) span a larger area than a LAN. This could range
   from interconnections between buildings covering several blocks within a city or

1

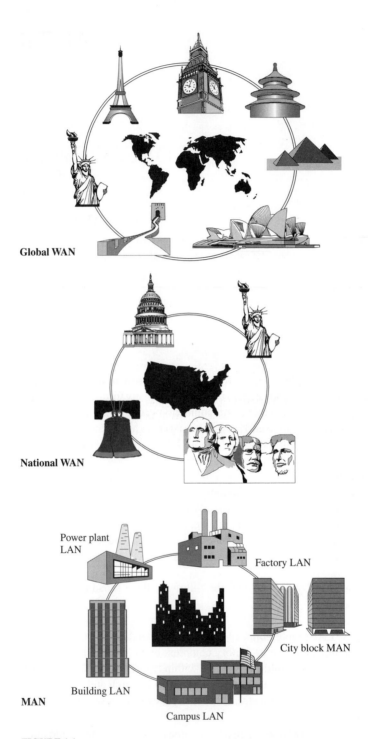

FIGURE 1.1
The three basic categories of networks include local, metropolitan, and wide area networks.

could encompass an entire city and the metropolitan area surrounding it. There is also some means of interconnecting the MAN resources with communication entities located in both LANs and wide area networks. MANs are owned and operated by many organizations.

3. *Wide area networks* (WANs) span a large geographical area. The links can range from connections between switching facilities in neighboring cities to long-haul terrestrial or undersea transmission lines running across a country or between countries. WANs invariably are owned and operated by many transmission service providers.

In this book we will concentrate on LANs since these types of networks play a major role in our lives at both work and home. LANs have found applications in every conceivable area where humans work and interact, including businesses, educational institutes, research organizations, medical facilities, government buildings, warehouses, and stock exchanges. In addition, wireless LANs are used in homes and small offices for voice and data transfer among computing and communication devices, such as personal computers, cordless telephones, a personal digital assistant (PDA), computer games, and other portable devices. Another application of LANs in a home is the interconnection of smart devices that allow users to control and monitor events in consumer-based appliances, home electronics, and home security systems.

LANs arose from the growing implementation of powerful desktop workstations. Since these workstations provide low-cost computing capabilities, they quickly came into widespread use. The basic drive for developing LANs was the desire to interconnect these relatively inexpensive workstations and desktop computers with each other and with more expensive resources, such as high-quality printers, disk storage systems, central files, and databases on a *shared basis.* The goal in these network developments was to provide high-speed, reliable interconnections between localized computing elements with an emphasis on simplicity and the low cost of the transmission links. Since these elements are located in a moderately sized geographical area, the distances range from 1 m (meter) to nominally 1 km (kilometer). Extensions to remote clusters of elements or other LAN segments located several kilometers away also are possible.

In addition to being configured as a shared network, a LAN may be set up as a *switched network*, where a switch replaces a passive central distribution device. As later chapters describe, this increases the capacity and flexibility of a local network since a LAN switch can make intelligent decisions as to where to send a message and can segment user traffic on the LAN.

With the emergence of the Internet and the widespread usage of personal computers both at home and in businesses, the needs arose to interconnect diverse LANs, to provide users on LANs with access to MAN and WAN resources, and to segment large LANs into manageable groups of devices. For example, an organization may have various types of LANs at different locations which need to be linked. Furthermore, a corporate site may have different types of LANs that handle a variety of needs (e.g., engineering, manufacturing, and marketing) or that segregate departmental functions for security reasons (e.g., keeping payroll records or corporate legal issues confidential).

In this chapter Sec. 1.1 defines basic LAN terminology. Next Sec. 1.2 gives a top-level overview of standards activities related to LANs. We then look at how LANs operate in Sec. 1.3, which includes the client/server concept, connection schemes, and transmission methods. This is followed by descriptions of fundamental LAN topologies in Sec. 1.4. To help understand the motivations behind constructing LANs, Sec. 1.5 describes some general applications for these networks. Finally Sec. 1.6 gives an overview of the various chapters in the text, Sec. 1.7 points to further supplementary resource material, and Sec. 1.8 lists the resources available on the website for the book.

1.1 BASIC LAN TERMINOLOGY

A basic item that appears throughout any communications book is the prefix used in metric units for designating parameters such as length, speed, and data rates. Although many of these are well known, a few may be new to some readers. As a handy reference, Table 1.1 lists standard prefixes, their symbols, and their magnitudes, which range in size from 10^{24} to 10^{-24}. As an example, a data rate of 1×10^9 bits per second (bps) = 1 Gbps (gigabits per second). The three highest and lowest designations are not especially common in communication systems (yet!) but are included in Table 1.1 for completeness.

Figure 1.2 shows an example of a shared LAN. Let us first look at some terminology used in describing a typical shared network and its elements.[1-8] In this case all the network devices are attached to a shared transmission medium. This means that a message sent from one device can be received by all the other devices that are attached to the same medium. The end devices that wish to communicate on the LAN may be multipurpose computers, workstations, personal computers, servers, or other equipment, such as printers, fax machines, and data storage elements. The computing devices are generally called *stations*. The points where stations and other devices connect to the

TABLE 1.1
Metric prefixes, their symbols, and their magnitudes

Prefix	Symbol	Magnitude
yotta-	Y	10^{24}
zetta-	Z	10^{21}
exa-	E	10^{18}
peta-	P	10^{15}
tera-	T	10^{12}
giga-	G	10^{9}
mega-	M	10^{6}
kilo-	k	10^{3}
centi-	c	10^{-2}
milli-	m	10^{-3}
micro-	μ	10^{-6}
nano-	n	10^{-9}
pico-	p	10^{-12}
femto-	f	10^{-15}
atto-	a	10^{-18}
zepto-	z	10^{-21}
yocto-	y	10^{-24}

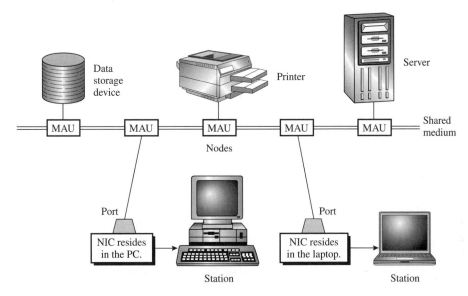

FIGURE 1.2
Example of a shared medium LAN and the terminology used to describe it.

network are referred to as *nodes*. A node can belong to either a media access device on a LAN cable or a switching device. Note that some devices, for example, switches and routers, can have more than one network connection so that they have a number of nodes associated with them. The term *circuit* refers to a point-to-point physical or logical path between two nodes, which can support continuous communications in one or both directions. A collection of nodes joined by transmission links and arranged in some topology constitutes a *communication network*.

At this point we need to note the meaning of the word "server," which can refer to both a network device and a functional role in a peer-oriented communication service, as described in Sec. 1.3.1. As a network device, a *server* provides specific functions to the whole network or to a significant segment of a network. For example, a network commonly has the following servers:

- A *file server*, which is a centralized device having disks that are dedicated to storing files or software programs that users on a network can access.
- A *print server*, which accepts print jobs from computers attached to the network, queues these requests, and then sends them to an attached printer.
- A *mail server*, which interacts with a mail application in network computers to enable users to exchange e-mail messages across both internal and external networks.

The physical attachment point in a station or a switch node is called a *port*. Note that a network device may have more than one port, for example, a switch generally has numerous input and output ports. As shown later, the shared transmission medium also can be reduced to a single-signal concentrating point, with all network devices connected directly to this point. The concentrator simply acts as a repeater since any station connected to this network point will see the transmission from another station.

A section of cable connects a microprocessor-based LAN access controller, or *network access unit* (NAU), in a station with a *media access unit* (MAU). The MAU connects directly to the shared medium so that it can broadcast and receive information over the network cable. The NAU coordinates the transfer of information between the station and the network. It contains the hardware, software, and control information stored on *read-only memory* (ROM) and usually resides on a circuit card called the *network interface card* (NIC). Since the elements attached to a network usually come from several manufacturers, they may not conform to a common data transmission scheme. Thus, in addition to providing media access, another function of the NIC, if necessary, is to transform the data rate and transmission format of the attached device to that of the LAN, as shown in Fig. 1.3. When data arrives for the attached station, the NIC temporarily stores it in an internal buffer while it is converted to match the data rate and format of the attached device. Likewise, data sent out from a station is buffered temporarily in the NIC while it is encoded to match the data transmission characteristics of the LAN. Other functions of the NIC include timing, buffering data from the attached equipment until medium access is achieved, scanning each message on the medium to see if it is destined for its attached device, and monitoring the incoming messages for errors.

As Fig. 1.4 illustrates, one can interconnect two or more LANs or LAN segments at either the physical level or through higher-level communication protocols. As Chap. 2 describes, a *protocol* is a set of rules that governs communication between peer entities on network devices, that is, between the same type of hardware components and/or

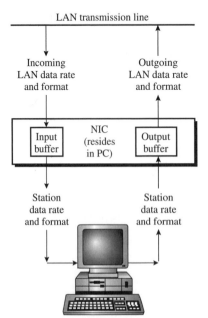

FIGURE 1.3
A NIC can function as a conversion interface if the data rate and protocol differ between a LAN and an attached device.

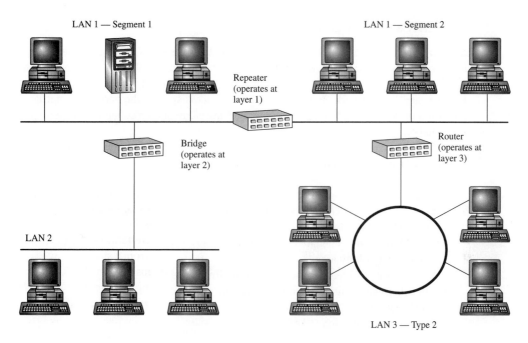

FIGURE 1.4
Interconnections of LANs and LAN segments through layered protocols.

software applications running on each machine. A common way of applying protocols is to partition them into layers, with each layer relying on lower layers to carry out more elementary functions and to offer total transparency to upper layers in regards to the operational details of those functions. Therefore if a networking function operates at layer x, then the associated protocol would define the rules for machine-to-machine communications between the functions at this level. The lowest layer is the physical level, which simply transmits information bits over a physical medium. At this level LAN segments are connected using a device called a *repeater*.

For the next two higher-level communication protocols the interconnecting devices are bridges and routers, respectively. A *bridge* is a relatively inexpensive device that may be used to segment a large LAN into smaller parts that have distinct communities of interest. If each of these segments has its own server, then most of the traffic will stay within a segment. A *router* has capabilities beyond those of a bridge since it operates at a higher protocol level. In addition to segmenting the network into smaller domains, it can limit broadcast traffic, provide firewall protection, and perform intelligent routing of packets. A *firewall* is a device that inspects incoming packets and determines whether or not to let them into the network. Chapter 10 gives further explanations of bridges and routers. Chapter 12 addresses the concepts of using a firewall. In addition, people often apply the word *switch* not only to equipment that performs switching functions, but also to bridges and routers since their original functions may have been enhanced with new additional capabilities.

1.2 LAN STANDARDS

Standards are national or international agreements that specify factors such as equipment installation procedures, test procedures for equipment or physical plant operation, and interface requirements that will allow equipment from different manufacturers to interoperate. For network applications these standards specify the hardware interfaces and software procedures through which networking elements can communicate correctly and reliably.

The key standards organizations promoting standards for telecommunication issues related to LANs include the following:

- The Telecommunication Standardization Sector of the International Telecommunication Union (ITU-T), which is an organization that operates under the auspices of the United Nations.[9]
- The International Standards Organization (ISO), which works mainly in the information technology area.[10]
- The Institute of Electrical and Electronic Engineers (IEEE).[11]
- The American National Standards Institute (ANSI).[12]
- The Electronic Industries Association in conjunction with the Telecommunication Industries Association (EIA/TIA).[13,14]

Among the LAN-related standards that originate from these organizations, the principal ones are as follows:

1. The OSI Reference Model, which recommends a baseline for a network architecture that defines the relationships and interactions between network services and functions through common interfaces and protocols. Chapter 2 describes the details of this model and its modifications for LANs and other networks.
2. Various EIA/TIA procedures for installing and testing LANs.
3. The IEEE-802 committee deals with a variety of LAN standards such as Ethernet, token rings, and wireless LANs.
4. ANSI addresses high-speed LANs such as Fibre Channel.

1.3 HOW LANS OPERATE

Here we look at some concepts related to the operation of LANs. These include the client/server interaction, the formation of data units, connectionless versus connection-oriented services, and message transfer methods.[15–18]

1.3.1 Client/Server Concept

The exchange of information between processes running in two different stations connected through a LAN may be characterized by a *client/server interaction*. The terms *client* and *server* describe the functional roles of the stations in the network, as Fig. 1.5 illustrates. The process that requests access to a file is called the *client,* and the process that supports access to the file is called the *server.* For reading a file the client sends a

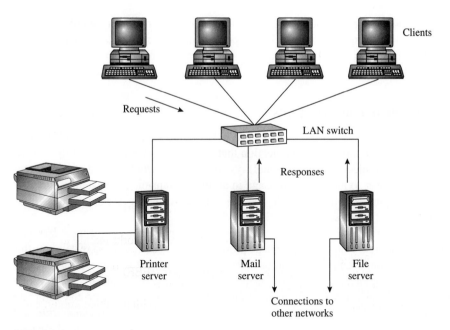

FIGURE 1.5
The networking concept of a client/server interaction.

small *request* message to a server. The server then sends back a *response* to this request, which is a larger message that contains the requested file. When writing a message, a client sends a large message containing data to be written to the server, and the server responds with a small confirmation message to verify that the data has been written to the storage disk.

Clients and servers communicate with each other through an *application program interface* (API) or *middleware*. Examples of middleware include the *Distributed Computing Environment* (DCE) specification established by the Open Software Foundation and the *Object Request Broker* (ORB) created by the Object Management Group.[19] For example, a client communicates with a server through the services of the ORB. The ORB receives a request from a client, finds a server that can satisfy the request, sends the request to the server, and returns the response from the server to the client. The server process typically resides on a computer that differs from the one on which the client process is running. In addition, the server process may not be running at the time of the request, so the ORB needs to initiate it on the other machine. Furthermore, the server process could be on a machine attached to a different LAN. The ORB handles these situations and thus provides client and server independence. If a client can access the ORB, then it is able to interact with any server that can communicate with the ORB. These features offer hardware and software independence between the client and the server.

An example of a client/server process is the interaction between an e-mail user and an e-mail server. The e-mail server functions as a post office for its clients through operations such as supplying mail addresses for a specified user name, distributing mail, interfacing to other e-mail servers, coordinating mail from different e-mail programs, and providing mail agent functions. One type of mail agent is a *vacation agent,* which can collect incoming mail in an electronic folder, reroute mail to another address, or notify senders that the recipient is away and will return on a specific date.

1.3.2 Formation of Data Units

From the standpoint of an interactive session between two or more network users a *message* is a single unit of communication that is sent from one participant to another. For example, in an electronic mail (e-mail) system a message would consist of a document sent from one user to another. A message in an image transmission system could be a fax, a single figure, an image, or a diagram. A critical factor in message transmission is that the recipient must receive the entire message.

A message transmitted over a network usually is represented as a string of *bits,* that is, a series of logical 1s and 0s. To manage properly factors such as message delay, buffer capacity, and congestion control, long messages normally are broken up into shorter data blocks or segments, as Fig. 1.6 illustrates. These data blocks then are sent through a network, such as a LAN, as individual units and are reassembled into the complete original message at the destination station. This process is known as *segmentation and reassembly.* To enable routers or switches in the communication path to direct these data blocks to their destination, a *header* consisting of source and destination address fields plus additional control bits must be added to form a *packet* or a *frame* (depending on the protocol layer), as illustrated in Fig. 1.6 for segment $N - 1$. These *control bits* offer features such as the indication of the beginning and end of a frame (frame delimiting), error detection and correction mechanisms, designation of the priority of a packet, and possible acknowledgment schemes for verifying that a packet arrived at its destination.

1.3.3 Connectionless and Connection-Oriented Services

The process of creating a communication path between two nodes can be characterized as either a connectionless or a connection-oriented service. In a *connection-oriented* operation a single logical network path (called a *virtual circuit*) is established between the two communicating elements for the duration of the connection. The logical path

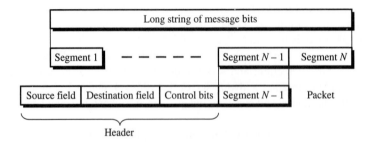

FIGURE 1.6
Segmentation of a long message into smaller manageable length packets and the addition of address and control fields.

is set up first and then information messages are exchanged. This path consists of the concatenation of a series of logical connections that join the two users across the network. Typically network resources are reserved at the time of path establishment in order to ensure the availability of a particular grade of service, such as a guaranteed throughput rate. During the data transfer phase packets are sent sequentially over the path that has been established. This means that the packets always arrive at the destination station in the order in which they were sent. When the information transfer is completed, the connection is terminated.

In a *connectionless* operation the path and its bandwidth are selected dynamically for each packet of an information exchange. Dynamic path selection allows traffic to be routed easily around network failures and congestion points since the paths are selected on a packet-by-packet basis. In addition, dynamic bandwidth allocation allows the network resources to be used more efficiently. When a packet is sent through a series of routers or switches in a connectionless path, each device makes an independent decision for every packet as to what the next hop should be for that packet. Thus different packets may follow different routes between source and destination stations. With a connectionless service, factors such as packet sequencing and data throughput are not guaranteed and the information flow must be able to tolerate some delay.

1.3.4   Message Transfer Methods

From a top-level classification networks can interconnect users by either a broadcast or a switching scheme. A *switched network* uses transmission lines, multiplexing equipment, concentrators, and switches to interconnect users, as illustrated in Fig. 1.7. The network equipment can be connected either directly to the central switch with dedicated lines, through a shared medium concentrator (which allows only one station in its attached

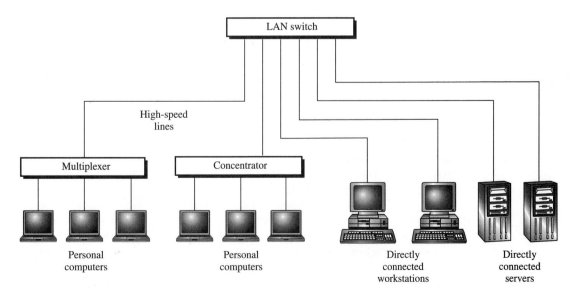

FIGURE 1.7
Example of a switched LAN.

group to communicate with the switch at one time), or via a multiplexer that interleaves the signals from a number of stations onto a single line. To direct packets from a source to a destination, the network needs to use routing tables by which the switches can determine the path between these two stations.

In contrast, *broadcast networks* are much less complex since all information is sent to each station. Thus routing is not necessary in this case. A simple addressing scheme is sufficient to indicate the destination of a given packet. However, since it is a multiple access network, a broadcast network needs some type of *medium access control* (MAC) protocol to coordinate the transmissions among the various network users. Initially LANs were based on a broadcast scheme, owing to the simplicity and low cost of this type of network. In a broadcast method each LAN station has a unique physical address, which is usually burned into a ROM that resides in the NIC.

Despite the success of broadcast LANs, in the mid-1990s it was found that a dramatic surge in bandwidth demand was causing the performance of large shared media broadcast-based LANs to sag. This was alleviated by adding LAN switches into the picture. The individual chapters in this book on various LAN types give more operational and performance details on specific LAN switches. In particular, switched Ethernet and LANs based on ATM switching have become popular, as discussed in Chap. 5 and Chap. 7, respectively.

1.4   LAN TOPOLOGIES

The manner in which nodes are arranged and connected geometrically is known as the *topology* of the network. There are two major classes of LAN topologies: These include the mesh (unconstrained) interconnection and the three basic constrained topologies known as the bus, ring, and star configurations. Each of these methodologies has its own particular advantages and limitations in terms of reliability, expandability, and performance characteristics.

In a *bus topology* all the network nodes are connected to a common transmission medium, as shown in Fig. 1.8a. As a result, only one pair of users on the network can exchange a packet of information at the same time. When a station sends a data packet, it appends an address field to the packet that designates either a unique address of a single destination device, a multicast address sent to a group of stations, or a broadcast made to all stations. The packet then propagates throughout the medium and arrives at each station. To receive messages, each station continuously monitors the medium and copies those messages that contain its address as the packets go by. Since the transmission medium in a bus is time-shared, there must be some type of control mechanism to prevent several stations from transmitting simultaneously. Chapter 4 describes these in detail, and Chap. 5 shows applications for Ethernet LANs.

In a *ring topology* point-to-point links connect consecutive nodes, which are arranged to form a single closed path as shown in Fig. 1.8b. Information in the form of data packets travels around the ring from node to node. The interface at each node is an active transceiver that has the ability to recognize its own address in a data packet in order to accept messages. The interface serves not only as a NAU, but also as an active repeater for forwarding messages that are addressed to other nodes. Chapter 6 gives more details on the operation of ring networks.

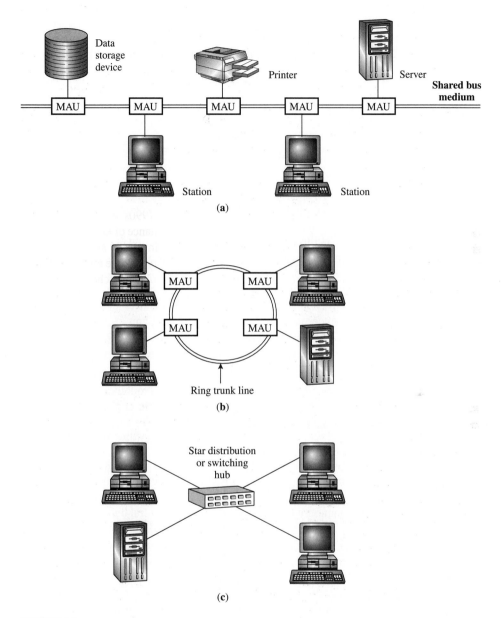

FIGURE 1.8
Illustration of three constrained topology LANs.

In a *star architecture* illustrated in Fig. 1.8c all the nodes are joined at a single point called the *concentrator* or *hub*. Hubs can be active or passive. *Active hubs* retransmit signals sent through them to a specified number of other output lines, whereas a *passive hub* only divides an arriving signal with a power splitter so that it is forwarded simultaneously to all other destinations. An active hub generally is used when it is responsible

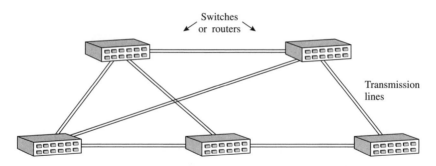

FIGURE 1.9
Illustration of a mesh network having an arbitrary interconnection.

for control of the network. In this case the hub performs all routing of messages between the network nodes. Star networks with an active hub are used mostly when the bulk of the communications is between the hub and outlying nodes. When there is a great deal of traffic between groups of outlying nodes, a heavy switching burden is placed on the central hub if a simple switched star is used. In this case localized switching hubs can be placed at the outlying nodes to reduce traffic to the central hub.

In the early days of LAN applications networks were mainly linear bus configurations with the stations connected to a single cable. This was adequate when the number of stations was small since cable problems were relatively easy to isolate. However, when networks grew much larger, the bus wires started to be run under floors, inside walls, and in ducts or cable trays hidden in a ceiling. Locating a loose connection or a cable break in this scenario became a difficult, time-consuming, and expensive process. To solve this problem, a star-coupled network using wiring centers or hubs started to be deployed since a star is logically equivalent to a bus network.[20,21] Although this requires some additional cabling, the attractive feature of the star network is that all MAUs can be located in the same wiring closet for ease of implementation, management, and maintenance. To increase the flexibility and capacity of a LAN even further, network interconnections now commonly use a LAN switch as the central hub.

In a *mesh network* shown in Fig. 1.9, point-to-point links connect the nodes in an arbitrary fashion that can vary greatly from one implementation to another. Network cost constraints usually determine the connection scheme. Although a mesh topology allows significant configuration flexibility, the associated routing problems are quite complex. Nodes that make routing decisions often must execute many network-related functions. This is not desirable for LANs since it can introduce delay, add unwanted overhead, and lead to higher network costs.

1.5 EXAMPLE APPLICATIONS OF LANS

To get an appreciation of the uses for different types of LANs, this section illustrates some generic applications. These include interconnected computing equipment in an office environment, a high-speed localized backbone network, a wireless LAN, and a specialized LAN called a storage area network. Each of these areas will be discussed in more detail in later chapters.

1.5.1   Office Computer Network

A typical LAN is an office network, which consists of numerous interconnected personal computers (PCs) that are used for functions such as preparing documents, project management, spreadsheet applications, accounting, e-mail exchanges, and Internet access. As Fig. 1.10 shows, such a network must allow access to a central processing computer that can handle more complex or specialized functions, it must provide printing resources, and users must be able to retrieve stored information. By connecting these computers to each other, staff members of a project or a particular department are able to share work and information. In addition, connections to external networks through a communications server allow access to Internet resources and to employees and information resources located at corporate facilities in other geographic locations.

Figure 1.10 shows both broadcast and switched LAN configurations. Each of these is configured as a star network. For the broadcast LANs the passive central hub merely splits arriving signals so that they are redirected to other stations on that LAN. In contrast, the LAN switch performs intelligent routing of arriving packets. Note that the LAN switch shown here has the capability to interface with both a 10-Mbps and a 100-Mbps broadcast LAN.

1.5.2   High-Speed Localized Backbone

To provide a higher degree of network flexibility and to segment a large corporate LAN into a number of independent but yet interconnected LANs, it is often advantageous

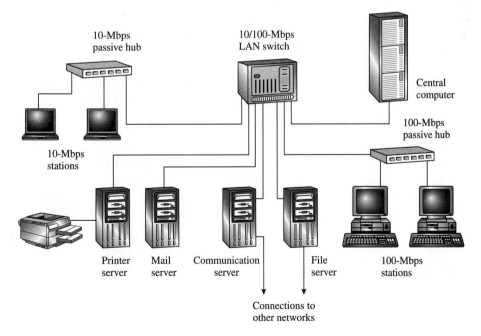

FIGURE 1.10
Typical LAN for an office environment.

to link such individual LANs with a high-capacity LAN. This type of interconnecting network is referred to as a *backbone LAN*. Figure 1.11 illustrates a high-speed LAN backbone consisting of three large-capacity switches connecting various LANs in a local environment. These backbone switches might run at 622 or 1000 Mbps and have 100- or 155-Mbps interfaces to end equipment. Examples of the possible connections to the backbone include high-capacity corporate servers or workstations that have internal high-speed network interface cards, smaller 100- or 155-Mbps access switches to individual LAN segments, or concentrators that interface to a large number of lower-speed devices. In addition, there is an access to WAN services.

1.5.3   Wireless LAN

The rapid increase of Internet usage has created new concepts and devices for mobile communications within a localized area. A *wireless LAN* has the advantage of allowing a great deal of user mobility, but generally with a lower transmission rate than a wired LAN

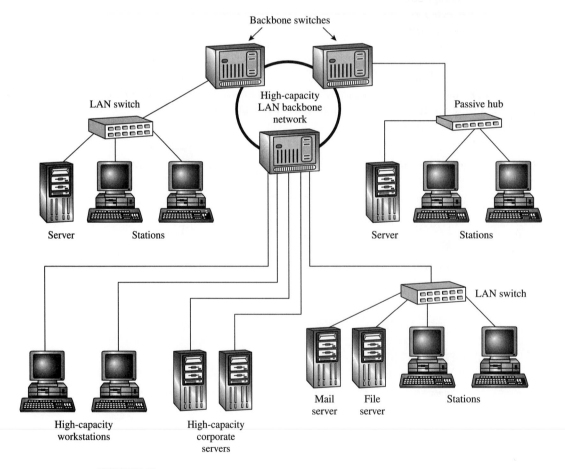

FIGURE 1.11
Example of a backbone LAN.

offers.[22,23] Typical applications of a wireless LAN include inventory control or product retrieval in warehouses, data transfers between workstations in large open manufacturing areas, information exchanges among personnel in office buildings where installing cable upgrades may be difficult, communications among medical staff members in a health care facility, or voice and data transfer among computing and communication devices in a home.

Figure 1.12 shows a simple example of a wireless LAN. Normally there is a wired backbone network that ties together equipment such as workstations, printers, servers, or hubs. Attached to this LAN is a wireless interface device called an *access point* (AP), which acts as a central base station or a bridge between the wireless equipment and the wired network.

1.5.4 Storage Area Network

A *storage area network* is a separate LAN that is dedicated to connecting computing systems to data storage devices.[24] As Fig. 1.13 shows, information-processing equipment that may be connected to a storage area network include computers, workstations, and servers. Connections between this equipment and storage devices or subsystems are made using elements such as LAN switches, hubs, and bridges. The advantage of such a network is that it relieves LAN servers from data storage tasks and provides users with a shared storage facility. In addition to having local storage capabilities, by using link extenders that can provide cable distances of up to nominally 100 km, one can store information safely in remote locations for data backup and recovery purposes in case any type of disaster occurs at the main facility.

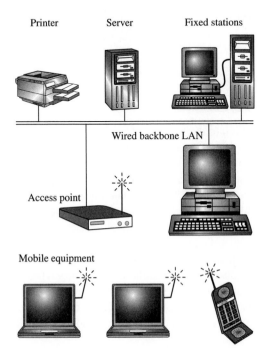

FIGURE 1.12
Simple illustration of a wireless LAN.

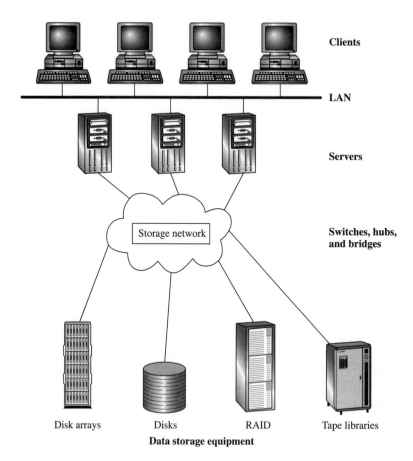

FIGURE 1.13
Illustration of a storage area network.

1.6   OVERVIEW OF THE CHAPTERS

The following chapters present an introduction to the field of LANs. The various topics describe the fundamental concepts needed to design and implement a LAN. The sequence of topics systematically takes the reader from the underlying theory, through descriptions of fundamental LAN types, to the internetworking of a LAN with other networks, and finally to the management and security issues of LANs. Thus the material presented here will provide a broad and firm basis with which to analyze, design, and implement LANs.

In general the equipment that users wish to connect to a LAN consists of many diverse products developed by numerous manufacturers. The difficulty in connecting such a group of heterogeneous machines is that each manufacturer could use different data formats and message exchange conventions. This is particularly true for new types of equipment that are developed. The only solution to achieving effective communications between such equipment is to have vendors abide by a common set of rules or protocols. Chapter 2 addresses this topic in terms of standard network architecture models and their associated protocols.

Chapter 3 gives a basic overview of fundamental data communication concepts. To exchange information between any two elements in a LAN, some type of signal has to be transmitted via a communication channel. This channel could be a wire, radio, microwave, satellite, infrared, or optical fiber link. Each medium has unique performance characteristics associated with it. Regardless of its type the medium degrades the fidelity of the transmitted signal because of both an imperfect response to the signal and the presence of electrical and/or optical noise and interference. This can lead to misinterpretations of the signal at the receiving end. To help readers understand the various factors that affect the physical transfer of information-bearing signals, Chap. 3 examines how communication theory applies to the physical and data link layers for LAN applications. These concepts will provide technical reference material in understanding the following chapters. They are given at an introductory level for those readers with limited background in data communications.

Chapter 4 discusses access protocols that have been devised for LANs. The two basic types of operational network architectures used for LANs are broadcast networks and switched networks. In a *broadcast LAN* all users receive the information sent by any particular transmitting station. The schemes for sharing the medium are random-access and controlled access methods. With *random access* no control is used to determine which station may transmit. This means that the users must *contend* for access to the LAN. In contrast, *controlled access* approaches attempt to produce an orderly collision-free access to the shared transmission medium. Two possible ways of doing this are through either a *token-passing* scheme or a *polling* mechanism. In a *switched LAN architecture* a switch employs forwarding logic and routing tables to transfer information units from source to destination. The switch provides input and output ports that are dedicated to either a single user or a small group of users.

The next five chapters present details on the operational principles, basic network designs, and associated standards of various types of LANs.

- Chapter 5 gives details on conventional Ethernet, Fast Ethernet, Gigabit Ethernet, and switched Ethernet. This technology has undergone a number of attractive enhancements since its conceptualization in the 1970s. The Ethernet transmission speed has gradually increased from 10 Mbps to 10 Gbps, and speeds of up to 1 Tbps are contemplated. To keep up with these increases in speed and to enhance the installation flexibility, the transmission media have changed from stiff limited-capacity coaxial cable to flexible high-capacity optical fiber links. In addition, the topologies have changed from a broadcast configuration to a switched LAN scheme. Since Ethernet has become the most widely used LAN implementation, this chapter should be studied most extensively.
- Chapter 6 describes the basis of *token-passing ring LANs*. Although these are no longer receiving much support from vendors or developers, there is a large installed base of these networks. Therefore, although coverage of this chapter is optional, the lessons learned from this technology are valuable for evaluating other types of LANs.
- Chapter 7 presents the concepts of *asynchronous transfer mode* (ATM) LANs. A key attraction of ATM is that it enables carriers to offer multiple classes of service over a network, to connect devices operating at different speeds, and to mix a variety of traffic types having different transmission requirements. In addition,

ATM can serve as a backbone for high-speed LANs and can be used to interconnect widely separated high-capacity LANs.

- Chapter 8 addresses the implementation of a *wireless LAN* (WLAN). This is a LAN using over-the-air infrared light waves or radio waves instead of relying on copper wires or optical fibers as the transmission means. Examples of such networks include configurations that allow the application of standard and Fast Ethernet over a wireless LAN, a *wireless personal area network* (PAN) based on the Bluetooth short-range radio specification for wire replacement in a room-sized area, and the applications of WLAN technology, such as HomeRF, for interconnecting communication and computing assets in either the home or an office.

- Chapter 9 describes a specialized LAN called a *storage area network* (SAN). This is a dedicated network that connects one or more computing systems to a collection of data storage devices. Fibre Channel has become a principal interconnection and networking technology for specialized networks that are used for information storage functions.

Following the details of the major types of LANs, Chap. 10 addresses internetworking issues. A LAN as an isolated entity has limited potential and usefulness. It is necessary for users to have the ability to share not only resources that belong to their own LAN, but also to be able to access stations, mainframes, servers, and data storage devices on other LANs, MANs, or a WAN. The concept for achieving this is known as *internetworking* and effectively creates a single large loosely coupled network from many different local, metropolitan, and wide-area networks.

Chapter 11 presents an overview on network management. Once the hardware and software elements of a LAN have been installed properly and integrated successfully, they need to be managed to ensure that the required level of network performance is met. This is carried out through *network management*. This service uses a variety of hardware and software tools, applications, and devices to assist human network managers in monitoring and maintaining networks. Implementation of network management concerns five fundamental functional areas: performance, configuration, accounting, fault, and security management.

Chapter 12 addresses network security issues. The topics covered include security policies, functions and uses of firewalls to protect LANs from external intrusions, authentication and access control methods, data encryption techniques, public-key infrastructure, IP security, and concepts of virtual private networks (VPNs).

1.7 REFERENCE MATERIAL AND FURTHER RESOURCES

Numerous references are given at the end of each chapter as a start for delving deeper into any given topic. Since local area networking brings together research and development efforts from many different scientific and engineering disciplines, there are hundreds of articles in the literature relating to the material covered in each chapter. Even though not all of these articles can be cited in the references, the selections represent some of the major contributions to the LAN field and can be considered a good introduction to the literature. An attempt was made to select all references on the basis of easy accessibility and they should be available in a good technical library or via web-based resources.

Additional references include major technical journals, such as those listed in Refs. 25 through 30. Further supplementary material can be found in the books listed in Refs. 31 through 41.

1.8 BOOK WEBSITE

A website for the book is available at http://www.mhhe.com/keiser2. This website includes instructor and student resources, corrections or revisions to the text, contact information, links to other related websites, and updates on new technical developments or standards. The site will be updated periodically with material such as suggestions for new homework problems, design projects, or modeling and simulation ideas; descriptions of recent technology or implementation developments; and a listing of web addresses of vendors offering components, transmission equipment, and measurement instruments. The website also contains a mechanism for readers to provide feedback and suggestions to the author.

1.9 SIMULATION PROGRAM ON A CD-ROM

Computer-aided modeling and simulation software programs are essential tools to predict how a network will function and perform. These programs are able to integrate component, link, and network functions, thereby making the design process more efficient, cheaper, and faster. These tools typically include library modules that contain the operational characteristics of devices such as routers, switches, workstations, and servers, plus the transfer characteristics of communication channels such as various wire lines, optical fiber cables, and wireless links. To check the performance of the network or the capacity that devices such as switches and servers need to handle, network designers invoke different traffic loads, routing protocols, and applications in the simulation programs.

An example of such programs is the suite of software-based modeling tools from VPIsystems, Inc.[42–43] These design and planning tools are intended for use across all levels of network analyses, performance evaluations, and technology comparisons ranging from components to modules, to entire networks. They are currently in use by component and system manufacturers, system integrators, network operators, and access service providers for functions such as capacity planning, comparative assessments of various technologies, optimization of transport and service networks, syntheses and analyses of optical network and link designs, and component designs.

One particular program from this suite is the VPIserviceMaker_IP, which is a capacity planning tool that can help to design networks of any size. This tool can be used by either an equipment vendor or an Internet service provider in network capacity estimation. The VPIserviceMaker_IP tool allows IP (Internet Protocol) network capacity design for best-effort services [e.g., web browsing, file transfers (using FTP), e-mail, news services], voice-over-IP (VoIP), and other services in an access IP network. It deploys traffic characterization models that include self-similarity and statistical multiplexing. The modeling program provides many functions such as routing topology checks, effective bandwidth calculations, automatic calculations of interface costs and number of links, networkwide or individual computer group overloads, bottleneck identifications, failure simulations, exports and imports of user-definable access profiles and device libraries, and detailed reports of all planning data.

The CD-ROM packaged with this book contains an introductory version of the VPIserviceMaker_IP program, which is based on a Microsoft Windows operating system. In addition to the software, the CD-ROM contains the user manual for this tool. This manual describes the suite of VPI modeling tools and their interactions, lists the PC hardware requirements to operate the program, provides installation instructions for the software, presents an overview of the fundamentals of IP networks, and gives details on how to use the program. Further information may be found on the book website.

PROBLEMS

1.1. List some of the equipment resources that could be shared on a LAN and state what are the advantages and possible limitations of sharing them.

1.2. Using web resources, find an example of an Ethernet NIC and describe its functions.

1.3. Look at the websites of the ITU-T, IEEE, and ANSI and describe in a few sentences what the standards activities of each is in relation to LANs.

1.4. Section 1.3.1 gives an example of e-mail as a client/server process. Discuss the functions of another client/server process, for example, as provided by a database server or an electronic appointment calendar system.

1.5. Using books or web resources, look up some details on the Object Request Broker (ORB) and write a one-page summary on its operation and application.

1.6. In client/server architectures *remote procedure calls* (RPCs) or *standard query language* (SQL) statements are typically used to communicate between a client and a server. Using books or web resources, look up some details on this and write a one-page summary.

1.7. A user wishes to transmit a large 1.2-MB (megabyte) file and a smaller 1.6-kB (kilobyte) file [*Note:* One byte $= 8$ bits.] Compare the times needed to transfer these files if the line rates are 28.8 kbps, 10 Mbps, and 1 Gbps.

1.8. Consider a file server that has 2 GB (gigabytes) of data stored on it. If 1.4-MB diskettes are used to back up the data, how many diskettes are needed? What would be some other means of backing up the data?

1.9. Consider a LAN that transmits data at 100 Mbps. If there is a 1-ms (millisecond) noise pulse that corrupts the data, how many bits are affected?

1.10. A two-story office building has two 10-foot-wide hallways per floor which connect four rows of offices with eight offices per row, as shown in Fig. 1.14. Each office is 15 by 15 feet square. The office ceiling height is 9 feet with a false ceiling hung 1 foot below the actual ceiling. Also, as shown in Fig. 1.14, there is a wiring room for LAN interconnection and control equipment in one corner of each floor. Every office has a local-area-network socket on each of the two walls that are perpendicular to the hallway wall. If we assume cables can be run only in the walls and in the ceilings, estimate the length of cable (in feet) that is required for the following configurations:
(a) A cable bus with a wire drop from the ceiling to each outlet
(b) A star configuration that connects each outlet to the wiring room on the corresponding floor and a vertical cable riser that connects the stars in each wiring room

1.11. Consider the M-by-N grid of stations shown in Fig. 1.15 which are to be connected by a LAN. Let the stations be spaced a distance d apart and assume interconnection cables will be run in ducts that connect the nearest neighbor stations (i.e., ducts are not run diagonally

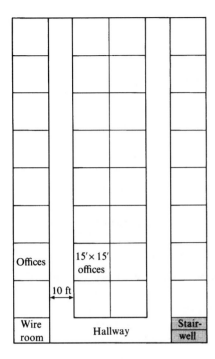

FIGURE 1.14
Diagram for Prob. 1.10.

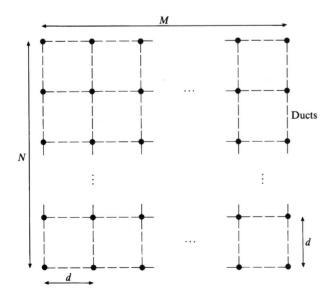

FIGURE 1.15
Diagram for Probs. 1.11 and 1.12.

in Fig. 1.15). Show that for the following configurations the cable length for interconnecting the stations is as stated:

(a) $(MN - 1)d$ for a bus configuration

(b) MNd for a ring topology

(c) $MN(M + N - 2)d/2$ for a star topology where each subscriber is connected *individually* to the network hub, which is located *in one corner* of the grid.

1.12. Consider the M-by-N rectangular grid of computer stations shown in Fig. 1.15, where the spacing between stations is d. Assume these stations are to be connected by a star-configured LAN using the duct network shown in the figure. Further assume each station is connected to the central star by means of its own dedicated cable.

(a) If m and n denote the relative position of the star, show that the total cable length L needed to connect the stations is given by

$$L = [MN(M + N + 2)/2 - Nm(M - m + 1) - Mn(N - n + 1)]d$$

(b) Show that if the star is located in one corner of the grid, then this expression becomes

$$L = MN(M + N - 2)d/2$$

(c) Show that the shortest cable length is obtained when the star is at the center of the grid.

1.13. What are some situations in which it is advantageous to implement a wireless LAN instead of a wired LAN?

1.14. Describe the differences between a LAN that uses a shared medium and a switched LAN. What are some advantages of each one?

1.15. What are some functions of a passive hub or a wiring center? What additional features does an active hub offer?

REFERENCES

1. S. Saunders, *The McGraw-Hill High-Speed LANs Handbook,* McGraw-Hill, New York, 1996.
2. A. S. Tanenbaum, *Computer Networks,* Prentice-Hall, Upper Saddle River, NJ, 2nd ed., 1996.
3. Ed Taylor, *The Network Architecture Design Handbook,* McGraw-Hill, New York, 1998.
4. A. Leon-Garcia and I. Widjaja, *Communication Networks,* McGraw-Hill, Burr Ridge, IL, 2000.
5. L. L. Peterson and B. S. Davie, *Computer Networks,* Morgan-Kaufmann, San Francisco, 2nd ed., 2000.
6. W. Stallings, *Local and Metropolitan Area Networks,* Prentice-Hall, Upper Saddle River, NJ, 6th ed., 2000.
7. J. Goldman and P. Rawles, *Local Area Networks: A Business-Oriented Approach,* 2nd ed., Wiley, 2000.
8. B. A. Forouzan, *Introduction to Data Communications and Networking,* McGraw-Hill, Burr Ridge, IL, 2nd ed., 2001.
9. Telecommunication Standardization Sector of the International Telecommunication Union (ITU-T), Place des nations, CH-1211 Geneva 20, Switzerland (http://www.itu.ch).
10. The International Standards Organization (ISO), Geneva, Switzerland (http://www.iso.ch).
11. Institute of Electrical and Electronic Engineers (IEEE), 345 E. 45th St., New York, NY 10017 (http://www.ieee.org).
12. American National Standards Institute (ANSI), 1430 Broadway, New York, NY 10018 (http://www.ansi.org).
13. Electronic Industries Association (EIA), 2001 Eye Street, Washington, DC 20006.
14. Telecommunication Industries Association (TIA) (http://www.tiaonline.org).
15. L. W. Couch II, *Digital and Analog Communication Systems,* Prentice-Hall, Upper Saddle River, NJ, 6th ed., 2001.
16. R. Perlman, *Interconnections: Bridges, Routers, Switches, and Internetworking Protocols,* Addison-Wesley, Reading, MA, 2nd ed., 2000.

17. W. Stallings, *Data and Computer Communications,* Prentice-Hall, Upper Saddle River, NJ, 6th ed., 2000.
18. R. J. Bates and D. W. Gregory, *Voice and Data Communications Handbook,* McGraw-Hill, New York, 3rd ed., 2000.
19. Object Management Group (http://www.omg.org).
20. J. Trulove, *LAN Wiring,* McGraw-Hill, New York, 2nd ed., 2001.
21. B. J. Elliott, *Cable Engineering for Local Area Networks,* Dekker, New York, 2001.
22. A. Santamaria and F. López-Hernández, eds., *Wireless LAN Standards and Applications,* Artech House, Boston, 2001.
23. G. Held, *Data over Wireless Networks,* McGraw-Hill, Burr Ridge, IL, 2001.
24. M. Farley, *Building Storage Networks,* McGraw-Hill/Osborne, Berkeley, CA, 2000.
25. *IEEE Network,* a bimonthly journal devoted to computer communications.
26. *IEEE/ACM Transactions on Networking,* a bimonthly journal reflecting the multidisciplinary nature of communication networks.
27. *IEEE Communications Mag.,* a monthly journal providing the latest information on all communications technologies including LANs.
28. *Computer Communications;* this journal covers practical developments in computer and telecommunications technology including LANs; published by Elsevier Science (http://www.elsevier.nl/locate/comcom).
29. *IEEE J. on Select Areas in Communications;* encompasses leading-edge communications research.
30. *Journal of High-Speed Networks,* IOS Press, Amsterdam (http://www.iospress.nl).
31. M. Nemzow, *Fast Ethernet,* McGraw-Hill, New York, 1997.
32. M. Smith, *Virtual LANs,* McGraw-Hill, New York, 1997.
33. G. Held, *Internetworking LANs and WANs,* Wiley, New York, 2nd ed., 1998.
34. C. Lewis, *Cisco TCP/IP Routing Professional Reference,* McGraw-Hill, New York, 3rd ed., 2000.
35. E. Tunmann, *Practical Multiservice LANs,* Artech House, Boston, 1999.
36. R. Seifert, *The Switch Book: The Complete Guide to LAN Switching Technology,* Wiley, New York, 2000.
37. R. O'Hara and A. Petrick, *The IEEE 802.11 Handbook,* IEEE Press, New York, 2000.
38. P. Izzo, *Gigabit Networks,* Wiley, New York, 2000.
39. L. R. Rossi, L. D. Rossi, and T. Rossi, *Cisco Catalyst LAN Switching,* McGraw-Hill, New York, 2000.
40. G. Keiser, *Optical Fiber Communications,* McGraw-Hill, Burr Ridge, IL, 3rd ed., 2000.
41. D. A. Stamper, *Local Area Networks,* Prentice-Hall, Upper Saddle River, NJ, 3rd ed., 2001.
42. Details on these and related design tools can be found on the website for VPIsystems, Inc. (http://www.vpisystems.com).
43. A. Lowery and D. Hewitt, "Network architectures combine broadband, data, and voice services," *Lightwave,* vol. 18, pp. 160–164, Jan. 2001.

CHAPTER
2

NETWORK ARCHITECTURE AND PROTOCOLS

The interconnection of multiple networks into a single large communication system is known as an *internetwork* or an *internet*. Thus the designation "Internet" (capital I) arose for the ubiquitous worldwide network that is in use today. The individual networks of such an internet may differ significantly in their underlying technology and operation. For example, they could be different types of LANs or point-to-point links, with transmission speeds of individual LANs or links ranging from 10 Mbps (megabits per second) to 10 Gbps (gigabits per second) and beyond. The information that is exchanged could be audio (e.g., voice, music, sound track), video (e.g., live news coverage or playback movies), data (e.g., e-mail, stock or banking information or transactions, business information), or images (e.g., faxes, photos, technical drawings, cartoons). Furthermore, the attached equipment typically comes from a wide variety of manufacturers. Obviously a common language is required for users to have meaningful dialogs in such a diverse collection of networks and communication devices. For a client/server example from human interactions, if the professor (the server) shown in Fig. 2.1 does not speak the same language as the student (the client), then the message of the lecture is lost.

The difficulty encountered when trying to interconnect diverse communications products is that the data formats and the data exchange conventions of this equipment can vary between manufacturers. How then can two distinct systems exchange information? Here the word *system* is used to denote a collection of workstations, desktop or laptop computers, printers, telephones, and other data-handling devices, together with their associated software, peripheral equipment, and users that are capable of information processing and/or transfer. The only solution to effective communications among various

FIGURE 2.1
Clients and servers need to speak the same language in order to communicate.

system components residing on either the same or different networks is to have vendors abide by a common set of rules or protocols.

Two different, but somewhat parallel, approaches were taken in the 1970s to address this issue. First the Advanced Research Projects Agency (ARPA) of the U.S. Department of Defense began to develop protocols for connecting their diverse and widely scattered communication assets. This work resulted in a robust network called the ARPANET and a set of specifications called the *Transmission Control Protocol/Internet Protocol* (TCP/IP) *suite.*[1–5] This name resulted from two important protocols contained in the suite: TCP and IP. Over time the TCP/IP suite underwent significant modifications and the ARPANET evolved into the commercial Internet, which is in global use today. Thus the evolved TCP/IP protocol suite has now become the conventional standard for worldwide communication between networked heterogeneous computers.

On the commercial side in 1978 the International Standards Organization (ISO) recognized the importance of and the need for *universality* in exchanging information between and within networks and across geographical boundaries. This resulted in the *Open System Interconnect (OSI) Reference Model* for network architecture, which defines seven hierarchical layers of networking functions.[6–8] The term *open* means the concepts are nonproprietary and can be used freely by anyone. The purpose of the OSI model is to enable communications between different network systems without requiring changes to the logic of the underlying hardware and software. An important point to keep in mind is that the OSI model is not a protocol. It is a model for understanding and designing a network architecture that is flexible, robust, and interoperable.

In this chapter we first look at some broad high-level concepts and terms that will provide a basis for examining local area network design and implementation in Sec. 2.1. This considers the overall *network architecture,* which is the structure that determines how the various logical and physical components of a network are interconnected. To obtain an understanding of how the layering works, in Sec. 2.2 we look at the functions of the various OSI-model layers and examine how information is formatted at each layer as it flows through a network from source to destination. Next Sec. 2.3 examines the structure of the TCP/IP protocol suite. Analogous to the OSI model, the TCP/IP model describes a hierarchical communication architecture, but in this case it uses a five-layer model. Section 2.3 addresses the upper three layers of the TCP/IP protocol suite. The bottom two layers are network-specific. Section 2.4 gives an overview of these layers for LAN applications. Details of the specific protocols are given in chapters dealing with each LAN technology.

2.1 NETWORK ARCHITECTURE CONCEPTS

Before we get into specifics of network architecture, let us first look at some concepts and terminology. The term *architecture* can be confusing since it has been used to describe everything from a framework for system development to actual hardware. An architecture is basically a set of rules and conventions by which something is built. The network architectures of the OSI model and the TCP/IP model define the rules and conventions for information exchanges between various peer functions residing within devices or software applications of communicating nodes. It specifies the general relations among these functions and notes the constraints on the types of functions and their relations. Neither the details of the implementation nor the specification of the functional interfaces are part of the architecture. Thus a network architecture model is just that—a model. It cannot be implemented and it does not represent a preferred implementation approach.[9]

2.1.1 Basic Concepts of Layering

The conceptualization, design, and implementation of a computer network is understandably a rather complex task. For users to be able to communicate the networks to which they are attached must adhere to a common set of protocols. A *protocol* is a set of rules or conventions that governs the generation, formatting, control, and interpretation of information that is transmitted through a network or that is stored in a database. Basically a protocol defines what is communicated, how it is sent, and when it is transmitted. Syntax, semantics, and timing are the key protocol elements:

- *Syntax* describes the ordered structure or format of the data. For example, the protocol might identify the first 8 bits to be the address of the sender, the next 8 bits to be the address of the intended recipient, and the rest of the block to be the message itself.
- *Semantics* refers to the meaning of a structured block of bits. For example, it tells how to interpret a particular pattern of bits, what action must be taken based on that interpretation, and whether the address contained in a block of bits identifies the route to be taken by the block or its final destination.
- *Timing* describes when data should be sent and at what rate. The importance of agreeing on timing is clear when considering a station that tries to transmit data at 100 Mbps to a station that can only process it at 10 Mbps. If there is no timing control, the recipient will be overloaded quickly and data might be lost.

Many design decisions must be made when setting up protocols. Traditionally this problem has been approached by subdividing it into a number of individual pieces of manageable and comprehensible size. The result is a layered structure of services. This type of layered structure is referred to as a *protocol stack.* The communication between two layers in a protocol stack is known as an *interface.* The idea behind this is that each layer is responsible for providing a service to the layer above it by using the services of the layer below. In this approach a user at the highest layer is offered the full set of services needed to interact with other users and peripheral equipment distributed on the network. When carrying out this layering, partitioning the protocols at each layer into independent functions will allow additions or updating of individual functions to be carried out without destabilizing the entire set of rules.[10,11]

The OSI model is an example of such a structured approach.[12] It modularizes a set of system interconnection protocols in a particular way by defining seven layers of functions, as Fig. 2.2 illustrates. This seven-layer hierarchy loosely groups the functional requirements for communication between two devices regardless of the software, hardware, or geographical distance between these elements. By convention the OSI-model layers are viewed as a vertical sequence with the numbering starting at the bottom layer. As one progresses up the protocol stack, a larger number of functions are

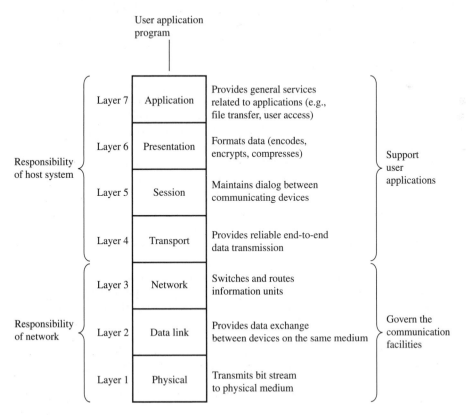

FIGURE 2.2
General structure and functions of the seven-layer OSI Reference Model.

provided and the level of abstraction of the service increases. The lower layers govern the *communication facilities:* the physical connections, data link control, and routing and relaying functions that support the actual transmission of data. The upper layers support *user applications* by structuring and organizing data for the needs of the user.

Note that there is nothing inherently unique about using seven layers or about the specific functionality in each layer. The reference model was designed before the protocols were established so that later (as is the case with TCP/IP) some of the layers were omitted from actual applications and other layers were subdivided into further sublayers. Thus the layering mechanism should be viewed as a framework for discussions of implementation and not as an absolute authority.

For simplicity in discussing the layers any layer is referred to as *layer n* or the *n-layer,* whereas its next lower and higher levels are denoted as the $(n-1)$ layer and the $(n+1)$ layer, respectively. The same notation is used to designate all concepts relating to layers; for example, entities in layer n are referred to as *n-entities.* The word *entity* denotes anything that is capable of sending, processing, or receiving information such as an application program, a file transfer package, a database management system, or a terminal.

The same set of layered functions must exist on each system in order for the two systems to communicate. Layer n on one machine communicates with the corresponding layer n on another machine. The entities that make up the corresponding layers on different machines are called *peer processes,* as indicated in Fig. 2.3. Thus information exchange between the two systems is carried out by having the layers on one system communicate with their peer layers in the other system. The orderly exchange of information between peers at a given layer is achieved via protocols specific to that layer.

In an actual system data is not directly transmitted from layer n on one machine to layer n on another machine, except at the lowest level. The solid lines in Fig. 2.3 indicate the real path of the information flow. For example, if host A wishes to send a message to host B, each layer in protocol stack A passes data and control information to the layer immediately below it. When the lowest layer is reached, there is an actual *physical connection* from host A to host B. In protocol stack B the information then is passed up from one layer to the next until it reaches layer n.

A data unit that gets passed from one layer to another is referred to as a *protocol data unit* (PDU). To make it precisely clear at what layer the exchange of PDUs is taking place, the ISO has suggested adding a single-letter prefix to the acronym PDU. The results are listed on the right-hand side in Fig. 2.3. For example, the data link layer communicates with a peer data link in another node through the use of LPDUs. Likewise, network layers communicate with each other through the exchange of NPDUs. Note that often an NPDU is called a *packet,* an LPDU is referred to as a *frame,* and PhPDUs are data *bits.*

2.1.2 Services

The term *service* represents a boundary between functions in different layers. In this sense a service is a statement of the set of capabilities of layer n that is provided to the entities of layer $n+1$, which are collectively called the *user of the service.* The

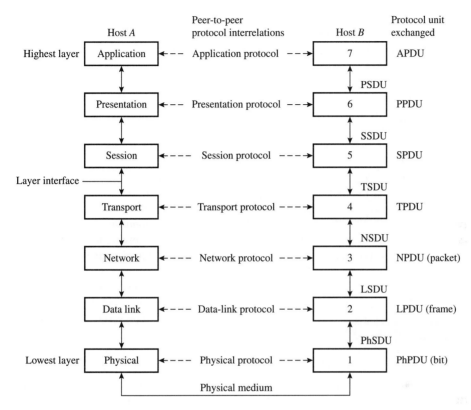

FIGURE 2.3
Peer-to-peer information exchange between two systems based on the OSI model.

parts of layer n which provide the set of capabilities to the above layer are called the *service provider,* as shown in Fig. 2.4. The service provider does not need to reside in one particular location but can be distributed across a number of physically distinct pieces of equipment. When layer $n + 1$ passes information to layer n for transmission, the information is called a *service data unit* (SDU), as shown before in Fig. 2.3. Analogous to PDUs, a single-letter prefix is added to the SDU acronym to avoid ambiguity about which layer is involved.

The transmission of a PDU between peer $(n + 1)$-entities is accomplished by first passing a block of information from layer $n + 1$ to layer n through a software port called a layer-n *service access point* (SAP). The SAP represents the logical interface between an n-entity and an $(n + 1)$-entity, as shown in Fig. 2.4. The block of information consists of control information and an nSDU, which together is the $(n + 1)$PDU itself. The layer n-entity then uses the control information to form an nPDU, which then gets transmitted from one node to the other. Upon receiving this nPDU, the peer layer-n process at the destination node executes the necessary layer-n protocol and delivers the nSDU to the peer layer $(n + 1)$-entity.

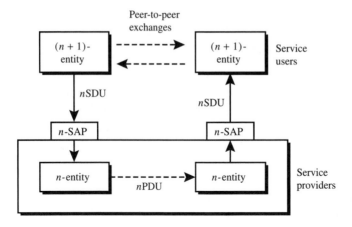

FIGURE 2.4
Service model showing the layered interaction between the service user and the service provider through service access points (SAPs).

EXAMPLE 2.1

When the network layer wishes to transmit an NPDU to a network layer in another node, it first passes control information and an LSDU to the lower data link layer, as shown in Fig. 2.5. The data link layer modifies the control information by adding any necessary header and trailer information to form an LPDU, and then transmits it through the physical layer to the other node. Upon receiving this LPDU, a process in the peer data link layer at the destination node executes the necessary protocol and delivers an LSDU to the peer network layer entity.

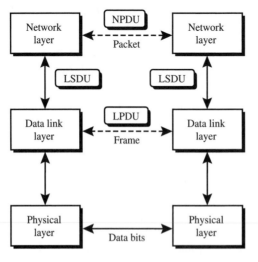

FIGURE 2.5
Peer-to-peer transmission process of an NPDU.

In defining services the ISO standard introduces the concept of *service primitives* as abstract, implementation independent elements of the interaction between the service user and the service provider. When an information exchange takes place between two users, the following four service primitives can occur at various instances in the dialog:

1. *Request.*   A service user issues this primitive to invoke some procedure.
2. *Indication.*   A service provider issues this primitive either to invoke some procedure or to indicate that the service user at the peer SAP has invoked a procedure.
3. *Response.*   This primitive is issued by a service user to complete, at a particular SAP, some procedure previously invoked by an indication at that SAP.
4. *Confirm.*   A service provider issues this primitive to complete, at a particular SAP, some procedure previously invoked by a request at that SAP.

The following two service types occur repeatedly in an information exchange between users, depending on whether the sender must eventually be informed of the outcome:

- *Confirmed.*   In this service element a *request* at one SAP produces an *indication* at the other SAP; this indication leads the service user into issuing a *response,* which in turn leads to a *confirm* at the originating SAP. Thus this service has all four of the primitives in the preceding list.
- *Unconfirmed.*   In this service element a *request* at one SAP produces only an *indication* at the other SAP.

The occurrence of a service primitive is a logically instantaneous and indivisible event. This event occurs at a specific instance, which cannot be interrupted by another event. Each primitive has a particular direction. This can be from either the service user to the service provider or vice versa, as shown in the example in Fig. 2.6. As illustrated here, the order in which related service primitives can occur is conventionally depicted in a *time-sequence diagram.* Each diagram is divided into three parts. The central field represents the service provider and the other two side parts represent the two service users. The passage of time increases downward so that the position of events along the vertical lines indicates their relative time sequence. Arrows in the user-service areas denote the propagation direction of the primitives, either to or from the service provider.

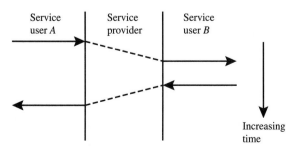

FIGURE 2.6
Time-sequence diagram showing the order in which related service primitives can travel.

EXAMPLE 2.2

An example of a protocol executing the layer-2 (data link) service is given in Fig. 2.7. The users are system A and system B, and the protocols which support the services are indicated by dashed lines. (The dashed lines represent generic protocol actions. The specific actions of the dashed lines depend on the particular data link protocol that is implemented.) As shown here, a *connection request* is first issued by user A. User B then issues a *connect indicate* and a *connect response,* which in turn is confirmed by user A. Similar procedures then are followed for data exchange and link disconnection.

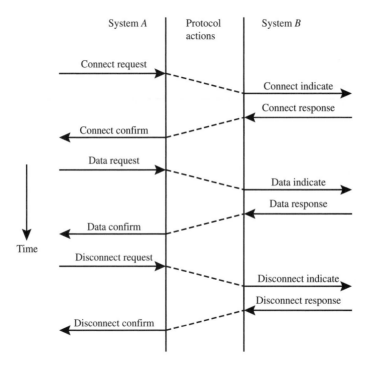

FIGURE 2.7
Example of a protocol executing a layer-2 (data link) service.

2.2 LAYERS OF THE OSI MODEL

Now let us look at how data is formatted as it flows through the seven layers of the OSI model.[13–15] We start with a user accessing an application at layer 7 and end up at the physical layer for interconnection to another user. Figure 2.8 shows the flow of information through a network from user A to user B based on an architectural view of the OSI model. Here we use the notation nPDU described earlier to designate a data unit at layer n, and the notation "Hn" to indicate the header that is added at each layer n to the PDU coming from a higher layer. At layer 2 a trailer T2 also must be added, as

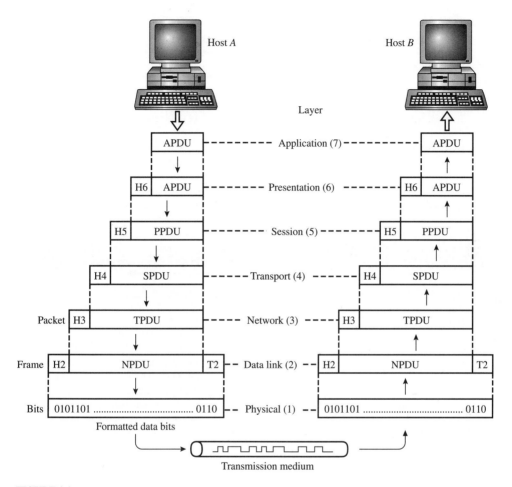

FIGURE 2.8

Flow of information through a typical layered network. The arrows show the direction of the flow from host *A* to host *B*. The PDU plus overhead information in a header at a particular layer becomes the data field for the next lower layer.

explained in Sec. 2.2.6. When the formatted information finally reaches the physical layer, it is transformed into either an electrical or an optical signal that is compatible with the characteristics of the transmission medium.

After passing through the transmission medium, the reverse process takes place. That is, header H*n* is stripped off at each layer *n* and the resultant PDU is passed to the next higher layer until it reaches user *B*.

2.2.1 The Application Layer

The application layer contains protocols that allow users to access the network.[16] Popular ones include those described in Table 2.1. Note that the application layer protocols do not include the end-user application programs, such as electronic mail, web browsers, and

TABLE 2.1

Examples of protocols operating at the application layer

Protocol	Abbreviation	Function
File Transfer Protocol	FTP	Transfers files between two remote machines.
Terminal Networking	TELNET	TCP/IP's client/server process for remote login.
Hypertext Transfer Protocol	HTTP	Downloads documents from a remote server when using a web browser.
Simple Mail Transfer Protocol	SMTP	Used to transfer electronic-mail messages between hosts.
Network File System	NFS	Used to make a file system on a remote machine visible without actually transferring the files.
Wide Area Information Service	WAIS	A content-search service that finds the name of a file given some information about the contents.
Real-time Transfer Protocol	RTP	Designed to transmit audio and video over the Internet with little latency.
Domain Name System	DNS	Identifies each host on the Internet with a unique name called a domain name, for example, "photonicscomm.com."
Trivial File Transfer Protocol	TFTP	Intended for file transfer applications that do not require complex interactions between client and server.
Simple Network Management Protocol	SNMP	Provides a set of fundamental operations for monitoring and maintaining an internet.

office applications since these reside in the user's computer as software applications. Rather, the protocols encompass the utilities and network-based services that support these applications. For example, the application layer protocols could support electronic mail (known as e-mail) via SMTP (Simple Mail Transfer Protocol), remote login with TELNET, Internet access via HTTP, file transfer using FTP, and network management through SNMP (Simple Network Management Protocol).

The interactions of the end users, the application layer, and the presentation layer are shown in Fig. 2.9. Of the available services, suppose user A wants to send an e-mail message to user B with the SMTP service. First user A prepares an e-mail message that includes the address of user B, a subject line, and a message body. When user A clicks on *Send,* the e-mail application prepares a file with the message information and passes it to the SMTP that resides in a local server. The SMTP formats a layer-7 PDU [i.e., an APDU (Application Protocol Data Unit)], which it passes to the next lower layer. After this data unit passes down through the protocol stack at the source end, travels across the transmission medium, and goes up the protocol stack at the destination end, the SMTP in the application layer at the destination receives the APDU and passes the e-mail message to user B.

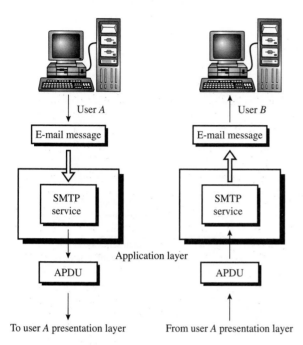

FIGURE 2.9
Exchanges of data units with neighboring layers at the application layer.

2.2.2 The Presentation Layer

The goal of the presentation layer is to ensure that communicating machines can interoperate properly. For application programs to understand the information transferred between devices that have different internal data representations, a common syntax must be used. This *syntax* represents information such as character codes, data types, and file formats. Thus the presentation layer protocols determine what syntax to use when applications in different machines exchange information.[17]

The presentation layer also may provide for encryption and decryption of data for transmission security, and for data compression and expansion. *Encryption* is a technique whereby data is transformed into an unintelligible format at the sending end to protect it against unauthorized disclosure, modification, utilization, or destruction as it travels through the network. *Data compression* is a methodology for reducing the total number of bits that must be transmitted. This is done either to conserve bandwidth or to reduce the size of very large files when transmission efficiency is needed.

Figure 2.10 shows the relationship between the presentation layer and the adjacent application and session layers. The APDU is accepted from the application layer, properly encoded, and optionally encrypted and/or compressed. Then a layer-6 header (H6) is added to form a PPDU (Presentation Protocol Data Unit). This header includes information on the type and parameters of the transmission and the length of the transmission. The PPDU then gets passed to the session layer. At the destination the presentation layer receives the PPDU from the session layer, strips off the header H6 that was added on at the source side, and passes the resultant APDU to the service protocol in the application layer.

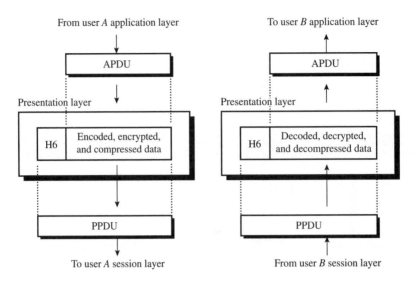

FIGURE 2.10
Exchanges of data units with neighboring layers at the presentation layer.

2.2.3 The Session Layer

The intent of the session layer is to perform orderly and reliable data exchange interactions by providing specialized user-oriented services, such as *dialog control* (enforcing a particular pattern of communication between systems), *synchronization* (placing checkpoints or synchronization points into the data stream), and *chaining* (combining groups of PDUs so that either all or none of the PDUs in the group get delivered).[18,19] Since these types of services are rare, the session layer is seldom used.

If a session layer is used, Fig. 2.11 shows the relationship between it and the adjacent presentation and transport layers. The PPDU is accepted from the presentation layer, and a layer-5 header (H5) is added to form an SPDU (Session Protocol Data Unit). This header includes control information, such as the type of the data unit that is sent and synchronization point information. Figure 2.11 also gives an example of placing synchronization checkpoints in the data flow. The SPDU then gets passed to the transport layer. The reverse process occurs at the destination.

2.2.4 The Transport Layer

The transport layer is responsible for reliably delivering the complete message from the source to the destination.[20] The major objective is to provide end-to-end error recovery and flow control in order to satisfy a *quality of service* (QoS) requested by the upper layer. The QoS is expressed in terms of parameters such as throughput, transit delay, residual error rate, delay time to establish a connection, cost, security, and priority. For example, if the upper layer requests a *throughput* (the amount of useful information processed or communicated during a specific time period) which is higher than the network access rate,

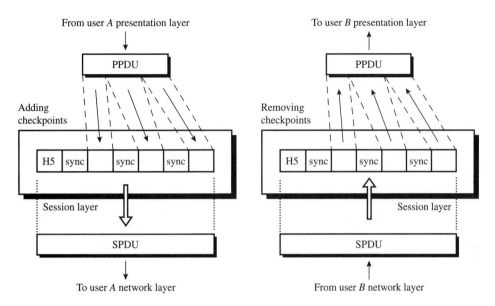

FIGURE 2.11
Exchanges of data units with neighboring layers at the session layer.

the transport layer would need to establish several network connections and to provide a line-sharing protocol. On the other hand, if the requested throughput is much less than the data-handling capacity of the network line, a protocol for multiplexing several user connections would be needed. In providing these services, the transport layer must know the quality and limitations of the network connection offered by the underlying network layer.

The transport layer also may need to *segment* (and reassemble at the receiving end) large messages coming from the session layer in order to have the segments match the sizes of NPDUs (Network Protocol Data Units) that can be handled by the network layer.

Figure 2.12 shows the relationship between the transport layer and adjacent layers. An SPDU is accepted from the session layer, and a layer-4 header (H4) is added to form a TPDU (Transport Protocol Data Unit). In this example a large SPDU is segmented and converted to several TPDUs to match the network layer packet sizes. Thus the header also includes sequence, or segmentation, numbers that allow a segmented SPDU to be properly reassembled at the destination.

2.2.5 The Network Layer

The function of the network layer is to deliver NPDUs (or packets) from the source to the destination across multiple network links.[21,22] This function is of importance for LANs when delivering messages from one LAN to another across a more expansive network. Typically the network layer must find a path through a series of connected nodes, and the

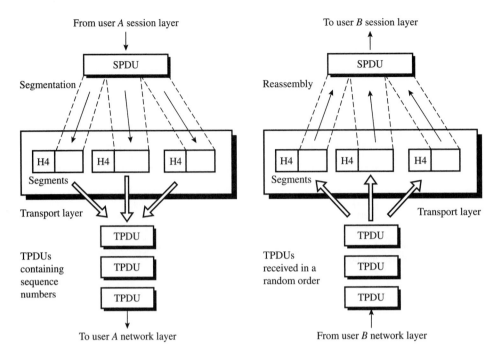

FIGURE 2.12
Exchanges of data units with neighboring layers at the transport layer.

nodes along this path must forward the NPDUs to the appropriate destination. In addition to dealing with route determination, the network layer must handle the following:

- *Fragmentation* of NPDUs into smaller units (and their reassembly at the receiving end) when different links in the path have different data unit size restrictions.
- An *error control service* to assure that the packets are received in the correct sequence and that all packets arrive correctly.
- A *flow control service* to prevent a slow receiver from being overwhelmed with data from a faster transmitter or to stop transmissions if a receiving station finds that it is about to run out of buffer space for incoming messages.

Figure 2.13 shows the relationship between the network layer and the adjacent transport and data link layers. The TPDU is accepted from the transport layer, and a layer-3 header (H3) is added to form an NPDU (i.e., a packet). In this case H3 contains the original source and final destination addresses of the packet. These addresses do not change during the end-to-end packet transmission and are called *logical addresses.*

2.2.6 The Data Link Layer

The data link layer is of particular importance to LANs since this is the layer where LAN architecture standards, such as the IEEE-802 family, are defined.[23,24] The basic purpose

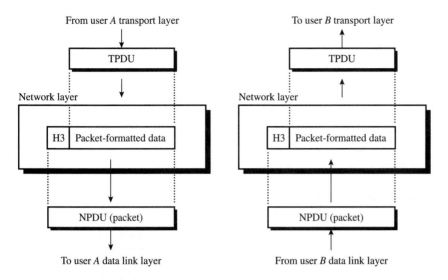

FIGURE 2.13
Exchanges of data units with neighboring layers at the network layer.

of this layer is to establish, maintain, and release data links that *directly* connect two network nodes. A data link connection between the nodes can consist of one or more physical paths, including wire cable, optical fiber cable, microwave links, radio links, infrared links, or satellite channels.

The basic structure of a link control protocol is derived from the nature of the transmission means that is used. Any transmission medium or mechanism can only support a finite data rate, the signals travel over a communication channel at a finite speed, and various types of electrical interference can introduce errors into the transmitted information. Since the integrity of the information being transferred is of paramount importance, the data link protocol must account for these limitations, plus the finite data processing speed of the devices connected to the network. In addition to the ability to accommodate the characteristics of the transmission mechanism, the data link protocol must take into account the application and nature of the information, that is, the user requirements.

These requirements are accomplished through the following set of functions that are common to all data link protocols:

- *Initialization.* This function establishes an active connection over an already existing transmission path. How to set up the path and how to move bits over it are the responsibilities of the physical layer processes.
- *An information-segmenting mechanism.* The segmenting mechanism breaks up long streams of data into structured segments of information called *blocks* or *frames.* These blocks or frames consist of data and control bits that are surrounded (i.e., the bit group is delimited or "framed") by either reserved bit patterns (e.g., 01111110) or reserved character sequences (special bit patterns that define a particular character or symbol). This segmenting mechanism allows the selection of a block length that is most likely to survive transmission.

- *Error checking.* Since errors inevitably occur during transmission, the data link protocol must have the ability to detect and correct errors to maintain a high degree of information integrity.
- *Data synchronization.* For the receiver to decode correctly the information that has arrived, a technique for acquiring and maintaining synchronization between the transmitter and the receiver is essential. That is, this information alerts the receiver that a frame is arriving, and the framing bit pattern allows the receiver to know the duration of each bit so that it can synchronize its timing to that of the transmitter.
- *Flow control.* Flow control functions allow a receiver to regulate the incoming data to an input rate that does not exceed the receiver's capacity to accept and process the data. At the data link level flow control is limited to the ability to accept or not to accept information transfers. No overload notification is sent to the transmitter.

As shown in Fig. 2.14, the data link layer accepts an NPDU (packet) from the network layer and then adds the appropriate header (H2) and trailer (T2) bits that contain address and other control information. As noted previously, a data unit with this structure is called an LPDU or a *frame* in the data link layer. Once a receiver node accepts a frame, it removes the header and trailer and forwards the remaining data unit (i.e., a packet) to the network layer.

2.2.7 The Physical Layer

The function of the physical layer[25,26] is to transmit any arbitrary arrangement of data bits (referred to as either a *raw bit stream* or an *unstructured bit stream*) over a physical medium connecting two pieces of communications equipment. It is concerned with

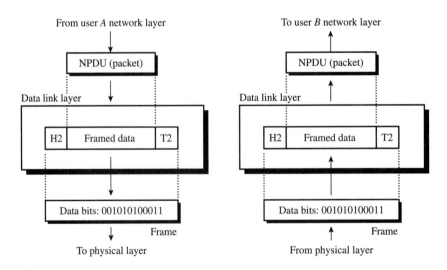

FIGURE 2.14
Exchanges of data units with neighboring layers at the data link layer.

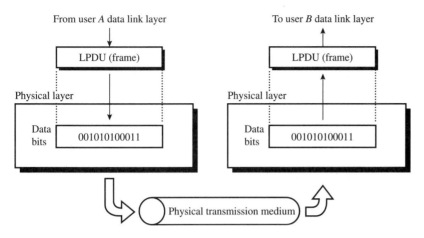

FIGURE 2.15
Exchanges of data units with neighboring layers at the physical layer.

mechanical and electrical network interface specifications; that is, it deals with issues such as signal durations, voltage or optical power levels, connector types, and pin assignments on the connectors. Typically the physical layer is broken into two or more sublayers. The two major divisions are a lower-level *physical media-dependent* (PMD) sublayer and a higher-level *physical media-independent* sublayer, which may have several further subdivisions. The PMD sublayer is concerned with the characteristics and methods of transmitting a signal over the actual physical communication channel. The functions of the media-independent sublayer (or layers) includes accepting a serial bit stream from the PMD, converting it into the data format used by a specific LAN, and interfacing to the data link layer, which may call for specific data-formatting characteristics. Chapters 5 through 9 describe the different physical layer subdivisions for specific LANs.

As shown in Fig. 2.15, the physical layer accepts an LPDU (frame) from the data link layer and converts it into a format that is appropriate to be carried over the physical transmission medium. Chapter 3 discusses these signal types in more detail.

2.3   THE TCP/IP ARCHITECTURE

Figure 2.16 shows the layers of the TCP/IP protocol suite[4,5,27–29] and how they relate to the OSI model. First we give some definitions of message encapsulation in Sec. 2.3.1 and then we examine the application layer in Sec. 2.3.2. The application layer is equivalent to the combined OSI session, presentation, and application layers. TCP/IP has two protocols at the transport layer: the User Datagram Protocol (UDP) and the important Transmission Control Protocol (TCP). Section 2.3.3 defines these two protocols. The fundamental protocol at the internet layer is the Internet Protocol (IP), which is supported by three other protocols (ICMP, ARP, and RARP). These are defined in Sec. 2.3.4. Note that the TCP/IP suite does not define any specific protocol at the data link and physical layers. At these layers TCP/IP supports all standard and proprietary protocols of the underlying networks, whether from a LAN, a MAN, or a WAN. Sometimes these two layers are jointly called the *network access layer* in the TCP/IP suite.

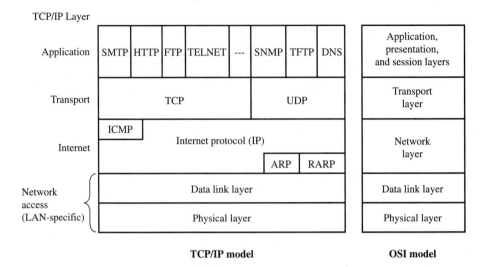

TCP/IP Layer

FIGURE 2.16
Comparison of the TCP/IP and OSI models.

2.3.1 Message Encapsulation

We will now look at each of the TCP/IP layers in more detail. For this we again will follow the flow of information from a user to the physical layer, as in Sec. 2.2 for the OSI model. However, in this section we address only the top three layers of TCP/IP. Section 2.4 discusses the bottom two network-specific layers in terms of the IEEE-802 family of LAN protocols.

Figure 2.17 illustrates how the TCP/IP protocol suite encapsulates data units at the various layers of the model. Analogous to the OSI model, the *message* is the data unit created at the application layer. The transport layer adds a header to form either a *segment* with TCP or a *user datagram* with UDP. Next the network layer adds another header to form a datagram (without the word "user"). A *datagram* is a self-contained message unit which contains sufficient information to allow it to be routed from the source to the destination without dependence on previous message interchanges between the source and the destination. From this point on, to transmit a message physically from one network to another, the protocols of the specific network type that is used need to encapsulate the datagram in a frame at the data link layer and to transmit it as properly encoded bits across the transmission medium.

2.3.2 The Application Layer

Many protocols exist for use at the TCP/IP application layer. Table 2.1 given earlier in the OSI model discussion lists some of the more popular ones. To illustrate these protocols, let us look at the following three examples: an e-mail exchange between two users, web browsing, and a FTP (File Transfer Protocol) process.

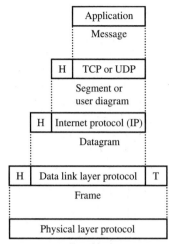

FIGURE 2.17
Encapsulation of data units using the TCP/IP protocol suite.

EXAMPLE 2.3

Figure 2.18 shows the client/server view of an e-mail exchange between user *A* on one network and user *B* on another. Here user *A* prepares a message with the help of an e-mail client application residing in a local computer. Generally a mail server is always running and ready to handle messages. Thus in an e-mail client/server application a user can send anything from short notes

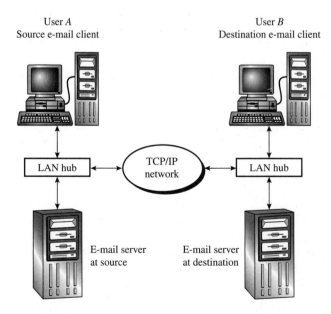

FIGURE 2.18
Client/server view of an e-mail exchange.

to long and complex files without having concern about whether the receiving host is prepared at that moment to receive these messages. The e-mail client typically queues mail to be sent in a separate application located in a local e-mail server. This server sets up communications with remote hosts, stores and delivers messages locally, and transmits mail to destination e-mail servers. At the destination the mail is stored in the private mailbox of the user to be read immediately or at a later time. SMTP (simple mail transfer protocol) defines the specifications for this process using TCP/IP.

EXAMPLE 2.4

The hypertext transfer protocol (HTTP) is the application layer protocol that enables linking to a worldwide web (WWW) page when using a web browser. HTTP uses TCP to get textual or image documents from an information base on the Web. In this case the web browser is the client and the server is the remotely located machine on which the document is stored. As shown in Fig. 2.19, a request command is sent from the client to the WWW server, and a response command is sent from the server to the client. When a user clicks on a web link, HTTP opens a connection to the server, and the server checks for authorization and possibly for a password. The server then sends the requested document and closes the connection to the client, after which the client closes the connection to the server.

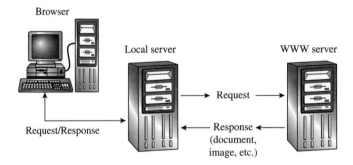

FIGURE 2.19
Linking to a web page using HTTP.

EXAMPLE 2.5

The FTP is used to copy a file from one host to another. It offers many options for creating, changing, or consulting a remote directory, deleting or retrieving a remote file, and choosing the transfer mode, either as a continuous data stream without modification, as partitioned blocks of information, or in a compressed format. FTP messages are encapsulated in TCP and are both reliable and secure. FTP differs from other client/server applications in that it establishes two virtual circuit connections between the communicating end stations, as shown in Fig. 2.20. One connection is for exchange of control messages and the other is for transferring the requested file and sending acknowledgments. When a user initiates a file transfer, FTP first sets up a TCP connection to the document server in order to exchange control messages. This enables the user to supply any required login and password identifiers and allows the user to specify the file and the transfer actions. After a file transfer is approved, a second TCP connection is set up for the data transfer. With this setup a file can be transferred over the data connection without incurring the normal overhead of headers or control information in the data stream at the application level.

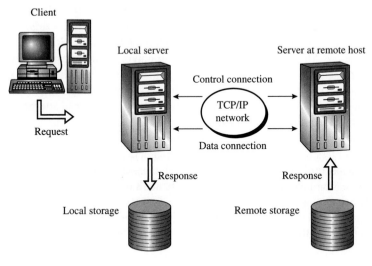

FIGURE 2.20
FTP process in a client/server setting.

2.3.3 The Transport Layer

The transport layer offers two basic types of services. The first of these is the *Transmission Control Protocol* (TCP), which is a *connection-oriented protocol*. This service provides a *reliable* connection for information exchange between different hosts. Typically when using a connection-oriented protocol, the network will guarantee that all packets will be delivered in the correct order, without loss or duplication. If this cannot be done, the network will terminate the call. Thus it is not possible to send a broadcast packet using a connection-oriented protocol since by definition such a packet is sent to multiple hosts on the same network. Examples of upper-level protocols using TCP are FTP, SMTP, and HTTP.

The second type of protocol at the transport layer is the *User Datagram Protocol* (UDP). This service is very basic since it simply offers a best-effort connectionless transfer of individual messages. The term *best effort* means that no error checking or tracking is done. A *connectionless protocol* transmits its data onto the network with a destination address and assumes it will get to the recipient. As such, it provides no mechanism for error recovery or flow control. Since multiple paths can exist when using this service, the service will likely deliver the packets in a different sequence from that in which they were sent. Thus the application at the destination is responsible for rearranging the packets into the correct order. Examples of upper-level protocols using UDP are Trivial File Transfer Protocol (TFTP), network file systems (NFS), and broadcast or multicast.

2.3.4 The Internet Layer

The *internet layer* deals with the transfer of information across one or more networks by using routers, as Fig. 2.21 shows. A *router* is a device that intelligently forwards packets from one network to another, as Chap. 10 describes in detail. There are four protocols at this layer, the most important one is the Internet Protocol (IP). The other peripheral protocols are the *Internet Control Message Protocol* (ICMP), the *Address Resolution Protocol* (ARP), and the *Reverse Address Resolution Protocol* (RARP). These are described in Table 2.2. All traffic, whether incoming or outgoing, must pass through the IP. The addressing scheme of IP accomplishes the primary purpose of the network layer, which is to route packets between different hosts. In the continuous improvement of the TCP/IP protocol suite the IP is evolving to encompass a larger number of addresses and enhanced routing capabilities. Thus in the literature there are numerous articles dealing with migration from IPv4 (version 4) to IPv6 (version 6).[30,31]

IP is a connectionless protocol so that it does not guarantee delivery of packets to adjacent layers. If connection-oriented service is desired, high-level protocols in either the transport or application layer must take care of it. In addition to handling the routing of packets between stations connected to different networks, the internet layer also deals with congestion control. When congestion occurs, the routers that interconnect the intermediate networks may discard packets. The transport layer then is responsible for recovery from these losses.

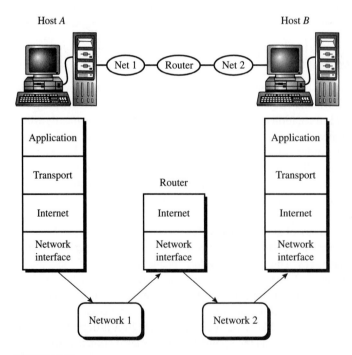

FIGURE 2.21
Use of routers to transfer information between networks.

TABLE 2.2
Protocols operating at the TCP/IP internet layer

Protocol name	Acronym	Function
Internet Protocol	IP	Responsible for addressing packets, packet routing, fragmentation, reassembly, and moving data between its neighboring transport and data link layers.
Internet Control Message Protocol	ICMP	Performs flow control, issues unreachable destination alerts, redirects routes, and checks remote hosts using an echo packet known as a *ping* packet.
Address Resolution Protocol	ARP	Translates the software address of a host to a hardware address.
Reverse Address Resolution Protocol	RARP	Determines a software address from a hardware address. Dynamic Host Configuration Protocol (DHCP) is now used more commonly than RARP.

2.4 LAN PROTOCOLS

The key features that distinguish how a particular LAN operates are its architecture and the protocols to which it adheres. The IEEE has standardized an extensive set of protocols for some of the major LAN architectures, such as Ethernet, token rings, and wireless LANs.[32,33] We will look at the foundations of protocols for these LANs in this section. Other standards organizations that have released LAN protocols are ANSI[34] and the ATM Forum.[35,36] Details of these protocols are given in Chaps. 6, 7, and 9.

2.4.1 IEEE Project 802

The Working Group 802 of the IEEE has been a major creator of specifications for LAN architectures. The IEEE-802 LAN standards are modularly structured, which makes them a powerful set of protocols. By means of this modularity it subdivides the LAN management functions into those that can be generalized and those that must remain specific to a particular LAN architecture. Table 2.3 lists the various IEEE-802 subgroups and technical advisory groups (TAG). Occasionally some of these groups are not active ("hibernating") because either the standards are mature at the moment or the technology is now obsolete. See the website "http://www.ieee802.org" for the most current status.

Some representative IEEE-802 LAN standards are listed in Table 2.4 and are based on the three-layer model shown in Fig. 2.22, that is, the LLC, MAC, and physical layers, where the physical layer may be further subdivided, as noted in Sec. 2.2.7. Note that these specifications may have addenda, which get added when the technology or the operating trends change. For example, IEEE 802.1, which deals with higher-layer LAN protocols, has addenda such as 802.1D for MAC-layer bridging and 802.1Q for virtual bridges. These bridging schemes are discussed further in Chap. 10. The basic 802 layers correspond to the two lower levels of the OSI and the TCP/IP models so that they specify the physical and data link layer characteristics. The data

TABLE 2.3

Functions of the various IEEE-802 Commitee Working Groups and Technical Advisory Groups

IEEE 802 designation	Subcommittee name	Function
802.0	Sponsor executive committee	Consists of all WG and TAG chairpersons.
802.1	Higher layer LAN protocols WG	Standards for bridging and virtual LANs; overall architecture of IEEE 802 LANs.
802.2	Logical link control WG	Hibernating (mature standard).
802.3	Ethernet WG	Access method and signaling for Fast Ethernet and Gigabit Ethernet.
802.4	Token bus WG	Hibernating (Industry is no longer pursuing the technology.)
802.5	Token ring WG	Hibernating (Industry is no longer pursuing the technology.)
802.6	Metropolitan area network WG	Hibernating.
802.7	Broadband TAG	Hibernating (Industry is no longer pursuing the technology.)
802.8	Fiber optics TAG	Group has been disbanded.
802.9	Integrated services LAN WG	Develops standards for isochronous LANs (hibernating).
802.10	Standards for interoperable LAN security (SILS) WG	Hibernating: The SILS WG has completed its work in providing standards for LAN/MAN security.
802.11	Wireless LAN WG	Access method and signaling for wireless LANs.
802.12	Demand priority WG	Hibernating.
802.14	Cable-TV based broadband communication network WG	Group has been disbanded.
802.15	Wireless personal area network	Develops standards for short-distance wireless networks.
802.16	Broadband wireless access	Standards for fixed broadband wireless access systems in MANs.
802.17	Resilient packet ring (RPR) WG	Defining a RPR access protocol for rates up to many Gbps.

link layer is partitioned into the *logical link control* (LLC) and the *media access control* (MAC) sublayers. The LLC layer, as specified by IEEE 802.2, is common to all LANs and deals with supervising transmission between nodes. The MAC layer handles access to the shared medium and is specific to the type of LAN that is implemented.

The next two subsections look at the functions of the LLC and MAC layers in more detail. Specific descriptions of the LAN-specific 802.3 and 802.9, 802.5, and 802.11 standards are given in Chaps. 5, 6, and 8, respectively. As described in these chapters, each LAN standard normally has various physical layer options.

TABLE 2.4
Some representative IEEE-802 LAN and MAN standards

Specification	Title
802, 1999 (update)	Architecture and overview
802.1B, 1995	LAN/MAN management
802.1D, 1998	Media access control (MAC) bridges
802.1E, 1994	System load protocol
802.1F, 1998	IEEE 802 management information
802.1G, 1998	Remote media access control (MAC) bridging
802.1Q, 1998	Virtual bridge local area networks
802.2, 1998	Logical link control (LLC)
802.3, 2000	CSMA/CD access method and physical layer specifications
802.5, 1998	Token-ring access method and physical layer specifications
802.6, 1994	Distributed queue dual bus (DQDB) access method
802.7, 1997	IEEE recommended practices for broadband LANs
802.9, 1996	Integrated services LAN interface at the MAC and physical layers
802.10, 1998	Interoperable LAN/MAN security (SILS)
802.11, 1999	Wireless LAN MAC and physical layer (PHY) specifications
802.12, 1998	Demand priority access method for 100 Mbps operation
802.14, 1998	Cable-TV access method and physical layer specification
802.15, 2001	Wireless personal area networks (PANs)

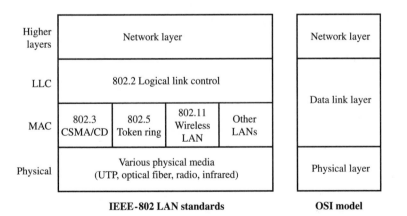

FIGURE 2.22
The IEEE-802 LAN model.

2.4.2   The Logical Link Control (LLC) Layer

The LLC is the upper sublayer of the IEEE-802 data link layer and is common to all LAN protocols. The IEEE-802 standards group the data link functions such as connection setup, initialization, data formatting, address recognition, error control, flow control, and connection termination within the LLC sublayer. Thus this sublayer supervises the transmission of a packet between nodes. For example, since the MAC protocols normally do not include error control mechanisms, the LLC can provide this by retransmitting a packet until its destination acknowledges its receipt. In some applications the higher layer arranges for reliable transmission. In these situations the LLC merely delivers the packets and discards erroneous ones.

The LLC builds on the underlying MAC datagram service to provide the following three fundamental end-to-end services:

- *Unacknowledged connectionless service* that uses unnumbered frames to transfer nonsequenced information. This service, which does not require the overhead of establishing a logical connection, is used to support highly interactive traffic.
- *Reliable connection-oriented service* that uses information frames. This requires connection setup and release processes, and the connection offers error control, sequencing, and flow control. This is helpful when the end systems do not use a transport layer protocol to provide reliable service.
- *Acknowledged connectionless service* that transfers individual frames with acknowledgment.

The data unit at the LLC level is called the *LLC protocol data unit* (LLC PDU) or frame. As shown in Fig. 2.23, it consists of the following fields:

- *DSAP and SSAP address fields.* These 8-bit fields identify the source and the destination SAP addresses in that they identify the receiving and sending machines that use the link layer service. The first bit of the DSAP field indicates whether the frame goes to an individual or to a group of users. The first bit of the SSAP field shows whether the frame is a command or a response PDU.
- *Control field.* The control field is either 8 or 16 bits long depending on whether the PDU is an information frame, a supervisory frame, or an unnumbered frame.
- *Information field.* The information field is a variable-length packet from the network layer.

The LLC PDU is encapsulated in IEEE MAC frames, as shown in Fig. 2.23 and described subsequently.

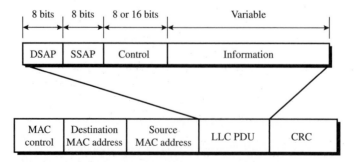

FIGURE 2.23
Formats of an LLC PDU and a generic media access control (MAC) frame.

2.4.3 The Media Access Control (MAC) Sublayer

The MAC sublayer regulates network access by dividing a shared link into virtual point-to-point links between pairs of stations. When a higher layer sends a LLC PDU to the MAC with a destination address, the MAC sublayer delivers it to the destination as if there were a dedicated link between the two end stations. In doing this, it constructs a *frame* that includes the source and the destination MAC addresses in a header and a frame check sequence (FCS) in a trailer. The MAC addresses specify the physical connections of the communicating stations to the LAN.

Although the exact MAC frame format differs slightly for the various MAC protocols, a common format is shown in Fig. 2.23. The fields within this frame are the following:

- The *control field* contains control information for proper functioning of the MAC protocol.
- The *destination MAC address field* indicates the destination physical attachment point on the LAN for this frame.
- The *source MAC address field* indicates the source physical attachment point on the LAN for this frame.
- The LLC PDU field is described in Sec. 2.4.2.
- The *cyclic redundancy check* (CRC) field, which also is known as the *frame check sequence* (FCS) field, is a function of the bits in the control, address, and LLC fields. First it is calculated and attached by the sender. The receiver calculates it again; if the results differ, then a transmission error has occurred.

The specific details of MAC frame formats are given in the chapters relating to individual LAN standards. Section 3.3.3 shows how to calculate the CRC.

2.5 SUMMARY

Since the conceptualization, design, and implementation of a computer network is a rather complex task, traditionally this problem has been subdivided into a number of individual pieces of manageable and comprehensible size. This has resulted in a layered structure of services, with the five-layer hierarchically structured TCP/IP model as the most widely used. This model establishes a common set of protocols that governs the generation, formatting, control, and interpretation of transmitted information through a network. The upper layers of the model support user applications, and the lower layers govern the transmission facilities.

The TCP/IP suite does not define any specific protocol at the two lowest layers, that is, the data link and physical layers. For these TCP/IP supports all standard and proprietary protocols of the underlying networks, whether from a LAN, a MAN, or a WAN. For LAN implementations the lower two layers are divided into three sublayers. These are the logical link control (LLC), the media access control (MAC), and the physical layer. The LLC is the upper sublayer of the IEEE-802 data link layer and is common to all LAN protocols. Its functions include connection setup, initialization, data formatting, address recognition, error control, flow control, and connection termination. The MAC sublayer regulates network access by dividing a shared link into virtual point-to-point links between pairs of stations. The function of the physical layer is to transmit any arbitrary arrangement of data bits over a physical medium connecting two pieces of communications equipment. It is concerned with mechanical and electrical network interface specifications, such as signal durations, voltage or optical power levels, connector types, and pin assignments on the connectors.

Of interest in this book are how a particular LAN operates, its architecture, and the protocols to which it adheres. The IEEE-802 Working Group has standardized an extensive set of protocols for some of the major LAN architectures, such as Ethernet, token rings, and wireless LANs. Other standards organizations that have released LAN protocols are ANSI and the ATM Forum. The information concerning protocol structures given in this chapter is a basis for examining the details of these various LANs, which are described in Chaps. 5 through 9.

PROBLEMS

2.1. In a *positive acknowledgment retransmit* (PAR) data link protocol, framed message blocks are checked at the receiver to assure that they arrived in the proper sequence. If they arrived correctly, a positive acknowledgment is returned; if errors occurred, the block must be retransmitted. To recover from lost messages, whenever a transmitter sends a message it starts a retransmit timer. If no positive acknowledgment is received at the expiration of the retransmit time, the message is sent out again. To avoid confusion as to which message is acknowledged, the acknowledgments must be numbered to correspond to the messages they verified.

(a) Using this type of protocol, draw a time-sequence diagram for the following message exchange scenario:
- Message 1 transmitted and acknowledged
- Message 2 transmitted and lost on first try
- Message 3 received incorrectly on first try

(b) What are some pitfalls that must be avoided in this protocol?

2.2. The utilization U (or efficiency) of a transmission channel depends on the following parameters:
- A = number of bits in an ACK frame
- C = channel capacity in bits per second (bps)
- D = number of data bits per frame
- H = number of bits in the frame header
- $F = D + H$ = total frame length
- I = propagation delay time + message processing time at the receiver (before an ACK is sent out)
- L = probability that a frame or its ACK is lost or damaged
- R = mean number of retransmissions per data frame
- T = time-out interval (set by the transmitter before another message is sent)

(a) Show that the probability of failure L is given by

$$L = 1 - (1 - P_2)(1 - P_1)$$

Here P_1 is the probability that a data frame is lost or damaged and P_2 is the probability that an ACK frame is lost or damaged.

(b) Show that $R = L/(1 - L)$.

(c) Show that the channel utilization U is given by

$$U = \frac{D}{[L/(1 - L)](F + CT) + (F + A + 2CI)}$$

2.3. A channel has a transmission capability of 56 kbps and a propagation delay (time for a bit to travel over the channel) of 20 ms.

  (a) For what range of frame sizes does the PAR protocol in Prob. 2.1 have an efficiency of at least 50 percent for error-free transmission? For simplicity assume there is no overhead and the length of an ACK frame is negligible compared to a data frame.

  (b) What is the minimum time interval at which the retransmit timer can be set?

2.4. Consider the following frame format for a bit-oriented data link protocol:

8-bit flag	8 bits	8 bits	≤ 1024 bits	16 bits	8-bit flag
01111110	Address	Control	Data	FCS	01111110

Here the special 8-bit sequence (01111110) is called a *flag*. These bits indicate the beginning and the end of a frame. The 16-bit FCS field is the frame check sequence described in Sec. 2.4.3. Use the parameter values and equations from Prob. 2.2.

  (a) What is the maximum data transfer efficiency that is possible?

  (b) Consider the PAR data link protocol described in Prob. 2.1. What is the transmission overhead (bandwidth wasted on headers and retransmission) if the error rate for data frames is 1 percent and the positive acknowledgment (ACK) frames are 40 bits long? Assume the error rate for ACK frames is negligible, and let the message processing time at the receiver (before the ACK is sent out) be 5 ms.

2.5. To distinguish data from the flag sequence 01111110 in a bit-oriented protocol, a procedure called *bit stuffing* is used. Whenever the transmitter sees five consecutive 1s in the data, it automatically inserts a 0 bit into the outgoing bit stream. At the receiving end whenever the receiver detects five consecutive 1 bits followed by a 0 bit, it automatically deletes the 0 bit. Determine the data stream appearing on the line for the following original data sequences:

  (a) 01101111111111111110010

  (b) 01111011111011111110111100

2.6. Describe the main differences between connectionless service and connection-oriented service. List some protocols that can be used with each type of service.

2.7. Describe the differences between a confirmed service and an unconfirmed service. Do the following functions fall into the category of confirmed service, unconfirmed service, both types, or neither:

  (a) Connection establishment

  (b) Data transfer in a connection-oriented service

  (c) Data transfer in a connectionless service

  (d) Connection release

2.8. Discuss some of the technical differences between virtual circuits using TCP and datagrams using UDP. Consider factors such as error control, flow control, packet sequencing, and overhead involved in setting up a circuit.

2.9. Flow control often is specified in both the data link layer and the network layer. Explain the difference between these two functions.

2.10. List the similarities between a communication network and the following delivery systems:

  (a) *The postal system.* Consider the steps involved from the time a letter is deposited in a mailbox to the time it is delivered to the addressee.

  (b) *Airline ticketing.* Consider the steps involved from the time a ticket reservation is initiated to the time the passenger receives the ticket.

  (c) *Pizza delivery.* Consider the steps involved from the time a customer decides on an order to the time the customer receives the pizza.

2.11. Which TCP/IP layers are responsible for the following functions when a message is sent from user *A* on network 1 to user *B* on network 2:
   (a) Selecting a route for message flow through the network
   (b) Performing error control
   (c) Ensuring security of the message transfer
   (d) Formatting message bits into frames

2.12. What is the need and advantage of UDP? Is it possible for a user program to bypass UDP and to go directly to the IP layer?

2.13. What would happen if one tried using the following application layer protocols with UDP?
   (a) Requesting a file transfer via FTP
   (b) Sending an e-mail via SMTP

2.14. Suppose the TCP entity receives an 800-kilobyte file from the application layer and that the IP layer can accommodate data units that have a maximum size of 1200 bytes. What is the overhead that is incurred from segmenting this data unit into the appropriately sized packets?

2.15. Routers are devices that connect nodes and networks of different architectures by performing protocol translations. Discuss some of the functions that routers would need to perform for the following:
   (a) Connections between dissimilar LANs (e.g., one supporting datagrams and one supporting virtual circuit connections).
   (b) Connections between devices on the same LAN that understand different higher-level protocols.

2.16. Consider the GEK Corporation, which distributes office products that come from manufacturers in both the United States and overseas (through importers). The customers are in three geographically separated localities, one of which is near the main business office of GEK. Each geographical location has a central warehouse that fulfills orders. Salespersons call in their orders to the appropriate local warehouse using portable terminals, which operate in a remote-job-entry mode. When warehouse personnel receive orders, they adjust inventories for committed stock and make shipping invoices. The two remotely located warehouses report their inventory and business activity to the home office on a daily basis.
   To remain competitive, the central offices of GEK require access to the web-based ordering sites of their suppliers, and they access the inventory databases of their remotely located warehouses via TELNET.
   (a) Discuss the networking and protocol issues of this corporation with respect to local area networking, database access, remote job entry, and electronic mail.
   (b) What are some of the applications that would need to be performed by a LAN in the headquarters building?

2.17. A LAN is to be installed in a three-story office building. The LAN will need to accommodate the following devices and services:
   (a) One hundred twenty desktop personal computers from various vendors, all based on the same operating system
   (b) Three shared black-and-white laser printers per floor
   (c) One color printer per floor for authorized users
   (d) A shared server housing specialized applications
   (e) Internet accesses for all users
   Describe some of the protocol issues that need to be considered when implementing this LAN.

2.18. (a) Consider a system with a five-layer protocol hierarchy. Suppose an application generates a message that is 1024 bits long. If each of layers 5 through 2 add a 16-bit header and there is a 16-bit trailer appended at layer 2, what fraction of the network bandwidth is filled with overhead bits?

(b) How does this fraction change in a seven-layer model?

2.19. A popular application layer protocol is a file transfer protocol (FTP). Its purpose is to transfer a file or a portion of a file from one system to another under the command of an FTP user. To carry out a file transfer, a connection first must be established between the sending and receiving nodes. Once this has been made, the following operations are carried out:

(a) A READ exchange initiated by the requestor

(b) One or more DATA exchanges initiated by the file recipient

(c) A DATA-END exchange initiated by the file recipient

(d) A TRANSFER-END exchange initiated by the requestor

What logical sequence of connections is required in order for a user located at node *A* to request that a file be exchanged between node *B* and node *C*?

REFERENCES

1. J. M. McQuillan and D. C. Walden, "The ARPA network design decision," *Comput. Networks,* vol. 1, pp. 243–289, Aug. 1977.
2. V. G. Cerf and E. Cain, "The DoD Internet architecture model," *Comput. Networks,* vol. 7, pp. 307–318, Oct. 1983.
3. B. M. Leiner, R. Cole, J. Postel, and D. Mills, "The DARPA Internet protocol suite," *IEEE Comm. Mag.,* vol. 23, pp. 29–34, Mar. 1985.
4. Chris Lewis, *Cisco TCP/IP,* McGraw-Hill, New York, 3rd ed., 2000.
5. B. A. Forouzan, *TCP/IP Protocol Suite,* McGraw-Hill, Burr Ridge, IL, 2000.
6. R. J. Bates and D. W. Gregory, *Voice and Data Communications Handbook,* McGraw-Hill, New York, 3rd ed., 2000, Chap. 15.
7. J. D. Day, "The (un)revised OSI Reference Model," *Comput. Commun. Rev.,* vol. 25, pp. 39–55, Oct. 1995.
8. ITU-T Recommendation X.200, *OSI Basic Reference Model,* Jul. 1994.
9. B. Jain and A. Agrawala, *Open Systems Interconnection,* McGraw-Hill, New York, 1990.
10. L. Pouzin and H. Zimmermann, "A tutorial on protocols," *Proc. IEEE,* vol. 66, pp. 1346–1370, Nov. 1978.
11. T. Russell, *Telecommunication Protocols,* McGraw-Hill, New York, 2nd ed., 2000.
12. ITU-T Recommendation X.210, *Basic Reference Model: Conventions for the Definitions of OSI Services,* Nov. 1993.
13. A. Tanenbaum, *Computer Networks,* Prentice-Hall, Upper Saddle River, NJ, 3rd ed., 1996.
14. A. Leon-Garcia and I. Widjaja, *Communication Networks,* McGraw-Hill, Burr Ridge, IL, 2000.
15. W. Stallings, *Data and Computer Communications,* Prentice-Hall, Upper Saddle River, 6th ed., 2000.
16. ITU-T Recommendation X.207, *OSI Application Layer Structure,* Nov. 1993.
17. ITU-T Recommendation X.216, *OSI Presentation Service Definition,* Jul. 1994.
18. W. F. Emmons and A. S. Chandler, "OSI Session Layer: Services and protocols," *Proc. IEEE,* vol. 71, pp. 1397–1400, Dec. 1983.
19. ITU-T Recommendation X.215, *OSI Session Service Definition,* Nov. 1995.
20. ITU-T Recommendation X.214, *OSI Transport Service Definition,* Nov. 1995.
21. C. Ware, "The OSI Network Layer: Standards to cope with the real world," *Proc. IEEE,* vol. 71, pp. 1384–1387, Dec. 1983.
22. ITU-T Recommendation X.213, *OSI Network Service Definition,* Nov. 1995.
23. ITU-T Recommendation X.212, *OSI Data Link Service Definition,* Nov. 1995.
24. J. W. Coward, "Services and protocols of the data-link layer," *Proc. IEEE,* vol. 71, pp. 1378–1383, Dec. 1983.
25. ITU-T Recommendation X.211, *OSI Physical Service Definition,* Nov. 1995.

26. F. M. McClelland, "Services and protocols of the physical layer," *Proc. IEEE,* vol. 71, pp. 1372–1377, Dec. 1983.

27. D. E. Comer, *Internetworking with TCP/IP Vol. I: Principles, Protocols, and Architecture,* Prentice-Hall, Upper Saddle River, 4th ed., 2000.

28. G. Held, *Managing TCP/IP Networks: Techniques, Tools, and Security Considerations,* Wiley, New York, 2000.

29. D. M. Piscitello and A. L. Chapin, *Open Systems Networking: TCP/IP and OSI,* Addison-Wesley, Reading, MA, 1993.

30. D. C. Lee, D. L. Lough, S. F. Midkiff, N. J. Davis IV, and P. E. Benchoff, "The next generation of the Internet: Aspects of the Internet Protocol version 6," *IEEE Network,* vol. 12, pp. 28–33, Jan./Feb. 1998.

31. M. Goncalves and K. Niles, *IPv6 Networks,* McGraw-Hill, New York, 1998.

32. The Institute of Electrical and Electronics Engineers (IEEE) (http://www.ieee.org).

33. J. Carlo, "The IEEE 802 organization," *IEEE Network,* vol. 12, pp. 8–9, Jan./Feb. 1998.

34. The American National Standards Institute (ANSI) (http://www.ansi.org).

35. ATM Forum (http://www.atmforum.com).

36. G. H. Dobrowski, "The ATM Forum: Developing implementation agreements," *IEEE Commun. Mag.,* vol. 36, pp. 121–125, Sept. 1998.

CHAPTER

3

DATA
COMMUNICATION
CONCEPTS

To exchange information between any two devices in a LAN (local area network), some type of electrical or optical signal which carries this information has to be transmitted from one device to the other via a communication channel. This channel could consist of either a wire, a radio, a microwave, a satellite, an infrared, or an optical fiber link. Each of the media used for such communication channels has unique performance characteristics associated with it. Regardless of its type, the medium degrades the fidelity of the transmitted signal because of both an imperfect response to the signal and the presence of electrical and/or optical noise and interference. This can lead to misinterpretations of the signal at the receiving end.

To help readers understand the various factors that affect the physical transfer of information-bearing signals, this chapter gives a basic overview of fundamental data communication concepts. In particular, we examine how communication theory applies to the physical and data link layers for LAN applications. These concepts will provide technical reference material in helping to understand the following chapters. They are given at an introductory level for those readers with limited background in data communications. Readers who desire more detailed information may consult the references given at the end of this chapter.[1–12]

We start by giving some basic concepts and definitions used in data communications and the possible formats of a signal. The signal format is an important factor in efficiently and reliably sending information both within a LAN and from a LAN across a more extensive network to another LAN. Section 3.1 addresses these formats and the types of impairments that can affect a signal as it traverses a channel. Then in Sec. 3.2 we examine the various data encoding techniques used to match the signal properties with the transmission characteristics of the channel. This is significant because the receiver must be able to interpret correctly the information contained in the incoming signal.

As a signal travels along a transmission medium, it will become attenuated and distorted owing to power loss and a variety of signal degradation effects in the line. Thus no matter what type of modulation scheme is used, errors are unavoidable in any real communication system because of noise bursts, data dropouts (e.g., switches temporarily open), or long transient interferences. Sections 3.3 and 3.4 describe the origins of these errors, show what limitations the errors impose on signal transmission fidelity, and discuss how to detect and possibly correct errors in a digital data stream. There also must be mechanisms in a network to handle the possibility of transmission errors and to regulate the rate at which traffic arrives at the destination. Two important functions for addressing these mechanisms at the data link layer are flow control and error control, which are the topics of Sec. 3.5.

The choice of a transmission medium has a major impact on the type of data the LAN can handle, the transmission speed, and the degree of flexibility for accommodating a variety of users. Section 3.6 describes the characteristics of various media that are used in LANs. To utilize efficiently the capacity of a transmission medium when many lower-capacity devices are attached to it, one turns to the concept of multiplexing, whereby many users simultaneously share a large-capacity transmission medium. This is the topic of Sec. 3.7.

3.1 BASIC CONCEPTS

This section first presents some basic terminology used in data communications and then describes two elementary formats of a signal. This is followed by discussions of how attenuation, distortion, and noise impairments change the characteristics of a signal as it travels along a communication channel. Later sections address encoding schemes and methods that may be used to mitigate the occurrence of errors introduced by signal impairments. Finally we see how the unwanted noise components that are added to a signal place an upper bound on the capacity of a communication channel.

3.1.1 Terminology

Three basic terms used in describing a communication system are data, information, and signal. First, *data* is an entity that conveys information. Data has to do with the form of something, such as arrays of integers, video frames, lines of text, or images. The word *information* refers to the content or meaning of the data or how it is interpreted. For example, information could be facts, concepts, or instructions. Although each of the words *data* and *information* has a specific definition, these terms, along with the word *message,* often are used loosely in the literature to refer to the same thing. *Signals* are electromagnetic waves (in electrical or optical formats) that are used to transport the data over a physical medium.

A block diagram of a typical communication link is shown in Fig. 3.1. The purpose of such a link is to transfer a message from an originating LAN user called a *source* to another LAN user called the *destination.* Here we assume the users could be on the same or different LANs. The output of the source serves as the message input to a transmitter.

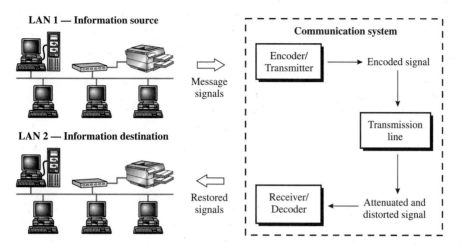

FIGURE 3.1
Diagram of a typical communication link between two LANs.

The function of the *transmitter* is to couple the message onto a transmission channel in the form of a signal that matches the transfer properties of the channel. This process is known as *encoding.*

As the signal travels through the channel, various imperfect properties of the channel induce impairments into the signal. The function of the *receiver* is to extract the weakened and distorted signal from the channel, to amplify it, and to restore it as close as possible to its original encoded form before *decoding* and passing it on to the message destination.

3.1.2 Signal Characteristics

Both the user information and the signals that represent this information can be of either an analog or a digital form. *Analog* information is generated in a continuous form, such as audio or video signals. *Digital* information refers to something that is discrete, such as numbers from a computer or letters of the alphabet, or it can be a digitized form of an analog signal. To be transmitted from one user to another, this information must be transformed into some type of time-varying electrical or optical waveform or *signal.* These signals likewise can be of either an analog or a digital form.

The most fundamental *analog signal* is the periodic *sine wave,* shown in Fig. 3.2. Its three main characteristics are its amplitude, period or frequency, and phase. The *amplitude* is the size or magnitude of the waveform. This is generally designated by the symbol "A" and is measured in either *volts, amperes,* or *watts,* depending on the signal type. The *frequency* (designated by f) is the number of cycles per second that the wave undergoes, which is expressed in units of *hertz* (Hz). The *period* (generally represented by the symbol T) is the inverse of the frequency; that is, *period* $= T = 1/f$. The term *phase* (designated by the symbol ϕ) describes the position of the waveform relative to time zero, as illustrated in Fig. 3.3. This is measured in *degrees* or *radians* ($180° = \pi$ rad).

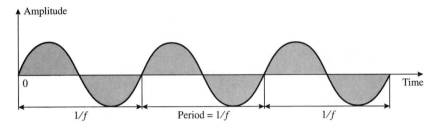

FIGURE 3.2
The periodic sine wave is a fundamental analog signal.

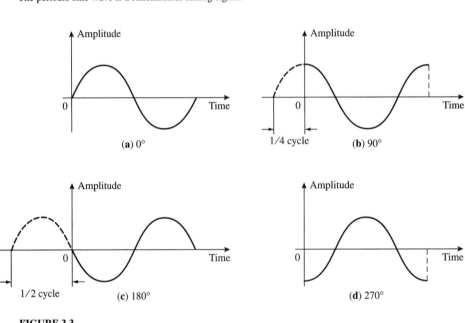

FIGURE 3.3
Concept of phase shifts relative to time zero.

EXAMPLE 3.1

- A sine wave has a frequency $f = 5$ kHz. Its period is $T = 1/5000$ s $= 0.20$ ms.
- A sine wave has a period $T = 1$ ns (nanosecond). Its frequency is $f = 1/(10^{-9}$ s$) = 1$ GHz (gigahertz).
- A sine wave is offset by one-quarter of a cycle with respect to time zero. Since one cycle is $360°$ the phase shift is $\phi = 0.25 \times 360° = 90° = \pi/2$ rad (radians).

Two further common characteristics in communications are the frequency spectrum (or simply spectrum) and the bandwidth of a signal. The *spectrum* of a signal is the range of frequencies that it contains. That is, the spectrum of a signal is the combination of all the individual sine waves of different frequencies which make up that signal. The *bandwidth* (designated by B) refers to the width of this spectrum.

EXAMPLE 3.2

If the spectrum of a signal ranges from its lowest frequency $f_{low} = 2$ kHz (kilohertz) to its highest frequency $f_{high} = 22$ kHz, then the bandwidth $B = f_{high} - f_{low} = 20$ kHz.

Digital signals can have two or more different amplitudes. A common configuration is the *binary* waveform shown in Fig. 3.4. A binary waveform is represented by a sequence of two types of pulses of known shape. The information contained in a digital signal is given by the particular sequence of the presence (a *binary one,* or simply either *one* or 1) and absence (a *binary zero,* or simply either *zero* or 0) of these pulses, which are commonly known as *bits* (this word was derived from *binary digits*). Since digital logic is used in the generation and processing of 1 and 0 bits, these bits often are referred to as a *logic one* (or *logic* 1) and a *logic zero* (or *logic* 0), respectively. The binary arithmetic used by this logic follows the rules of addition and multiplication given in Table 3.1. A block of 8 bits frequently is used to represent an encoded symbol or word and is referred to as an *octet* or a *byte.*

The time slot T in which a bit occurs is called either the *bit interval, bit period,* or *bit time.* (Note that this T is different from the T used for designating the period of a

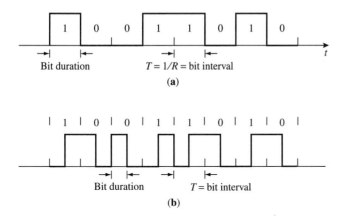

FIGURE 3.4
Examples of two binary waveforms showing their amplitude, period, and bit duration. (*a*) The bit fills the entire bit period; (*b*) the bit fills half a bit period.

TABLE 3.1
Arithmetic rules for binary logic

Addition	Multiplication
$0 + 0 = 0$	$0 \times 0 = 0$
$0 + 1 = 1$	$0 \times 1 = 0$
$1 + 0 = 1$	$1 \times 0 = 0$
$1 + 1 = 0$	$1 \times 1 = 1$

waveform.) The bit intervals are regularly spaced and occur every $1/R$ seconds (s), or at a rate of R *bits per second* (abbreviated as *bps* in this book), where R is called the *bit rate* or the *data rate*. A bit can fill the entire bit interval or part of it.

The term *baud* refers to the number of signal units per second that are needed to represent those bits, which means it represents the efficiency with which one can transmit data bits. The signal units, which are called *symbols,* are measured by the modulation rate of a signal or the number of transitions the signal makes per second. When fewer signal units are required to represent a certain number of bits, the communication system is more efficient and less bandwidth is needed to transmit these bits. For example, as shown in Sec. 3.3, in some data encoding schemes a signaling symbol may represent 1 bit, whereas in other schemes it may represent 2 or more bits.

EXAMPLE 3.3

A certain analog signal can carry 2 bits in each signaling element or symbol. If 10^6 symbols are sent per second, then we have

$$\text{Bit rate} = \text{symbol rate} \times \text{bits per symbol}$$
$$= 10^6 \text{ transitions per second} \times 2 \text{ bits per transition} = 2 \text{ Mbps}$$

3.1.3 Signal Impairments

Regardless of what type of transmission means is used, as the signal traverses the medium it becomes progressively attenuated, distorted, and corrupted by noise with increasing distance since no transmission medium is perfect.

Attenuation

Attenuation (reduction) of the signal strength arises from various loss mechanisms in a transmission medium. For example, electric power is lost through heat generation as an electric signal flows along a wire, and optical power is attenuated through scattering and absorption processes in a glass fiber or in an atmospheric channel. To compensate for these energy losses, amplifiers are used periodically along a channel to boost the signal level, as shown in Fig. 3.5.

A convenient method for establishing a measure of attenuation is to reference the signal level to some absolute value or to a noise level. For guided media the signal strength normally decays exponentially so that for convenience one can designate it in terms of a logarithmic power ratio measured in *decibels* (dB). In unguided (wireless) media the attenuation is a more complex function of distance and the composition of the atmosphere. The dB unit is defined by

$$\text{Power ratio in dB} = 10 \log \frac{P_2}{P_1} \tag{3.1}$$

where P_1 and P_2 are the electrical or optical power levels of a signal at points 1 and 2 in Fig. 3.6, and *log* is the base-10 logarithm. The logarithmic nature of the decibel allows

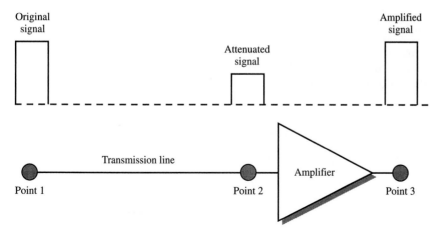

FIGURE 3.5
Amplifiers periodically compensate for energy losses along a channel.

FIGURE 3.6
P_1 and P_2 are the electrical or optical power levels of a signal at points 1 and 2.

a large ratio to be expressed in a fairly simple manner. Power levels differing by many orders of magnitude can be compared easily when they are in decibel form. Another attractive feature of the decibel is that to measure the changes in the strength of a signal, one merely adds or subtracts the decibel numbers between two different points.

EXAMPLE 3.4

Assume after traveling a certain distance in some transmission medium the power of a signal is reduced to half; that is, $P_2 = 0.5P_1$ in Fig. 3.6. At this point the attenuation or loss of power is

$$10 \log \frac{P_2}{P_1} = 10 \log \frac{0.5 P_1}{P_1} = 10 \log 0.5 = 10(-0.3) = -3 \text{ dB}$$

Thus −3 dB (or a 3-dB attenuation) means that the signal has lost half its power. If an amplifier is inserted into the link at this point to boost the signal back to its original level, then that amplifier has a 3-dB gain.

EXAMPLE 3.5

Consider the transmission path from point 1 to point 4 shown in Fig. 3.7. Here the signal is attenuated by 9 dB between points 1 and 2. After getting a 14-dB boost from an amplifier at point 3, it is again attenuated by 3 dB between points 3 and 4. Relative to point 1, the signal level in dB at point 4 is

$$\text{dB level at point 4} = (\text{loss in line 1}) + (\text{amplifier gain}) + (\text{loss in line 2})$$
$$= (-9\text{ dB}) + (14\text{ dB}) + (-3\text{ dB}) = +2\text{ dB}$$

Thus the signal has a 2-dB gain in power.

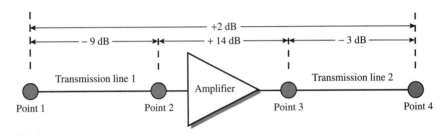

FIGURE 3.7
Example of attenuation and amplification in a transmission path.

Since the decibel is used to refer to ratios or relative units, it gives no indication of the absolute power level. However, a derived unit can be used for this. Such a unit that is particularly common in optical fiber communications is the *dBm*. This unit expresses the power level *P* as a logarithmic ratio of *P* referred to 1 mW (milliwatt). In this case the power in dBm is an absolute value defined by

$$\text{Power level (in dBm)} = 10 \log \frac{P}{1\text{ mW}} \tag{3.2}$$

An important rule-of-thumb relationship to remember for optical fiber communications is 0 dBm = 1 mW. For electrical systems one may see the unit dBW, which is the power level referred to 1 W.

Distortion

Delay effects in a transmission medium cause signals to change their shape as they travel along the channel. For a wireless channel, signal distortion is caused by multipath propagation effects. In such a channel the signal travels not only directly to the receiver, but part of it also may be reflected off nearby surfaces, thereby arriving at the receiver somewhat later than the direct signal. This causes a spread in the received signal and is the main degradation mechanism for wireless systems. Chapter 8 gives more details on this phenomenon. Here we address delay distortion in guided media.

In general a signal is made up of many frequency components, each of which has a slightly different propagation speed through a guided medium. Thus the various frequency components of a signal will arrive at the receiver at different times, which results in phase shifts between the frequencies. This effect is called *delay distortion* since the received signal is distorted as a result of varying delays of its constituent frequencies. In a digital system delay distortion will cause each bit to spread out in time so that the signal components of a particular bit position will spill over into adjacent bit positions. This is a major limitation to the maximum bit rate that is achievable over a transmission channel and is known as *intersymbol interference.* Since after a certain distance the receiver no longer can distinguish the beginning and end of a pulse, slightly ahead of that point the pulse needs to be reshaped or regenerated.

Noise

In addition to delay distortion, various noises and disturbances associated with the signal transmission and detection mechanisms can cause errors in interpreting the received signal. The term *noise* refers to unwanted components of a signal that may be imposed on the signal during its journey from the source to the receiver or that may arise at the receiver itself. Possible sources of noise include the following:

- *Thermal noise* arises from the random motion of electrons. It is present in all electronic devices and is a function of temperature. Since it is uniformly distributed across the frequency spectrum, thermal noise often is referred to as *white noise.* Transmission errors due to white noise are referred to as *random errors* since the occurrence of an error in a particular bit interval generally does not affect the system performance during the following bit interval. The thermal noise N_{th} in watts that is present in a bandwidth of B hertz can be expressed as

$$N_{th} = k_B TB \tag{3.3}$$

  where k_B is Boltzmann's constant $= 1.3803 \times 10^{-23}$ J/K $= 1.3803 \times 10^{-23}$ (W/Hz)/ K and T is temperature in degrees kelvin.

EXAMPLE 3.6

At room temperature $T = 17°C = 290$ K. The thermal noise power density in W/Hz is given by

$$N_{th}/B = [1.3803 \times 10^{-23} \text{ (W/Hz)/K}] \times 290 \text{ K} = 4 \times 10^{-21} \text{ W/Hz} = -204 \text{ dBW/Hz}$$

- *Intermodulation distortion* results from the mixing of signals at different frequencies to produce energy at another frequency. For example, signals at frequencies f_1 and f_2 might produce energy at other frequencies such as $f_1 + f_2$, $2f_1 - f_2$, or $2f_2 - f_1$. The energy at such new frequencies may interfere with the original signals if they fall within the bandwidths occupied by intended signals.
- *Crosstalk* is an unwanted coupling of a signal from one signal channel to another. For example, when using the telephone, one sometimes can hear another weak conversation in the background, which may arise from electromagnetic coupling between adjacent wires in a cable. This is rare in transmission media such as optical fibers but can be large in certain types of twisted-pair wires (see Sec. 3.6).
- *Impulse noise* is characterized by long, quiet intervals that are interrupted by noise bursts. These bursts consist of noncontinuous irregular pulses or noise spikes of

short duration and of relatively high amplitude. They can arise from external electromagnetic disturbances such as lightning, high-voltage switching transients, power-line surges, and sudden or erratic faults in the communication system. In this case errors in digital systems usually occur in bursts that affect two or more successive transmitted symbols or bits.

- *Shot noise* or *quantum noise* arises in optical systems from the statistical nature of the production and collection of photoelectrons when an optical signal is incident on a photodetector.

3.1.4 Channel Capacity

In the analysis of any communication network an important factor is *channel capacity*. This is the maximum rate at which data can be sent across a channel from the message source to the user destination. A fundamental and important theorem for this is the *Shannon capacity formula*. This theorem states that the maximum information transmission *capacity* C of a channel with bandwidth B is given in *bits per second* by the relationship[13,14]

$$C = B \log_2(1 + S/N) \tag{3.4}$$

Here $\log_2$ represents the base-2 logarithm, and S and N are the average signal power and noise power, respectively. Typically these powers are measured at the receiver since it is at this point that a signal is extracted from the channel and processed. *Note:* For simplicity of calculation the following relationship may be useful to find $\log_2 x$:

$$\log_2 x = (\log_{10} x)/(\log_{10} 2) = (\log_{10} x)/0.3 \tag{3.5}$$

The parameter S/N is the *signal-to-noise ratio* (SNR), which is the ratio of the power in a signal to the power contained in the noise at a particular measurement point. This ratio is often expressed in decibels:

$$\text{SNR}_{\text{dB}} = 10 \log \frac{\text{signal power}}{\text{noise power}} = 10 \log \frac{S}{N} \tag{3.6}$$

The Shannon formula indicates the theoretical maximum capacity that can be achieved. In practice this capacity cannot be reached since the formula takes into account only thermal noise and does not consider factors such as impulse noise, attenuation distortion, or delay distortion. Furthermore intuitively it might seem that the capacity can be increased merely by raising the signal strength. However, raising the signal level also increases nonlinear effects in the system, which leads to higher noise powers. Also note that increasing the bandwidth B decreases the ratio S/N since the wider the bandwidth is, the more noise is introduced into the system.

EXAMPLE 3.7

Suppose we have an extremely noisy channel with a 1-MHz (megahertz) bandwidth in which the SNR is 1. From Eq. (3.4) the maximum capacity for this channel is

$$C = B \log_2(1 + S/N) = 10^6 \log_2(1 + 1) = 10^6 \log_2(2) = 10^6(1.0) = 1 \text{ Mpbs}$$

$$\text{(megabits per second)}$$

EXAMPLE 3.8

Let us find the capacity of a channel that operates between 3 and 4 MHz and in which the SNR is 20 dB. Then the bandwidth is

$$B = (4 \text{ MHz}) - (3 \text{ MHz}) = 1 \text{ MHz}.$$

and from Eq. (3.6)

$$S/N = 10^{20/10} = 100$$

Then

$$C = 10^6 \log_2(1 + 100) = [10^6 \log(101)]/0.3 = 10^6(2.0)/0.3 = 6.7 \text{ Mbps}$$

3.2 SIGNAL ENCODING TECHNIQUES

In designing a communication link, one should consider the format of the transmitted digital signal.[1–4,6,7,15–19] This is significant because the receiver must be able to extract precise *timing information* from the incoming signal. The three main purposes of *timing* are:

- To allow the signal to be sampled by the receiver at the time the SNR is a maximum
- To maintain a proper spacing between pulses
- To indicate the start and end of each timing interval

In addition, since errors resulting from channel noise and distortion mechanisms can occur in the signal detection process, it may be desirable for the signal to have an inherent error-detecting capability, as well as an error correction mechanism, if it is needed or practical. These features can be incorporated into the data stream by structuring (or *encoding*) the signal. Generally one does this by introducing extra bits into the raw data stream at the transmitter on a regular and logical basis and by extracting them again at the receiver. This process is called *channel* or *line coding*. This section presents some examples of generic encoding techniques. Chapters 5 through 9 present further details of specific line codes for different LAN architectures.

Here we concentrate on the encoding of digital bit streams for transmission over either analog or digital channels. For sending digital data over an analog channel, one superimposes the digital bit stream onto a sinusoidally varying waveform that matches the transfer properties of the transmission medium. This sine wave is called a *carrier wave*. This encoding process is known as *modulation* or *shift keying,* which is the systematic variation of the carrier waveform. Depending on the type of message to be sent, the modulation process can vary the amplitude, phase, or frequency (or some combination of these) of the carrier waveform. In addition to matching the signal properties to channel characteristics, modulation is used to reduce noise and interference, to transmit several independent signals simultaneously over a single channel, and/or to overcome equipment limitations.

When sending message bits over a digital channel, the encoding process could include schemes such as changing the bit stream into a form that has inherent timing capabilities, adding redundant bits for error control, or rearranging the symbols in a random pattern to prevent long strings of 1s or 0s in order to improve timing extraction from the bit stream.

Both analog and digital signals can be sent by either analog or digital transmission systems, as illustrated in Fig. 3.8. This shows that we have the following four possible combinations:

- An analog signal sent over an analog line: For example, a voice signal can be sent directly in its original form over an analog telephone line.
- An analog signal can be approximated by a digital bit stream and sent over a digital channel.
- A *modem* (modulator/demodulator) superimposes a digital signal (or a digitized analog signal) onto a sinusoidally varying carrier wave, which then is sent over an analog channel.
- A digital signal can be sent directly over a digital line.

Current wire and optical fiber-based LANs mostly use a digital format on their transmission lines. On the other hand, wireless LANs need to use an analog carrier wave to send digital data since this is compatible with the wireless transmission media.

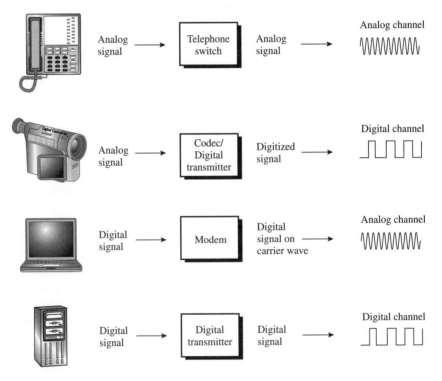

FIGURE 3.8
Both analog and digital signals can be sent by either analog or digital transmission systems.

TABLE 3.2
Representative encoding schemes for different types of LANs

LAN type	Encoding scheme
10Base-T (Ethernet)	Manchester
100Base-T (Fast Ethernet)	4B5B, NRZI (optical fiber); MLT-3 (UTP)
Gigabit Ethernet	8B10B (optical fiber); 4D-PAM5 (UTP)
4/10-Mbps token ring	Differential Manchester
FDDI	4B5B, NRZI (optical fiber); MLT-3 (UTP)
Fibre Channel	8B10B
Wireless LANs	BPSK, QPSK, QAM

Table 3.2 lists some encoding schemes for representative LAN types. Since the TCP/IP encapsulation scheme is based on digitized data, in this section we first look at how to convert analog signals that may originate from a LAN host into a digital form so that they can be properly encapsulated in the TCP/IP (Transmission Control Protocol/Internet Protocol) stack. We then concentrate on the encoding techniques for formatting digital data to be sent over wireless or wired LANs.

3.2.1 Transforming Analog Signals into a Digital Form

Examples of analog information include speech, audio signals, and video. All of these are important in human communications and are used in a variety of multimedia applications. The process of converting an analog signal to a digital format is known as *digitization*. The device for carrying out this process, and for recovering the analog signal from the digitized format, is known as a *codec*, which is an abbreviation for *coder-decoder*.

To convert an analog signal to a digital form, one starts by taking instantaneous measures of the height of the signal wave at regular intervals, which is called *sampling* the signal. One way to convert these analog samples to a digital format is simply to divide the amplitude excursion of the analog signal into N equally spaced levels designated by integers and to assign a discrete binary word to each of these N integer values. Each analog sample then is assigned one of these integer values. This process is known as *quantization*. Since the signal varies continuously in time, this process generates a sequence of real numbers.

EXAMPLE 3.9

Figure 3.9 shows an example of digitization. Here the allowed voltage-amplitude excursion is divided into eight equally spaced levels ranging from 0 to V volts. In this figure samples are taken every second and the nearest discrete quantization level is chosen as the one to be transmitted, according to the binary code listed next to the quantized levels shown in Fig. 3.9. At the receiver this digital signal then is demodulated. That is, the quantized levels are reassembled into a continuously varying analog waveform.

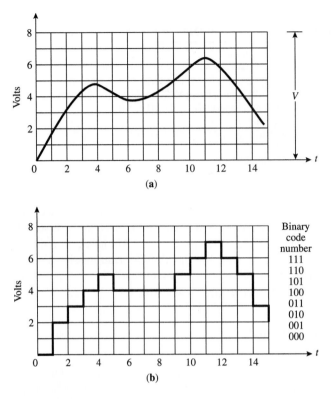

FIGURE 3.9
Digitization of analog waveforms: (*a*) original signal varying between 0 and *V* volts; (*b*) quantized and sampled digital version.

Note that the equally spaced levels in Fig. 3.9 are the simplest quantization implementation, which are produced by a *uniform quantizer.* Frequently it is more advantageous to use a *nonuniform quantizer* where the quantization levels are proportional to the signal level, for example, the quantization intervals may be smaller for larger signal levels. The companders used in telephone systems are an example of this.

Intuitively one can see that if the digitization samples are taken frequently enough relative to the rate at which the signal varies, then to a good approximation the signal can be recovered from the samples by drawing a straight line between the sample points. The resemblance of the reproduced signal to the original signal depends on the fineness of the quantizing process and on the effect of noise and distortion added into the transmission system. According to the *Nyquist theorem,* if the sampling rate is at least two times the highest frequency, then the receiving device can reconstruct the analog signal faithfully. Thus if a signal is limited to a bandwidth of *B* hertz, then the signal can be reproduced without distortion if it is sampled at a rate of $2B$ times per second. These data samples are represented by a binary code. As noted in Fig. 3.9, eight quantized levels having upper bounds $V_1, V_2, \ldots, V$ can be described by three binary digits ($2^3 = 8$). More digits can be used to give finer sampling levels. That is, if n binary digits represent each sample, then one can have 2^n quantization levels.

EXAMPLE 3.10

Consider a high-quality color video signal having a 6-MHz bandwidth. To digitize this signal, we sample at 12×10^6 samples per second (twice the bandwidth). Using 8 binary bits per sample to give $2^8 = 256$ quantization levels creates a signal of very high fidelity. The resultant digital signal then would be sent at 96 Mbps (12×10^6 samples/second $\times$ 8 bits/sample = 96 Mbps).

3.2.2 Analog Encoding of Digital Signals

One can modulate a sinusoidal carrier wave by varying its amplitude, phase, or frequency in accordance with the signal that is transmitted. This can be either an analog or a digital signal. Mathematically the carrier wave $x_c(t)$ has the form

$$x_c(t) = A_c(t) \cos[\omega_c t + \phi(t)] \tag{3.7}$$

where

$$A_c(t) = \text{instantaneous amplitude of the carrier at time } t$$
$$f_c = \omega_c/2\pi = \text{carrier frequency}$$
$$\phi(t) = \text{instantaneous phase deviation of the carrier}$$

Let us first examine the case of analog signals. If the temporal variation of a message signal $x(t)$ is linearly related to $A(t)$, then we have *amplitude modulation* (AM). An example of this is the familiar commercial AM radio application. When the phase $\phi(t)$ or its time derivative is linearly related to $x(t)$, then we have *phase modulation* (PM) and *frequency modulation* (FM), respectively. The name *angle modulation* is commonly used to denote both phase and frequency modulations. Figure 3.10 shows typical AM, FM, and PM waveforms for representative analog and digital message waveforms.

An important point to note in Fig. 3.10 is that in the analog case the amplitude, frequency, or phase of the carrier varies continuously in response to the message waveform. However, in the binary digital case these three parameters switch between one of two possible values, depending on whether a 0 or a 1 pulse is transmitted. For the AM case the amplitude of the carrier switches between a low level (the *off* state) and a predetermined higher level (the *on* state). This type of modulation is referred to as an *on-off-keyed* (OOK) or *amplitude-shift-keyed* (ASK) system. Both frequency and phase remain constant as the amplitude changes. A limitation of ASK is its high susceptibility to noise effects, such as stray voltages introduced on a line by electromagnetic interference (EMI).

For the *frequency-shift-keyed* (FSK) case the carrier wave takes on one of two predetermined constant frequencies depending on whether a logic 1 or a logic 0 was sent. Both the amplitude and the phase remain constant as the frequency switches from one value to another. FSK overcomes most of the noise problems of ASK, but its limiting factor is the physical bandwidth capability of the carrier.

In *phase-shift keying* (PSK) the phase of the carrier is changed. PSK is not susceptible to the noise degradation that affects ASK nor does it have the bandwidth limitations of FSK. This means that a receiver can detect small variations in the signal. Therefore instead of using only two-phase variations (each representing 1 bit), one can establish four- or eight-phase variations, for example. In this case each phase shift is a

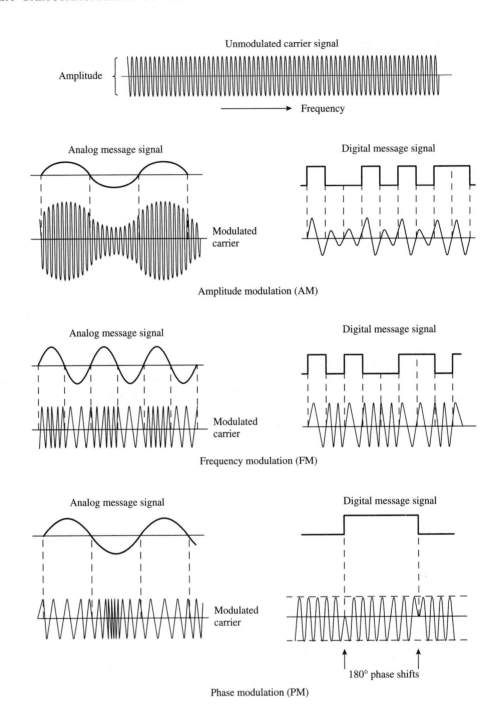

FIGURE 3.10
Typical AM, FM, and PM waveforms for representative analog and digital message signals.

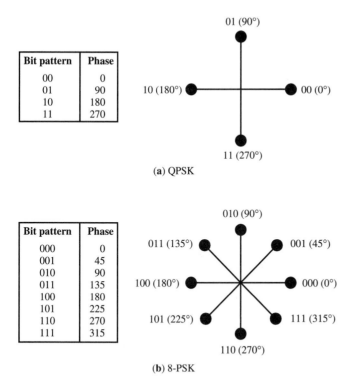

Bit pattern	Phase
00	0
01	90
10	180
11	270

(a) QPSK

Bit pattern	Phase
000	0
001	45
010	90
011	135
100	180
101	225
110	270
111	315

(b) 8-PSK

FIGURE 3.11
Representation of the phase and amplitude relationships by a constellation or phase-state diagram for QPSK and 8-PSK.

signaling *symbol* that represents 2 or 3 bits, respectively. The four-phase technique is called 4-PSK or *quadrature PSK* (QPSK) and the eight-phase technique is called 8-PSK, in contrast to the *binary PSK* (BPSK) that uses two phase shifts. One can represent the phase and amplitude relationships by a *constellation* or *phase-state diagram*. Figure 3.11 shows the bit representations for each signaling symbol and the corresponding constellations for QPSK and 8-PSK. The BPSK and QPSK methods have applications in wireless LANs, as described in Chap. 8.

As a further variation one can combine ASK and PSK to form *quadrature amplitude modulation* (QAM). This technique offers a selection from several variations in phase (e.g., 2, 4, 8, 16, or 64) and at least two variations in amplitude, yielding numerous possible types of QAM, as shown in Table 3.3. Popular versions for wireless LANs are 16-QAM and 64-QAM. Figure 3.12 shows two possible constellations for 16-QAM for different amplitude and phase combinations, which are based on signal points that fall on a rectangular grid.[3] The one on the left has three amplitudes, which are represented by the dots, and 12 phases, which are indicated by the dashed lines. The right-hand one has four amplitudes and eight phases. Note that in each case the number of amplitude changes is less than the number of phase changes since amplitude changes are more susceptible to noise than phase changes.

TABLE 3.3

Baud and bit rate comparison of possible quadrature amplitude modulation (QAM) schemes

Modulation scheme	Bits/symbol	Baud (symbol rate)	Bit rate
ASK, FSK, 2-PSK	1	N	N
4-PSK, 4-QAM	2	N	$2N$
8-PSK, 8-QAM	3	N	$3N$
16-QAM	4	N	$4N$
32-QAM	5	N	$5N$
64-QAM	6	N	$6N$
128-QAM	7	N	$7N$
256-QAM	8	N	$8N$

3 amplitudes, 12 phases

4 amplitudes, 8 phases

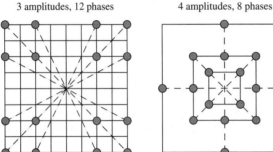

FIGURE 3.12
Two possible constellations for 16-QAM for different amplitude and phase combinations.

Table 3.3 shows the number of bits that each signaling symbol represents for different encoding methods. For example, with 64-QAM each symbol represents 6 bits, so here an N-baud modulation rate yields a $6N$-bps bit rate. From this table one also can see that the relationship between the number of bits per symbol and the number of symbols is a power of 2. When there are four possible symbols, one can send 2 bits at a time since $2^2 = 4$. With eight possible symbols, one can send 3 bits at a time since $2^3 = 8$, and so on.

3.2.3   Sending Digital Signals in a Digital Form

In a digital link one of the principal functions of a line code is to enable recovery of timing information from the digital signal. In addition, some line codes have built-in error-detecting capabilities, and others may offer better immunity to noise and interference effects. Although large system bandwidths are attainable with high-capacity links, signal-to-noise considerations at the receiver show that larger bandwidths result in larger noise contributions. Thus from noise considerations, minimum bandwidths are desirable. However, a larger bandwidth may be needed to have timing data available from the bit stream. In selecting a particular line code, one therefore must make a trade-off between timing and noise bandwidths. Normally these are largely determined by the expected characteristics of the raw data stream. Two line coding methods described here are the NRZ codes and block codes.

NRZ Codes

Figure 3.13 shows several commonly used line codes. The coded patterns in this figure are for the data sequence 1010110. The simplest method is the *unipolar nonreturn-to-zero (NRZ) code*. This also is called an NRZ-level (NRZ-L) code. *Unipolar* means that a logic 1 is represented by a voltage or light pulse that fills an entire bit period, whereas for a logic 0 no pulse is transmitted. If 1 and 0 pulses occur with equal probability and if the amplitude of the voltage pulse is A, then the average transmitted power for this code is $A^2/2$. The *polar NRZ code* maps a binary 1 into a $+A/2$ voltage level and a 0 into a $-A/2$ level. This code is more efficient than unipolar NRZ since its average power is $A^2/4$. These codes are simple to generate and decode, but they possess no inherent error-monitoring or correcting capabilities and they have no timing features.

The lack of timing capabilities in NRZ codes can lead to misinterpretations of the bit stream at the receiver. For example, since there are no level transitions from which to extract timing information in a long sequence of NRZ 1s or 0s, a long string of N identical bits could be interpreted as either $N + 1$ or $N - 1$ bits, unless highly stable (and expensive) clocks are used. This problem can be avoided with a code that has transitions at the beginning of each bit interval when a binary 1 is transmitted and no transition at the start of a bit interval for a binary 0. This can be accomplished with *differential encoding* or an *NRZ-inverted (NRZI) code*.

The Manchester encoding methods shown in Fig. 3.13 are used in basic Ethernet and in token-ring LANs. In normal *Manchester encoding* a binary 1 is represented by a transition from $+A/2$ to $-A/2$ in the middle of the bit period, whereas a binary 0

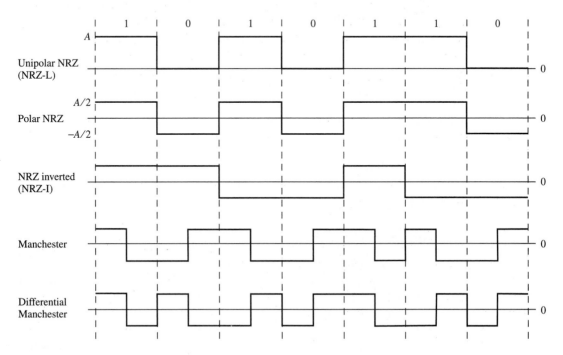

FIGURE 3.13
Examples of several commonly used line codes.

is denoted by a transition from $-A/2$ to $+A/2$. The transitions in the middle of every bit interval make timing recovery simple. *Differential Manchester encoding* is used in token-ring LANs. This method retains the transitions in the middle of each bit interval, but the binary sequence is mapped into the presence or absence of transitions at the beginning of bit periods, indicating 1 or 0 pulses, respectively.

Block Codes

As noted earlier, introducing *redundant bits* into a data stream can be used to provide adequate timing and to have error-monitoring features. A popular and efficient encoding method for this is the class of *mBnB block codes*. In this class of codes, blocks of m binary bits are converted to longer blocks of $n > m$ binary bits. As a result of the additional redundant bits, the required bandwidth increases by the ratio n/m. Note that the Manchester encoding method is an example of an *mBnB* code with $m = 1$ and $n = 2$. In these codes a binary 1 is mapped into the binary pair 10, and a binary 0 becomes 01.

Suitable *mBnB* codes for high data rates are the 3B4B, 4B5B, 5B6B, and 8B10B codes. If simplicity of the encoder and decoder circuits is the main criterion, then the 3B4B format is the most convenient code. The 5B6B code is the most advantageous if bandwidth reduction is the major concern. Various versions of Ethernet use either the 3B4B, 4B5B, or 8B10B formats, as Chap. 5 describes. Token-ring LANs discussed in Chap. 6 use 4B5B encoding and Fibre Channel employs an 8B10B code, as discussed in Chap. 9.

3.2.4 Multilevel Digital Transmission

Another way of increasing the bit rate in a digital system is by sending pulses with more than two levels. For example, suppose the pulses can take on amplitudes from the set $\{-A, -A/3, +A/3, +A\}$. Analogous to the QPSK case, one can use these pulses to transmit the pairs of bits $\{00, 01, 10, 11\}$. In this case since each pulse conveys 2 bits of information, then from the Nyquist theorem we can send a bit rate of 4B bps, compared to 2B bps for binary signaling. In general if we use *multilevel transmission* pulses that can take on $M = 2^n$ levels, then the bit rate R will be

$$R = 2B \text{ pulses per second} \times n \text{ bits per pulse} = 2Bn \text{ bps} \tag{3.8}$$

Other multilevel coding schemes, such as MLT-3, are given in Chap. 5 in relation to Ethernet.

3.3 ERROR DETECTION

In any digital transmission system errors are likely to occur even when there is a sufficient SNR to provide a low bit error rate. To control errors and to improve the reliability of a communication line, first we must be able to detect the errors and then either to correct them or to retransmit the information.[2,6,7]

For LAN applications the most common error detection scheme is the cyclic redundancy check, which we look at in Sec. 3.3.3. Other available error detection schemes include the parity check (also known as a vertical redundancy check or VRC), the longitudinal redundancy check (LRC), and the checksum, which is used by upper protocol layers. For information on these schemes, the reader is referred to the literature.[1-4,6-8]

3.3.1 Bit Error Rate (BER)

In practice there are several standard ways of measuring the rate of error occurrences in a digital data stream. One method is to divide the number N_e of errors appearing over a certain time interval t by the number N_t of 1 and 0 pulses transmitted during this interval. This is called either the *error rate,* the *bit error rate* (BER), or the *bit error ratio* (also BER). Thus we have

$$\text{BER} = \frac{N_e}{N_t} = \frac{N_e}{Rt} \tag{3.9}$$

where $R = 1/T$ is the bit rate and T is the bit period. The BER is expressed by a number, such as 10^{-9}, for example, which states that on the average one error occurs for every billion pulses sent. A typical BER for optical fiber communication systems may range from 10^{-9} to 10^{-12}. Since the error rate depends on the SNR at the receiver, the system error rate requirements and the receiver noise levels set a lower limit on the signal power level that is required at the receiver.

3.3.2 Types of Errors

An error in a data stream can be categorized as a single-bit error or a burst error. As its name implies, a *single-bit error* means that only 1 bit of a data unit (e.g., a byte, code word, a packet, or a frame) is changed from a 1 to a 0, or vice versa. Single-bit errors are not very common in a typical transmission system since most bit-corrupting noise effects last longer than a bit period.

A *burst error* refers to the fact that more than 1 bit in a data unit has changed. This type of error happens most often in a typical transmission system since the duration of a noise burst lasts over several bit periods. A burst error does not necessarily change every bit in a data segment that contains errors. As shown in Fig. 3.14, the length of an error burst is measured from the first corrupted bit to the last corrupted bit. Not all the bits in this particular segment have been damaged.

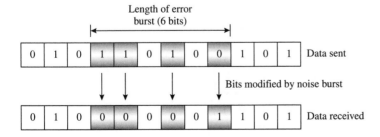

FIGURE 3.14
The length of an error burst is measured from the first corrupted bit to the last corrupted bit.

EXAMPLE 3.11

The number of bits affected by a burst error depends on the data rate and the duration of the noise burst. For example, if a bit-corrupting burst noise lasts for 1 ms, then 10 bits are affected for a 10-kbps data rate, whereas a 10,000-bit segment is damaged for a 10-Mbps rate.

3.3.3 Cyclic Redundancy Check

The *cyclic redundancy check* (CRC) technique is based on a binary division process involving the data portion of a packet and a sequence of redundant bits. Figure 3.15 outlines the following basic CRC procedure:

- *Step 1.* At the sender end a string of n zeros is added to the data unit on which error detection will be performed. For example, this data unit may be a packet. The characteristic of the redundant bits is such that the result (packet plus redundant bits) is exactly divisible by a second predetermined binary number.
- *Step 2.* The new enlarged data unit is divided by the predetermined divisor using binary division. If the number of bits added to the data unit is n, then the number of bits in the predetermined divisor is $n + 1$. The remainder which results from this division is called the *CRC remainder* or simply the CRC. The number of digits in this remainder is equal to n. For example, if $n = 3$ it may be the binary number 101. Note that the remainder also might be 000, if the two numbers are exactly divisible.
- *Step 3.* The n zeros that were added to the data unit in step 1 are replaced by the n-bit CRC. The composite data unit then is sent through the transmission channel.
- *Step 4.* When the data unit plus the appended CRC arrives at the destination, the receiver divides this incoming composite unit by the same divisor that was used to generate the CRC.
- *Step 5.* If there is no remainder after this division occurs, then the assumption is that there are no errors in the data unit and it is accepted by the receiver. A remainder indicates that some bits became corrupted during the transmission process and therefore the data unit is rejected.

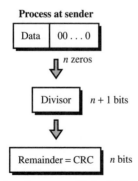

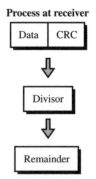

Replace the n zeros with the CRC and send the composite data unit.

Accept data if remainder is zero; otherwise reject.

FIGURE 3.15
The basic procedure for the cyclic redundancy check (CRC) technique.

TABLE 3.4

Commonly used polynomials and their binary equivalents for CRC generation

CRC type	Generator polynomial	Binary equivalent
CRC-8	$x^8 + x^2 + x + 1$	100000111
CRC-10	$x^{10} + x^9 + x^5 + x^4 + x + 1$	11000110011
CRC-16	$x^{16} + x^{15} + x^2 + 1$	11000000000000101
CRC-32	$x^{32} + x^{26} + x^{23} + x^{22} + x^{16} + x^{12} + x^{11} +$ $x^{10} + x^8 + x^7 + x^5 + x^4 + x^2 + x + 1$	100000100110000010001110110110111

Instead of using a string of 1 and 0 bits, the CRC generator normally is represented by an algebraic polynomial with binary coefficients. The advantage of using a polynomial is that it is simple to visualize and perform the division mathematically. Table 3.4 shows examples of several commonly used polynomials and their binary equivalents for the CRC generation. These are designated as CRC-8, CRC-10, CRC-16, and CRC-32. The numbers 8, 10, 16, and 32, respectively, refer to the size of the CRC remainder. Thus the CRC divisors for these polynomials are 9, 11, 17, and 33 bits, respectively. The first two polynomials are used in ATM (asynchronous transfer mode) networks, whereas CRC-32 is used in IEEE-802 LANs. CRC-16 is used in bit-oriented protocols, such as the High-Level Data Link Control (HDLC) Standard, where frames are viewed as a collection of bits.

EXAMPLE 3.12

The generator polynomial $x^7 + x^5 + x^2 + x + 1$ can be written as

$$1 \times x^7 + 0 \times x^6 + 1 \times x^5 + 0 \times x^4 + 0 \times x^3 + 1 \times x^2 + 1 \times x^1 + 1 \times x^0$$

where the exponents on the variable x represent bit positions in a binary number and the coefficients correspond to the binary digits at these positions. Thus the generator polynomial given here corresponds to the 8-bit binary representation 10100111.

EXAMPLE 3.13

The generator polynomial $x^3 + x + 1$ can be written in binary form as 1011. For the information unit 11110 the CRC can be found through either binary or algebraic division using steps 1 through 3 outlined earlier. Since there are 4 bits in the divisor, three 0s are added to the data for the binary arithmetic operation. Figure 3.16 shows the two different procedures using polynomial and binary arithmetic division. For the polynomial division process the remainder is $x^2 + 1$, which is equivalent to the remainder 101 found by the binary division method (it better be!). The resulting composite data unit plus CRC that gets transmitted is 11110101. Note that when following the binary division method, if the leftmost bit of a remainder is zero, one must use 0000 as the divisor instead of the original 1011 divisor.

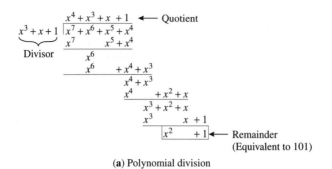

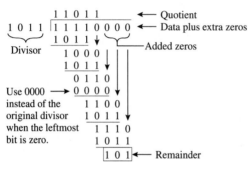

(a) Polynomial division

(b) Binary division

FIGURE 3.16

Two different procedures for finding the CRC using polynomial and binary arithmetic division.

A polynomial needs to have the following properties:

- It should not be divisible by x. This condition guarantees that the CRC can detect all burst errors that have a length less than or equal to the degree of the polynomial.
- It should be divisible by $x + 1$. This allows the CRC to detect all bursts that affect an odd number of bits.
- Given these two rules, the CRC also can detect with a probability

$$P_{ed} = 1 - 1/2^N \tag{3.10}$$

any burst errors that have a length greater than the degree N of the generator polynomial.

EXAMPLE 3.14

The CRC-32 given in Table 3.4 has a degree of 32. Thus it will detect all burst errors affecting an odd number of bits, all burst errors with a length less than or equal to 32, and from Eq. (3.10) more than 99.99 percent of burst errors with a length of 32 or more.

3.4 ERROR CORRECTION

Error correction may be done by the use of *redundancy* in the data stream.[20–22] With this method extra bits are introduced into the raw data stream at the transmitter on a regular and logical basis and are extracted again at the receiver. These digits themselves convey no information but allow the receiver to detect and even correct errors in the information-bearing bits. The degree of error-free transmission that can be achieved depends on the amount of redundancy introduced. Note that the data rate which includes this redundancy must be less than or equal to the channel capacity. In addition, the cost and complexity of implementing the encoding method must be reasonable.

If an error-correcting code is used, corrupted bits in the transmitted data can be corrected at the receiver. However, owing to the large number of redundant bits needed to correct burst errors and the complexity of the associated circuitry, most error correction is limited to rectifying 1-, 2-, and 3-bit errors. Generally since this is not adequate, it is more common to retransmit any defective data. Section 3.5.2 addresses this topic.

3.5 DATA LINK CONTROL

During the exchange of information between two network users there should be mechanisms to handle the possibility of transmission errors and to regulate the rate at which traffic arrives at the destination. Two important functions for addressing these mechanisms at the data link layer are flow control and error control.

3.5.1 Flow Control

In any communication system the receiving devices have a limited speed at which they can process incoming data and a limited block of memory, called a *buffer,* in which to store incoming information. *Flow control* enables a receiver to regulate the flow of data from a sender so that the receiver does not receive data faster than it can be processed, thereby avoiding its buffers from overflowing. To achieve this, the receiver invokes a flow control procedure that uses an *acknowledgment* (called an ACK) frame to inform the sender when more data can be sent. Thus the transmitter can send only a certain amount of data before it must stop and wait for an ACK from the receiver. Normally the receiver stops sending ACKs before its buffer is full in order to prevent the buffer from overflowing and losing data. Two common flow control methods are the stop-and-wait and the sliding window schemes.

Stop-and-Wait Flow Control

The simplest form is the *stop-and-wait flow control* method. Here the sender waits for an ACK after every frame it sends, as shown in Fig. 3.17. The sender will transmit another frame only after it receives the ACK for a previous frame. Therefore the sender must wait a time equal to at least two propagation delays ($2t_{\text{prop}}$) plus the time t_f needed to process a frame. The destination thus can stop the flow of data merely by withholding the acknowledgment. Although this method is simple, it is slow and inefficient, particularly for LAN applications. It is slow since each frame must travel all the way to the receiver and an ACK must travel all the way back to the sender before another frame can be sent, which can be quite time-consuming. In addition, the stop-and-wait method is inefficient

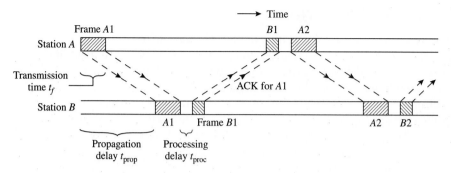

FIGURE 3.17
Example of the stop-and-wait flow control method.

since the bit length of an ACK only occupies a small portion of the line at any one time, which means that the line utilization is low.

Sliding Window Flow Control

Sliding window flow control is more efficient than the stop-and-wait method since the source can transmit several frames before it needs an ACK. This means that the transmission link acts like a pipeline that may be filled with frames in transit to the receiver while acknowledgments are returned to the sender. A single ACK can confirm the receipt of multiple data frames. The *sliding window* refers to imaginary variable-length boxes at both the source and the destination, as illustrated in Fig. 3.18. To remember which frames were transmitted and which were received, the sliding window method uses an identification scheme based on the size of the window. The frames are numbered modulo n, which means that their sequence numbers run from 0 through $n - 1$. For example, suppose an overhead field in a series of frames contains a 3-bit sequence number that identifies the frames. With this 3-bit sequence number one can identify eight frames since $n = 2^3 = 8$. In this case the frames are numbered 0 through 7 (modulo 2^3). The maximum size of the window is $n - 1$ since it is not allowed to cover all eight frames.

Suppose the window size is seven frames, as shown in Fig. 3.18. The top of the figure shows the situation at the transmitter. Frames 0 through 5 that are to the left of the vertical bar have been sent out and acknowledged. Frames 6 and 7, which are between the vertical bar and the leftmost window boundary, have been sent out but have not as yet been acknowledged. Since these two frames are buffered and waiting for an ACK, the five frames that are contained within the shaded window are those that may be sent out. As frames are sent out, the left boundary of the window moves to the right (inward), thereby shrinking the window size and decreasing the number of frames that may be transmitted. Once an ACK arrives, the rightmost boundary of the window expands to allow more frames to enter the window. The number of new frames that may enter the window is equal to the number just acknowledged by the ACK.

The bottom portion of Fig. 3.18 shows the corresponding situation at the receiver. Initially the receiver window is empty but contains spaces equal to the maximum window size for frames. The size of the receiver window shrinks as frames come in and expands as frames are acknowledged. Frames 6 and 7 that are between the vertical bar and the

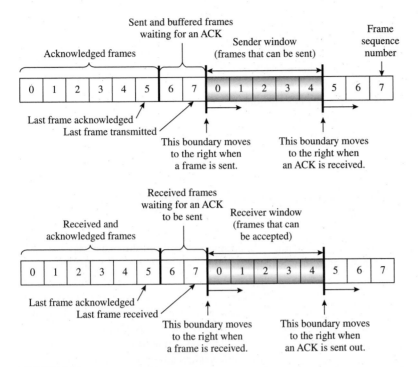

FIGURE 3.18

Concept of the sliding window protocol operation at the transmitter and the receiver.

window have been received but are not as yet acknowledged. Therefore the receiver can accept five more frames, as indicated by the shaded frames in the window, without sending an ACK. Note that normally a receiver returns an ACK before the window size is reduced to zero.

3.5.2 Error Control

Error control refers to the methods used to detect and correct errors that occur in the transmission of frames. It allows the receiver to inform the sender that certain frames have been lost or corrupted. Error control also coordinates with the sender the process of retransmitting those lost or damaged frames. In the data link layer error correction is implemented through the combined use of an error detection mechanism, an ACK showing successful receipt of a frame, a *negative acknowledgment* (NAK) indicating unsuccessful receipt of a frame, and the specification of which frames are in error. Collectively these mechanisms are referred to as *automatic repeat request* (ARQ). Three ARQ versions that have been standardized are the stop-and-wait ARQ, the go-back-*N* ARQ, and the selective-repeat ARQ.

Stop-and-Wait ARQ

The simplest retransmission protocol is *stop-and-wait ARQ*. Basically it uses the stop-and-wait flow control method described in Sec. 3.5.1, but with the extension of a capability to retransmit lost or corrupted frames. With this additional feature, if the receiver discovers an error in a data frame, it returns a NAK to the sender indicating that the frame should be retransmitted. Therefore the source sends out one frame and then waits until it receives either an ACK or a NAK before sending the next frame. The sending device also is equipped with a timer that indicates how long it should take for an acknowledgment to come back. If none is received within the allotted time period, the source assumes the last data frame was lost in transit and sends it again. As noted previously, since the stop-and-wait mechanism is very inefficient it is not widely used.

Go-Back-*N* ARQ

The most common form of error control that is based on the sliding window flow control is *go-back-N ARQ,* which also is known as *continuous ARQ.* In this method a series of data frames is sent continuously without waiting for an acknowledgment. The number *N* specifies how many successive frames can be sent in the absence of an ACK or a NAK. When the receiving station detects an error in a frame, it sends a NAK to the transmitter for that frame. The receiver then discards all further incoming frames, whether or not they are good, and now waits to receive correctly the frame that was in error before accepting any other frames. Thus when the transmitting station receives a NAK, it must retransmit the frame in question plus all succeeding frames. Hence the name *go-back-N,* since frames that were transmitted after the damaged frame also must be resent. This may affect up to *N* previously transmitted frames when an error occurs.

As is the case with stop-and-wait ARQ, the go-back-*N* ARQ uses a timer mechanism that informs the transmitter how long it should wait for an acknowledgment to come back before it retransmits unacknowledged frames.

EXAMPLE 3.15

Figure 3.19 gives an example of frame retransmission. Here frames 1 and 2 sent by station *A* have been received correctly by station *B*, but frame 3 is in error. Before the NAK returns, station *A* has sent out frames 4, 5, and 6. When the NAK for frame 3 arrives at station *A*, frame 3 plus frames 4, 5, and 6 must be retransmitted.

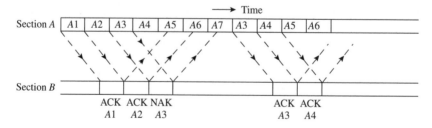

FIGURE 3.19
An example of a frame retransmission using go-back-*N* ARQ. Frame 3 was received in error.

Selective-Repeat ARQ

With *selective-repeat ARQ* only the specific lost or damaged frame is retransmitted. Intuitively this may seem more efficient than the go-back-N ARQ, where all good frames following the error also are retransmitted. Although this does offer better performance, the implementation can be quite involved. This is because the receiver has the added major burdens of storing frames that follow an error, keeping track of which frame was incorrect, and inserting the correct retransmitted frame into the proper sequence when it arrives. Since the additional logic needed for such functions is complex and expensive to implement, selective-repeat ARQ is used much less than go-back-N ARQ.

3.6 TRANSMISSION MEDIA

At first glance it may seem straightforward to select a transmission medium for interconnecting equipment in a particular LAN. However, its choice has a major impact on the type of data that the LAN can handle, the transmission speed, and the degree of flexibility for accommodating a variety of users. In addition, the continuous migration to higher-speed LANs places greater demands on the transmission medium since the susceptibility of information signals to factors such as electromagnetic interference (EMI) and far-end crosstalk increases with increasing data rate. *Far-end crosstalk* is noise on a wire pair at the receiver that is caused by signal leakage from adjoining wire pairs. Because of these factors, cables that work fine at 10 Mbps may not be suitable for service speeds at 100 Mbps and higher.

Transmission media can be broadly classified as either *guided* or *unguided*. For LAN applications guided media include twisted-pair wires and optical fibers. Older LAN installations also used coaxial cables, which we will not discuss here. Unguided media are the so-called *airwaves* for wireless systems, which use radio, microwave, and infrared signals for sending information. Wireless LAN applications are described in Chap. 8.

3.6.1 Twisted-Pair Wire

High-performance *unshielded twisted-pair* (UTP) cables that are used for LAN applications within buildings consist of four copper wire pairs. A thin polyvinyl chloride (PVC) jacket protects each wire. The wires are twisted together in pairs in a regular spiral pattern to minimize the interference that is created between adjacent pairs when they are combined into a cable. The advantage of this medium is that it is relatively inexpensive and one can install it with readily available tools. The cable types are designated as Category-X (or Cat-X) UTP cable, where X is a number ranging from 3 through 7. In going to higher numbers, the copper pairs are twisted in a tighter spiral pattern to enhance their transmission performance, as shown in Table 3.5. Signal attenuation and distortion limit the transmission distances for UTP cables to 100 m without the use of repeaters. The two most common types are Cat-3 and Cat-5 cables.[23]

To ensure that cables are installed correctly, the ANSI/EIA/TIA-568A Standard defines how high-performance cabling should be installed and it gives the performance

TABLE 3.5
Categories and uses of UTP cables

Cable type	Data rate over 100 m, Mbps	Traditional use
Category 3	10	Supports data rates up to 10 Mbps (10Base-T)
Category 4	16	16-Mbps token rings
Category 5	100	10Base-T and 100Base-T Ethernet
Category 5E (enhanced)	100	Includes requirements to measure far-end crosstalk and return loss
Category 6	200	High performance (in development)
Category 7	600	Ultra-high performance (in development)

parameters that the cable should meet.[24] The EIA/TIA TSB-67 technical service bulletin provides cable-testing information.[25] Current versions of cable-testing instruments incorporate these test functions.

3.6.2 Optical Fibers

To overcome the distance and capacity limitations of UTP cables, LAN designers have the option of using optical fiber cables.[5,26–28] Although fibers are used largely on a LAN backbone to interconnect buildings or remote sites, many installations also have fiber running within buildings. The dielectric nature of optical fibers makes them an attractive alternative to wire cables since they are immune to EMI effects and there is virtually no crosstalk between different fibers within the same cable. An *optical fiber* is a dielectric waveguide that operates at optical frequencies. This fiber waveguide structure is a single solid dielectric cylinder of radius a and an index of refraction n_1, as Fig. 3.20 shows. This cylinder is known as the *core* of the fiber. A solid dielectric *cladding* having an index $n_2 < n_1$ surrounds the core. Since the core refractive index is larger than that of the cladding, light propagates along the waveguide through internal reflection at the core-cladding interface. For LAN applications the core can be either glass or plastic. An elastic buffer material surrounds the core-cladding structure in order to provide protection and further mechanical strength.

As shown in Fig. 3.21, variations in the material composition of the core give rise to two common fiber types known as step-index and graded-index fibers. In *step-index fiber*

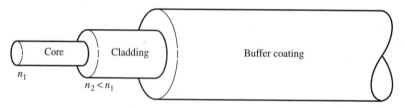

FIGURE 3.20
Structure of an optical fiber waveguide.

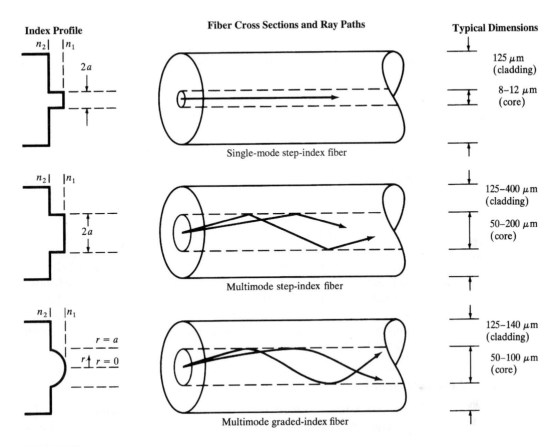

FIGURE 3.21
Comparison of single-mode and multimode step-index and graded-index optical fibers.

the index of the core material is uniform throughout and undergoes an abrupt change (or step) at the core-cladding boundary. In the *graded-index fiber* the core refractive index varies as a function of the radial distance from the center of the fiber. Depending on their core size, both fiber types can be further divided into multimode and single-mode classes. As the name implies, a *single-mode fiber* sustains only one mode of propagation, whereas *multimode fibers* contain many hundreds of modes.

Table 3.6 gives a comparison of different multimode fiber types for LAN applications. Popular multimode sizes are 50 and 62.5 μm. Graded-index multimode fibers used in LANs have bandwidth-distance products ranging from 160 to 500 MHz-km. Thus data rates of 1 Gbps can be sent over distances of up to 550 m in these fibers. In high-quality, single-mode fibers the core sizes are nominally 9 μm and the bandwidth-distance products are several hundred GHz-km. Plastic optical fibers (POF) have a significantly higher attenuation than glass fibers.[29] However, they are useful for connections to the desktop since cable lengths in these applications are generally short and the installation of plastic fibers is easier than for glass fibers.

TABLE 3.6
Comparison of multimode optical fiber types

Core diameter, μm	Bandwidth, MHz-km	Transmission distance, m
62.5	160	2–220
62.5	200	2–275
50	400	2–500
50	500	2–550

3.6.3 Radio Links

In a wireless LAN a set of laptop computers, personal organizers, cordless telephones, or other communication devices are linked together through a base station to share a wireless medium, as Fig. 3.22 illustrates. The initial IEEE-802.11 Standard for wireless LANs specifies using radio waves in the 2.4-GHz band to support data rates ranging from 1 to 11 Mbps.[30,31] An option to transmit in a 300-MHz-wide spectrum at 5.2 GHz was approved later. Table 3.7 gives the available frequency bands in different countries and the maximum allowed output power. Here "UNII" designates a category of unlicensed equipment called *unlicensed national information infrastructure* devices. The parameter B is the 26-dB emission bandwidth in MHz. Chapter 8 provides more detail on using these frequency bands for wireless LANs.

3.6.4 Infrared Links

As Chap. 8 describes in more detail, wireless infrared LANs are aimed at providing a simple, low-cost, and reliable means of communication over a limited distance be-

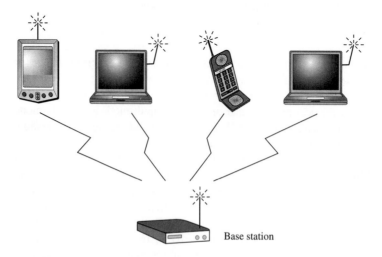

FIGURE 3.22
Example of communication devices sharing a wireless LAN.

TABLE 3.7
Available unregulated wireless frequency bands

Region	Operating range	Maximum output power
North America	2.400–2.4835 GHz	1000 mW
Europe	2.400–2.4835 GHz	100 mW
Japan	2.471–2.4897 GHz	10 mW
United States (UNII lower band)	5.150–5.250 GHz	Minimum of 50 mW or 4 dBm $+10\log B^2$
United States (UNII middle band)	5.250–5.350 GHz	Minimum of 250 mW or 11 dBm $+10\log B$
United States (UNII upper band)	5.725–5.825 GHz	Minimum of 1000 mW or 17 dBm $+10\log B$

tween devices such as laptop and desktop computers, printers, modems, and other LAN devices.[32,33] The connections are point-to-point links that use diffused infrared light beams transmitted through the air. Data rates up to 4 Mbps are possible. Since infrared radiation has properties similar to visible light, the infrared signals propagate through multiple reflections in the networking environment (e.g., within a room or large office area). However, this generally creates multiple paths for the signals so that time dispersion results in the received signals. This effect, which is called *multipath dispersion,* results in intersymbol interference at data rates that are higher than 10 Mbps.

In setting up such a LAN, one must take into account that indoor illumination sources, such as sunlight and artificial light, radiate power in the same wavelength band as the infrared signals. Thus the ambient light is the main source of signal degrading noise created in the receiver photodetector.

Since users of an infrared wireless LAN are directly exposed to the infrared radiation, international safety regulations specify the maximum levels to which a user can be safely exposed. In practice these regulations limit the average optical power emitted by the source to a few hundred milliwatts.

3.7 MULTIPLEXING

In any kind of network, whether it is a LAN, a MAN, or a WAN, the capacity or bandwidth of the transmission medium generally far exceeds that of any single attached user. Thus various schemes for allowing many attached users to share the larger transmission-line capacity have been developed. The technique for doing this is called *multiplexing.* Three general forms of multiplexing are frequency division multiplexing, time division multiplexing, and wavelength division multiplexing.[1–10,34]

The fundamental concept of each of these schemes is to allow the simultaneous transmission of multiple independent signals across a single common link, which is referred to as a *line,* as shown generically in Fig. 3.23. The device used for combining the signals onto a line is referred to as a *multiplexer* or *mux,* whereas at the receiving end a *demultiplexer* or *demux* separates the signals into their original independent information streams. In discussing multiplexing, one often uses the word *channel* to indicate an individual information stream within the multiplexed line.

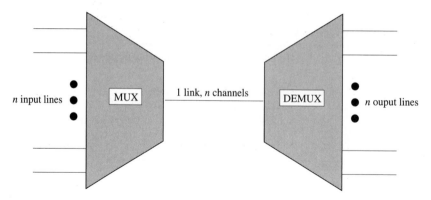

FIGURE 3.23
The fundamental concept of multiplexing.

3.7.1 Frequency Division Multiplexing

Frequency division multiplexing (FDM) may be used if a transmission line has a bandwidth (measured in hertz), which exceeds that required by individual connections. In FDM the bandwidth of the line is divided into a number of *frequency carrier slots,* each of which can accommodate the signal bandwidth of an individual channel. The multiplexer assigns a different carrier frequency to each connection and uses modulation to place the signal of the connection in the appropriate slot. Thus the line can carry a number of signals simultaneously if the carrier frequencies are sufficiently separated so that the bandwidths of the signals do not overlap.

Figure 3.24 illustrates the FDM process. Here the bandwidth B of a line is divided into N frequency slots, each having a bandwidth B_I, where $I = 1, 2, \ldots, N$. The center frequency of each slot i is designated by f_i. To prevent interference from adjacent channels, the slots are normally separated by *guard bands,* which are unused portions of the spectrum so that $B > \Sigma B_i$. Now N signals, each of which has a bandwidth of W_i Hz, can be multiplexed onto the line into a bandwidth B_i Hz by modulating each signal onto a different carrier frequency f_i.

3.7.2 Time Division Multiplexing

In *time division multiplexing* (TDM) one uses transmission *time slots,* in contrast to frequency slots as in the FDM case. The TDM scheme can be used when the data rate of individual sending and receiving devices is much less than the data rate capacity of a transmission link. In this case the simultaneous transmission of multiple independent signals on the same line can be achieved by sequentially interleaving bits from the individual data sources into these time slots. TDM can be implemented in either a synchronous or an asynchronous fashion, as described next.

Synchronous Time Division Multiplexing

If each of a number of lower-speed lines presents a relatively steady stream of traffic to a higher-speed line, then one traditionally uses *synchronous time division multiplexing.*

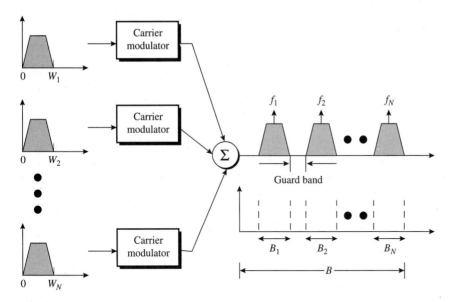

FIGURE 3.24

Illustration of the frequency divison multiplexing (FDM) process with adjacent channels separated by guard bands.

Synchronous TDM usually is referred to simply as TDM. In this scheme transmission time is divided into blocks or *frames* of N equal-sized slots, as shown in Fig. 3.25. If there are N input links, each operating at k bits per second, then TDM combines their information streams into a higher-rate bit stream of $(Nk + \Delta)$ bps. The factor Δ accounts for the possibility of including additional synchronization bits into the composite data stream. In the TDM scheme each incoming line is given a chance to send its data over the physical link in a round-robin fashion. This means that each line is allocated a fixed time slot in repetitive frames of N slots, as shown in Fig. 3.25. Data from input line 1 is sent during slot 1, data from input line 2 is sent during slot 2, and so on. This process continues until all input lines have had a turn to transmit, and then the process repeats. Note that the term *synchronous* means that the multiplexer allocates exactly the same time slot to a particular input line at all times, whether or not there is any data to be transmitted on that input line. For example, there are empty slots in the frames generated during cycles 1, 3, and 4 in Fig. 3.25.

Statistical Time Division Multiplexing

The synchronous TDM scheme is not efficient when the lines carry "bursty" traffic. This can occur when the user generates bursts of information separated by long idle times, as is the case in modern networks, particularly in LANs. In this case *statistical TDM* or *asynchronous TDM* is an efficient line utilization method. Statistical TDM takes advantage of the fact that the network traffic sources are not all transmitting at the same time. By dynamically allocating time slots for message bursts from many users, the data rate on the multiplexed transmission line is less than the summation of the data rates of the attached devices.

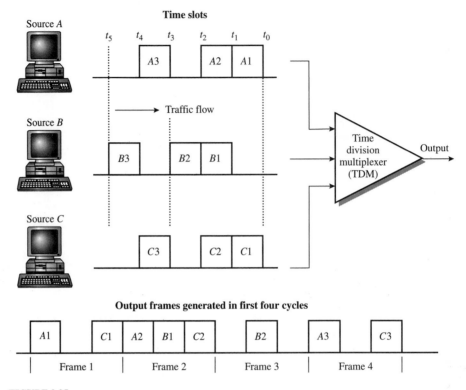

FIGURE 3.25
Illustration of synchronous time division multiplexing (TDM).

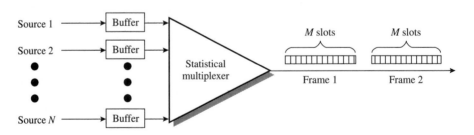

FIGURE 3.26
The concept of statistical TDM, which interleaves packets from N sources into $M < N$ time slots.

Figure 3.26 shows the concept of statistical TDM. Here the packets from N input lines are waiting to be multiplexed into M available time slots. The number of time slots M in an asynchronous TDM frame is less than the number of input lines N. It is based on a statistical estimate of the number of input lines that may be transmitting at any given time. Each line coming from a terminal has a buffer associated with it, where message packets are queued up to await transmission on the output line. The function of the statistical multiplexer is to scan the contents of the buffers, to arrange the waiting packets in a queue, and to create a frame of packets to be sent out. Normally the packets are sent in a *first-in first-out* (FIFO) manner if they all have the same priority (transmission urgency). However, some types of statistical multiplexers can send the packets based on their priority, which is usually indicated by a preassigned control bit in the packet header.

If there is insufficient data to fill all the time slots in a frame, the frame is sent only partially filled. Thus the full capacity of a link is not necessarily used. However, the dynamic allocation of time slots together with the lower ratio of time slots to input lines make statistical TDM more efficient than synchronous TDM.

EXAMPLE 3.16

In Fig. 3.27 packets from three sources get statistically multiplexed into two time slots. Here we assume all packets have the same priority. One output time slot is empty in frame 5 since no packet is waiting to be transmitted during that cycle.

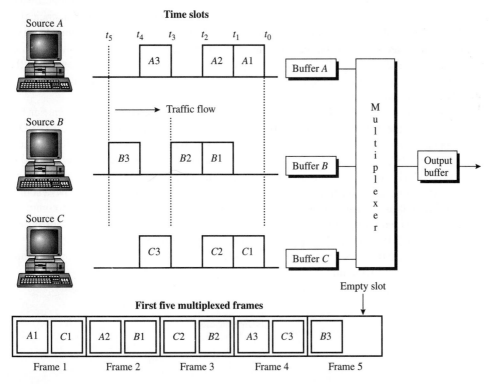

FIGURE 3.27
Example of statistical TDM for three input lines and two output time slots.

3.7.3 Wavelength Division Multiplexing

Multiplexing of signals also can be done optically. When talking about optical signal transmission, one normally refers to the *wavelength* of the light wave that is carrying a signal. Generally optical links are simplex point-to-point optical lines. In its most elementary format such a link consists of a single fiber line with one light source at the transmitting end and one photodetector at the receiving end. The light source in a high-quality optical link nominally is a laser diode that has a very narrow frequency spectrum so that it occupies only a very small spectral slice, which is a small fraction of a nanometer. Since the spectral bands for optical fibers used for LANs and optical fiber communications cover the (nominal) 800- to 900-nm and the 1300- to 1600-nm wavelength ranges, by using sources operating at different wavelengths, many independent signals can occupy these wavelength bands simultaneously. The technology of combining a number of wavelengths onto the same fiber is known as *wavelength division multiplexing* or WDM.[5,34] When the wavelengths are closely spaced with a peak wavelength separation of 1 nm or less, the term *dense wavelength division multiplexing* (DWDM) is used.

Figure 3.28 shows the concept of DWDM for a wavelength band centered around 1552.524 nm. Conceptually the WDM scheme is the same as FDM used in microwave radio and satellite systems. Just as in FDM the wavelengths (or optical frequencies) in a DWDM link must be properly spaced to avoid interference between channels. In an optical system this interference may arise from the fact that the center wavelength of laser diode sources and the bandpass characteristics of other optical components in the link may drift with temperature and time, thereby giving rise to the need for a guard band between wavelength channels.

Since WDM is essentially frequency division multiplexing at optical carrier frequencies, the ITU (International Telecommunication Union) has developed DWDM standards that specify channel spacings in terms of frequency. The ITU-T Recommendation G.692 specifies selecting the channels from a grid of frequencies referenced to 193.100 THz (1552.524 nm in glass) and spacing them 100 GHz (0.8 nm at 1552 nm) apart, as Fig. 3.28 illustrates. As implied by the line width of the heavy arrow, a source emitting at any particular peak wavelength λ_N has a narrow spectral width compared to the channel width. Table 3.8 shows the ITU-T G.692 grid for a 32-channel system with 100-GHz spacings.[35] Suggested alternative spacings include 25, 50, and 200 GHz. These optical frequency spacings correspond to wavelength bands of 0.2, 0.4, and 1.6 nm, respectively, at 1552 nm.

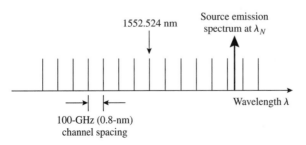

FIGURE 3.28
The concept of wavelength division multiplexing or WDM based on the ITU-T G.692 grid.

TABLE 3.8
Wavelength grid for DWDM recommended by ITU-T document G.692

	Channel	Wavelength, nm	Channel	Wavelength, nm
	1	1557.36	17	1544.53
	2	1556.55	18	1543.73
	3	1555.75	19	1542.94
ITU-T reference	4	1554.94	20	1542.14
frequency	5	1554.13	21	1541.35
(193.100 THz)	6	1553.33	22	1540.56
→	7	<u>1552.52</u>	23	1539.77
	8	1551.72	24	1538.98
	9	1550.92	25	1538.19
	10	1550.12	26	1537.40
	11	1549.31	27	1536.61
	12	1548.51	28	1535.82
	13	1547.72	29	1535.04
	14	1546.92	30	1534.25
	15	1546.12	31	1533.47
	16	1545.32	32	1532.68

3.8   SUMMARY

This chapter presented a basic overview of how data communication theory applies to the physical and data link layers for LAN applications. Some key *definitions* that are helpful for understanding how information flows from user to user within a LAN or between LANs include the following:

- The *spectrum* of a signal is the range of frequencies it contains. The *bandwidth* is the width of this spectrum.
- As a signal traverses a physical medium it becomes progressively attenuated, distorted, and corrupted by noise with increasing distance since no transmission medium is perfect. *Attenuation* of the signal strength arises from various loss mechanisms in a transmission medium. Attenuation typically is measured in *decibels* (dB). *Distortion* arises from delay effects in a transmission medium, which cause signals to change their shape as they travel along the channel. The term *noise* refers to unwanted components that are added to a signal during the transmission and detection processes and that can cause errors in interpreting the received signal.
- The *Shannon capacity formula* defines the *channel capacity,* which is the maximum rate at which data can be sent across a channel from the message source to the user destination.
- The parameter S/N is the *signal-to-noise ratio* (SNR), which is the ratio of the power in a signal to the power contained in the noise at a particular measurement point. This ratio often is expressed in decibels.

In designing a communication link, one should consider the format of the transmitted digital signal since the receiver must be able to extract precise *timing information* from it. In addition, since errors resulting from channel noise and distortion mechanisms can occur in the signal detection process, it may be desirable for the signal to have an inherent error-detecting capability. This feature can be implemented by introducing extra bits into the raw data stream at the transmitter on a regular and logical basis and extracting them again at the receiver. This process is called *channel* or *line coding.*

For sending digital data over an analog channel one superimposes the digital bit stream onto a sinusoidally varying waveform that matches the transfer properties of the transmission medium. This sine wave is called a *carrier wave.* This encoding process is known as *modulation* or *shift keying,* which is the systematic variation of the carrier waveform. For LAN applications the common methods are various forms and combinations of *amplitude-shift keying* (ASK) and *phase-shift keying* (PSK).

When sending message bits over a digital channel, one could include in the encoding process schemes such as changing the bit stream into a form that has inherent timing capabilities, adding redundant bits for error control, or rearranging the symbols in a random pattern to prevent long strings of 1s or 0s in order to improve timing extraction from the bit stream.

Error control refers to the methods used to detect errors that occur in the transmission of frames and to coordinate with the sender the process of retransmitting those lost or damaged frames. In the data link layer error correction is implemented through the combined use of an error detection mechanism, an ACK indicating successful receipt of a frame, a *negative acknowledgment* (NAK) indicating unsuccessful receipt of a frame, and the specification of which frames are in error. Collectively these mechanisms are referred to as *automatic repeat request* (ARQ). Three ARQ versions that have been standardized are the stop-and-wait ARQ, the go-back-N ARQ, and the selective-repeat ARQ mechanisms.

Transmission media can be broadly classified as either *guided* or *unguided.* For LAN applications guided media include unshielded twisted-pair (UTP) wires and optical fibers. Unguided media are the so-called *airwaves* for wireless systems, which use radio, microwave, and infrared signals for sending information. The IEEE-802.11 Standard for wireless LANs specifies using radio waves in the 2.4- and 5.2-GHz bands.

Multiplexing schemes allow many low-bandwidth users to share a large-capacity transmission line. Three general forms of multiplexing are:

- *Frequency division multiplexing* (FDM), in which the bandwidth of the line is divided into a number of *frequency carrier slots,* each of which can accommodate the signal bandwidth of an individual channel.
- *Time division multiplexing* (TDM), which uses *time slots* for the simultaneous transmission of multiple independent signals on the same line. The sequentially interleaving of bits from the individual data sources into these slots can be implemented in either a synchronous or an asynchronous (statistical) manner.
- *Wavelength division multiplexing* (WDM), wherein many independent optical signals, each using a different wavelength, can be sent along a single optical fiber simultaneously.

PROBLEMS

3.1. Three sine waves have the following periods: 25 μs, 220 ns, and 125 ps (picosecond). What are their frequencies?

3.2. A sine wave is offset one-sixth of a cycle with respect to time zero. What is its phase in degrees and in radians?

3.3. Two signals have the same frequency but when the amplitude of the first signal is at its maximum, the amplitude of the second signal is at half its maximum. What is the phase shift between the two signals?

3.4. What is the duration of a bit for each of the following three signals which have bit rates of 200 kbps, 5 Mbps, and 1 Gbps?

3.5. (a) Convert the following absolute power gains P_2/P_1 to decibel power gains: 10^{-3}, 0.3, 1, 4, 10, 100, 500, and 2^n.

    (b) Convert the following decibel power gains to absolute power gains: -30, 0, 13, 30, and $10n$ dB.

3.6. (a) Convert the following absolute power levels to decibel levels referenced to 1 mW: 1 pW, 1 nW, 1 mW, 10 mW, 50 mW, 1 W, and 13 W.

    (b) Find the absolute power levels in units of mW of the following dBm values: -13, -6, 6, and 20 dBm.

3.7. A signal travels from point A to point B.

    (a) If the signal power is 10 W at point A and 2.5 W at point B, what is the attenuation in dB?

    (b) What is the signal power at point B if the attenuation is 9 dB?

3.8. A signal passes through three cascaded amplifiers, each of which has a 6-dB gain. What is the total gain in decibels? How much is the signal amplified?

3.9. (a) Consider the cable system illustrated in Fig. 3.29. Calculate the signal levels in both dBm and volts at points A, B, C, and D. Recall that $P = V^2/R$, where V is the voltage and R is the resistance.

    (b) What gain in dB is needed in the final amplification stage so that its nominal output is 3 volts across a 50-ohm load?

3.10. A 30-km long optical fiber has a total attenuation of 24 dB. If 200 μW of optical power is launched into the fiber, what is the output optical power level in dBm and in μW (microwatts)?

3.11. A transmission line has a bandwidth of 2 MHz. If the signal-to-noise ratio (SNR) at the receiving end is 30 dB, what is the maximum data rate that this line can support?

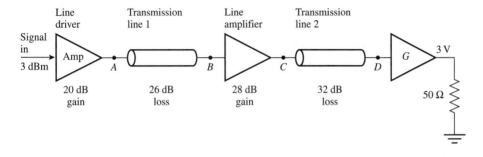

FIGURE 3.29
Figure for Prob. 3.9.

3.12. The human voice is an analog signal that normally contains frequencies ranging from 0 to 4000 Hz. If we want to digitize this signal with a uniform quantizer, what is the resulting bit rate if 8 bits per sample are used?

3.13. If the bandwidth is 20 kHz for an 8-PSK signal, what are the baud and the bit rate?

3.14. A QAM-constellation diagram consists of 64 phase and amplitude variations. If the bit rate is 48 Mbps, what is the symbol rate?

3.15. Consider a 16-QAM constellation that is based on the intersections of eight radial lines with four concentric circles. This means that there are eight phases and four amplitudes. How many possible symbol variations could this yield? Why are only 16 of these symbols used in practice?

3.16. Draw a 16-QAM constellation that uses two amplitudes and eight phases.

3.17. A 3B4B code converts blocks of 3 bits to blocks of 4 bits according to the rules given in Table 3.9. When there are two or more consecutive blocks of three 0s, the coded binary blocks 0010 and 1101 are used alternately. Likewise, the coded blocks 1011 and 0100 are used alternately for consecutive blocks of three 1s.
  (a) Using these translation rules, find the coded bit stream for the data input 010001111111101000000001111110.
  (b) What is the maximum number of consecutive identical bits in the coded pattern?

3.18. If a bit-corrupting burst noise lasts for 2 ms, how many bits are affected for data rates of 64 kbps, 10 Mbps, and 155 Mbps?

3.19. If the probabilities of occurrence for 1 and 0 pulses are equally likely, then the BER may be approximated by

$$\text{BER} \approx \frac{1}{\sqrt{2\pi}} \frac{e^{-Q^2/2}}{Q}$$

where Q is related to the SNR by $Q = 0.5 \, S/N$. Plot the BER as a function of Q (i.e., the SNR) for values of Q ranging from 0 to 8.

3.20. Consider the case where the *threshold voltage* v_{th} for deciding whether a binary 1 or 0 pulse was sent is given by $v_{th} = V/2$, where V is the peak voltage of a 1 pulse. In this case $Q = V/2\sigma$, where σ is the *root-mean-square (rms) noise,* and the ratio V/σ, is the *peak signal-to-rms-noise ratio.*
  (a) Suppose a transmission system sends out information at 200 kbps and that the rms noise voltage is 0.2 V. If 1 and 0 bits are equally likely to be transmitted, what is the average time in which an error occurs?

TABLE 3.9
3B4B code conversion rules

| Original code | 3B4B code | |
	Mode 1	Mode 2
000	0010	1101
001	0011	
010	0101	
011	0110	
100	1001	
101	1010	
110	1100	
111	1011	0100

    (b) How is this time changed if the voltage amplitude is doubled with the rms noise voltage remaining the same?

3.21. (a) Find the binary equivalent of the polynomial $x^8 + x^7 + x^3 + x + 1$.

    (b) Find the polynomial equivalent of 10011011110110101.

3.22. Consider the 10-bit data unit 1010011110 and the divisor 1011. Use both binary and algebraic division to find the CRC (cyclic redundancy check).

3.23. Consider the generator polynomial $x^3 + x + 1$.

    (a) Show that the CRC for the data unit 1001 is given by 110.

    (b) If the resulting code word has an error in the first bit when it arrives at the destination, what is the CRC calculated by the receiver?

3.24. Suppose station A has four frames to be sent to station B using the stop-and-wait ARQ method. If the frames are unnumbered, draw a time-sequence diagram to show what frames arrive at the receiver and what ACKs are sent back to station A if the ACK from frame 2 is lost.

3.25. Suppose the time-out value for a stop-and-wait ARQ system is less than the time required to receive an ACK. Draw the sequence of frame and ACK exchanges when station A sends five frames to station B and no errors occur in the transmissions.

3.26. (a) If station A and station B are 3600 km apart, how long does it take an ACK to come back to station A. Assume the line speed is 3×10^8 m/s.

    (b) Suppose the frames are 1000 bits long and the data rate on the line is 10 Mbps. If the stations use the stop-and-wait protocol, what is the efficiency of the transmission line between stations A and B?

3.27. Suppose two stations are using go-back-2 ARQ. Draw the time-sequence diagram for the transmission of seven frames if frame 4 was received in error.

3.28. (a) A sliding window protocol uses a window size of 15. How many bits are needed to represent the sequence number?

    (b) A sliding window protocol uses 6 bits to define the sequence number. What is the size of the window?

3.29. The attenuation of optical fibers typically is specified in units of dB/km at a certain wavelength. Assume a certain fiber has attenuations of 0.6 dB/km at 1300 nm and 0.3 dB/km at 1550 nm. Suppose the following two optical signals are launched simultaneously into the fiber: an optical power of 150 μW at 1300 nm and an optical power of 100 μW at 1550 nm. What are the power levels in μW of these two signals at (a) 8 km and (b) 20 km?

3.30. Research the characteristics of some commercially available multimode optical fibers, connectors, transmitters, and receivers for LAN use. Assume the LAN data rates are 10 and 100 Mbps, and the transmission distances could range up to 500 m.

3.31. What are some differences between Cat(Category)-3 and Cat-5 UTP cable? You may want to consult vendor data sheets that can be found on the Internet.

3.32. Research the operational characteristics of some commercially available line-of-sight IR links for indoor use.

3.33. A four-channel FDM system is to be implemented using the following design strategy. Channel 1 will be retained directly at baseband. A guard band equal to 25 percent of the bandwidth of channel 1 will be maintained between the upper edge of channel 1 and the lower edge of channel 2. Similarly, a guard band equal to 25 percent of the bandwidth of channel 2 will be maintained between the upper edge of channel 1 and the lower edge of channel 3, and so on.

    (a) Draw a spectral diagram for the composite baseband spectrum, label the frequencies where the channels begin and end, and compute the total transmission bandwidth for four data channels each having a 4-kHz baseband bandwidth.

(b) Repeat (a) for four data channels having the following baseband bandwidths:
- Channel 1: 4 kHz
- Channel 2: 6 kHz
- Channel 3: 14 kHz
- Channel 4: 20 kHz

3.34. (a) TDM is an essential tool for digital telephone service. At the lowest level of the *digital service* scheme (designated as DS-0), each of the 24 channels of 64 kbps is multiplexed into a 1.544-Mbps channel, which is designated as a DS-1 service. The line over which this service is sent is called a T-1 line. How much is the overhead that is added?

(b) The next higher multiplexed level is called DS-2 and the line handling this service is called a T-2 line. If the DS-2 rate is 6.312 Mbps, how many DS-1 channels can be accommodated and what is the overhead?

(c) The third multiplexed level is DS-3 and the line for this service is a T-3 line. If the DS-3 rate is 44.376 Mbps, how many DS-2 channels can be accommodated and what is the overhead?

(d) Using the preceding results, find how many DS-0 channels can be sent over a T-3 line. What is the total added overhead?

3.35. A time division multiplexer combines the outputs of 50 modems with data rates of 28.8 kbps each onto a T-1 line. If 25 kbps are used for overhead, how much of the line is unused?

3.36. Ten digital lines, each of which can have a maximum output of 56 kbps, are combined onto a single 400-kbps line using statistical TDM. By how much is the data rate of each input line reduced if all 10 lines are sending data? How many stations can transmit simultaneously with full capacity?

3.37. To find the optical bandwidth (the frequency band occupied by a light signal) corresponding to a particular spectral width, one needs to make use of the basic relationship $c = \lambda f$. This equation relates the speed of light c to the wavelength λ and the optical frequency f. Show that by differentiating this equation, we have

$$|\Delta f| = \left(\frac{c}{\lambda^2}\right)|\Delta\lambda|$$

where the deviation in frequency Δf corresponds to the wavelength deviation $\Delta\lambda$ around a center wavelength λ.

3.38. A WDM optical transmission system is constrained to have 500-GHz channel spacings. How many wavelength channels can be utilized in the 1536- to 1556-nm spectral band?

REFERENCES

1. A. B. Carlson, *Communication Systems,* McGraw-Hill, Burr Ridge, IL, 4th ed., 2002.
2. B. A. Forouzan, *Introduction to Data Communications and Networking,* McGraw-Hill, Burr Ridge, IL, 2nd ed., 2001.
3. J. G. Proakis, *Digital Communications,* McGraw-Hill, Burr Ridge, IL, 4th ed., 2001.
4. W. Hioki, *Telecommunications,* Prentice-Hall, Upper Saddle River, NJ, 4th ed., 2001.
5. G. Keiser, *Optical Fiber Communications,* McGraw-Hill, Burr Ridge, IL, 3rd ed., 2000.
6. A. Leon-Garcia and I. Widjaja, *Communication Networks,* McGraw-Hill, Burr Ridge, IL, 2000.
7. W. Stallings, *Data and Computer Communications,* Prentice-Hall, Upper Saddle River, NJ, 6th ed., 2000.
8. L. W. Couch II, *Digital and Analog Communication Systems,* Prentice-Hall, Upper Saddle River, NJ, 6th ed., 2000.
9. R. J. Bates and D. W. Gregory, *Voice and Data Communications Handbook,* McGraw-Hill, New York, 3rd ed., 2000.
10. L. L. Peterson and B. S. Davie, *Computer Networks,* Morgan-Kaufmann, San Francisco, 2nd ed., 2000.

11. R. L. Freeman, "Bits, symbols, bauds, and bandwidth," *IEEE Commun. Mag.,* vol. 36, pp. 96–99, Apr. 1998.
12. M. Schwarz, *Information Transmission, Modulation, and Noise,* McGraw-Hill, New York, 4th ed., 1990.
13. C. E. Shannon, "A mathematical theory of communication," *Bell Sys. Tech. J.,* vol. 27, pp. 379–423, July 1948; vol. 27, pp. 623–656, Oct. 1948.
14. A. J. Jerri, "The Shannon sampling theorem—Its various extensions and applications: A tutorial review," *Proc. IEEE,* vol. 65, pp. 1565–1596, Nov. 1977.
15. J. G. Proakis and D. Manolakis, *Digital Signal Processing: Principles, Algorithms and Applications,* Prentice-Hall, Upper Saddle River, NJ, 3rd ed., 1996.
16. R. B. Wells, *Applied Coding and Information Theory for Engineers,* Prentice-Hall, Upper Saddle River, NJ, 1999.
17. M. K. Simon, S. M. Hinedi, and W. C. Lindsey, *Digital Communication Techniques: Signal Design and Detection,* Prentice-Hall, Upper Saddle River, NJ, 1995.
18. M. K. Simon, S. M. Hinedi, and W. C. Lindsey, *Digital Communications: Synchronization,* Prentice-Hall, Upper Saddle River, NJ, 2002.
19. S. Haykin, *Communication Systems,* Wiley, New York, 4th ed., 2000.
20. A. M. Michelson and A. H. Levesque, *Error-Control Techniques for Digital Communication,* Wiley, New York, 1985.
21. S. B. Wicker, *Error Control Systems for Digital Communication and Storage,* Prentice-Hall, Upper Saddle River, NJ, 1995.
22. V. Pless, *Introduction to the Theory of Error-Correcting Codes,* Wiley, New York, 3rd ed., 1998.
23. J. Trulove, *LAN Wiring,* McGraw-Hill, New York, 1997.
24. ANSI/TIA/EIA-568-A-5-2000, *Transmission Performance Specifications for 4-pair 100-Ohm Category 5e Cabling,* Feb. 2000.
25. EIA/TIA-TSB-67, *Transmission Performance Specifications for Field Testing of Unshielded Twisted-Pair Cabling Systems,* Oct. 1995.
26. J. Hecht, *Understanding Fiber Optics,* Prentice-Hall, Upper Saddle River, NJ, 4th ed., 2002.
27. R. Ramaswami and K. N. Sivarajan, *Optical Networks,* Morgan-Kaufmann, San Francisco, 1998.
28. J. Powers, *An Introduction to Fiber Optic Systems,* Irwin, Chicago, 2nd ed., 1997.
29. T. Ishigure, Y. Koike, and J. W. Fleming, "Optimum index profile of the perfluorinated polymer-based GI polymer optical fiber and its dispersion properties," *J. Lightwave Tech.,* vol. 18, pp. 178–184, Feb. 2000.
30. R. O'Hara and A. Petrick, *The IEEE 802.11 Handbook,* IEEE Press, New York, 2000.
31. R. van Nee, G. Awater, M. Morikura, H. Takanashi, M. Webster, and K. W. Halford, "New high-rate wireless LAN standards," *IEEE Commun. Mag.,* vol. 37, pp. 82–88, Dec. 1999.
32. R. T. Valadas, A. R. Tavares, A. M. de Oliveira Duarte, A. C. Moreire, and C. T. Lomba, "The infrared physical layer of the IEEE 802.11 standard for wireless local area networks," *IEEE Commun. Mag.,* vol. 36, pp. 107–112, Dec. 1998.
33. J. Kahn and J. Barry, "Wireless infrared communications," *Proc. IEEE,* vol. 85, pp. 265–298, Feb. 1997.
34. S. V. Kartalopoulos, *Introduction to DWDM,* IEEE Press, New York, 2000.
35. ITU-T Recommendation G.692, *Optical Interfaces for Multichannel Systems with Optical Amplifiers,* Oct. 1998.

CHAPTER
4

LAN
ACCESS
TECHNIQUES

A basic characteristic of a local area network (LAN) is that its community of users must share the capacity of the transmission links that interconnect them. To utilize this capacity efficiently, standardized procedures are needed for users to access the LAN medium. This is the function of protocols at the medium access control (MAC) layer.

The two basic types of operational network architectures used for LANs are *broadcast networks* and *switched networks*. In a broadcast LAN all users receive the information sent by any particular transmitting station. Here the schemes for sharing the medium are random-access and controlled access methods. With *random access* no control is used to determine which station can transmit. This means that the users must *contend* for access to the LAN. When two or more stations attempt to transmit simultaneously in such a contention-based LAN, their signals will collide and interfere with each other. Various methods for listening to the network before sending a message (and sometimes during its transmission) have been devised to minimize such collisions. In contrast to random-access methods, *controlled access* approaches attempt to produce an orderly collision-free access to the shared transmission medium. Two possible ways of doing this are through either a *token-passing* scheme or a *polling* mechanism.

Switched LANs evolved from broadcast LANs because of a growing urgency to make better use of the LAN transmission-line capacities. This came about because the ever-growing complexity and communications demands of new user applications started to overburden the transmission lines. In a switched LAN architecture a switch employs forwarding logic and routing tables to transfer information units from the source to the destination. The switch provides input and output ports that are dedicated to either a single user or a small group of users. The group of stations may share the capacity of the line running to the switch either through a multiplexing scheme or by means of contention access, in which case collisions may appear on that particular line.

In this chapter Sec. 4.1 first defines some performance measures used to evaluate different LAN medium access methods. Among these are terms such as *throughput, transfer delays,* and *channel utilization* or *efficiency.* Sections 4.2 through 4.5 then present the fundamentals on various random-access techniques that are used when many stations share and contend for a common broadcast channel. These include ALOHA (a ground-based radio packet broadcast network developed in Hawaii), carrier sense multiple access (CSMA), and CSMA with collision detection (CSMA/CD). We note here that although ALOHA is not a LAN, its broadcast concept is applicable to the local networking environment, and as such it may be compared to random-access broadcast schemes used in LANs. In addition, an understanding of ALOHA will assist the reader in grasping the concepts behind the CSMA techniques. Another variation on CSMA, the CSMA with collision avoidance (CSMA/CA) method used in wireless LANs, is described in Chap. 8.

Controlled access to a LAN can be performed in either a centralized or a distributed fashion, as Sec. 4.6 describes. A popular centralized technique is polling, in which a master node decides which node may access the channel at any one time. A well-known distributed controlled access scheme is *token passing* in a ring-based network architecture.

Section 4.7 describes the basic characteristics of switched LANs. Chapter 5 on Ethernet, Chap. 7 on ATM, and Chap. 10 on internetworking give more details beyond these descriptions. The appendixes at the end of the chapter present the mathematical derivations of the performance equations for several variations of contention-based access schemes. Appendix 4A shows the analysis of network stability as exemplified by slotted ALOHA. Appendix 4B presents the analysis of nonpersistent CSMA.

4.1 PERFORMANCE MEASURES AND NOTATION

Before examining the details of LAN access methods, let us consider what performance measures are needed to evaluate and compare them. The evaluations of the performance of access methods usually is done in terms of the *average packet delay* (also called the *average transfer delay*) versus channel *throughput,* which is a key performance measure.

The performance of a network depends on the interaction of the traffic load and the network resources. A successful method for calculating the throughput is based on the use of a *queuing model.* Figure 4.1 shows a simple example of this, where a node is represented by a *single-server queue.* This means that the node has a single buffer in which arriving packets of length L_p that come from some arbitrary collection of message sources queue up and wait to be processed. The number of message sources in the network affects the packet arrival rate; that is, the larger the number of sources is, the higher the packet arrival rate will be. How these packets then are processed for transmission onto a common LAN channel is a function of the medium access method that is used.

A traditional analysis technique for describing the throughput of a network is to use the heuristic concept of packets arriving according to *Poisson statistics.*[1,2] These statistics are based on the concept that network traffic has a limited memory of the past

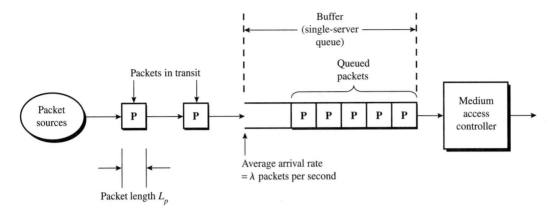

FIGURE 4.1
General concept of a simple queuing model.

so that averaging of "bursty" traffic over a long period of time gives rise to a smooth data stream. However, studies have shown that bursty traffic may retain similar bursty statistical properties over time scales ranging from milliseconds to days. This property is known as *self-similarity*.[3] Since a full explanation and application of the effects of self-similarity on network performance is beyond the scope of this book, we will use the traditional Poisson model, which is computationally easy. Thus under the assumption that a large number of packets can arrive at a buffer with a Poisson distribution, the probability $P_n(t)$ of exactly n packets arriving during a time interval of length t is given by

$$P_n(t) = \frac{(\lambda t)^n e^{-\lambda t}}{n!} \qquad (4.1)$$

where $n = 0, 1, 2, \ldots$ and λ is the *average packet arrival rate*.

The *throughput* of a link is a measure in bits per second of the *successful* traffic transmitted between stations; that is, since packets can become corrupted in traveling from station to station, it is customary to count only the error-free bits (error-free packets) when measuring throughput. To make the analysis completely independent of the actual channel rate, the throughput S often is expressed in a dimensionless normalized form

$$S = \frac{\lambda L_p}{R} \qquad (4.2)$$

where L_p is the packet length in bits and R is the channel transmission rate in bits per second. The values of S thus range from 0 to 1.

The throughput is expressed in terms of the *offered load G*, which is the actual message load or traffic demand presented to the network. We note that because some packets may need to be retransmitted, the total offered traffic λ_T is the sum of the packets that were delivered successfully on the first transmission attempt and repetitions of those that were damaged in transit. The normalized offered load G thus is given by

$$G = \frac{\lambda_T L_p}{R} \qquad (4.3)$$

where $\lambda_T \geq \lambda$. Analogous to the throughput, G is given by a dimensionless number which ranges from 0 to ∞ since λ_T can become arbitrarily large. The maximum achievable throughput for a particular type of access scheme is called the *capacity* of the channel under that access scheme and is found by maximizing S with respect to G.

Another important performance measure is the *average transfer delay* or *latency T*. The latency is the time that elapses from the generation of the first bit of a packet at the information source until the reception of the last bit at the destination. Since a packet encounters different elements in its path from the source to the destination, the time delay likewise consists of different components. The three main delay components are:

1. The *queueing delay* t_{queue} or waiting time in a buffer at the source before the packet is processed for transmission. As the traffic load increases, there is more contention for the channel, so packets have to wait increasingly longer before they can be sent out.
2. The *transmission delay* or *packet transmission time* t_p is the amount of time it takes to transmit a unit of data. This is a function of the link data rate R and the length L_p of the data unit sent out so that $t_p = L_p/R$.
3. The *propagation delay* t_{prop} is the time required to transmit a packet along the link connecting the source and the destination. Note that this time depends on the transmission medium that is used. For example, an electromagnetic signal travels at 3×10^8 m/s in free space, 2.3×10^8 m/s in a wire cable, and 2×10^8 m/s in an optical fiber.

EXAMPLE 4.1

Suppose we want to transmit a 1.5-kB (kilobyte) e-mail message and a 1.5-MB (megabyte) image file. Table 4.1 gives their transmission times for three different data rates.

TABLE 4.1
Transmission times for two types of files with different data rates

Data rate	Transmission times		
	1.5 Mbps	10 Mbps	100 Mbps
1.5-kB e-mail	8 ms	1.2 ms	0.12 ms
1.5-MB image	8 s	1.2 s	120 ms

Given the definitions of these various time parameters, we can define the *channel utilization* or *efficiency U* as the ratio of the packet transmission time to the average total transfer delay.

4.2 RANDOM-ACCESS OVERVIEW

Random-access or *contention* techniques are used in systems where many users try to send messages to other stations through a common broadcast channel. The term "random access" means that there is no definite or scheduled time when any particular station should transmit. In addition, all stations must *contend* for time on the network since there is no control mechanism for determining whose turn it is to transmit (hence the term *contention*).

Early work in this area resulted in the ALOHA scheme,[4,5] where each individual user transmits at any arbitrary time when there is a message to be sent. If more than one user attempts to transmit at the same time, the messages collide and have to be retransmitted later. This scheme is the simplest possible since it is completely asynchronous; that is, there is no coordination among users. However, since there is a high-interference possibility between messages from different simultaneously transmitting users, the maximum achievable channel utilization is only about 18 percent.

To improve the efficiency, a scheme called *slotted ALOHA* was proposed[6,7] which doubled the capacity of the ALOHA system. Here the channel is divided into discrete uniform time slots, each interval being equal to one frame transmission time. All users then are synchronized by means of a central clock or other technique so that transmission can start only at the beginning of a time slot. Thus the partial overlapping of colliding messages is eliminated and the maximum achievable channel utilization was raised to about 37 percent.

The next improvement in efficiency was made through a scheme in which the user listens to the channel to see if it is free before transmitting a message packet. If the user senses the channel to be idle, the packet is transmitted; if the channel is sensed to be busy, the packet transmission is delayed to a later time. Through this scheme, which is called *carrier sense multiple access* (CSMA), the chance of packet collision is greatly reduced.[8]

Although the CSMA scheme is a great improvement over ALOHA methods, packet collisions still can occur. To improve channel utilization further by shortening the collision time duration, a user can listen to the channel while sending out a message and immediately can cease a transmission before it is completed when a collision with another simultaneously transmitting user is detected. This scheme is called *CSMA with collision detection* (CSMA/CD) and is the basis of the Ethernet Protocol.[9–11] Sections 4.4 and 4.5 discuss the fundamentals of CSMA and CSMA/CD.

Another variation on the CSMA scheme is the *carrier sense multiple access with collision avoidance* (CSMA/CA) method, which is used for a wireless LAN. Here there is no collision detection function since this is not practical in a wireless network. This is due to the large dynamic range of signals on the medium, which makes it difficult to distinguish weak incoming signals from noise. Obviously a station must wait for the channel to be idle before transmitting. Once the channel becomes idle, a smooth and fair mechanism must be used to gain access to the channel since other stations also may be waiting to transmit. Without this mechanism all waiting stations would transmit at once and collisions would occur, thereby wasting transmission time. To solve this, the CSMA/CA Protocol uses a random set of delays to allow stations to transmit. Chapter 8 presents more details on the operation of this access method.

4.3 ALOHA

To set a basis with which to compare various random-access methods, let us first look at ALOHA, which is the simplest possible broadcast protocol,[3–6,12–14] and the enhanced slotted ALOHA version. The original ALOHA method often is called *pure ALOHA* to distinguish it from the slotted ALOHA scheme. Appendix 4A at the end of the chapter gives a mathematical analysis of the stability of slotted ALOHA since the results are applicable to any random-access method in general.

4.3.1 Pure ALOHA

The basic idea of pure ALOHA is simple since users transmit immediately whenever they have data to send. To determine whether a transmission was successful, a sender waits for an acknowledgment from the receiver for a time period equal to two propagation times $2t_{prop}$, which is the time it takes a packet to travel from the sender to the receiver and back again. If no acknowledgment is received after this time, a backoff algorithm is used to select a random retransmission time. If no acknowledgment is received after K retransmission attempts, the packet is dropped. The *average backoff time B* can be selected in a number of ways. For example, if it is distributed uniformly between 1 and K packet transmission times t_p, then $B = t_p(K + 1)/2$.

Obviously there will be collisions between packets sent within a packet transmission time t_p from different users as is indicated in Fig. 4.2. We first assume all packets have the same length and each requires one time unit t_p (called a *slot*) for transmission. Consider an attempt by a user to send packet A starting at time $t_0 + t_p$ and ending at time $t_0 + 2t_p$. If another user had started generating packet B between t_0 and $t_0 + t_p$, the end of packet B will collide with the beginning of packet A. This can occur because, owing to long propagation delays, the sender of packet A did not know that packet B was already underway when the transmission of packet A was started. Similarly, if another user attempts to transmit between $t_0 + t_p$ and $t_0 + 2t_p$ (packet C), the beginning of packet C will collide with the end of packet A. Thus if two packets overlap by even the slightest amount in the *vulnerable period* of length $2t_p$ shown in Fig. 4.2, both packets will be corrupted and will need to be retransmitted later.

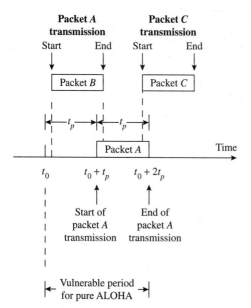

FIGURE 4.2
Vulnerable period during which packets can collide in the pure ALOHA scheme.

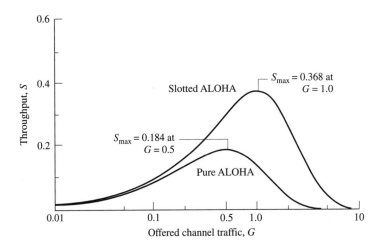

FIGURE 4.3
Comparison of the throughput as a function of the offered load for pure and slotted ALOHA.

Now let S be the channel throughput (the average number of successful transmissions per time period t_p), and let G be the total traffic entering the channel from an infinite population of users (i.e., G denotes the number of packet transmissions that are attempted in a time period t_p). To find the throughput, we first assume the probability p_k of k transmission attempts per packet time follows a Poisson distribution with a mean G per packet time. From Eq. (4.1) this probability is given by

$$p_k = \frac{G^k e^{-G}}{k!} \tag{4.4}$$

The throughput S then is just the offered load G times the probability of a transmission that is successful. Thus

$$S = Gp_0 \tag{4.5}$$

where p_0 is the probability that a packet does not suffer a collision (i.e., p_0 is the probability that no other traffic is generated during a vulnerable period which is two packet times long). From Eq. (4.4) the probability of zero packets being generated in an interval two packet times long is

$$p_0 = e^{-2G} \tag{4.6}$$

so that from Eq. (4.5)

$$S = Ge^{-2G} \tag{4.7}$$

The throughput given by Eq. (4.7) is plotted in Fig. 4.3. The maximum value of S occurs at $G = 0.5$, where $S = 1/(2e)$, which is about 0.184. This means that the best channel utilization that can be achieved is around 18 percent for the pure ALOHA method.

4.3.2 Slotted ALOHA

To increase the efficiency of the ALOHA method, the slotted ALOHA scheme was introduced. Here the channel is divided into time slots which are exactly equal to a

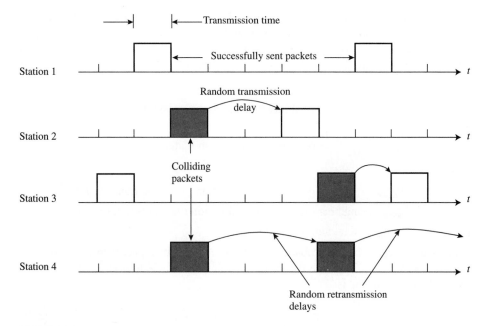

FIGURE 4.4
Examples of transmission attempts and random retransmission delays for colliding packets in
slotted ALOHA.

packet transmission time. All users then are synchronized to these time slots so that
whenever a user generates a packet, it must synchronize exactly with the next possible
channel slot. Consequently the vulnerable period in which this packet can collide with
other data is reduced to *one* packet time period versus *two* for pure ALOHA. Examples of
transmission attempts and random retransmission delays for colliding packets are shown
in Fig. 4.4 for four network users.

Since the vulnerable period is now reduced in half, the probability of no other
traffic occurring during the same time period as the packet we wish to send is $p_0 = e^{-G}$.
This in turn leads to a throughput

$$S = Ge^{-G} \tag{4.8}$$

As shown in Fig. 4.3, the maximum efficiency for the slotted ALOHA system occurs at
$G = 1$, where $S = 1/e$ or about 0.368, which is twice that of pure ALOHA.

EXAMPLE 4.2

Consider an ALOHA radio network that uses a 19.2-kbps channel for sending messages and
assume the message packets are 100 bits long. The system therefore is capable of transmitting at
(19.2 kbps) × (1 packet/100 bits) = 192 packets per second. The maximum throughput for ALOHA
then is 192(0.184) ≈ 35 packets per second. For slotted ALOHA the maximum throughput is
192(0.368) ≈ 70 packets per second.

The curves shown in Fig. 4.3 were obtained for an infinite number of users. Let us now consider a slotted ALOHA system with a *finite* number of users.[12] To start, we first examine the relative-frequency concept of probability so that for station i we can define the steady-state average throughput S_i and the offered traffic G_i by the following expressions:

$$S_i = \frac{N_{i,\text{good}}}{N_T} = \text{probability that station } i \text{ successfully transmits} \qquad (4.9)$$

$$G_i = \frac{N_{i,\text{attempt}}}{N_T} = \text{probability that station } i \text{ attempts transmission} \qquad (4.10)$$

where

$$N_{i,\text{good}} = \text{number of slots used by station } i \text{ for good transmissions}$$

$$N_{i,\text{attempt}} = \text{number of slots in which station } i \text{ attempts to transmit}$$

$$N_T = \text{total number of slots}$$

For M users let G_i be the probability that user i transmits a packet in any given slot where $i = 1, 2, \ldots, M$. Since the average traffic per slot due to user i is G_i, the total average channel traffic is

$$G = \sum_{i=1}^{M} G_i \quad \text{packets per slot} \qquad (4.11)$$

Similarly, let S_i be the probability of a successful transmission for a packet generated by user i. This means that the average throughput per slot due to user i is S_i so that the average total throughput is

$$S = \sum_{i=1}^{M} S_i \quad \text{packets per slot} \qquad (4.12)$$

The probability S_i that user i has a successful transmission in a particular time slot then is merely the probability G_i that user i sends a packet, multiplied by the probability that none of the other $M - 1$ users sends packets; thus

$$S_i = G_i \prod_{j \neq i} (1 - G_j) \qquad (4.13)$$

EXAMPLE 4.3

Consider the case where all M users are identical. Then each user has a throughput $S_i = S/M$ packets per slot and a total transmission rate of $G_i = G/M$ packets per slot, where G and S are given by Eqs. (4.11) and (4.12), respectively. Substituting these expressions into Eq. (4.13) then yields

$$S = G \left(1 - \frac{G}{M} \right)^{M-1} \qquad (4.14)$$

Note that as $M \to \infty$, we have $S = Ge^{-G}$, which is the expected expression of Eq. (4.8) for an infinite population slotted ALOHA system.

4.4 CARRIER SENSE MULTIPLE ACCESS (CSMA)

Since LANs span a limited geographical area, the propagation delay between a sending and a receiving node is small compared to the packet transmission time. In this case when a station sends a packet, all the other stations in the network are aware of it within a fraction of the packet transmission time. This observation led to the development of the *carrier sense multiple access* (CSMA) scheme.[15–18] In this scheme a station that wishes to transmit attempts to avoid collisions by first listening to the medium to determine if another transmission is in progress.

When the channel is sensed to be idle, a station can take one of three different approaches (depending on the network design) to insert a packet onto the channel. These three protocols are known as *nonpersistent CSMA, 1-persistent CSMA,* and *p-persistent CSMA.* Actually the 1-persistent protocol is a special case of the *p*-persistent scheme, but we consider it separately here. As shown subsequently, these protocols differ by the action that a station with a packet to transmit takes after sensing the readiness state of the channel. However, when a station notes that a transmission was unsuccessful, in each protocol the rescheduling of the packet transmission is the same. In these reschedulings the packet is sent again according to a randomly distributed retransmission delay. A comparison of these three CSMA protocols is given in Table 4.2.

Here we look at the basic concepts of the three CSMA protocols. Appendix 4B at the end of the chapter gives details on the analyses of the throughputs for the first two. In this section we simply state the derived results.

4.4.1 Nonpersistent CSMA

For the nonpersistent CSMA scheme the throughput S is expressed in terms of the offered traffic rate G and the dimensionless parameter a, which is defined as

$$a = \frac{\text{propagation delay}}{\text{packet transmission time}} \qquad (4.15)$$

The parameter a corresponds to the vulnerable period during which a transmitted packet

TABLE 4.2
Characteristics of the three basic CSMA protocols

CSMA Protocol	Characteristics
Nonpersistent	If medium is idle, transmit.
	If medium is busy, wait random amount of time and resense channel.
1-persistent	If medium is idle, transmit.
	If medium is busy, continue listening until channel is idle; than transmit immediately.
p-persistent	If medium is idle, transmit with probability p.
	If medium is busy, continue listening until channel is idle; then transmit with probability p.

can suffer a collision. Since the propagation delay is much smaller than the packet transmission time, a is a small quantity, say, on the order of 0.01 for a typical LAN.

EXAMPLE 4.4

Table 4.3 gives some examples of the values of the parameter a for various data rates, packet sizes, and link lengths, assuming a signal speed along a wire of 2.3×10^8 m/s. For example, at a Fast Ethernet rate of 100 Mbps, $a = 0.017$ for a 25000-bit packet and a transmission distance of 1 km.

TABLE 4.3
**Examples of the value of a for various data rates,
packet sizes, and link lengths**

Data rate, Mbps	Packet size, bits	Link length, km	a
1	100	0.1	0.004
1	1500	1	0.003
10	100	0.1	0.043
10	1500	1	0.029
100	25000	0.1	0.002
100	25000	1	0.017

To see how the CSMA Protocol operates, consider Fig. 4.5 which shows the successful and unsuccessful attempts at transmitting packets. This figure also shows that the activity on the channel may be divided into both busy periods during which transmission attempts are made and idle periods during which no stations transmit. (Note that in Fig. 4.5 and in the following discussions we will normalize the time scale to units of the packet transmission time t_p.) Now consider the packet that is sent at time $t = 0$ when the channel was sensed to be idle. We let this packet originate at station 1. It now will take a time interval a for all other stations on the channel to become aware that station 1 is transmitting. Thus by the definition of a if no other station transmits between time $t = 0$ and $t = a$, then the transmission attempt will be successful because for $t > a$ all other stations will sense the channel to be busy. The busy period for successful transmission then is $1 + a$, which is the propagation delay plus the packet transmission time (in normalized time units). The busy period is followed by an *idle period* during which no station transmits, and this in turn is followed immediately by another busy period. Thus we define a *cycle* as consisting of a busy period plus an idle period.

Now assume station 3 has a packet to send during the vulnerable time interval a associated with packet B. The station will transmit this packet since it senses the channel to be idle (the packet from station 1 has not arrived as yet), and thereby will cause a collision. As shown in Fig. 4.5, we let Y be the arrival time of the last packet which collides with the one sent by station 1 so that $0 \leq Y \leq a$. The transmission of all packets arriving in the time interval Y will be completed after $Y + 1$ time units. Since any station still can transmit during the time period a, the channel finally will be sensed unused at time $Y + 1 + a$. Thus the time duration $Y + 1 + a$ is the busy period for an unsuccessful

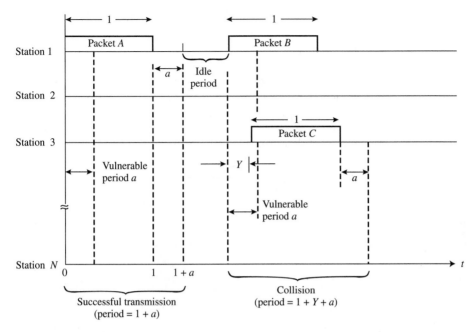

FIGURE 4.5

Successful and unsuccessful transmission attempts for nonpersistent CSMA. Time is measured in units of the packet transmission time t_p.

transmission attempt. It is important to note that there can be at most one successful transmission during a busy period.

From Appendix 4B we have that the throughput for nonpersistent CSMA is

$$S = \frac{Ge^{-aG}}{G(1 + 2a) + e^{-aG}} \tag{4.16}$$

In the limit as $a \to 0$ we have

$$S \to \frac{G}{1 + G} \tag{4.17}$$

Thus when $a = 0$, a throughput of 1 theoretically can be achieved for an infinitely large offered channel load G. This is shown in Fig. 4.6 where the throughput given by Eq. (4.16) is plotted as a function of G for various values of a.

4.4.2 Slotted Nonpersistent CSMA

A variation of the nonpersistent CSMA method is *slotted nonpersistent CSMA*. The concept is similar to the slotted ALOHA scheme. Here the time axis is slotted into intervals of length τ as shown in Fig. 4.7. All stations are synchronized and required to start transmission only at the beginning of a slot. All packets are assumed to be of a length t_p (i.e., they require a transmission time t_p), which is an integral number of time slots. When a packet arrives during a time slot, the station senses the state of the channel

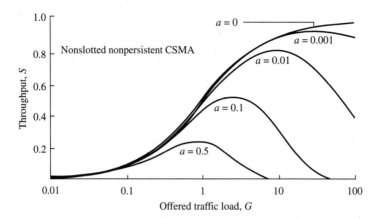

FIGURE 4.6
Throughput S as a function of the offered load G for various values of a for nonslotted nonpersistent CSMA.

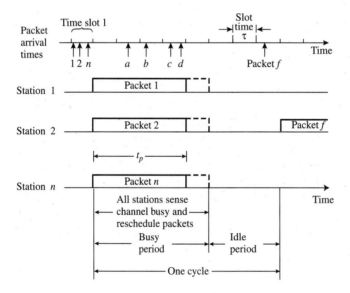

FIGURE 4.7
Example of packet arrivals in busy and idle periods in slotted nonpersistent CSMA.

at the beginning of the next slot and then either transmits if the channel is idle or defers to a later time slot if traffic is present.

An example of this is given in Fig. 4.7. Here packets from stations 1, 2, and n arrive during the first time slot. If the next slot is empty, all three stations will transmit as shown in the figure. All stations, including the ones at which packets arrive in the busy period (shown as packets a, b, c, and d in Fig. 4.7), then will sense the channel to be busy. These stations thus defer their packets for transmission at a later time. As can be seen in Fig. 4.7, the length of each busy period is exactly $(t_p + \tau)$ or, in normalized time units $(1 + a)$, where $a = \tau/t_p$ as given by Eq. (4.15). Therefore the end of the transmission can be determined by all stations since the busy period is longer than the transmission time by the amount τ (or a in normalized time units). Analogous to the unslotted CSMA case, an idle period consisting of an integral number of slots with no arrivals follows a busy period. This is shown as three slots long in Fig. 4.7. The first two slots are empty and there is an arrival (packet f, which we take as coming from station 2) in the third slot. This packet is sent in the next slot, thereby ending a cycle.

From Appendix 4B we have that the throughput for the slotted nonpersistent CSMA method is

$$S = \frac{aGe^{-aG}}{1 - e^{-aG} + a} \tag{4.18}$$

4.4.3 The 1-Persistent CSMA

The 1-persistent CSMA Protocol was devised to avoid situations in which a station has to wait before transmitting even though the channel is idle. As noted in Table 4.2, the 1-persistent CSMA scheme operates by transmitting a packet with probability 1 if the channel is sensed to be idle. If the channel is busy when a station has a packet to transmit, the station waits until the channel becomes idle and then transmits immediately with probability 1. (This is the reason for the name "1-persistent"; the station persists on transmitting when the channel is busy and then sends its packet with probability 1.) When two or more stations are waiting to transmit, a collision is guaranteed since each station will transmit immediately at the end of the busy period. In this case each station will wait a random amount of time and then will reattempt to transmit.

As is the case with nonpersistent CSMA, the performance of the 1-persistent CSMA Protocol depends on the channel delay time. Suppose just after a station begins sending, another station has a packet to transmit and checks to see if the channel is idle. If the packet from the first station has not yet arrived at the second station, the latter will assume the channel is idle and will send its packet, thereby creating a collision. As the delay time becomes longer, this effect becomes more important since the performance of the protocol decreases.

The throughput of 1-persistent CSMA is given by

$$S = \frac{Ge^{-G(1+2a)}[1 + G + aG(1 + G + aG/2)]}{G(1 + 2a) - (1 - e^{-aG}) + (1 + aG)e^{-G(1+a)}} \tag{4.19}$$

The analysis for finding this expression is fairly involved and the interested reader is referred to the literature.[18]

4.4.4 The p-Persistent CSMA

To reduce the interference resulting from collisions and to improve the throughput, the p-persistent CSMA scheme was developed. This is a general case of the 1-persistent CSMA Protocol and applies to slotted channels. In this protocol when a station becomes ready to send and it senses the channel to be idle, it either transmits with a probability p or defers transmission by one time slot (which is typically the maximum propagation delay) with a probability $q = 1 - p$. If the deferred slot also is idle, the station either transmits with a probability p or defers again with probability q. This process is repeated until the packet is transmitted or the channel becomes busy. When the channel becomes busy, the station acts as though there had been a collision; that is, it waits a random time and then starts the transmission attempt again. In case the channel originally was sensed to be busy, the station waits until the next slot and applies the preceding procedure.

The analysis and the resulting expression for the throughput of this protocol are rather involved. We will not consider this method further here since it has no conceptual advantage over nonpersistent CSMA. The interested reader should consult Refs. 8, 16, and 17 for details.

4.5 CSMA WITH COLLISION DETECTION (CSMA/CD)

A considerable performance improvement in the basic CSMA protocols can be achieved by means of the *carrier sense multiple access with collision detection* (CSMA/CD) technique.[19,20] As noted in Chap. 5, the concept of the CSMA/CD method of randomly accessing a LAN was started at the Xerox Corporation. This was developed subsequently through a joint effort by Digital Equipment Corporation, Intel, and Xerox into a detailed specification for a system called *Ethernet*. The IEEE-802.3 CSMA/CD Standard for LANs is based on the Ethernet specification and is almost identical to it. The CSMA/CD protocols are essentially the same as those for CSMA with the addition of the collision detection feature. With this feature, when a CSMA/CD station senses that a collision has occurred, it immediately ceases transmitting its packet and sends a brief jamming signal to notify all the stations of this collision. The same variations exist as in CSMA; that is, there are nonpersistent, 1-persistent, and *p*-persistent methodologies.

The basic operating characteristics of the CSMA/CD Protocol are outlined in Fig. 4.8. One key feature of the CSMA/CD Protocol is a *deference mechanism*. Even when there is no packet waiting to be transmitted, the CSMA/CD MAC sublayer monitors the physical medium for traffic. When the station becomes ready to transmit, the behavior of the deference mechanism depends on which protocol variation is used. In particular, if the channel is idle, then one of the following actions is taken:

- The packet is transmitted if nonpersistent or 1-persistent CSMA/CD is used.
- For *p*-persistent CSMA/CD the packet is sent with probability *p* or is delayed by the propagation delay with probability $(1 - p)$.

If the channel is busy, then:

- The packet is backed off and the algorithm is repeated for the nonpersistent case.
- The station defers transmission until the channel is sensed to be idle and then immediately transmits in the 1-persistent case.
- For the *p*-persistent protocol the station defers until the channel is idle and then follows the idle-channel procedure.

In each of the busy channel cases when there is a packet ready to be sent out, the MAC sublayer defers to the passing frame that is in transit by delaying the transmission of its own waiting packet. After the last bit of the frame from the other station has passed

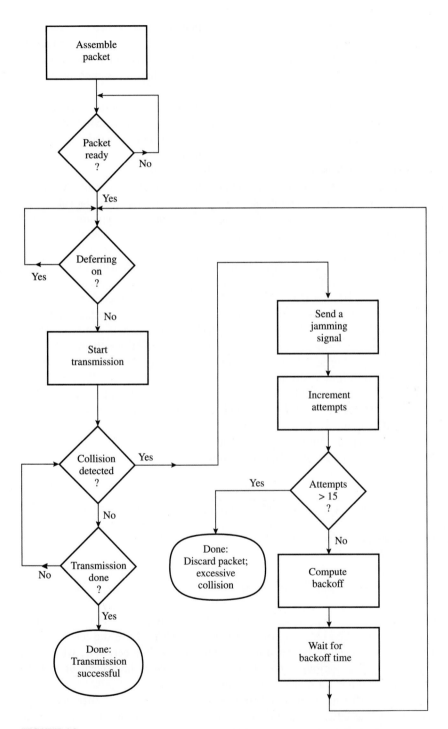

FIGURE 4.8
Flow diagram for the CSMA/CD Protocol.

by, the MAC sublayer continues to defer for a certain time period, called an *interframe spacing*. Transmission of any waiting packet is initiated at the end of this time. When the transmission is completed (or immediately at the end of the interframe spacing time if no packet is waiting in the transmission buffer), the MAC sublayer resumes monitoring the carrier sense signal.

Once the deference at a station is finished and transmission has started, collisions still can occur until acquisition of the network by that station has been achieved through the deference of all the other stations. If a collision is detected, the station aborts the packet that is transmitted and sends a jamming signal of duration b (this time parameter is measured in dimensionless units, analogous to the parameter a).

After the jamming signal has been transmitted, the stations that were involved in the colliding packets wait random amounts of time and then try to send their packets again. By using a random delay, these stations are not likely to have another collision on the next transmission attempt. However, to ensure that this backoff technique maintains stability, a method known as *truncated binary exponential backoff*[19,21] is used in Ethernet, for example. In this method a station will persist in trying to transmit when there are repeated collisions. These retries will continue until either the transmission is successful or 16 attempts (the original attempt plus 15 retries) have been made unsuccessfully. At this point (if all 16 attempts fail) the packet is discarded and the event is reported as an error.

The backoff strategy is quite simple. If a packet has been transmitted unsuccessfully n times, the next transmission attempt is delayed by an integer r times the base backoff time (which usually is chosen to be twice the round-trip propagation delay). The integer r is selected as a uniformly distributed integer in the range $0 \le r \le 2^k$, where $k = \min(n, 10)$; that is, k is the minimum of the number of presently attempted transmissions n and the integer 10. Thus as the Ethernet load becomes increasingly heavy, the stations automatically adapt to the load.

The derivations of the throughput for unslotted and slotted nonpersistent CSMA/CD are rather complex,[20] so we merely state the results here. For the unslotted case

$$S = \frac{Ge^{-aG}}{Ge^{-aG} + bG(1 - e^{-aG}) + 2aG(1 - e^{-aG}) + (2 - e^{-aG})} \qquad (4.20)$$

and for slotted nonpersistent CSMA/CD

$$S = \frac{aGe^{-aG}}{aGe^{-aG} + b(1 - e^{-aG} - aGe^{-aG}) + a(2 - e^{-aG} - aGe^{-aG})} \qquad (4.21)$$

Figure 4.9 gives a comparison of pure ALOHA, slotted ALOHA, 1-persistent CSMA, nonpersistent CSMA, and nonpersistent CSMA/CD. Here the length of the jamming signal b is taken to be equal to the vulnerability time period a, which was chosen to be 0.01. The various curves show the performance improvement that the CSMA/CD method offers for higher traffic loads.

The expression for the throughput S for 1-persistent CSMA/CD is rather messy,[18,20] so we merely plot it as a function of the offered load G. This is shown in Fig. 4.10 with $a = 0.01$ for several values of b. From this figure we see that the 1-persistent CSMA/CD Protocol is able to maintain throughput near capacity over a large range of loads.

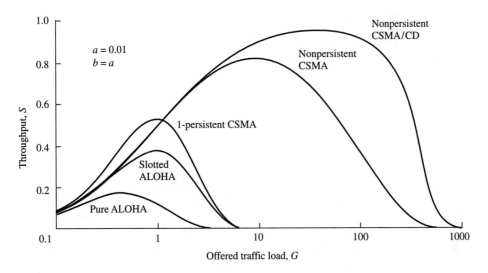

FIGURE 4.9
Performance comparison of pure ALOHA, slotted ALOHA, 1-persistent CSMA, nonpersistent CSMA, and nonpersistent CSMA/CD.

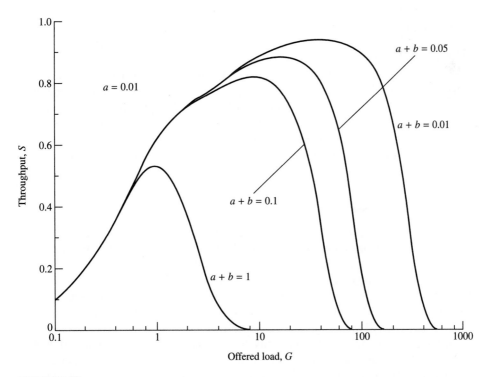

FIGURE 4.10
Throughput as a function of G for $a = 0.01$ and with $b + a = 1.0, 0.1, 0.05$, and 0.01. (*Reprinted with permission from Takagi and Kleinrock,*[17] *©1987, IEEE.*)

4.6 CONTROLLED ACCESS SCHEMES

In contrast to the stochastic nature of contention-based access methods, a *controlled access technique* is a *deterministic* method since it employs a specific digital signal to grant permission to transmit to *one station at a time.* Thereby packets from two different stations cannot collide since only one user has the right to send messages at any instance. The responsibility for the control signal can be assigned to one station on the network (centralized control), or it may be distributed among all the nodes.

4.6.1 Polling

A common *centralized control* method is known as *polling.*[22] Polling techniques determine the order in which stations can take turns to access the network. Figure 4.11 shows three different polling processes. In Fig. 4.11a the controller uses the outbound line to query each of N stations in some prescribed order, asking whether or not the station has a message to send. The polled station then transmits on the inbound line if it has data to send. When it has completed its transmission, the polled station sends a *go-ahead message* back to the controller. If it does not have anything to transmit, the station sends back a special negative response. Usually the controller polls the station sequentially, but in special circumstances important terminals may be polled several times per cycle.

Figure 4.11b shows a central controller that uses a certain radio-frequency band to transmit polling messages to N stations. The polled stations can use either the same or a different frequency band to transmit inbound messages. If the controller and the stations use the same frequency, the system would have to alternate between transmissions from the controller and messages from the polled stations.

Polling also can be done without a central controller, as Fig. 4.11c illustrates. Here there are N stations, each of which can receive the transmissions from all the other stations. For example, this network may consist of mobile laptop computers configured as a wireless LAN. The stations use some particular protocol to make a list that establishes the order in which the stations are allowed to transmit. After a station has finished sending its message, it is responsible for transferring a polling message to the next station on the polling list.

4.6.2 Token Passing

Distributed control access methods commonly are referred to as *token controlled.* These techniques are employed in token-ring topologies.[23] *Tokens* are special bit patterns or packets, usually several bits in length, that circulate from node to node when there is no message traffic. When a station wants to send data, it removes the token from the line and holds it. Now the station has exclusive access to the network for transmitting its message. In the meantime other stations are continuously monitoring the messages that pass by on the network. All the stations are responsible for identifying and accepting messages addressed to them. In addition, they must forward messages that are addressed to other stations. When a station is finished transmitting its message, it puts the token back into circulation. This indicates to the network that the station has finished sending and gives other stations a chance to transmit. Chapter 6 presents more details and illustrations on this access method.

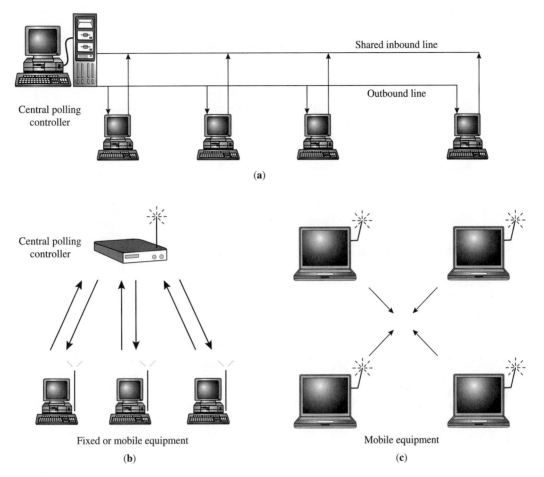

Shared inbound line

Outbound line

Central polling
controller

(a)

Central polling
controller

Fixed or mobile equipment

(b)

Mobile equipment

(c)

FIGURE 4.11
Examples of three types of polling schemes.

4.7 SWITCHED ACCESS METHODS

To increase the network capacity significantly over that achievable with broadcast LANs, developers have implemented *switched LAN* solutions.[24,25] The advantage of a LAN switch is that it eliminates the collision detection timing restrictions, thereby offering longer cable distances between stations. Furthermore it can provide an individual user with a private or dedicated link to the LAN switch and can allow multiple ports on the switch to be active simultaneously, which leads to significantly greater network capacity. For example, by having a dedicated link, a user receives instant access to the full available bandwidth and does not have to contend for this bandwidth with other LAN users. In addition, the implementation of various types of LAN switches allows the creation of larger networks than can be achieved with a broadcast scheme.

Figure 4.12 illustrates the use of a central LAN switch in a star network architecture. The switch provides input/output (I/O) ports that are dedicated to either a single user or

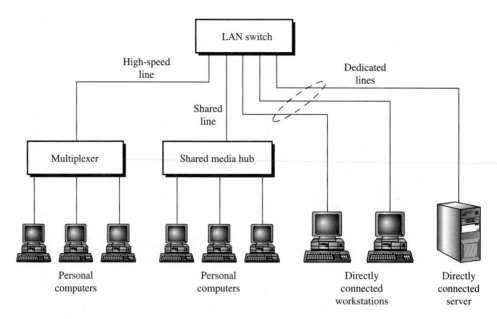

FIGURE 4.12
The use of a central LAN switch in a star network architecture.

a small group of users. A group of stations may share the capacity of the line running to the switch either through a multiplexing scheme or by means of contention access, in which case collisions may appear on that particular line. Other applications include a LAN-to-LAN switch or a switch that interconnects a LAN to other networks, as shown in Fig. 4.13. Chapter 10 gives further details on these applications.

Figure 4.14 shows the basic concept of a LAN switch. The two major components of any switch are the forwarding logic and the I/O ports. The I/O ports are classified as access ports and network uplink ports. *Access ports* are the physical interfaces that a switch uses to connect to stations on the LAN. *Network uplink ports* are the ports that connect the LAN switch to other LAN switches. Each access port has a buffer, which is used for queuing up incoming frames while they wait for the outgoing port to become free for transmission.

The IEEE-801.1D Standard defines the *forwarding logic* of a LAN switch.[26] The basic function of the forwarding logic is to examine the incoming frames and to transfer them to the appropriate output port when this port is free for transmission. With this setup each incoming line constitutes a single collision domain. Thus no collisions will occur if only a single station is attached to the line. However, if several stations share an input line by means of another hub, then this group of stations will constitute a collision domain.

More details on LAN switches are given in Chap. 5 in the discussions concerning Ethernet and in Chap. 10 on switching techniques used for the internetworking of a LAN to other networks.

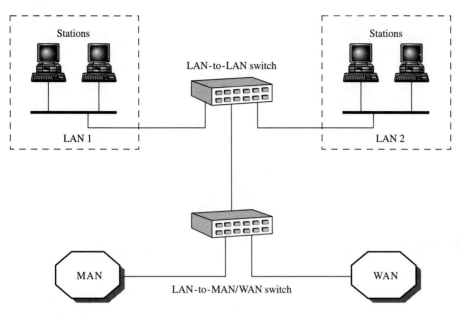

FIGURE 4.13
Applications of a LAN-to-LAN switch and a switch that interconnects a LAN to other networks.

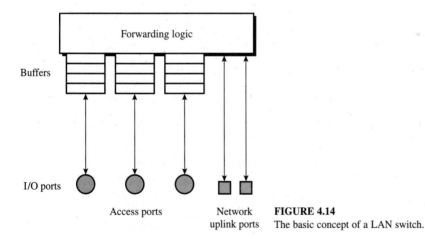

FIGURE 4.14
The basic concept of a LAN switch.

4.8 SUMMARY

The two basic types of operational network architectures used for LANs are *broadcast networks* and *switched networks:*

1. In a broadcast LAN all users receive the information sent by any particular transmitting station. The schemes for sharing the medium are random-access and controlled access methods.

- No control is used with *random access,* so all stations contend for access to the LAN. When two or more stations attempt to transmit simultaneously in a contention-based LAN, their signals will collide and interfere with each other.
- *Controlled access* approaches attempt to produce an orderly collision-free access to the shared transmission medium. Two possible ways of doing this are through either a *token-passing* scheme or a *polling* mechanism.

2. Among the possible random-access concepts are the following:
   - In *pure ALOHA,* which is a ground-based radio packet broadcast network developed at the University of Hawaii, users transmit immediately whenever they have data to send. When traffic is light, the probability of collisions is very small. However, an increasing number of collisions starts to occur with heavier traffic loads, thereby resulting in a low maximum achievable throughput of 18 percent. The *slotted ALOHA* scheme improves the performance of the pure ALOHA scheme by constraining the stations to transmit in a synchronized fashion. This allows a maximum achievable throughput of about 37 percent
   - Various forms of *carrier sense multiple access* (CSMA) were devised in order to stop the wastage of bandwidth because of packet collisions. The idea of the CSMA protocols is to avoid transmissions that are certain to cause collisions. This is done by monitoring the medium for the presence of a carrier signal, which would indicate that there is an ongoing transmission.
   - To improve further on the CSMA method, *CSMA with collision detection* (CSMA/CD) was developed to allow a station to cut off an ongoing transmission immediately when it detects a collision with a transmission from another station. Ethernet-based LANs use this concept, which is outlined in the IEEE-802.3 Standard.
   - *CSMA with collision avoidance* (CSMA/CA) is another variation on the CSMA scheme. This method is used for a wireless LAN, such as that based on IEEE-802.11. CSMA/CA has no collision detection function since this is not practical in a wireless network. This is due to the large dynamic range of signals on the medium, which makes it difficult to distinguish weak incoming signals from noise. To provide a smooth and fair mechanism for gaining access to the channel, the CSMA/CA Protocol uses a random set of delays to allow stations to transmit.

3. *Controlled access techniques* are *deterministic* methods since they employ a specific digital signal to grant permission in order to transmit to *one station at a time.* Thus packets from two different stations cannot collide since only one user has the right to send messages at any instance. The control can be assigned to one station on the network (centralized) or it may be distributed among all the nodes.
   - A common *centralized* control method is *polling,* which determines the order in which stations can take turns to access the network. Usually the controller polls the station sequentially, but in special circumstances important high-priority terminals may be polled several times per cycle.
   - Distributed access control methods commonly use *tokens,* which are special bit patterns or packets that circulate from node to node when there is no message traffic. When a station wants to send data, it removes the token from the line

and holds it, thereby giving it exclusive access to the network. When a station is finished transmitting its message, it puts the token back into circulation for other stations to use.

4. A *switched LAN* can significantly increase the network capacity over that achievable with broadcast LANs. The advantage of a LAN switch is that it eliminates the collision detection timing restrictions, thereby offering longer cable distances between stations. A LAN switch also can provide an individual user with a private or dedicated link to the LAN switch and it allows multiple ports on the switch to be active simultaneously, which leads to significantly greater network capacity.

APPENDIX

4A

STABILITY
OF SLOTTED
ALOHA

An important factor in any network is its stability. Let us look at this for slotted ALOHA. We will go into this in some detail here since the results hold for any random-access method in general. To study the stability, we assume there are N identical stations, each of which can hold at most one packet. Thus if a new packet arrives at a station with a full buffer, the newly arriving message is lost since the station is busy or *blocked;* that is, the station controller prevents any more inputs. We further assume the station generates new packets according to a Poisson distribution with a mean transfer probability $p \ll 1$ packets per slot when the station is not blocked.

To carry out a tractable analysis, it is necessary to adopt a memoryless model in connection with packet retransmission. Normally in slotted ALOHA a station waits a random integral number of time slots before trying to retransmit. Instead here we assume a previously collided packet (called a *backlogged* packet) is retransmitted with probability α in every succeeding time slot until a successful transmission occurs. Note that this does not accurately reflect the behavior of a realistic system if a constant interval of time is needed to detect a collision. However, simulation studies have shown that this is a very good approximation when the condition

$$\frac{1}{\alpha} = R + \frac{K+1}{2} \tag{4.22}$$

holds, where R is the number of slots that fit into one round-trip propagation time, and K is the number of time slots required for successful retransmission to take place.

The state of the ALOHA system then can be described by determining how many stations are backlogged. First let state k be the condition wherein k of the N stations are backlogged (i.e., the stations contain packets that have undergone collision). Each of these k stations then may decide either to resend its backlogged packet with probability α

or to skip the present slot with probability $1 - \alpha$. In addition to the mean retransmission attempts of $k\alpha$ packets per slot, the remaining $N - k$ unblocked stations are generating new packets at a collective rate of $(N - k)p$ packets per slot.

There will be a successful transmission in state k only if exactly one packet, either backlogged or new, is sent. Suppose we let n represent the number of new packets generated by the $N - k$ unblocked stations during a given time interval, and let r represent the number of retransmission attempts by the k backlogged stations during the same slot. These parameters obviously need to satisfy the conditions $0 \leq n \leq N - k$ and $0 \leq r \leq k$. Further we let $P\{n = 0\}$ be the probability that no new packets are generated during the present time slot, $P\{n = 1\}$ be the probability that a new packet is generated, and $P\{r \geq 1\}$ be the probability that one or more of the backlogged stations attempt a retransmission. The probability P_k of a successful transmission then is

$$
\begin{aligned}
P_k &= P\{n = 1\}P\{r = 0\} + P\{n = 0\}P\{r = 1\} \\
&= [k\alpha(1 - \alpha)^{k-1}][(1 - p)^{N-k}] + [(1 - \alpha)^k][(N - k)p(1 - p)^{N-k-1}] \\
&= S_{\text{out}, k}
\end{aligned}
\tag{4.23}
$$

where $S_{\text{out}, k}$ is the rate at which packets leave the system when k stations are backlogged. Under the same conditions the rate at which packets enter the system is

$$
S = (N - k)p
\tag{4.24}
$$

For a large number of stations N and for small transfer probability p Eq. (4.23) reduces to

$$
S_{\text{out}, k} = k\alpha(1 - \alpha)^{k-1}e^{-S} + (1 - \alpha)^k S e^{-S}
\tag{4.25}
$$

When the channel input rate S given by Eq. (4.24) is equal to the channel output rate $S_{\text{out}, k}$ for given values of k and α, the network is in *equilibrium*. A plot of an equilibrium contour is given in Fig. 4.15 as a function of the number of backlogged stations k for $\alpha = 0.03$, $N = 200$, and $p = 0.001$. In the shaded region under the curve $S_{\text{out}, k}$ is greater than S so that the number of backlogged stations tends to decrease in the next time slot. Elsewhere $S_{\text{out}, k} < S$, which means the network capacity is exceeded. Note that for $k = 0$ we have $S_{\text{out}} = 0.164$.

At high-transmission rates there will be many collisions between packets and many stations will become backlogged. Since a substantial portion of the traffic then consists of retransmitted messages, there will be many collisions in the succeeding time slots and the throughput will be small, as shown in Fig. 4.15. By making the retransmission probability α smaller, the shaded area in Fig. 4.15 is increased. Plots of equilibrium contours for various values of α are given in Fig. 4.16. Although this shows that by decreasing α a finite throughput is achieved even when the network is heavily backlogged, the result is very long retransmission intervals. This also can be seen from Eq. (4.22), which shows that small values of α correspond to large values of the number of time slots K required for successful retransmission.

When both the number of stations N and the new packet generation probability p are constant in time, we have what is called a *stationary* input. Let us look at the conditions under which a stationary channel is unstable. For this we use Eq. (4.24) for the system input to define the *channel load line*. With N and p constant Eq. (4.24) defines a straight line in the (k, S) plane. An example is shown in Fig. 4.17 for $N = 200$ and

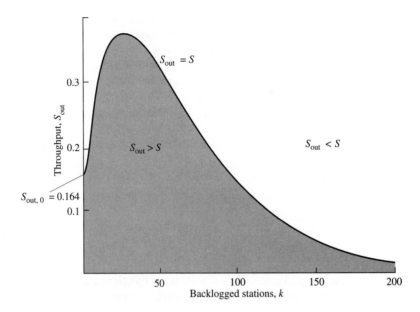

FIGURE 4.15
Equilibrium throughput curve as a function of the number of backlogged stations in slotted ALOHA; at $k = 0$, $S_{out} = 0.164$.

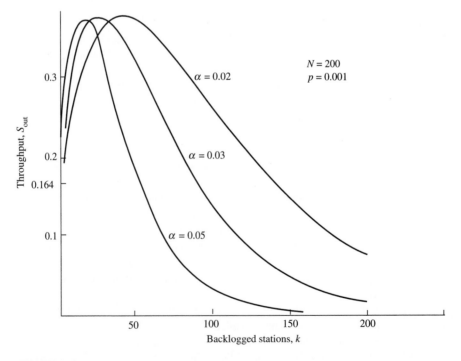

FIGURE 4.16
Equilibrium contours for various values of the retransmission probability α for slotted ALOHA. All curves go to 0.164 at $k = 0$.

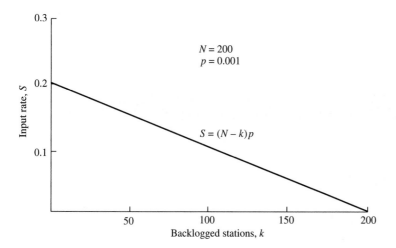

FIGURE 4.17
Example of a channel load line showing the input rate as a function of backlog.

$p = 0.001$. This line has a slope $-p$ and its intercepts on the k and S axes are N and Np, respectively.

The intersection of the load line and the throughput-backlog curve are the points at which the packet input rate S is equal to the packet output rate. These points therefore specify possible operating, or equilibrium, values of throughput. There are three possible equilibrium points. A point is *stable* if operation can remain at or about that point for a finite period of time. Furthermore if it is the only stable equilibrium point, then it is said to be *globally stable*. If more than one stable equilibrium point exists, each is *locally stable*. An equilibrium point is *unstable* if operation immediately drifts away from it.

There are four possible ways in which the load line and equilibrium curve can intersect. In the first case shown in Fig. 4.18 N is small, the system is lightly loaded, and the backlog is low at the equilibrium operating point D. The input traffic in this case is so small that packets rarely collide and only a very small backlog builds up (point k_1). However, let us see what happens if a sudden fluctuation in input traffic moves the operation point from D to A where the backlog is much higher (point k_2). The input is now at point B. Since A is higher than B, the throughput is greater than the input rate. The backlog thus is driven back to point D as indicated by the arrow on the load line. Similarly, as shown in the inset in Fig. 4.18, if the input load momentarily moves outside of the equilibrium region to point C (to the left of D on the load line), the throughput decreases sharply to point F and a backlog builds up again. That is, the system is driven back to the equilibrium point D. Thus point D is a globally stable equilibrium point since it is the only point where the load line crosses the equilibrium curve.

Figure 4.19 shows the case where the number of stations N is increased while keeping α constant. For this example we take $N = 200$, $p = 0.001$, and $\alpha = 0.035$. The load line then moves up so that it now intersects the equilibrium throughput curve in three places. Although each of these points is a possible equilibrium point, only two of them are stable. Point D_1 is a stable point as we saw in the preceding argument. The opposite holds at point D_2. If the backlog at this point increases momentarily from k_2, the throughput drops faster than the input rate, thereby making the backlog even greater.

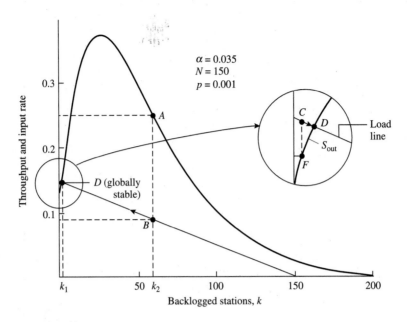

FIGURE 4.18
Example of a globally stable, lightly loaded system.

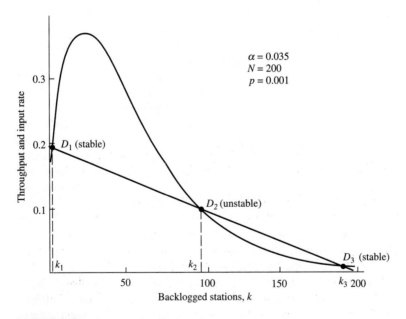

FIGURE 4.19
Bistable system having two locally stable and one unstable equilibrium points.

This trend increases until the high backlog point D_3 is reached. Here the system is again stable since the throughput is greater than the input rate.

This operation thus is bistable with two locally stable equilibrium points. The point D_1 gives a large throughput and a small delay, whereas at point D_3 there is almost zero throughput and very large delay so that almost every station is backlogged. This situation is not desirable in a network since the operation can oscillate between the two locally stable points. If the system is operating at point D_1, then a momentary input excursion in which the backlog becomes greater than k_2 will drive the operation to point D_3. Similarly, equilibrium operation changes from D_3 to D_1 when the backlog momentarily becomes less than k_2.

An even further increase in the number of stations N with α held constant yields the condition shown in Fig. 4.20a. Here the channel is completely overloaded. Even though

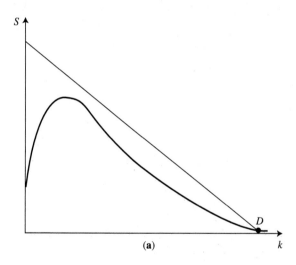

(a)

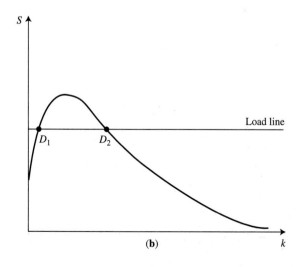

(b)

FIGURE 4.20
Behavior of systems which are
(a) stable but overloaded (N and p
are large); (b) unstable with an
infinite number of users.

the network is globally stable, the only equilibrium point occurs at channel saturation where both the input rate and the throughput are very close to zero.

Figure 4.20b shows what happens when there is an infinite number of users. As $N \to \infty$, the load line becomes horizontal with two possible equilibrium points (a third one exists at $N = \infty$). Again point D_1 is locally stable (as is the point at infinity) but point D_2 is unstable. If this system happens to get into a high backlog state, the input rate will continue to exceed the throughput and the backlog will grow without bound to the equilibrium point at infinity.

Unstable systems such as those shown in Figs. 4.19 and 4.20a can be made stable by decreasing α. By doing so, then analogous to Fig. 4.18 there will be a single stable point where the load line and the equilibrium curve meet.

APPENDIX
4B

THROUGHPUT ANALYSIS FOR CSMA

This appendix presents the analyses of the throughput for nonpersistent CSMA and slotted nonpersistent CSMA. The analyses of the throughput for 1-persistent CSMA, nonpersistent CSMA/CD, and 1-persistent CSMA/CD are quite involved and can be found in the literature.[18,20]

Before we analyze the CSMA protocols, let us state the following assumptions on which these analyses are based:

- A station may not transmit and receive simultaneously.
- The state of the channel can be sensed instantaneously.
- All packets are of constant length t_p.
- The channel is noiseless (i.e., message errors resulting from random noise are negligible compared to errors caused by overlapping packets).
- Any fractional overlap of two packets results in destructive interference so that both must be retransmitted.
- The propagation delay is the same between all source-destination pairs and is small compared to the packet transmission time.
- The generation of packets (both new ones and retransmitted ones) from an infinite source of users follows a Poisson distribution. Each user generates traffic at an infinitesimally small rate so that the average channel traffic sums to G packets per packet time t_p.

4B.1   NONPERSISTENT CSMA

To find the channel throughput S, we let $E[B]$ be the expected duration of the busy period, $E[I]$ the expected length of the idle period, and $E[U]$ the average time during the cycle that the channel is used without collisions. The throughput then is given by

$$S = \frac{E[U]}{E[B] + E[I]} \tag{4.26}$$

This equation is based on the facts that all cycles are statistically similar, assuming steady-state conditions, and that the throughput is the ratio of the average successful packet transmission time for a cycle to the total cycle time.

To find $E[U]$, we note that having a successful transmission during a busy period is the probability that no station transmits during the first a time units of the period, so that from Eq. (4.1) we have

$$E[U] = e^{-aG} \tag{4.27}$$

The idle period is just the time interval between the end of a busy period and the next arrival to the network. Hence looking at the end of a busy period and noting that the packet arrivals follow a Poisson distribution, the average duration of an idle period is given by

$$E[I] = \frac{1}{G} \tag{4.28}$$

Now let us examine the busy periods. The time duration B of a transmission attempt is given by the random length (see Fig. 4.5)

$$B = 1 + a + Y \tag{4.29}$$

where $Y = 0$ for successful transmissions. The average value of B then is

$$E[B] = 1 + E[Y] + a \tag{4.30}$$

since Y is the only random quantity on the right-hand side of Eq. (4.29).

Equation (4.30) states that the last packet which collides with the one sent from station 1 arrives on the average $E[Y]$ time units after the busy period begins, spends one time unit in transmission, and finally clears the channel a time units later. The probability density function of Y is the probability that no packet arrival occurs in an interval of length $(a - y)$. Thus we have

$$f(y) = Ge^{-G(a-y)} \qquad \text{for } 0 \leq y \leq a \tag{4.31}$$

so that

$$E[Y] = \int_0^a yf(y)\,dy$$

$$= a - \frac{1}{G}(1 - e^{-aG}) \tag{4.32}$$

The expected duration of the busy period $E[B]$ then becomes

$$E[B] = 1 + 2a - \frac{1}{G}(1 - e^{-aG}) \tag{4.33}$$

Substituting Eqs. (4.27), (4.28), and (4.33) into Eq. (4.26), we have for nonpersistent CSMA

$$S = \frac{Ge^{-aG}}{G(1 + 2a) + e^{-aG}} \tag{4.34}$$

4B.2   SLOTTED NONPERSISTENT CSMA

The analysis for the slotted nonpersistent CSMA case parallels that of the unslotted case in that we calculate S using Eq. (4.26). First let us find $E[U]$, the average time during a cycle that a transmission is successful. In normalized time units this is given by

$$E[U] = P_s \tag{4.35}$$

where the conditional probability P_s is the fraction of time that a transmission is good. This is given by

$$P_s = P\{\text{one packet arrives in slot } a | \text{some arrival occurs}\}$$

$$= \frac{P\{\text{one packet arrives in slot } a \text{ and some arrival occurs}\}}{P\{\text{some arrival occurs}\}}$$

$$= \frac{P\{\text{one packet arrives in slot } a\}}{P\{\text{some arrival occurs}\}} \tag{4.36}$$

Using Poisson arrival statistics, we then have

$$P\{\text{one packet arrives in slot } a\} = aGe^{-aG} \tag{4.37}$$

and

$$P\{\text{some arrival occurs}\} = 1 - e^{-aG} \tag{4.38}$$

so that Eq. (4.35) becomes

$$E[U] = \frac{aGe^{-aG}}{1 - e^{-aG}} \tag{4.39}$$

Since in normalized time units the busy period is always $1 + a$, its average value is simply

$$E[B] = 1 + a \tag{4.40}$$

Now let us look at the average value of the idle period $E[I]$. First we need to recall the characteristics of the idle period. For slotted nonpersistent CSMA an idle period always consists of an integral number of time slots $I \geq 0$. If a packet arrives during the last time slot of a busy period, then the next slot immediately starts a new busy period so that $I = 0$. When there are no arrivals during the last slot of a busy period, then the next $I - 1$ slots will be empty until there is an arrival in the final Ith slot. This then marks the beginning of a new busy period.

To find $E[I]$, we first consider the case $I = 0$. The probability p of this occurring is merely the probability of some packet arriving in the interval a, which is given by Eq. (4.38); that is,

$$P\{I = 0\} = p = 1 - e^{-aG} \tag{4.41}$$

Next we look at the case $I = 1$. The probability of this is the joint probability that no arrival occurs in the last slot of the busy period and that some arrival occurs in the next time slot. This is given by

$$P\{I = 1\} = (1 - p)p \tag{4.42}$$

Extending this argument to an idle period of length $I = i$, we have the probability that for no arrivals in i consecutive time slots followed by some arrival in the next slot is

$$P\{I = i\} = (1 - p)^i p \tag{4.43}$$

This describes a geometrically distributed random variable V with a mean value of

$$E[V] = \sum_{i=0}^{\infty} i(1 - p)^i p = \frac{1 - p}{p} \tag{4.44}$$

The average length of the idle period then is a times $E[V]$ so that from Eqs. (4.41) and (4.44)

$$E[I] = aE[V] = \frac{ae^{-aG}}{1 - e^{-aG}} \tag{4.45}$$

Substituting Eqs. (4.39), (4.40), and (4.45) into Eq. (4.26) we have for the slotted non-persistent CSMA case

$$S = \frac{aGe^{-aG}}{1 - e^{-aG} + a} \tag{4.46}$$

PROBLEMS

4.1. Using Eqs. (4.7) and (4.8), show that the maximum values of the throughput S are $(1/2e)$ at $G = 0.5$ for pure ALOHA and $1/e$ at $G = 1.0$ for slotted ALOHA.

4.2. (a) If the average number of transmission attempts per packet in an ALOHA system is G/S, what is the average number of unsuccessful attempts per packet?

 (b) If the first transmission attempt requires $(t_p + t_{\text{prop}})$ seconds and each subsequent retransmission requires $(t_p + t_{\text{prop}} + B)$ seconds, show that the average packet transmission time $\langle T_{\text{ALOHA}} \rangle$ in an ALOHA system is

$$\langle T_{\text{ALOHA}} \rangle = t_p + t_{\text{prop}} + (e^{2G} - 1)(t_p + 2t_{\text{prop}} + B)$$

4.3. Suppose an ALOHA system uses a 9600-bps channel for sending 120-bit-long packets.

 (a) What is the maximum possible throughput?

 (b) If the offered load G is 40 percent of the maximum possible throughput and assuming the propagation delay time is negligible, use the expression in Prob. 4.2b to find the average packet transmission time in units of t_p.

4.4. Consider a slotted ALOHA system with a finite number of users M. Assume the M users form two groups so that M_1 of them have a throughput S_1 and $M_2 = M - M_1$ of them have a throughput S_2. Then $S = M_1 S_1 + M_2 S_2$ and $G = M_1 G_1 + M_2 G_2$.

 (a) Using Eq. (4.13) and the condition $G = 1$ for maximum throughput, find expressions for S_1 and S_2 in terms of M_1, M_2, and the offered load G_1.

 (b) For the case $M_1 = 1$ and $M_2 = 1$, show that $S_1 = G_1^2$ and $S_2 = (1 - G_1)^2$. Plot S_1, S_2, and S as a function of G_1 for values of G_1 ranging from 0 to 1.

4.5. Consider a slotted ALOHA system having four stations.

(a) If the offered loads are $G_1 = 0.1$, $G_2 = 0.5$, $G_3 = 0.2$, and $G_4 = 0.2$ packets per second, find the individual throughput rates for each user and the total throughput.

(b) What are the individual throughputs and the total throughput if all stations have the same offered load of 0.25 packets per second?

4.6. Make a graphical comparison of the throughput S as given by Eq. (4.20) for the unslotted nonpersistent CSMA/CD access method for values of $a = 0.1, 0.01, 0.001$, and 0. Choose values of G ranging from 0.1 to 100 and let $b = a$.

4.7. The difference between CSMA/CD and CSMA is that collision detection reduces the time that a station must continue transmitting a packet once a collision has occurred. For slotted CSMA this is a full transmission period $t_p = 1$, whereas for slotted CSMA/CD this time is reduced to $(b + a)$. Thus letting $b = 1 - a$ in Eq. (4.21), show that the result reduces to the slotted CSMA case given by Eq. (4.18).

4.8. A wireless LAN uses polling for M workstations to communicate with a central base station. Assume each workstation is 100 m from the base station and the channel operating speed is 2 Mbps. Let the polling messages be 64 bytes long and assume all the message packets have a length of 1250 bytes.

(a) What is the maximum possible packet arrival rate if the stations can transmit an unlimited number of packets per poll?

(b) What is the maximum possible packet arrival rate if the stations can transmit five packets per poll? Assume the stations send a 64-byte message to the base station when they are done transmitting.

REFERENCES

1. (a) A. M. Law and W. D. Kelton, *Simulation Modeling and Analysis,* McGraw-Hill, Burr Ridge, IL, 3rd ed., 2000.
   (b) P. Z. Peebles, *Probability, Random Variables, and Random Signal Principles,* McGraw-Hill, Burr Ridge, IL, 4th ed., 2001.
2. G. N. Higginbottom, *Performance Evaluation of Communication Networks,* Artech House, Boston, 1998.
3. (a) Z. Sahinoglu and S. Tekinay, "On multimedia networks: Self-similar traffic and network performance," *IEEE Commun. Mag.,* vol. 37, pp. 48–52, Jan. 1999.
   (b) W. Leland, M. Taqqu, W. Willinger, and D. Wilson, "On the self-similar nature of Ethernet traffic," *IEEE/ACM Trans. Networking,* vol. 2, pp. 1–15, Feb. 1994.
4. N. Abramson, "The ALOHA system—Another alternative for computer communications," *AFIPS Conf. Proc., Fall Joint Computer Conf.,* vol. 37, pp. 281–285, 1970.
5. N. Abramson, "Development of the ALOHANET," *IEEE Trans. Information Theory,* vol. IT-31, pp. 119–123, Mar. 1985.
6. L. G. Roberts, "ALOHA packet system with and without slots and capture," *ACM SIGCOM Computer Commun. Rev.,* vol. 5, pp. 28–42, Apr. 1975.
7. Y. C. Jenq, "Optimal retransmission control of slotted ALOHA systems," *IEEE Trans. Commun.,* vol. COM-29, pp. 891–895, June 1981.
8. L. Kleinrock and F. A. Tobagi, "Packet switching in radio channels: Part 1—Carrier sense multiple-access modes and their throughput-delay characteristics," *IEEE Trans. Commun.,* vol. COM-23, pp. 1400–1416, Dec. 1975.
9. IEEE 802.3 Standard, "CSMA/CD access method and physical layer specification," 2000.
10. G. Held, *Ethernet Networks,* Wiley, New York, 3rd ed., 1998.
11. P. Izzo, *Gigabit Networks,* Wiley, New York, 2000.
12. H. Kobayashi, Y. Onozato, and D. Huynh, "An approximate method for design and analysis of an ALOHA system," *IEEE Trans. Commun.,* vol. COM-25, pp. 148–157, Jan. 1977.

13. D. Raychandhuri, "ALOHA with multipacket messages and ARQ-type retransmission protocols—throughput analysis," *IEEE Trans. Commun.,* vol. COM-32, pp. 148–154, Feb. 1984.

14. V. C. M. Leung and R. W. Donaldson, "Effects of channel errors on the delay-throughput performance and capacity of ALOHA multiple access systems," *IEEE Trans. Commun.,* vol. COM-34, pp. 497–502, May 1986.

15. F. A. Tobagi and L. Kleinrock, "Packet switching in radio channels: Part II—The hidden terminal problem in carrier sense multiple access and the busy-tone solution," *IEEE Trans. Commun.,* vol. COM-23, pp. 1417–1433, Dec. 1975.

16. H. Takagi and L. Kleinrock, "Throughput analysis for persistent CSMA systems," *IEEE Trans. Commun.,* vol. COM-33, pp. 627–638, July 1985.

17. H. Takagi and L. Kleinrock, "Correction to 'Throughput analysis for persistent CSMA system'," *IEEE Trans. Commun.,* vol. COM-35, pp. 243–245, Feb. 1987.

18. K. Sohraby, M. L. Molle, and A. N. Venetsanopoulos, "Comments on 'Throughput analysis for persistent CSMA systems'," *IEEE Trans. Commun.,* vol. COM-35, pp. 240–243, Feb. 1987.

19. F. A. Tobagi and V. Hunt, "Performance analysis of carrier sense multiple access with collision detection," *Computer Networks,* vol. 4, pp. 245–259, Oct.–Nov. 1980.

20. G. Keiser, *Local Area Networks,* McGraw-Hill, New York, 1st ed., 1989.

21. D. Bertsekas and R. Gallager, *Data Networks,* Prentice-Hall, Upper Saddle River, NJ, 2nd ed., 1992.

22. A. Leon-Garcia and I. Widjaja, *Communication Networks,* McGraw-Hill, Burr Ridge, IL, 2000.

23. J. T. Carlo, R. D. Love, M. S. Siegel, and K. T. Wilson, *Understanding Token Ring Protocols and Standards,* Artech House, Boston, 1998.

24. J. J. Roese, *Switched LANs,* McGraw-Hill, New York, 1998.

25. L. R. Rossi, L. D. Rossi, and T. Rossi, *Cisco Catalyst LAN Switching,* McGraw-Hill, New York, 2000.

26. IEEE-802.1D Standard, *Information Technology—Local and Metropolitan Area Networks—Common Specifications—Media Access Control (MAC) Bridges,* 1998.

CHAPTER
5

ETHERNET

In the early 1970s a group of researchers at the Xerox Palo Alto Research Center (PARC) conceptualized the Ethernet local area network (LAN).[1,2] After further development in 1980 a consortium consisting of Digital Equipment Corporation, Intel Corporation, and Xerox Corporation (DIX) formulated the original Ethernet specification.[3] This "DIX" Ethernet Standard, which was for a 10-Mbps bus-based LAN using a coaxial cable, then was submitted to the IEEE. In 1982 the IEEE-802.3 document for *carrier sense multiple access with collision detection* (CSMA/CD) became the first IEEE standard for LANs. The basic intent of the IEEE-802.3 Standard is for use in commercial and light industrial environments. Today when talking about Ethernet, one typically refers to the IEEE-802.3 Standard since the vast majority of current Ethernet products adhere to the specifications in that standard. Thus now the terms *Ethernet* and *IEEE 802.3* are considered to be synonymous. Note, though, that the DIX and the current Ethernet standards differ slightly in some signaling and data-formatting methods (see Sec. 5.2.1).

This standard evolved significantly over the following years with the addition of a series of clauses or modifications that accommodate different media types and new operational concepts. These media included thick and thin coaxial cable, twisted-pair wires, single-mode and multimode optical fibers, and wireless infrared and radio links.

This chapter first gives an overview in Sec. 5.1 of the general characteristics that are common to all variations of Ethernet. Section 5.2 then describes the basic 10-Mbps Ethernet operating alternatives and how they are currently implemented. The next higher level of Ethernet operates at 100 Mbps and is called *Fast Ethernet* or 100BASE-T. The standard for this was approved in 1995 and is the topic of Sec. 5.3. To create larger networks with increased capacity, implementers turned to switched Ethernet systems. Section 5.4 discusses this briefly, with more details given in Chap. 10. Even greater speeds are achieved with *Gigabit Ethernet* and *10-Gigabit Ethernet,* which are discussed in Secs. 5.5 and 5.6, respectively.

141

5.1   OVERVIEW OF ETHERNET

5.1.1   Nomenclature

The result of the IEEE-802.3 Standards Committee was the family of specifications listed in Fig. 5.1 that encompasses a variety of speeds and media.[4] The nomenclature for the standards consists of three parts. The first part is either 10, 100, or 1000, which indicates the speed (in Mbps) at which the signal travels through the medium.

In the second part the word *BASE* refers to the baseband transmission mode. A baseband LAN uses digital signals, which are inserted directly on the network transmission medium. The frequency spectrum of the transmitted signal extends from zero hertz (0 Hz) to some upper limit that is dictated by the bandwidth requirements of the signal. The word *BROAD* specifies broadband signaling, which utilizes an analog carrier wave to transmit a digital information stream over one of the frequency bands of the cable. Since cable-based Ethernet LANs almost exclusively use baseband digital technology, the 10BROAD36 Standard is the only broadband Ethernet specification. This defines a broadband coaxial cable tree topology that can transport a 10-Mbps signal on a carrier wave over a 3600-m maximum end-to-end span. However, this architecture is outdated and rarely used.

The last part of the LAN designator is a number or a letter. In early LAN standards the number referred to the distance that a signal could be transmitted without significant attenuation. Thus 10BASE5 means the 10-Mbps baseband signal could travel 500 m

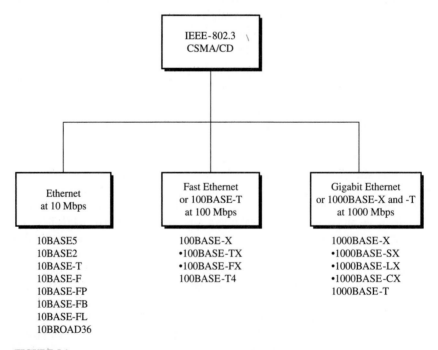

FIGURE 5.1
The IEEE-802.3 family of specifications.

over the LAN transmission medium. In later 802.3 standards the last part is a letter, which is a physical layer designation rather than a distance indicator. Table 5.1 gives the meanings of the various letters used. For example, 10BASE-F specifies a 10-Mbps baseband Ethernet LAN that uses optical fibers.

As the IEEE-802.3 Standard evolved, its scope expanded to include new technology developments and implementation concepts. As Table 5.2 shows, these include higher transmission speeds, the concept of virtual LANs (see Chap. 10), updated physical layer specifications, and repeater management.

The IEEE-802.3ae Standard for the 10-Gbps Ethernet operation uses the IEEE-802.3 Ethernet media access control (MAC) protocol, the IEEE-802.3 Ethernet frame format, and the minimum and maximum IEEE-802.3 frame sizes. However, it provides only full-duplex operation and does not support shared media implementations. This standard is discussed in Sec. 5.6.

TABLE 5.1
Definitions of the symbols used for identifying IEEE-802.3 standards

Symbol	Definition
T	Unshielded twisted pair
F	Optical fiber
FP	Optical fiber passive star
FS	Optical fiber backbone
FL	Optical fiber link
X	Two physical links between nodes
TX	Two pairs of STP or Cat-5 UTP
FX	Two optical fibers
T4	Four pairs of Cat-3 UTP
SX	Short-wavelength duplex optical fiber link
LX	Long-wavelength duplex optical fiber link
CX	One pair of short-UTP wire

TABLE 5.2
Selected addenda and extensions to the basic IEEE-802.3 Standard

IEEE Standard	Year issued	Description
802.3	2000	Latest consolidated standard
802.3u	1995	Suite of clauses relative to 100BASE-TX and 100BASE-FX
802.3x and y	1997	Defines full-duplex and flow operation
802.3ac	1998	Defines extensions for virtual LAN (VLAN) tagging
802.3z	1998	Defines gigabit operation for 1000BASE-SX/LX/CX and repeaters
802.3ab	1999	Physical layer specification for gigabit operation
802.3ad	2000	Multiple link segments
802.3ae	2002	10-Gigabit Ethernet

5.1.2 Basic Ethernet Concepts

All devices on an Ethernet network time-share the common communication medium, and all stations have equal-priority access to this medium. Multiple stations can receive data at the same time from the medium, but only one station is permitted to transmit at any time. To achieve this, Ethernet is based on the CSMA/CD Protocol described in Chap. 4. With this protocol when a station has a frame to transmit, it first listens to the medium to see if another station is currently using it. If there is no activity on the medium, the station sends its frame. If the medium is busy, the station continues to listen to the channel until it is idle and then transmits its frame immediately after a predetermined period of silence passes. This is the 1-persistent algorithm described in Sec. 4.4.3. The silence period is called the *interframe gap* (IFG), or alternatively in the literature, *interframe space* (IFS) or *interpacket gap* (IPG). This IFG is a 9.6-μs quiet time that delineates each frame and allows clock circuitry within all stations to recover. At a 10-Mbps transmission rate this gap is equivalent to 96 bits.

During transmission a station continues to listen to the medium to see if another station sent out a message within the signal propagation delay time in the medium. This is called a *carrier sense* process for the purpose of *collision detection.* If another station starts transmitting, then the two messages will overlap. This results in a *collision* between the messages and both become garbled. When the station detects a collision, it sends out a jamming signal to notify all other stations that a collision has occurred and then ceases transmission. The station then waits a random amount of time according to a prescribed randomization algorithm before again attempting to send a message (see Sec. 4.5). An important point to note is that in an Ethernet system the frames are sufficiently long so that collisions are detected before the end of the frame transmission. Transmission of the frame is stopped immediately at that point so that the efficiency of CSMA/CD is higher than the case without collision detection, where the entire frame always is transmitted. If no collisions occur within two end-to-end transfer delay times, then the station knows it has control over the channel since the transmission from the station will have reached all the other stations and thus they will refrain from transmitting until the first station is done.

5.1.3 Logical Link Control (LLC)

As noted in Sec. 2.4.2 and shown in Fig. 5.2, the *logical link control* (LLC) layer is the upper portion of the IEEE-802 data link layer and is common to all LAN protocols. This layer resides above the medium access control (MAC) layer. Its primary function is to provide addressing and control mechanisms to enable data exchange between end users across a MAC-controlled link or across a series of LANs joined by MAC-level bridges (see Chap. 10). The LLC Protocol is based on the *High-Level Data Link Control* (HDLC) Protocol. This is a general purpose ITU-T protocol that operates at the data link layer of the OSI (Open System Interconnection) reference model.[5] The LLC in the IEEE-802.3 Standard uses an unacknowledged, connectionless service and depends on a *best-effort mode of frame delivery.* This means that unless a frame was involved in a collision, there is no procedure for retransmission if it gets lost or becomes corrupted. For this case Ethernet depends on the upper-layer protocols to detect and schedule redelivery.

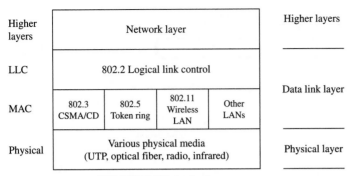

FIGURE 5.2

The IEEE-802 LAN model.

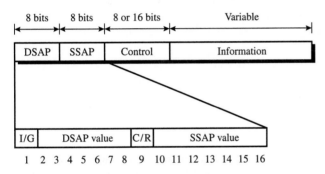

I/G: 0 = individual DSAP; 1 = group DSAP
C/R: 0 = command; 1 = response

FIGURE 5.3

Fields in the LLC (logical link control)-level protocol data unit (PDU).

The data unit in the LLC level is called a *protocol data unit* (PDU). The PDU contains the following four fields shown in Fig. 5.3: a 1-byte *destination service access point* (DSAP), a 1-byte *source service access point* (SSAP), an 8- or 16-bit control field, and a variable-length information field. The total length of the PDU can range from 46 to 1500 bytes. The DSAP and SSAP fields contain 7-bit addresses that identify the receiving and sending machines that use the link layer service. The first bit of the DSAP field indicates whether the frame goes to an individual (I) or a group (G) of users. The first bit of the SSAP field shows whether the frame is a command (C) or a response (R) PDU.

The control field identifies whether the PDU is an information frame (I-frame), a supervisory frame (S-frame), or an unnumbered frame (U-frame). Figure 5.4 shows the formats of these frames. Each type of frame serves as an envelope for the transmission of a different message type. If the first bit of the control field is a 0, then the frame is

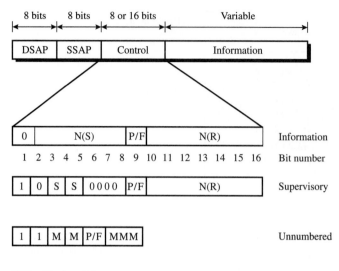

N(S) = Number of frames sent
N(R) = Number of frames received
S = Supervisory bit
M = Modifier bit
P/F = Poll/final bit

FIGURE 5.4
Formats of the LLC protocol data unit (PDU).

an I-frame. *I-frames* transport user data and related control information. Depending on the control field length an I-frame contains either 3-bit or 7-bit flow and error control sequences called $N(S)$ and $N(R)$. The $N(S)$ specifies the number of frames sent, and $N(R)$ acknowledges the number of frames expected in a two-way exchange.

If the first bit of the control field is a 1 and the second bit is a 0, then the frame is an S-frame. *S-frames* only transport control information, such as data link layer flow and error controls. Since they do not transmit data, they do not require an $N(S)$ field to identify them. The S bits are coded flow and error control information.

If both the first and second bits of the control field are set to 1, then the frame is a U-frame. *U-frames* are reserved for system management. Since they are not designed for user data exchange or acknowledgment, they have neither $N(S)$ nor $N(R)$ fields. The 2-bit and the 3-bit modifier (M) code fields identify the type of U-frame and its function. For example, the U-frame can establish the mode of exchange between users.

The control field of all three types of frames contains a *poll/final bit* (P/F). This bit has meaning only when it is set to 1 and can indicate poll or final. It means *poll* when a primary station sends the frame to a secondary station, that is, when the address field contains the address of the receiver. It means *final* when a secondary station sends the frame to a primary station, that is, when the address field contains the address of the sender.

Note that the PDU has no flag fields, no cyclic redundancy check (CRC), and no station addresses. These get added in the MAC layer.

5.2 STANDARD ETHERNET

5.2.1 Functional Overview

The original IEEE-802.3 Standard for a 10-Mbps LAN was defined for a bus topology, a coaxial cable transmission medium, and broadcast transmissions using CSMA/CD for the MAC Protocol. The basic Ethernet LAN operates at 10 Mbps over a maximum distance of 2500 m. The key parameter for evaluating the performance of the CSMA/CD scheme is the *round-trip delay time* since it forms the basis for the *contention resolution time,* or *contention slot,* that is required for a station to seize control of the channel. Chapter 4 presents a rigorous performance analysis of a CSMA/CD network under the assumption that messages arrive with a Poisson distribution. This distribution is used widely for ease of mathematical analysis but may not reflect the real traffic pattern in actual systems. This section gives a simplified version for the performance of an 802.3 network under a heavy and constant traffic load.

Given that k stations are always ready to send out a message, the analysis assumes a constant retransmission probability in each contention slot. First let t_{prop} be the end-to-end propagation delay so that the maximum round-trip time delay is $2t_{\text{prop}}$. Thus, $2t_{\text{prop}}$ is the duration of a contention slot. If each station transmits during a contention slot with probability p, then the probability P_A that a station acquires the channel in that time slot is

$$P_A = kp(1-p)^{k-1} \tag{5.1}$$

This parameter is a maximum when $p = 1/k$. As the number of stations gets large, that is, in the limit $k \to \infty$, then $P_A \to 1/e$. The probability that there are j contention slots in the time interval over which contention takes place is

$$P_j = P_A(1 - P_A)^{j-1} \tag{5.2}$$

Thus the mean number of slots per contention interval is

$$N = \sum_{j=1}^{\infty} jP_j = \sum_{j=1}^{\infty} jP_A(1 - P_A)^{j-1} = \frac{1}{P_A} \tag{5.3}$$

Since a contention slot has a duration $2t_{\text{prop}}$, the mean contention interval is $2t_{\text{prop}}/P_A$. For the optimum value of p (maximum value of P_A), the mean number of contention slots is $N = e$. Therefore the contention interval is at most $2t_{\text{prop}}e \approx 5.4t_{\text{prop}}$.

The maximum *throughput,* or *channel efficiency,* occurs when all the channel times are used up in packet transmissions followed by contention intervals. Let t_p be the mean packet transmission time. The total channel time then consists of the packet transmission time, a period t_{prop} during which stations learn that a packet transmission is completed, and a contention interval of duration $2et_{\text{prop}}$. The throughput S then is

$$S = \frac{t}{t_p + t_{\text{prop}} + 2et_{\text{prop}}} = \frac{1}{1 + (1 + 2e)a} \tag{5.4}$$

where from Eq. (4.15), the parameter a is defined by

$$a = \frac{\text{link length in bits}}{\text{packet length in bits}} = \frac{\text{propagation delay}}{\text{packet transmit time}} = \frac{t_{\text{prop}}}{t_p} \tag{5.5}$$

Note that $t_p = L_p/R$, where L_p is the packet length and R is the network transmission rate. Since t_{prop} depends on the maximum cable length between two stations, the contention interval increases for longer cable lengths so that from Eq. (5.4) the throughput or channel efficiency decreases.

EXAMPLE 5.1

If the parameter a is small, say, $a = 0.01$, then the maximum throughput is 94 percent. When a is larger for longer cable distances, for example, $a = 0.2$, then the maximum throughput $S = 44\%$.

EXAMPLE 5.2

Consider a 10-Mbps Ethernet LAN that has stations attached to a 2.5-km-long coaxial cable. Given that the transmission speed is 2.3×10^8 m/s in a coaxial cable, then the one-way propagation delay is

$$t_{prop} = \frac{2500 \text{ m}}{2.3 \times 10^8 \text{ m/s}} = 10.9 \ \mu s$$

If the packet size is 128 bytes, then the transmission time t_p of a packet is

$$t_p = \frac{128 \text{ bytes} \times 8 \text{ bits/byte}}{10 \times 10^6 \text{ bps}} = 102.4 \ \mu s$$

Using these two numbers, we have $a = t_{prop}/t_p = 0.11$. From Eq. (5.4) the throughput is

$$S = \frac{1}{1 + 6.44a} = 59\%$$

Thus the effective transmission rate is only 59 percent of 10 Mbps when many stations heavily load the network. If 30 bytes of a 128-byte packet are allocated to overhead, then only 77 percent of the packet consists of user data bits. The maximum rate at which the network can send data then is

$$(5.9 \text{ Mbps}) \times 77\% = 4.5 \text{ Mbps}$$

As noted earlier, this rate depends on the network span.

By restricting the cable length to be less than 2.5 km and by having at most four repeaters between any two transceivers, the round-trip delay time is less than 51.2 μs. At 10 Mbps this propagation delay equals 512 bits or 64 bytes. Therefore this is the minimum Ethernet frame length.

Figure 5.5 shows the layering relationship of the 10-Mbps Ethernet specification to the OSI model.[5-8] This illustrates the actual implementation within an Ethernet station, which the IEEE-802.3 Standard refers to as *data terminal equipment* (DTE). The data link layer encompasses the LLC and the MAC functions. The *physical signaling* (PLS) sublayer and the *attachment unit interface* (AUI) subsystems support the signaling scheme between the MAC layer and the *medium attachment unit* (MAU). The PLS carries out media access management by monitoring the state of the attached medium. The AUI can be either an external cable that connects the PLS function to the MAU or it can be embedded in an integrated circuit together with the MAC and PLS functions.

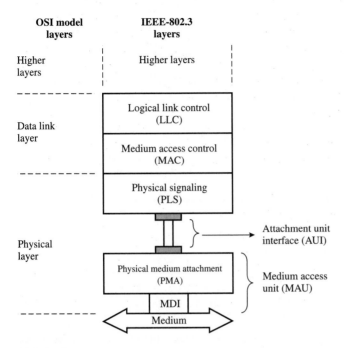

FIGURE 5.5
Layering relationship of the 10-Mbps Ethernet specfication to the OSI (Open System Interconnection) model.

In the latter case this integrated circuit is placed on a *network interface card* (NIC), which now is normally the case. The MAU consists of two sublayers and is responsible for the physical and electrical or optical interface between the station and the transmission medium. The first sublayer of the MAU is the *physical medium attachment* (PMA), which also is known as a *transceiver.* The PMA defines the electrical or optical signaling, line states, clocking guidelines, data encoding, and circuitry needed for data transmission and reception. The other part of the MAU is the *medium-dependent interface* (MDI), which is a connector that couples the transceiver to the physical transmission medium.

5.2.2 MAC Frame

The MAC layer is responsible for formatting frames it receives from the LLC layer and for resolving contentions for the transmission medium. It contains the synchronization, flag, flow, and error control information required for moving data from one user to another. In addition, it contains the physical address of the next station that will receive and route a packet. The frame formats for the IEEE-802.3 and the DIX Ethernet standards differ slightly in the fifth field, as Fig. 5.6 shows. The functions of the eight fields are as follows:

1. *Preamble.*   The frame begins with a 7-byte preamble that repeats the 8-bit pattern 10101010 seven times. This square-wave pattern alerts the receiving system that a frame is coming in and enables the receiver to synchronize its timing to the beginning of the frame.

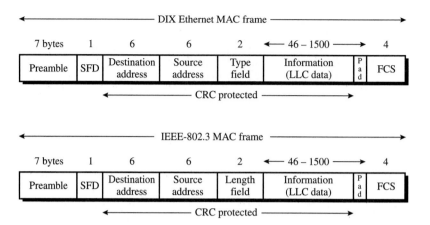

FIGURE 5.6
Frame formats for the IEEE-802.3 and the DIX Ethernet standards.

2. *Start frame delimiter (SFD).* The SFD field consists of the sequence 10101011, where the two consecutive 1s indicate the start of a frame. This enables the receiver to find the first bit of the frame.

3. *Destination address (DA).* This 6-byte field contains the physical address of the next destination for the packet. The first DA bit distinguishes between addresses for a single user and addresses used to multicast a frame to a group of stations. The second bit tells whether this is a local or global address. A physical address is the bit pattern that is encoded on the NIC of the station. Thus for a 6-byte DA field the Ethernet standard allows 2^{46} addresses. Each NIC has a unique address that distinguishes it from another NIC. The first 3 bytes designate the NIC vendor, so this allows up to $2^{24} - 1(16,777,215)$ addresses per vendor.

    If a packet needs to go across one or more LANs in order to reach its destination, the DA field contains the physical address of the router that connects the current LAN to the next LAN. When the packet arrives at the end network, the DA field contains the physical address of the NIC in the destination station. There are three types of physical addresses. A *unicast address* is assigned permanently to a NIC. A NIC normally compares transmissions to this address in order to identify frames destined for its attached station. A *multicast address* identifies a group of stations that are to receive a given frame. A host computer is responsible for setting its NIC to accept specific multicast addresses. A *broadcast address* contains all 1s, which indicates that all stations should receive the packet containing that destination address.

4. *Source address (SA).* The 6-byte SA field contains the physical address of the last device that forwarded the packet. This could be the original sending station or the most recent router that received and forwarded the packet.

5. *Length/type of PDU.* In the IEEE-802.3 Standard this 2-byte field indicates the number of bytes in the PDU (the LLC data field). In the earlier DIX Ethernet specification this field indicates the function of the PDU that is sent. The longest allowable frame is 1526 bytes.

6. *LLC Data.* This field contains the entire 802.2 PDU supplied by the LLC as a modular, removable unit. This field can be anywhere from 46 to 1500 bytes long depending on the type of frame and the length of the information field.

7. *Pad.* The pad field contains bytes that are added to ensure that the frame size is always at least 64 bytes long, which is the length required for proper collision detection operation.

8. *Frame check sequence (FCS).* This field contains the error detection information for the frame. For Ethernet it is based on a 32-bit cyclic redundancy check (CRC) that uses all fields except the preamble, the SFD, and the FCS itself (see Sec. 3.3.3). When a frame arrives, the NIC sees if the frame has the correct length and then checks the received CRC for errors. If the NIC detects errors, the frame is discarded and therefore it is not passed to the network layer.

5.2.3 Media Options for Basic Ethernet

Table 5.3 lists some characteristics of different copper wire-based versions of 10-Mbps Ethernet. The 10BASE5 specification is the original version of IEEE 802.3. This standard defines the use of a special purpose, 10-mm thick, 50-Ω (ohm) coaxial cable operating at 10 Mbps. Stations use a MAU to connect to the cable. The signaling is the Manchester encoding method and the maximum segment length is 500 m. A repeater can be used to extend the length of the network. Basically a repeater consists of two MAUs that are joined together and attached to two different segments of cable. The standard allows a maximum of four repeaters in the path between any two stations, thereby extending the length of the medium to 2500 m. A major drawback of 10BASE5 is that the thick coaxial cable is awkward to handle and install. The example of a 10BASE5 Ethernet LAN given in Fig. 5.7 implies the rigidity of the cable segment.

The 10BASE2 specification provides a lower-cost system for implementing personal-computer-based LANs. Similar to 10BASE5, this network uses 50-Ω coaxial cable and Manchester signaling at 10 Mbps. The difference is in the transmission medium, which is a thin (5-mm) coaxial cable. This flexible cable is less expensive and easier to handle. Stations use a simple T-shaped connector to attach to the cable, as shown in Fig. 5.8. Thus no electronics are needed across a drop cable between the station and the bus cable. However, the thinner cable supports fewer taps over a shorter distance than 10BASE5. The maximum segment length for 10BASE2 is 185 m. Since they both run at 10 Mbps and have the same signaling format, 10BASE5 and 10BASE2 segments can be combined in the same network by using a repeater. This device conforms to 10BASE5 on one side and to 10BASE2 on the other side.

TABLE 5.3
Characteristics of copper wire-based 10-Mbps Ethernet options

Characteristic	10BASE5	10BASE2	10BASE-T
Medium	50-Ω coaxial	50-Ω coaxial	UTP
Cable diameter	10 mm	5 mm	0.4 to 0.6 mm
Topology	Bus	Bus	Star
Maximum segment length	500 m	185 m	100 m

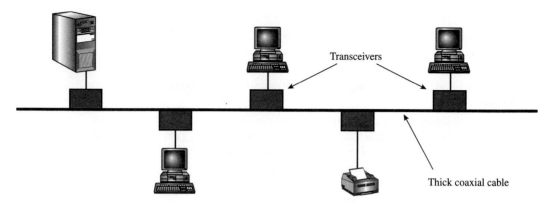

FIGURE 5.7
A 10BASE5 Ethernet LAN showing the rigidity of the thick coaxial cable.

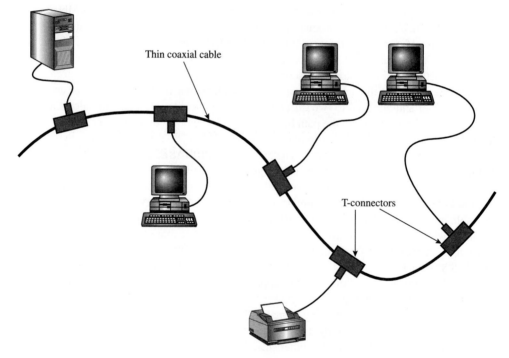

FIGURE 5.8
A 10BASE2 Ethernet LAN showing the flexibility of the thin coaxial cable.

In the simplest configuration a 10BASE-T network is wired in a star topology, as shown in Fig. 5.9. All stations are connected directly to a *central hub* or *concentrator,* which also is referred to as a *multipoint repeater.* The 10BASE-T network uses two unshielded twisted pairs of copper wires, such as Cat-3. The advantage of using Cat-3 UTP wire is that it is widely available in office buildings as excess telephone cable. Existing wiring layouts allow the hubs to be placed in telephone wiring closets.

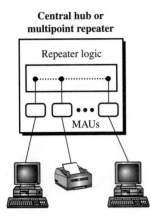

Central hub or multipoint repeater

Repeater logic

MAUs

FIGURE 5.9
In the simplest configuration a 10BASE-T network is wired in a star topology.

However, because the transmission quality of the line is poor at the relatively high data rate of 10 Mbps, the link length is limited to 100 m.

With a star topology the repeater is responsible for detecting collisions. The central concentrator monitors all transmissions from the stations. When there is only one station transmitting, the concentrator accepts a signal on any one incoming line and repeats it on all other lines (but not back to the originating port). In this sense the concentrator (repeater) acts just like a logical bus coaxial cable since any node connected to the network will see the transmission from another node. If there is a collision, the concentrator sends a jamming signal to all the stations, which then implement the backoff algorithm. Note that the function of sending a jamming signal is now concentrated at the central hub. Again, since 10BASE-T, 10BASE5, and 10BASE2 all run at 10 Mbps and have the same signaling format, different segments can be combined in the same network by using a repeater. For 10BASE-T the connection to a repeater is a link that appears the same to the hub as an ordinary station link.

Figure 5.10 shows two individual basic Ethernet networks connected by a bridge. The term *collision domain* defines a single CSMA/CD network. Within such a network a collision will occur if two stations transmit simultaneously. Stations that are attached to a simple multipoint repeater belong to the same collision domain, whereas stations that are separated by a bridge belong to different collision domains. Since the bridge acts as a store-and-forward device, it participates independently in the collision-detecting algorithms of the two collision domains it interconnects.

The IEEE developed the 10BASE-FL, 10BASE-FB, and 10BASE-FP Standards to take advantages of the increased distance and higher-performance transmission characteristics available with optical fibers. Each of these specifications uses a pair of multimode optical fibers, with one fiber dedicated for transmission in each direction between a station and the concentrator. The wavelength used on these $62.5\text{-}\mu$m core-diameter fibers is 850 nm. The 10BASE-FL Standard defines point-to-point fiber optical links up to 2 km long for connecting stations or repeaters. We note here that 10BASE-FL replaces the older fiber optical inter-repeater link (FOIRL) specification. The 10BASE-FB Standard was designed to provide a more optimized point-to-point interface for links between repeaters. Again the maximum distance between repeaters is 2 km. The 10BASE-FB links allow up to 15 cascaded repeaters to achieve greater length. The 10BASE-FP

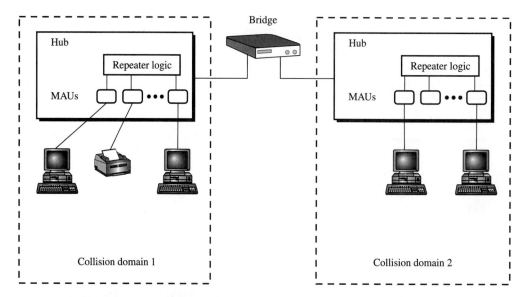

FIGURE 5.10
Two basic Ethernet networks connected by a bridge.

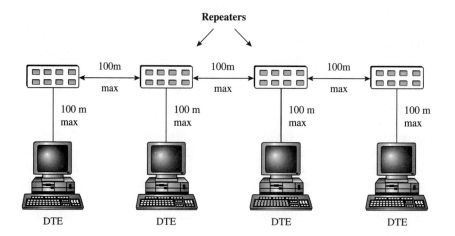

FIGURE 5.11
Timing constraints for collision detection limit the maximum interstation transmission path to five cable segments.

specification defines a passive star topology to interconnect a maximum of 33 stations and repeaters located up to 500 m from the concentrator.

As a result of timing constraints for the collision detection process, the maximum transmission path between any two stations can consist of up to five cable segments, as shown in Fig. 5.11. Thus there can be four repeater sets with three cable segments

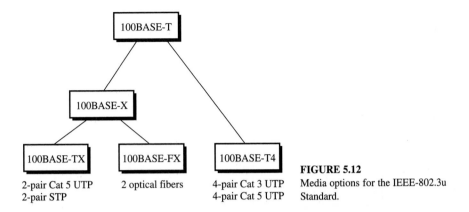

FIGURE 5.12
Media options for the IEEE-802.3u
Standard.

interconnecting them and two cable segments connecting the DTEs to the end hubs. For a four-hub topology that only uses UTP wires, all segments must not exceed 100 m in length. The repeaters typically are multiport devices, for example, an 8-port configuration. When fiber optical cable replaces some of the UTP wiring in the four-hub configuration, the propagation constraint for the collision detection process determines their maximum lengths.

5.3 FAST ETHERNET

Fast Ethernet or 100BASE-T was developed in the early 1990s to support the rapidly growing application of desktop computing in the business world. By retaining the fundamental structure of the Ethernet MAC Protocol in the Fast Ethernet Standard, the standard developers were able to benefit from the large body of existing Ethernet expertise, and implementers were able to exploit the extensive installed Ethernet base. The result was the IEEE-802.3u Standard,[9] which has the media options shown in Fig. 5.12. Fast Ethernet is similar to the 10BASE-T Ethernet with respect to employing a hub-based architecture and the use of the CSMA/CD access protocol. Besides the operating rate, the main differences concern the type of network cabling, the data encoding method, and the network spans. This section addresses these issues.

5.3.1 Fast Ethernet Architecture

Figure 5.13 shows the modifications that IEEE 802.3u makes to the physical layer of the basic IEEE-802.3 Standard.[10,11] The *medium-independent interface* (MII) separates the MAC layer from the physical layer (PHY) devices. Its function is essentially the same as the AUI for 10BASE-T, which is to decouple the MAC from the specific medium-independent characteristics of the underlying PHY. As such, it permits the MAC to operate unchanged with a variety of physical media, which generally require different physical signaling functions. One significant difference between the MII and the AUI is that the MII transfers data in blocks of 4 bits, which is known as a *nibble,* to and from the MAC in contrast to the 1-bit rate that the AUI supports. This allows the MII to operate with a 25-MHz clock for the 100-Mbps Fast Ethernet rate, instead of the 100-MHz clock

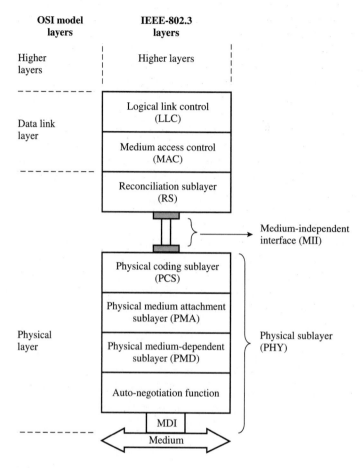

FIGURE 5.13
Modifications that IEEE 802.3u makes to the physical layer of the IEEE-802.3 Standard.

that would be needed for a 1-bit path. Another difference between the MII and the AUI is that the AUI can be up to 50 m in length, whereas the MII is restricted to a length of 0.5 m.

The MII can accommodate two specific data rates of 10 and 100 Mbps, thereby permitting the support of 10BASE-T nodes at Fast Ethernet hubs. To reconcile the MII signal with the MAC signal, the *reconciliation sublayer* (RS) is used. That is, it provides the mapping between the 1-bit data stream at the MAC interface and the nibblewide transmit and receives interfaces at the MII.

The physical layer has five different sublayers. The *physical coding sublayer* (PCS) is responsible for the data encoding, transmit, receive, and carrier sense functions. Since the data encoding is different for 100BASE-FX, 100BASE-TX, and 100BASE-T4 (see Sec. 5.3.3), a distinct PCS is needed for each version of Fast Ethernet. The *physical medium attachment* (PMA) sublayer provides a serialization service interface between the PCS and the underlying *physical medium-dependent* (PMD) sublayer. This service converts the parallel bit stream from the PCS into a serial bit stream, which is needed by the PMD to send information over the physical medium. In the reverse direction the PMA accepts a serial bit stream from the PMD and converts it into a specific parallel format, depending on the type of PCS used. In addition, the PMA sublayer extracts symbol-timing clock information from the received serial bit stream so that the receiver can frame the incoming data correctly.

The PMD sublayer translates the electrical serial bit stream coming from the PMA into a format that is suitable for transmission on the specific physical medium. Similar to 10BASE-T, the MDI (medium-dependent interface) is a connector that couples the transceiver to the physical transmission medium.

The purpose of the *auto-negotiation function* is to allow interoperability between 10BASE-T and 100BASE-TX subnetworks. It is defined only for a 100BASE-TX PHY. When a connection is established between network devices, the auto-negotiation mechanism senses the modes of operation that each device supports and automatically configures the link for the highest-performance mode of operation possible with these devices.

An operating characteristic of the CSMA/CD Protocol is that it is sensitive to the ratio of the round-trip propagation delay to the frame transmission time. To have good performance, this ratio must be small. Furthermore correct operation of the protocol requires the transmission time of the minimum-sized frame to be larger than the round-trip propagation delay. Otherwise an entire frame could be sent out before the station becomes aware of a collision. When the transmission speed goes from 10 to 100 Mbps, the frame transmission time is reduced by a factor of 10. This requires that either the minimum frame size must increase from 64 to 640 bytes or the maximum cable length between stations must be reduced by a factor of 10, for example, to a 200-m maximum length. The IEEE-802.3u Standard addresses these issues by maintaining the same frame size as that used in 10BASE-T, and by defining a reduced-sized hub-based topology that uses UTP and optical fiber cable.

We can make a simple estimate of the maximum theoretical throughput of Fast Ethernet by considering the efficiency of a single station in the absence of collision overhead. The throughput of an actual network consisting of a number of stations will be less than this. By letting L_p be the packet length (in bits), I be the interframe gap (which is 96 bits), and L_{preamble} be the length of the packet preamble (which is 64 bits), we can express the normalized throughput as

$$S = \frac{L_p}{L_p + I + L_{\text{preamble}}} \tag{5.6}$$

The worst-case throughput occurs for the minimum packet length of 512 bits (64 bytes), in which case $S = 76\%$.

5.3.2 Physical Media for 100BASE-T

As shown earlier in Fig. 5.12, there are four physical medium alternatives for Fast Ethernet. There is also a fifth version called 100BASE-T2, which 100BASE-T4 now supersedes.[12] The various 100BASE-X options all use two physical links between devices. One link is used for transmission and the other is used for reception and collision detection. 100BASE-TX uses either two pairs of shielded twisted-pair (STP) wire or two pairs of high-quality Cat-5 UTP cable, the latter being the most widely used in practice. The DTE-to-repeater distances are limited to 100 m. The 100BASE-FX option is similar to 100BASE-TX, except that it uses two multimode optical fibers. With these fibers transmission distances of up to 2 km are possible.

The 100BASE-T4 option was designed to transmit at 100 Mbps over lower-quality Cat-3 cable because a large amount of this type of cable exists in many office buildings for telephone usage. However, the transmission quality of this voice-grade cable is not suitable for sending a 100-Mbps data stream over a single twisted pair in this cable. Therefore the signal is split into three separate data streams, each having an effective data rate of 33 1/3 Mbps. These data streams are then sent over individual physical paths.

Altogether 100BASE-T4 uses four of the twisted-wire pairs in a Cat-5 cable. Six of these eight wires are available for data transmission and reception (three in each direction) and the other two wires are used for collision detection. Figure 5.14 shows the wiring configuration for communication between a node and a central hub. Data is transmitted over the wire pairs labeled D1, D3, and D4, and is received on the pairs labeled D2, D3, and D4. Note that pairs D1 and D2 are unidirectional and are used for transmitting and receiving data and for collision detection. Pairs D3 and D4 are bidirectional and are used for data only.

5.3.3 Data Encoding for Fast Ethernet

When going from 10 to 100 Mbps, an alternative for the Manchester encoding method is needed since this code has high-frequency side effects at increased data rates. The selected alternatives are the 4B5B code with NRZI encoding for 100BASE-FX use over

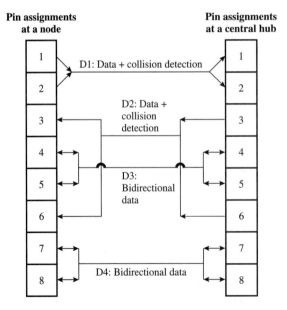

FIGURE 5.14
100BASE-T4 wiring configuration for communication between a node and a hub.

optical fiber links, the MLT-3 scheme for 100BASE-TX use over twisted-pair wires, and the 8B6T code with NRZ encoding for 100BASE-T4 use over twisted-pair wires.

As described in Sec. 3.2.3, the 4B5B code converts 4 binary bits into 5 binary bits in order to provide adequate timing and error-monitoring information. The efficiency of this code thus is 80 percent since to operate at an information rate of 100 Mbps requires a data rate of 125 Mbps. To ensure that the receiver can synchronize on the data stream, the 4B5B code is sent as an NRZI (NRZ, invert on "one") signal. In this code for a binary 1 there is a transition at the beginning of a bit interval, whereas for a binary 0 there is no transition at the beginning of a bit interval. The benefit of NRZI is that, compared to a threshold detection mechanism, it generally allows a more reliable detection of a signal level transition in the presence of noise and distortion. Figure 5.15 gives two examples of the 4B5B encoding and the final NRZI pattern for two sets of 4 information bits. Tables 5.4 and 5.5 give the complete set of data sequences and control symbols, respectively, used in 4B5B encoding.

Although the 4B5B-NRZI scheme works well for optical fiber links, it is not suitable for UTP cables. The problem is that the signal energy is spread over a 125-MHz-spectral band when sending a 100-Mbps information rate on a copper wire using a 4B5B code. If the transmission medium is a UTP wire, then this concentration pattern of the signal energy produces unacceptable spurious electromagnetic emissions from the cable. These emissions induce electromagnetic interference (EMI) and radio-frequency interference (RFI) effects in adjacent cables and neighboring electronic equipment. The alternative is the MLT-3 (*multilevel transmit*) code. First the transmitted code is scrambled to smooth the spectral content of the resulting waveform. Then an MLT-3 code is

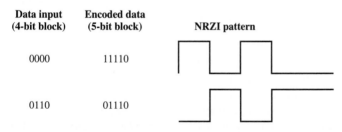

Data input (4-bit block)	Encoded data (5-bit block)	NRZI pattern
0000	11110	
0110	01110	

FIGURE 5.15

Two examples of the 4B5B encoding and the final NRZI pattern for two sets of 4 information bits.

TABLE 5.4

Data sequences used in 4B5B encoding

Data sequence	Encoded sequence	Data sequence	Encoded sequence
0000	11110	1000	10010
0001	01001	1001	10011
0010	10100	1010	10110
0011	10101	1011	10111
0100	01010	1100	11010
0101	01011	1101	11011
0110	01110	1110	11100
0111	01111	1111	11101

TABLE 5.5

Control symbols used in 4B5B encoding

Control symbol	Encoded sequence
Q (quiet)	00000
I (idle)	11111
H (halt)	00100
J (used in start delimiter)	11000
K (used in start delimiter)	10001
T (used in end delimiter)	01101
S (set)	11001
R (reset)	00111

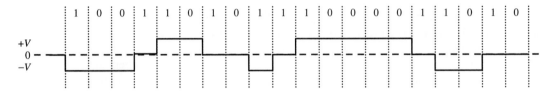

FIGURE 5.16

An example of MLT-3 encoding. A transition occurs each time there is an input of a 1 bit.

applied to the transmitted serial bit stream. The data rate on the line is still 100 Mbps, but the scrambling and coding steps concentrate most of the energy in the transmitted signal to below 30 MHz. This mitigates EMI and RFI effects.

Figure 5.16 gives an example of MLT-3 encoding. The method produces a waveform that has a transition for every binary 1. It uses three voltage levels: a positive voltage $(+V)$, a negative voltage $(-V)$, and a zero level. Since transitions only occur for 1 bits, the output value for a 0 is the same as that of the preceding bit. For a 1 bit if the preceding value was either $+V$ or $-V$, then its value is 0. If the preceding value was 0, then its value is nonzero and its sign is opposite to that of the last nonzero output; that is, the occurrences of $+V$ and $-V$ alternate.

The 8B6T block-coding method was developed specifically to enable 100-Mbps signaling over Cat-3 (or better) four-pair wire cable. This scheme uses three of the four wire pairs for data transmission and the other pair for detecting simultaneous activity from the device on the other end of the link, which would identify a collision condition. Figure 5.17 shows the basic operation of the 8B6T-encoding algorithm. This algorithm uses ternary signaling, which assigns one of three voltage levels $(+V, -V,$ or zero) to each signal bit. When a station transmits, the PHY layer takes two nibbles from the MII to form a byte. That is, the incoming data is handled in 8-bit blocks (or bytes). It then converts this 8-bit block to a 6-bit block. The encoding technique maps the 256 possible 8-bit bytes to a subset of the $3^6 = 729$ available 6T ternary codes. This allows the data code values to be picked such that they contain good clock transition information to simplify receiver clock recovery, to minimize high-energy transitions (from $+1$ to -1 and vice versa) to mitigate EMI and RFI effects, to maintain good DC balance on

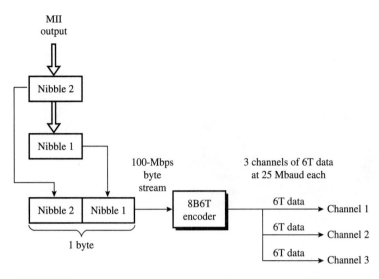

FIGURE 5.17
The basic operation of the 8B6T-encoding algorithm.

the lines, and to offer error detection capabilities. After the incoming bytes are ternary encoded, the stream of ternary code groups is transmitted in a round-robin fashion across the three output channels at a rate of

$$\frac{6 \text{ symbols}}{8 \text{ bits}} \times 33\frac{1}{3} \text{ bits/s} = 25 \text{ Mbaud}$$

5.3.4 Network Spans Using 100BASE-T

Analogous to 10BASE-T, in the simplest configuration a 100BASE-T network is wired in a star topology. All stations are connected directly to a central concentrator or repeater, which is responsible for detecting collisions. There are two types of 100BASE-T repeaters. A *Class I repeater* can support a *mixed-media topology,* which means it has the flexibility of interconnecting 100BASE-TX, FX, and T4 links. However, now the encoding scheme at each port can be different. The process within the repeater of converting from one coding format to another introduces additional delay, which is a critical parameter in Ethernet. This requires the Class I repeater to have additional margin in its time-delay budget. Thus a limitation of a mixed-media network is its restriction to a single Class I repeater in a single CSMA/CD collision domain. Figure 5.18 shows an example of a mixed-media topology using a Class I repeater. If all the DTE transmission links in the network are either type TX or FX, the FX optical fiber link is allowed to be 160 m long. If the repeater has any T4 port, then the FX link is restricted to 130 m. The 100BASE-TX and 100BASE-T4 twisted-pair cables running from the repeater to the DTEs can be up to 100 m long.

Class II repeaters are less flexible since they are optimized for either 100BASE-X or 100BASE-T4 operation, but not for both. One advantage of this is that the delay time a signal encounters in traversing a Class II repeater is less than that in a Class I repeater.

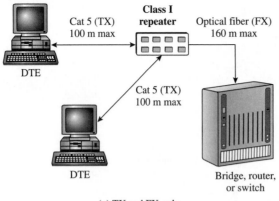

(a) TX and FX only

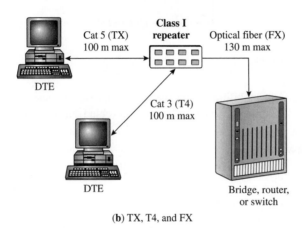

(b) TX, T4, and FX

FIGURE 5.18
Examples of Fast Ethernet mixed-media topologies using a Class I repeater.

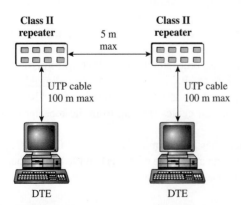

FIGURE 5.19
Two Fast Ethernet Class II repeaters in the same collision domain.

The extra time margin can be allocated to a longer span to another router or bridge, with 100BASE-FX link lengths of up to 200 m being possible. Two Class II repeaters can be in the same collision domain. However, as Fig. 5.19 illustrates, the separation between two Class II repeaters is limited to 5 m, but the UTP cables between a station and the repeater still can be up to 100 m long. Thus although a Class-II repeater topology enables some expansion capability between repeater products located in a wiring closet, it does not offer any substantial capability for increasing the network size. To overcome these limitations, a switch can replace the central concentrator hub, as Sec. 5.4 discusses.

5.4 SWITCHED ETHERNET

To create larger networks than can be achieved with a repeater at the central hub, and to increase the network capacity significantly, developers have implemented switched Ethernet solutions.[13–15] Chapter 10 addresses these topics in detail, so this section presents a concise basic overview. The advantage of a switch is that it eliminates the collision detection timing restrictions, thereby allowing longer cable distances between stations, and it allows multiple ports to be active simultaneously, which leads to a greater network capacity.

Figure 5.20 shows the basic concept of an Ethernet switch. The two major components of any switch are the forwarding logic and the input/output (I/O) ports. The I/O ports are classified as access ports and network uplink ports. *Access ports* are the physical interfaces that a switch uses to connect to stations on the LAN. *Network uplink ports* are the ports that connect the LAN switch to other LAN switches. Each access port has a buffer, which is used for queuing up incoming frames while they wait for the outgoing port to become free for transmission.

The IEEE-801.1D Standard defines the *forwarding logic* of a LAN switch.[16] The basic function of the forwarding logic is to examine the incoming frames and to transfer them to the appropriate output port when this port is free for transmission. With this setup each incoming line constitutes a single collision domain. Thus no collisions will occur

Basic Ethernet Switch

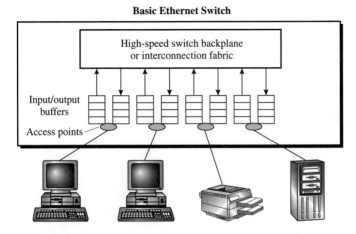

FIGURE 5.20
The basic concept of an Ethernet switch.

if only a single station is attached to the line. However, if several stations share an input line by means of another concentrator hub, then this group of stations will constitute a collision domain.

In addition, switches allow ports to implement either full- or half-duplex data exchanges over a transmission line. With *half-duplex transmission* only one of two stations on a point-to-point link is allowed to transmit at a time. To carry on an information exchange, the two stations need to alternate in transmitting. A CSMA/CD Ethernet network that uses a multiport repeater is an example of a network employing a half-duplex operation between stations and a hub. With *full-duplex transmission* two stations can simultaneously exchange data. When using digital signaling over a guided transmission medium, full-duplex operation requires two separate transmission lines, for example, two twisted-wire pairs or two optical fibers. Half-duplex operation needs only one path since this line is shared alternately in opposite directions. For analog signaling the duplex mode of operation depends on the signaling frequency. If two stations transmit and receive on the same frequency over a wireless link, then the link must be half-duplex. However, when using two guided transmission lines, the stations can exchange information at the same frequency in a full-duplex mode. If the stations use different frequencies for transmission and reception, then they can operate in a full-duplex mode over a wireless link or over a single guided transmission line.

Ethernet switches can be used with both 10- and 100-Mbps segments simultaneously on a port-by-port basis. Figure 5.21 gives an example of a hybrid 10- and

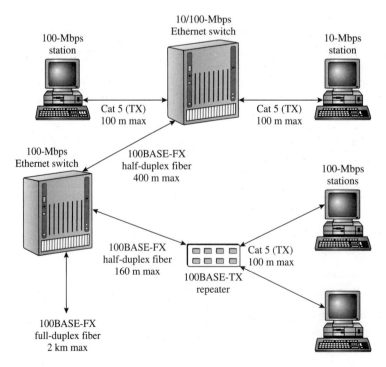

FIGURE 5.21
Example of a hybrid 10- and 100-Mbps switched Ethernet topology with full- and half-duplex links.

100-Mbps switched Ethernet topology that employs both full- and half-duplex links. The half-duplex fiber connections from the hybrid switch to a DTE or to another switch can be 400 m long, whereas it is limited to 160-m spans to a repeater. A full-duplex 100BASE-FX connection to another switch or a DTE can span 2 km using single-mode fiber.

5.5 GIGABIT ETHERNET

The IEEE-802.3z Gigabit Ethernet Standard was released in 1998.[17-21] This standard established an Ethernet LAN with a transmission speed of 1 Gbps. It specifies the use of optical fibers and short-haul (less than 25 m) STP (shielded twisted-pair) copper wire transmission media. Subsequent to the development of IEEE 802.3z, the IEEE-802.3ab Standard for 1-Gbps operation over Cat-5 UTP wire was created as a separate document.[22] The impetus for going to higher speeds came from the increasing use of bandwidth-hungry internet applications and the growing demand for time-sensitive communications between network users. The goal in creating this standard was to define not only new physical layers but also to keep the same frame structure and procedures used in the 10-Mbps IEEE-802.3 Standard. This makes Gigabit Ethernet compatible with 10BASE-T and 100BASE-T, which allows a smooth migration path within an organization from lower-speed to higher-speed Ethernet equipment.

5.5.1 Gigabit Ethernet Architecture

Figure 5.22 shows the layering structure for the IEEE-802.3z Gigabit Ethernet architecture. The function of the reconciliation sublayer is similar to that of the RS for Fast Ethernet. However, in this case it maps data in 1-byte blocks to and from the MAC layer, as opposed to nibblewide blocks for Fast Ethernet.

The *gigabit medium-independent interface* (GMII) provides the logical interaction between the MAC and the PHY layers. The GMII is optional for all medium alternatives except UTP. It is implemented as an integrated-circuit chip and allows the intermingling of MAC and PHY components from different vendors. The GMII is similar to the MII (medium-independent interface), but with some modifications. The major difference is that for the GMII the data path from the MAC to the PHY layer is 1-byte (8 bits) wide. Thus during each clock cycle 1 byte of data is moved across the GMII. The transmit and receive clocks operate at 125 MHz to provide a total data rate of 1 Gbps. When interfacing to 10BASE-T or Fast Ethernet networks, the GMII also can run at 10- and 100-Mbps data rates, in which case its operation is identical to an MII.

The physical layer of Gigabit Ethernet differs in several ways from that of Fast Ethernet. As shown in the left-hand side of Fig. 5.23, the PCS implements an 8B10B encoder and decoder for use with optical fibers and short-haul STP copper wires. In addition, the auto-negotiation and flow control functions now are specified in the PCS. The auto-negotiation process determines the link speed and whether the mode of operation should be full- or half-duplex. In the half-duplex mode of operation the PCS is responsible for carrier sense and collision detection. The PMA provides a 10-bit serialization function. It receives 10-bit blocks of 8B10B-encoded data that are clocked at a 125-MHz rate from the PCS and changes these to a serial bit stream for delivery to the PMD sublayer. In the reverse direction the PMA receives serialized data from the PMD sublayer and

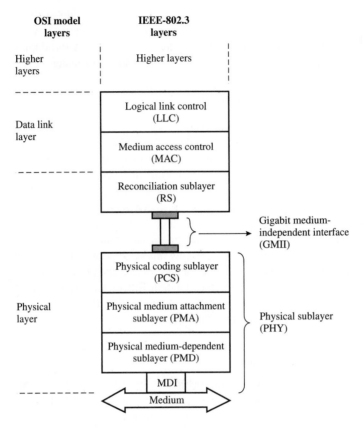

FIGURE 5.22
Layering structure for the IEEE-802.3z Gigabit Ethernet architecture.

converts it to 10-bit blocks of data for submission to the PCS. Similar to Fast Ethernet, the PMD and the MDI specify the transceivers and connectors, respectively, for the various media.

5.5.2 General Functions

Although the frame structure for Gigabit Ethernet remains the same, the factor of 10 increase in speed requires modifications to the MAC layer. The reason is that as the transmission speed increases, the maximum distance between stations must be shortened so that all stations on the shared medium can detect collisions successfully. This means that if the interstation distances are limited to 2000 m for 10-Mbps Ethernet and to 200 m for Fast Ethernet, then the diameter of a Gigabit Ethernet network could be only 20 m, which is not particularly useful. Thus the first modification was in the minimum allowed frame size. At a line rate of 1 Gbps if the frame size is 64 bytes (512 bits), its transmission can be completed before the sending station senses a collision. Therefore the slot time was extended to 512 bytes (4096 bits) for Gigabit Ethernet. Frames that are smaller than

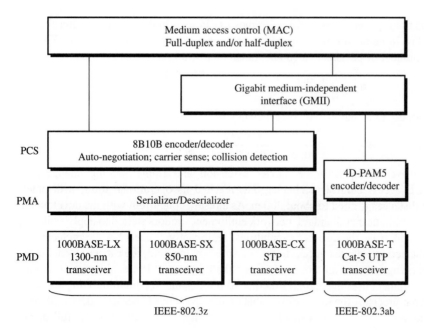

FIGURE 5.23
Architecture options for the IEEE-802.3z and IEEE-802.3ab standards.

this need to be lengthened by a process called *carrier extension,* which appends a set of special symbols to the end of short MAC frames.

Another change to the media access control layer specification is the addition of an approach called *frame bursting.* This method allows a station to send a limited burst of multiple short frames consecutively. This avoids the overhead of using carrier extension when a station has a number of small frames waiting to be sent.

Let us see what effect carrier extension and frame bursting has on the throughput for Gigabit Ethernet. With carrier extension only, the normalized efficiency is[18,23]

$$S = \frac{L_p}{\max[L_{\text{slot}}, L_p] + I + L_{\text{preamble}}} \tag{5.7}$$

Here $\max[L_{\text{slot}}, L_p]$ means the larger of L_{slot} or L_p, and the contention slot length L_{slot} is 512 bytes (4096 bits). For the smallest-sized packet of 64 bytes (512 bits), the worst-case throughput is

$$S = \frac{512}{4096 + 96 + 64} = 12\% \tag{5.8}$$

This is not particularly efficient. When frame bursting is added, the throughput becomes[18,23]

$$S = \frac{(n + 1)L_p}{\max[L_{\text{slot}}, L_p] + n(L_p + I + L_{\text{preamble}})} \tag{5.9}$$

Here n is the number of consecutive frames transmitted in the first burst after the first frame. Now if the burst timer is set to transmit a maximum length $L_{timer} = 65,536$ bits, then the number of packets that can be transmitted within the burst is

$$n = \frac{L_{timer} - L_{slot}}{L_p + I + L_{preamble}} = \frac{65,536 - 4096}{512 + 64 + 96} = 92 \tag{5.10}$$

Then from Eq. (5.9) the worst-case efficiency is

$$S = \frac{93 \times 512}{4096 + 92(512 + 64 + 96)} = 72\% \tag{5.11}$$

However, even with the carrier extension and frame-bursting changes, the CSMA/CD access control mechanism has reached its operational limit, with practical span distances limited to about 200 m. As a result, concurrent with the development of the Gigabit Ethernet Standard, network equipment vendors started to apply switching schemes to increase the distance capabilities significantly. Since a LAN switch can provide dedicated full-duplex access to the transmission medium, the carrier extension and frame-bursting features are not needed, and the CSMA/CD Protocol is not used. Full-duplex equipment uses the regular Ethernet 96-bit IFG and 512-bit minimum packet size so that it has precisely the same form as that used by 10-Mbps Ethernet and Fast Ethernet. Owing to these factors, all available Gigabit Ethernet equipment supports full-duplex switching operation.

Figure 5.24 shows an example of a switched Gigabit Ethernet configuration. Here a Gigabit Ethernet switch is connected by means of 1-Gbps links to Fast Ethernet and hybrid 100/1000-Mbps workgroup LAN switches. Each workgroup LAN switch supports two functions. First it provides 1-Gbps links to connect to the central Gigabit Ethernet switch. Secondly, it provides 100-Mbps connections to high-performance workstations, servers, and hybrid 10/100-Mbps switches.

5.5.3 Transmission Media

The physical layer alternatives for Gigabit Ethernet include the following:

- *1000BASE-LX* supports optical fiber backbones using wavelengths in the 1310-nm window (1270 to 1355 nm). For short-span backbones the maximum lengths are 550 m using multimode fibers with either 50- or 62.5-μm core diameters. Long-span campus-type backbones can have spans up to 5 km with single-mode fibers.
- *1000BASE-SX* is a lower-cost short-wavelength (770- to 860-nm range) option used in short-span backbones. The link lengths can be up to 275 m with 62.5-μm multimode fibers, or up to 550 m with 50-μm multimode fibers.
- *1000BASE-CX* supports short 1-Gbps spans between devices clustered within a single room or an equipment rack. The cables are specialized shielded twisted-pair (STP) copper wires with a maximum length of 25 m.
- *1000BASE-T* specifies characteristics of cables running from a wiring closet to a network node using four-pair Category-5 or -5e unshielded twisted-pair (Cat-5 or Cat-5e UTP) wires. The maximum cable run is 100 m, thereby enabling network managers to build networks with diameters of 200 m.

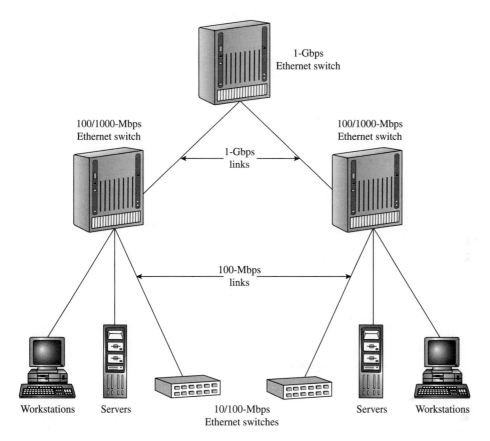

FIGURE 5.24
Example of a switched Gigabit Ethernet configuration.

The first three alternatives fall under the realm of IEEE 802.3z, which specifies using 8B10B encoding on the line. The UTP-based 1000BASE-T option is specified in IEEE 802.3ab and employs 4D-PAM5 encoding. Section 5.5.4 describes the bases of these encoding methods.

5.5.4 Gigabit Ethernet Encoding Schemes

The 8B10B coding method arose from Fibre Channel (see Chap. 9) and other fiber-oriented protocols. In this scheme an 8-bit group of data from the MAC is converted into a larger group of 10 signal bits used for transmission. Figure 5.25 illustrates the operation of this code. The encoding is actually accomplished as a combination of two separate 5B6B and 3B4B block codes. However, these two codes are not necessarily performed as separate functions since they generally serve as a tool that simplifies the mapping and implementation functions. Before encoding, the 8 bits are given the designations A, B, C, D, E, F, G, H. After encoding, the bits are designated by the letters a through j.

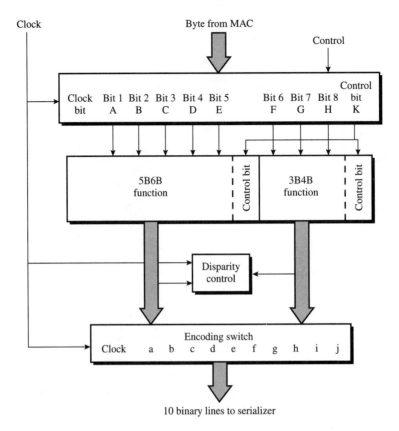

FIGURE 5.25
Operation of the 8B10B-encoding process.

As explained in Chap. 3, the 8B10B code has a good transition density for easier clock recovery; it is well DC-balanced to prevent baseline wander and provides a good error detection capability. As part of the encoding process, the control-line input K indicates whether the bits A through H are data or control bits. If they are control bits, a special 10-bit block is generated. There are 12 of these unique nondata blocks, which can be used for synchronization, signal control instructions, or other functions. The disparity control function monitors the number of 1 and 0 bits, where the *disparity* is the excess of one type of bit over another. The disparity controller determines the proper 8B10B encoding of the next data byte so that an equal balance of 1 and 0 bits is maintained.

The 1000BASE-T Gigabit Ethernet Standard employs the *four-dimensional five-level pulse amplitude modulation* (4D-PAM5) encoding scheme. The designation 4D refers to the eight-state trellis forward error correction coding that is used to mitigate the effects of noise and crosstalk on the adjacent wire pairs in the UTP cable.[24-25] The PAM5-coding scheme uses five different voltage levels to keep the symbol rate at or below 125 Mbaud per cable. Four of these voltage levels encode data bits, whereas the fifth is used for implementing forward error correction. Scrambling is applied to the input bits to produce a smoothed pattern of 1s and 0s for improving signal quality.

5.6 TEN-GIGABIT ETHERNET

In 1999 the IEEE created the 802.3ae[26–29] Task Force to develop the next iteration of Gigabit Ethernet, which is to transport Ethernet traffic at 10 Gbps. Whereas previous Ethernet standards were designed specifically for networking applications in LANs, the 802.3ae specification defines two PHY types. These are the LAN PHY and the WAN PHY. These physical layer definitions will allow network providers to establish low-cost, high-speed Ethernet links throughout an entire network of MANs and WANs to interconnect geographically dispersed LANs.

The IEEE-802.3ae Standard for 10-Gigabit Ethernet operation uses the IEEE-802.3 Ethernet MAC Protocol, the IEEE-802.3 Ethernet frame format, and the minimum and maximum IEEE-802.3 frame sizes. Ten-Gigabit Ethernet provides only full-duplex operation and does not support shared media implementations. Therefore it is not distance limited, as is the case with other versions of Ethernet.

To support a broad base of installed multimode and single-mode optical fiber types and to meet the destination requirements for connecting the more than 600 million existing Ethernet nodes, the 10-Gigabit Ethernet Standard defines the physical layer interfaces listed in Table 5.6. As shown in that table, the specification includes a long-haul optical transceiver or physical medium-dependent interface for single-mode fiber that can be used with either the LAN PHY or WAN PHY for building MANs. The WAN PHY option allows 10-Gigabit Ethernet to be transparently transported across existing OC-192 SONET infrastructures. Note, however, that the WAN PHY is not a SONET interface; it is an asynchronous Ethernet interface.

Figure 5.26 illustrates the implementation of 10-Gigabit Ethernet in a LAN environment for high-speed connections between large-capacity switches inside a data center, in a computer room, between buildings, or to the Internet. Extending out from this LAN environment are long-distance 10-Gigabit Ethernet connections between geographically dispersed enterprise facilities that can be located up to 40 km apart.

Among the applications of 10-Gigabit Ethernet links are the following:

- *High-speed Internet access.* More and more people are making a rapidly growing use of the Internet. As the sophistication of the applications they employ increases,

TABLE 5.6

Optical fiber medium options for 10-Gigabit Ethernet

Fiber type	Wavelength, nm	Distance
Multimode	850	65 m
Multimode	1310	300 m
Single mode	1310	10 km
Single mode	1550	40 km

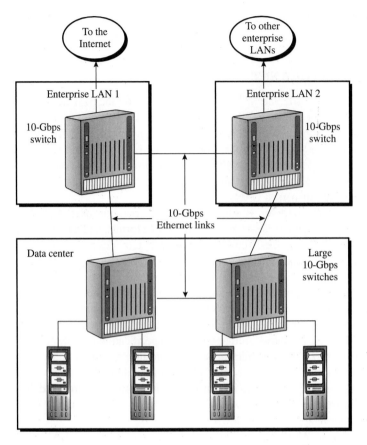

FIGURE 5.26
Implementation of 10-Gigabit Ethernet in a LAN environment.

their bandwidth demands also grow. Thus higher-speed links to the Internet are needed for people to use these applications effectively without incurring long delays.

- *Enterprise LAN interconnections.* Computers of employees, servers, standard and high-quality printers, fax machines, and other communicating devices within an enterprise all need to be joined by means of a seamless, high-speed Ethernet network to handle the growing bandwidth demand of applications used by these machines without encountering network congestion or delays.
- *Connections to server farms.* Clusters of servers that are located in data centers need very high-speed links to support the rapid transaction rates expected by users.
- *Telecommuting.* Employees who telecommute from a home office or a remote office should be capable of communicating at the same speed as colleagues at the corporate site. Gigabit-speed links between the outside office and the enterprise LAN are needed to fulfill this requirement.
- *High-speed data transport.* Applications such as software downloads, music or video distribution, and exchanges of information or images from interactive col-

laborations are most acceptable to users only if large amounts of data can be transferred in a short time.

- *Real-time streaming.* Real-time applications such as Internet radio, voice-over-IP, and video on demand need reliable, high-capacity transmission links to provide a reasonable quality of service.

5.7 SUMMARY

Ethernet has become the most widely used protocol for local area network applications and is being extended throughout both metropolitan and wide area networks. The standard has evolved from a contention-based method in which all users share the transmission medium to a switched network implementation. The operating speed of various versions of Ethernet range from 10 Mbps to 10 Gbps.

All devices on a basic legacy 10-Mbps Ethernet network time-share the common communication medium, and all stations have equal-priority access to this medium. Multiple stations can receive data at the same time from the medium, but only one station is permitted to transmit at any time. To achieve this, Ethernet is based on the CSMA/CD Protocol. With this protocol, when a station has a frame to transmit, it first listens to the medium to see if another station is currently using the network. If there is no activity on the medium, the station sends its frame. If the medium is busy, the station continues to listen to the channel until it is idle and then transmits its frame immediately after a predetermined period of silence passes.

Fast Ethernet or 100BASE-T was developed in the early 1990s to support the rapidly growing application of desktop computing in the business world. Since the standard retains the fundamental structure of the Ethernet MAC Protocol, implementers were able to apply Fast Ethernet to the extensive installed Ethernet base with few modifications. Fast Ethernet is similar to the 10BASE-T Ethernet with respect to employing a hub-based architecture and the use of the CSMA/CD access protocol. Besides the operating rate, the main differences between Ethernet and Fast Ethernet concern the type of network cabling, the data encoding method, and the network spans.

The IEEE-802.3z Gigabit Ethernet Standard for a transmission speed of 1 Gbps was released in 1998. This standard specifies the use of optical fibers and short-haul (less than 25 m) STP copper wire transmission media. The impetus for going to higher speeds came from the increasing use of bandwidth-hungry internet applications and the growing demand for time-sensitive communications between network users. The goal was to define new physical layers but to keep the same frame structure and procedures used in the 10-Mbps IEEE-802.3 Standard. This makes Gigabit Ethernet compatible with 10BASE-T and 100BASE-T, which allows a smooth migration path within an organization from lower-speed to higher-speed Ethernet equipment.

In 1999 the IEEE created the 802.3ae Task Force to develop the next iteration of Gigabit Ethernet, which is to transport Ethernet traffic at 10 Gbps. The 802.3ae Standard uses the IEEE-802.3 Ethernet MAC protocol, the IEEE-802.3 Ethernet frame format, and the minimum and maximum IEEE-802.3 frame sizes. Ten-Gigabit Ethernet provides only full-duplex operation and does not support shared media implementations. Therefore it is not distance limited, as is the case with other versions of Ethernet. Whereas previous Ethernet standards were designed specifically for networking applications in LANs, the 802.3ae specification defines a LAN PHY and a WAN PHY. These physical layer definitions will allow network providers to establish low-cost, high-speed Ethernet links throughout an entire network of MANs and WANs to interconnect geographically dispersed LANs.

PROBLEMS

5.1. Suppose 50 desktop personal computers used by engineers and support personnel are connected to an Ethernet LAN, which provides the following capabilities:
- Digital telephone service at 32 kbps
- Retrieval time of 250 ms for a 1-MB (megabyte) file from a server attached to the LAN.
- Ten e-mail messages per hour to and from a user. Assume 90 percent of the messages are less than 10 kB (kilobytes) and 10 percent contain a 100-kB attachment.
- Internet access at 56 kbps (kilobits per second).
- Full-duplex videoconferencing capability at 64 kbps.

(a) Estimate the bit rate requirements of the LAN.

(b) Draw possible topologies for a 10-Mbps hub-based Ethernet LAN and a 10-Mbps switch-based Ethernet LAN.

5.2. Suppose an Ethernet LAN services a group of 20 desktop computers. How much bandwidth is available to each computer station if:

(a) A 10-Mbps Ethernet repeater hub is used?

(b) The computers are connected to a 100-Mbps Ethernet repeater hub?

(c) The computers are connected to a 100-Mbps Ethernet switch?

5.3. Using web resources, check the configuration, price, and features of a typical 10/100-Mbps Ethernet network interface card (NIC). Consider features such as media support, transmission distance for a 10/100BASE-T operation, and driver support.

5.4. Using web resources, check the price, size, and capabilities of a nominally eight-port 10/100-Mbps Ethernet hub that is applicable for home or small office use.

5.5. Using web resources, check the price, size, and capabilities of a nominally 24-port 10/100-Mbps Ethernet hub that is applicable for use in a medium-sized enterprise LAN. Consider features such as transceiver options for support of different media, autosensing capability, how many units can be stacked, and status monitoring.

5.6. Consider an Ethernet LAN in which 80 percent of the traffic generated by the stations is destined for other stations on the LAN, and the remaining 20 percent goes to stations outside of the LAN. For this situation, is an Ethernet hub preferable to an Ethernet switch? Which device should be used if the percentages are reversed?

5.7. A personal computer (PC) typically has either built-in Ethernet ports or slots for inserting an Ethernet adapter card. Using web resources, describe the features of some Ethernet PC adapter cards for both desktop and laptop computers. What are the Ethernet capabilities of the PC you are using?

5.8. Two 10BASE-T LANs are located in separate buildings that are 8 km apart. One LAN has a total cable span of 1000 m and the other has a 2500-m cable span.

(a) Draw a basic topology showing what repeaters, bridges, and routers are needed to form a consolidated network.

(b) What connection alternatives are possible and why would they be used?

5.9. An engineer needs to set up a small 10BASE-T network to interconnect the following equipment:
- One server with at least 20 GB of disk storage and 64 MB of memory
- Fifteen identical desktop computers
- A backup storage device

- Two laser printers
- A bridge for Internet access

The network covers a 50- × 50-m area in an office building.

(a) Draw a topology and equipment layout for such a network.

(b) Consult recent trade magazines or vendor websites to select specific equipment, including cabling and LAN adapters.

(c) Make an estimate of the cost of this network.

5.10. Consider a switched LAN in which a station is transmitting 1500-byte frames at a 10-Mbps rate.

(a) If a 1-ms data-corrupting electrical noise pulse occurs on the link, how many frames could be corrupted if they are sent continuously?

(b) How many frames could be affected in a hub-based LAN?

5.11. Encode the following bit stream using 4B5B encoding:

$$0101110100101110101010100111$$

5.12. For the bit stream 01101010, draw the waveforms produced by 4B5B and MLT-3 encoding.

5.13. Consider a 10BASE-T Ethernet LAN in which the maximum distance between any two computers is 200 m. Suppose the transmission medium is twisted-pair wire in which signals travel at 1.75×10^8 m/s. Assume the hub takes at most 0.1 μs to detect a collision. What is the maximum time between when a station starts transmitting and when it notices that a collision has occurred?

5.14. Consider the hybrid network that has 25 computers attached to a 10/100-Mbps Ethernet switch via 10-Mbps links and a file server attached to the switch with a 100-Mbps link. Describe the throughput of the network as a function of the fraction of packets traveling between computers and between the computers and the server.

5.15. Consider a hub-based Ethernet LAN operating at R Mbps in which a dedicated pair of lines of length d attaches each of N stations to the central hub. Assume all packets are 12,500 bytes long and that the signal travels at 2.5×10^8 m/s in the medium. Compare the maximum achievable throughputs for the four possible combinations of the following parameters: $d = 25$ m or 2500 m; $R = 10$ Mbps or 1 Gbps.

5.16. (a) Derive Eq. (5.1) which gives the probability that exactly one Ethernet station transmits under the simplified condition that the traffic pattern is a constant, heavy load.

(b) Show that P_A is a maximum when $p = 1/k$.

5.17. Consider a 10-Mbps Ethernet LAN that spans 2.5 km. Assume the stations can transmit 64-byte packets that contain 30 bytes of overhead.

(a) What is the throughput of the network?

(b) What is the maximum rate at which the network can send user data bits?

(c) What is the maximum rate of sending user data bits for 1200-byte packets (again assuming 30 bytes of overhead)?

5.18. Before a station can successfully acquire an Ethernet channel, it must wait a mean number of slots N during a contention interval.

(a) Show that the probability that the contention interval has j slots in it is

$$P_j = P_A(1 - P_A)^{j-1}$$

where P_A is defined in Eq. (5.1).

(b) Show that the mean number of slots per contention interval is $N = 1/P_A$.

5.19. Using web resources, discuss the price and features of some typical print and terminal Ethernet LAN servers. Consider features such as the number of ports, memory size, and protocols supported.

5.20. Discuss the advantages of implementing switched Ethernet instead of contention-based Ethernet. Consider factors such as access delay, transmission distances, user and server isolation, and congestion control.

5.21. Using web resources, check the price, size, and capabilities of a nominally 12-port Gigabit Ethernet LAN switch. Consider features such as the number of ports, power dissipation, built-in fault tolerance, and management options. Draw a simple diagram to show how and where such a switch might be used within a large organization.

5.22. Consider two campus organizations that are located within 40 km of each other. Each campus has two branch offices with nominally 10 employees that are from 5 to 10 km away. Draw some possible network configurations connecting these sites using 10-Gigabit Ethernet, Gigabit Ethernet, and Fast Ethernet switches. Show what kinds of switches and links would be needed within the campus organizations to connect 100 employees and clusters of servers.

5.23. Discuss how 10-Gigabit Ethernet and SONET or SDH can interoperate to deliver 10-Gbps traffic to anyplace in the world. Use web resources to find what physical layer interfaces are needed to enable the attachment of packet-based IP/Ethernet switches to SONET/SDH links.

5.24. Examine the trade literature to find recent applications of 10-Gigabit Ethernet. Were these applications for local, metropolitan, or wide area networks? What was the purpose of these implementations? Who was using these systems? Why was 10-Gigabit Ethernet chosen versus another technology?

5.25. Using web resources, check the availability and capabilities of current 10-Gigabit Ethernet equipment for both LAN and WAN applications. What vendors are offering this equipment?

REFERENCES

1. R. M. Metcalfe and D. R. Boggs, "Ethernet: Distributed packet switching for local computer networks," *Commun. ACM,* vol. 19, pp. 395–404, June 1976.

2. J. F. Shoch, Y. K. Dalal, D. D. Redell, and R. C. Crane, "Evolution of the Ethernet local computer network," *Computer,* vol. 15, pp. 10–27, Aug. 1982.

3. Digital Equipment Corporation, Intel Corporation, and Xerox Corporation, *The Ethernet, A Local Area Network, Data Link and Physical Layer Specifications,* version 2.0, Nov. 1982.

4. ANSI/IEEE Standard 802.3, *Carrier Sense Multiple Access with Collision Detection (CSMA/CD) Access Method and Physical Layer Specifications,* 2000 ed. This consolidated edition includes all contents of IEEE Standard 802.3ab-1999, IEEE Standard 802.3ac-1998, and IEEE Standard 802.3ad-2000.

5. A. Leon-Garcia and I. Widjaja, *Communication Networks,* McGraw-Hill, Burr Ridge, IL, 2000.

6. G. Held, *Ethernet Networks,* Wiley, New York, 3rd ed., 1998.

7. W. Stallings, *Local and Metropolitan Area Networks,* Prentice-Hall, Upper Saddle River, NJ, 6th ed., 2000.

8. C. E. Spurgeon, *Ethernet: The Definitive Guide,* O'Reilly, Sebastopol, CA, 2000.

9. IEEE-802.3u Standard, *MAC Parameters, Physical Layer, MAUs, and Repeater for 100-Mbps Operation,* 1995; this specification now is included in the consolidated ANSI/IEEE-802.3 Standard listed in Ref. 4.

10. M. Nemzow, *Fast Ethernet,* McGraw-Hill, New York, 1997.

11. P. Izzo, *Gigabit Networks,* Wiley, New York, 2000.

12. G. Cherubini, S. Ölçer, G. Ungerboeck, J. Creigh, and S. K. Rao, "100BASE-T2: A new standard for 100-Mb/s Ethernet transmission over voice-grade cables," *IEEE Commun. Mag.,* vol. 35, pp. 115–122, Nov. 1997.

13. J. J. Roese, *Switched LANs,* McGraw-Hill, New York, 1998.

14. L. R. Rossi, L. D. Rossi, and T. Rossi, *Cisco Catalyst LAN Switching,* McGraw-Hill, New York, 2000.

15. See vendor websites for application notes and white papers on switched Ethernet.

16. IEEE-802.1D-1998, *Local Area Network MAC (Media Access Control) Bridges,* May 25, 1998.

17. IEEE-802.3z Standard for Gigabit Ethernet; this specification now is included in the consolidated ANSI/IEEE-802.3 Standard listed in Ref. 4.
18. J. Kadambi, I. Crayford, and M. Kalkunte, *Gigabit Ethernet,* Prentice-Hall, Upper Saddle River, NJ, 1998.
19. S. Saunders, *Gigabit Ethernet Handbook,* McGraw-Hill, New York, 1998.
20. The 10-Gigabit Ethernet Alliance (10GEA) (http://www.10gea.org).
21. H. Frazier, "The 802.3z Gigabit Ethernet Standard," *IEEE Network,* vol. 12, pp. 6–7, May–June 1998.
22. IEEE-802.3ab Standard for 1000BASE-T Ethernet; this specification now is included in the consolidated ANSI/IEEE-802.3 Standard listed in Ref. 4.
23. M. Molle, M. Kalkunte, and J. Kadambi, "Frame bursting: A technique for scaling CSMA/CD to gigabit speeds," *IEEE Network,* vol. 11, pp. 6–15, July/Aug. 1997.
24. R. B. Wells, *Applied Coding and Information Theory for Engineers,* Prentice-Hall, Upper Saddle River, NJ, 1999.
25. J. G. Proakis, *Digital Communications,* McGraw-Hill, New York, 4th ed., 2001.
26. IEEE-802.3ae Standard for 10-Gigabit Ethernet, Spring 2002.
27. P. Hochmuth, "10G Ethernet gains momentum," *Network World,* vol. 18, pp. 21, 24, Jan. 29, 2001.
28. See vendor websites for information on 10-Gigabit Ethernet products.
29. S. Harbour, "Ethernet will help telcos forge a quiet revolution," *Fibre Systems International,* vol. 2, pp. 43–46, Apr. 2001.

CHAPTER

6

TOKEN-PASSING LANS

In the late 1970s a few years after Ethernet was already in development for LAN applications, IBM started looking at the requirements of their customers for future networking. Among these customers were major banks and insurance companies that depended critically on reliable data transport. On a large scale these companies were using the IBM-developed Systems Network Architecture (SNA), which provided highly reliable message delivery, efficient bandwidth utilization, and a significant amount of built-in system redundancy to provide a high degree of network availability and reliability. For future networking these performance aspects needed to be migrated to a LAN environment.[1]

In examining the alternatives, one found that the stochastic access scheme inherent in Ethernet was quite acceptable for LANs (local area networks) operating in a general office environment. However, with the CSMA/CD method used in Ethernet, collisions can occur between messages from different senders. This is particularly true when the network is heavily loaded so that stations may have to make multiple attempts to send data before a message is successfully accepted onto the link. This may cause delays of indeterminable length. This type of uncertainty is not desirable for handling vital corporate network traffic. In addition, early Ethernet LANs did not have well-defined network management procedures and network maintenance could be a time-consuming process when trying to find a network fault. Although the current hub-based 10BASE-T Ethernet and switched Ethernet have overcome these problems, at that time IBM decided to develop a more robust and deterministic LAN type. The result was the token-ring LAN, which now is included in the IEEE-802.5 Standard.[2-7]

The first product release in 1985 operated at 4 Mbps. This was upgraded to 16 Mbps in 1988. The 16-Mbps version is now often referred to as the *classic token ring* (CTR) to distinguish it from enhanced higher-speed products.

TABLE 6.1
Some fundamental IEEE-802.5 standards for token rings

Number	Title	Year
802.5	Token-Ring Access Method (original base standard)	1985
802.5-1998	Token-Ring Access Method—Revision 3	1998
802.5r	Dedicated Token Ring	1998
802.5t	100-Mb/s Dedicated Token Ring	2000
802.5v	Gigabit Token-Ring Operation	2000
802.5w	Corrigenda to 802.5-1998	2000

Token rings resolve time-delay uncertainty by requiring that the attached stations take turns sending messages. The network allows only one device to transmit at a time. Depending on the particular token-passing method used, each station either transmits only one frame during its turn or sends as many frames as it can during an allotted access period. These methods are used in the classic token ring, which this chapter addresses in Sec. 6.1.

From 1995 to 1997 the performance-enhancing concepts of the *dedicated token ring* (DTR) were developed.[8,9] The DTR defines signaling protocols and attachment policies that provide a dedicated 16-Mbps bandwidth for each station. This greatly increases the transmission capacity of the attached stations by means of a centralized switching scheme. Section 6.2 presents the details of the DTR concept.

In the late 1990s a growing demand for greater backbone bandwidth to handle streaming video and other bandwidth-intensive applications led to concepts for 100-Mbps and 1000-Mbps token rings. Section 6.3 describes these concepts. Table 6.1 lists some of the fundamental IEEE standards for various token-ring concepts that have emerged from the 802.5 committee during the development and implementation of token-ring LANs.

The Fiber Distributed Data Interface (FDDI) is an optical fiber-based 100-Mbps Token-Ring LAN Protocol that is similar to the IEEE-802.5 Standard.[10] Starting in 1985, the standards organization ANSI (ASC X3T9.5) and the ITU-T (ITU-T X.3) developed the specifications for this protocol. FDDI is now an older technology and is mainly used for high-speed backbones. In 1994 a related copper-based specification called *copper distributed data interface* (CDDI) was created to provide 100-Mbps service over Cat-5 UTP wires. Section 6.4 describes the basics of FDDI and CDDI.

6.1 CLASSIC TOKEN RINGS

As the name implies, the stations on a token ring are logically arranged in a ring topology. The access scheme requires that stations take turns to transmit messages. Each station is allowed to transmit only during its turn and only for allotted time durations. To coordinate this, a unique type of placeholder frame called a *token* is used. Initially one station, called the *active monitor* (AM), releases the token. The network passes this token from node to node. When a station receives the token, it has the right to transmit information. This section looks at the various aspects of token-passing rings, including the access method, frame formats, some implementation factors, and performance characteristics.

6.1.1   Token-Ring Operation

Figure 6.1 shows the four basic steps in the operation of a token ring. When there is no traffic on the network, a simple 3-byte token circulates around the ring. This token is passed sequentially from one NIC (network interface card) to another until it reaches a station that has a message to transmit (step 1). If the token is free (i.e., if it is not reserved by a station with a higher priority, as described a few paragraphs later), then the station may send a data frame. To do this, it seizes the token by changing 1 bit in it. This action transforms the token into a start-of-frame sequence for a data frame. The station then adds and transmits the remaining set of fields needed to make a single frame (step 2). It also sets a bit inside its NIC as a reminder that it has possession of the token.

Once a station has seized a token and starts sending a data frame, there is no longer a token on the ring. As the frame travels around the ring, each station examines the destination address. If the frame is addressed to another station, it gets forwarded to the next station. When the intended recipient recognizes its own address in a frame, it copies the message, checks for errors, and changes 4 bits in the last byte of the frame (step 3). The last step is to indicate that the station has recognized its address and has copied the frame. The complete packet then continues around the ring until it reaches the originating station.

After the frame makes a round-trip, the sender receives the frame and recognizes itself in the source address. It examines the address-recognized bits to see if they are set, which will indicate that the recipient received the message. If they are set, the sender then discards the used data frame and releases a new token onto the ring (step 4).

Although a station could release a new token as soon as it has finished sending out its last bit, the IEEE-802.5 Standard requires that the following two conditions must be met for token release:

- A station has finished transmitting all its message bits.
- The first bit of the transmission has returned to the station after going completely around the ring.

In general the propagation time a around the ring is less than the frame transmission time. For this case the first transmitted bit returns before the station has sent out the last bit. Thus the station sends out a new token as soon as it finishes transmitting. When the propagation time a is greater than the frame transmission time, the station transmits its last bit before the first bit returns. In this case it has to wait a time a after the start of transmission before it is allowed to send out a token in order to ensure that only one data frame is on the ring at one time.

Once a new token is released onto the ring, in general the next station along the ring that has data to send is allowed to seize the token and to transmit its data. An exception to this is the *token-reservation* case in the IEEE-802.5 model, wherein another station farther along the ring that has a higher priority than the next station may have reserved the token for its transmission. This works in the following way. Each station has a *priority code* assigned to it. When a frame passes by, a station may reserve the next open token by entering its priority code in the access control field of the data frame (see Sec. 6.1.2). A station that has a higher priority can replace a lower-priority reservation with its own priority code. If the contending stations all have the same priority, the first station to reserve the token gets to transmit next regardless of its location on the ring.

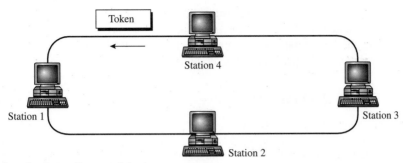

(1) A free token is traveling around the ring.

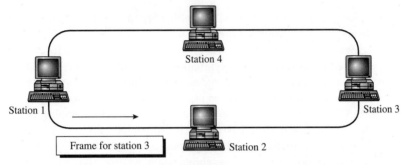

(2) Station 1 siezes the token and sends a data frame to station 3.

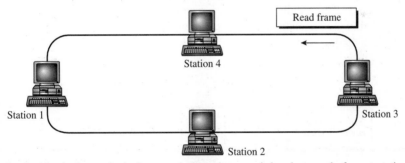

(3) Station 2 copies the frame, checks for errors, indicates it was copied, and returns the frame to station 1.

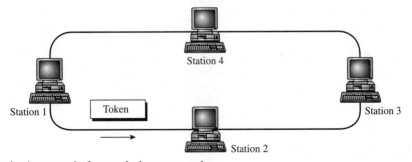

(4) Station 1 removes the frame and releases a new token.

FIGURE 6.1
Four basic steps in the operation of a token ring.

The IEEE-802.5 Token-Ring Protocol imposes a limit on the time that a station may hold the token. This is called the *token-holding time.* It is nominally 10 ms, unless the network administration sets a different time limit. The token-holding time thus limits the time a station is allowed to transmit continuously.

6.1.2 IEEE-802.5 Frame Structure

Figure 6.2 shows the structure of the two types of frames used by the IEEE-802.5 Protocol. These are the data (or command) frame and the token frame. The *token frame* is a truncated data frame. The *data frame* can contain either user data or management commands. It consists of the following nine fields:

1. *Start delimiter (SD).* The 1-byte SD is the first field and indicates the start of a data frame. In addition to alerting the receiving station to the arrival of a frame, it allows the receiver to synchronize its retrieval timer. Figure 6.3 shows the format of the SD field, which contains four nondata symbols to distinguish it from data. The form of a nondata symbol depends on the signal encoding scheme that is used. For example, when using the differential Manchester encoding method, the J and K bits are coding violations. These violations are created at the physical layer by changing the encoding pattern for the duration of the bit. Normally in differential Manchester encoding each bit can have two transitions, one at the beginning and one in the middle of the bit. The transition at the middle is used for synchronization, whereas the presence or absence of a transition at the beginning identifies the bit. Here a transition indicates a binary 0 and no transition indicates a binary 1, as shown in Fig. 6.4a. Both transitions are canceled in the J violation, and the middle transition is canceled in the K violation, as Fig. 6.4b illustrates.

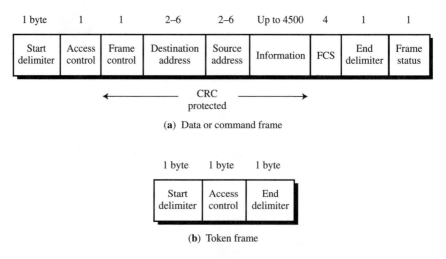

FIGURE 6.2
Structure of the two types of frames used by the IEEE-802.5 Protocol.

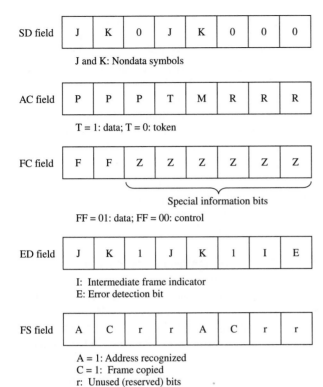

| SD field | J | K | 0 | J | K | 0 | 0 | 0 |

J and K: Nondata symbols

| AC field | P | P | P | T | M | R | R | R |

T = 1: data; T = 0: token

| FC field | F | F | Z | Z | Z | Z | Z | Z |

Special information bits

FF = 01: data; FF = 00: control

| ED field | J | K | 1 | J | K | 1 | I | E |

I: Intermediate frame indicator
E: Error detection bit

| FS field | A | C | r | r | A | C | r | r |

A = 1: Address recognized
C = 1: Frame copied
r: Unused (reserved) bits

FIGURE 6.3
Formats of the various fields in an IEEE-802.5 frame.

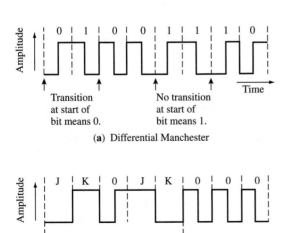

(a) Differential Manchester

Transition at start of bit means 0.

No transition at start of bit means 1.

Unique starting pattern

(b) Starting delimiter

FIGURE 6.4
(*a*) Illustration of the differential Manchester encoding method; (*b*) starting delimiter bit pattern showing the J and K encoding violations.

2. *Access control (AC).* The 1-byte AC field includes four subfields, as shown in Fig. 6.3. The 3-bit priority subfield PPP indicates the priority of the token. A station that wishes to reserve access to the ring sets the three RRR reservation bits. The PPP and RRR bits implement eight levels of ring access priority. The fourth bit T is the *token bit,* which indicates whether this is a data frame (T = 1) or a token (T = 0). Thus a station can convert an available token frame into a data frame by simply changing the T bit from 0 to 1. Following the token bit is the monitor bit M, which is used by a designated monitor station to remove persistent data frames or persistent high-priority tokens from the ring. For example, because of a station failure or crash, a station might not have removed the frame it sent or the high-priority token it reserved.

3. *Frame control (FC).* The 1-byte FC field indicates whether a frame contains data or MAC information. Data frames are identified by setting FF = 01, in which case the 6 Z bits are ignored. MAC control is identified by setting FF = 00, in which case the Z bits contain information used by the token-ring logic, for example, how to use the information in the AC field.

4. *Destination address (DA).* The 2- or 6-byte DA field contains the address of the next destination for the frame. The IEEE-802.5 Standard specifies both 16- and 48-bit addressing with the same format as that found in the IEEE-802.3 Ethernet Standard (see Sec. 5.2). If the final destination is a station on another network, the DA field contains the address of the router in the path that the frame follows to the next LAN. If the final destination is a station on the same LAN, the DA field contains the address of that station.

5. *Source address (SA).* Similarly, the SA is a 2- or 6-byte field that contains the address of the sending station. If the packet came from another LAN, the SA is the physical address of the most recent router. Again the SA field follows the same format as in the IEEE-802.3 Ethernet Standard (see Sec. 5.2).

6. *Data field.* The data field contains the protocol data unit (PDU) and can be up to 4500 bytes long. A token-ring frame does not have a PDU-length or type field.

7. *Frame check sequence (FCS).* The 4-byte FCS field contains the same 32-bit cyclic redundancy check (CRC) as in the IEEE-802.3 Standard (see Chap. 3). It is based on the FC, SA, DA, and information fields.

8. *End delimiter (ED).* Similar to the SD field, the 1-byte end delimiter (ED) field contains noncode symbols, such as the J and K code violations, to distinguish it from data. Its function is to indicate the end of the data or control information. In addition, as shown in Fig. 6.3, it contains an error detection bit (E) and an intermediate bit (I). The E bit is set if any station interface detects an error such as a line code violation in the data or a FCS error. The I bit indicates whether a frame is an intermediate or a final one in a multiple frame transmission.

9. *Frame status (FS).* The 1-byte frame status (FS) field, shown in Fig. 6.3, allows the receiving station to convey transfer status information to the sender. This is done with address-recognized (A) and frame-copied (C) bits that come at the beginning of the field. Since these bits are outside of the FCS, they are repeated at the fifth and sixth bits within the field to provide a redundancy check for detecting possible erroneous settings. The condition A = 1 states that the receiving station recognized the destination address. When C = 1, this indicates that the receiving station copied the frame into its buffer. The other 4 bits, designated by *r*, are unused (reserved) bits.

A *token* includes only three 1-byte fields since it is basically a placeholder and reservation frame. As shown in Fig. 6.2, these are the SD, AC, and ED fields, which are previously described.

6.1.3 Ring Configurations

In the simplest architecture a token ring has a series of stations connected by point-to-point links in a closed-loop configuration, as shown in Fig. 6.5. This simple loop has several disadvantages. First since the attached devices are wired together in a circle, any disruption in the electrical flow around the loop will bring down the LAN. This could include the failure of a NIC in a station, a break in the cable, or the need to remove a station from the network or to attach another one. Also the simple act of shutting off a machine turns off the power to the NIC at that station, which would disrupt service on the LAN.

These problems can be avoided through the use of *concentrators,* also called a *multistation access unit* (MAU), in *wiring centers* (or *wiring closets*) and by having a self-healing capability on the ring. Figure 6.6 shows a basic example of stations connected via a wiring center. The logical connection is still a ring, but now the physical layout is a star. Each station is connected to the wiring center by a cable containing at least two twisted pairs. This cable typically consists of Cat-5 UTP and is known as a *lobe cable.* One wire pair is for transmission to the station and the other is for transmission from the station. Inside the wiring centers the cables connect to bypass relays that are energized by current from the stations. For normal operation the relays connect the station to the

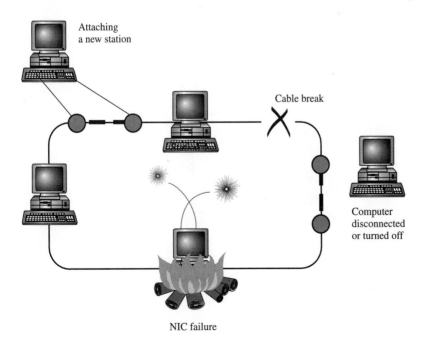

FIGURE 6.5
Basic closed-loop configuration and failure points for token rings.

Concentrator or multistation access unit (MAU)

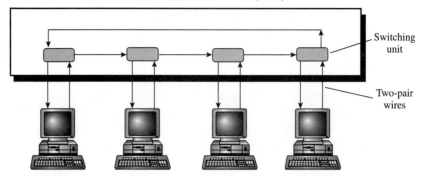

Switching unit

Two-pair wires

Station input/output lines

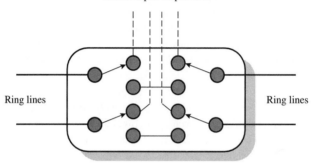

Ring lines

Ring lines

Switching unit in the "station-inserted" mode

Station input/output lines

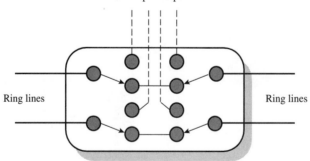

Ring lines

Ring lines

Switching unit in the "station-bypassed" mode

FIGURE 6.6
Basic example of stations connected via a switchable wiring center.

ring inside the MAU. In case the lobe cable breaks or a station goes down, this current will stop and the relay will close to bypass the failed station or cable segment. Thus the ring is automatically reconfigured to operate without that station. Once the station is back in full operation, it signals the concentrator to get patched into the ring again.

The MAUs generally reside in equipment racks within a wiring closet. A typical lobe cable length from the wiring closet to the office area that it supports ranges from 30 to 70 m. Distances between wiring closets can vary from 5 m from floor to floor in a multistory building, to more than 150 m in a large office or factory complex.

For the bigger LANs a series of MAUs can be connected into a larger ring, as shown in Fig. 6.7. Here there is a redundant standby loop in parallel with the primary ring linking the MAUs. This configuration can provide either a bypass function or a self-healing capability. In the *bypass technique* both the main and the standby rings transmit in the same direction, as shown in Fig. 6.8. When a failure occurs at the station, a bypass element routes the signal onto the standby ring. With the *self-healing technique* the main and the standby rings transmit in opposite directions, as shown in Fig. 6.9. In the event of a catastrophic failure at the station or when a break occurs in the cable, a *reconfiguration* or *loop-back switch* reroutes the signal stream so that it bends back on itself (via the standby loop) at either side of the failure. This switching technique uses the same principle as that shown in Fig. 6.6.

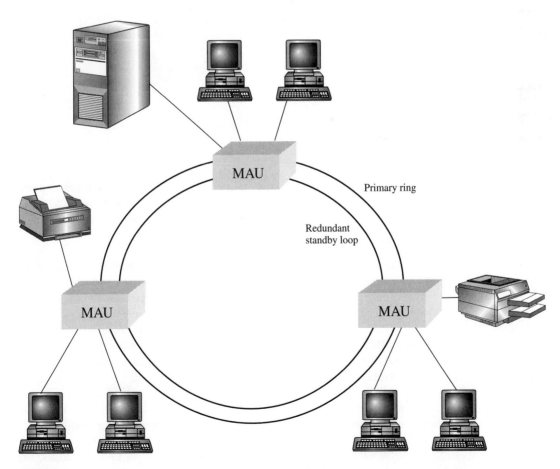

FIGURE 6.7
For big LANs a series of MAUs can be connected into a large ring.

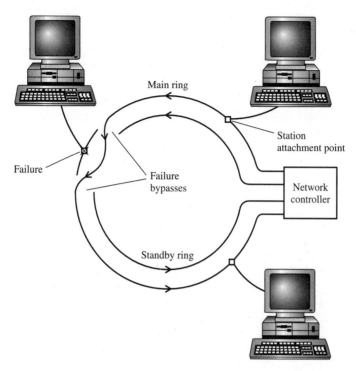

FIGURE 6.8
In the bypass technique both the main and the standby rings transmit in the same direction.

6.1.4   Ring Management

Various faults or error conditions can arise to disrupt the operation of a token-ring network. These are designated as either hard or soft errors. *Hard errors* generally cannot
be resolved through the token-ring access protocol. Thus they need some operator intervention and include conditions as listed here:

- *Streaming errors* occur when a station continuously transmits either a stream of bits
  or a continuous sequence of frames or tokens. This removes or destroys tokens and
  frames by writing over or replacing the data in other legitimate frames or tokens.
- A *frequency error* occurs when a station detects an excessive frequency difference
  between the input signal and the frequency of the crystal timing oscillator at the
  station. This causes the station to enter the claim-token mode.
- A *signal loss error* arises when, for example, a ring breaks, a receiver saturates,
  or a transmitter fails, which causes a station to reconfigure.

When soft errors occur, they either allow the token-ring access protocol to operate
normally or to restore the token ring to normal operation, but with some possible higher
layer performance degradation. They are usually resolved by one station designated
as the *active monitor* (AM) station. *Soft errors* include frame or token bit errors, lost
tokens or frames, multiple tokens on the ring, continuously circulating priority tokens
and frames, or a lost monitor station.

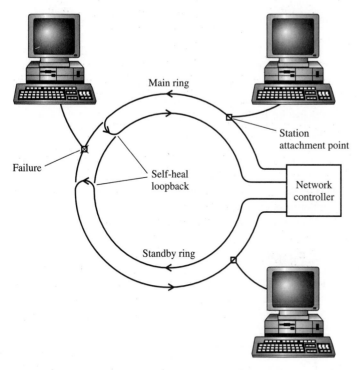

FIGURE 6.9
With the self-healing technique the main and the standby rings transmit in opposite directions.

To handle these situations, the monitor sets a timer whenever a token goes by. If the token does not reappear within this allotted time, the AM assumes it is lost and generates a new token. The AM station prevents unclaimed data frames from continuously circulating around the ring by setting a bit in the AC field of each frame. The AM station checks the status of this bit as a frame passes and removes and discards the frame if it has already gone by. It then inserts a new token onto the ring. If the AM station fails, a backup AM station takes over the monitoring function.

6.1.5   Token-Ring Performance Analysis

A major advantage of token rings over Ethernet is that because access is controlled, there are no collisions. Thus ring utilization rates near 100 percent are achievable. Let us look at a simple analysis of this. The literature gives a more detailed performance evaluation and comparison with other LAN access techniques.[11–13]

The *throughput* or *efficiency* η_{TR} of a token ring is defined as the fraction of time that the stations send out packets under a heavy load condition, that is, when all the stations have packets that are ready to transmit. Let T_m be the time a station is allowed to send messages. For the IEEE-802.5 Standard this is 10 ms. Let T_{token} be the token transmission time and take a to be the propagation time of a signal around the ring of N equally spaced stations. To evaluate the efficiency, we need to examine two separate cases, one where $a < T_m$ and the other where $a > T_m$.

First consider the timing diagram for the case $a < T_m$ shown in Fig. 6.10a. Here station 1 starts transmitting at time $t = 0$. Since $a < T_m$, the first bit sent out arrives back at the station before the last bit has been transmitted. Thus once the station has completed transmitting its last bit at time T_m, it can release a new token onto the ring. The new token takes a time T_{token} to transmit and a time a/N to arrive at the next station (under the assumption that the stations are equally spaced around the ring). Thus the total time T elapsed from the instant station 1 starts transmitting until the time station 2 can start sending its message is

$$T = T_m + T_{\text{token}} + \frac{a}{N} \approx T_m + \frac{a}{N} \tag{6.1}$$

The approximation on the right-hand side arises from the assumption that the transmission time of the token is much less than T_m since the token is much smaller than the average packet. If all N stations take turns during a time period NT to transmit for a

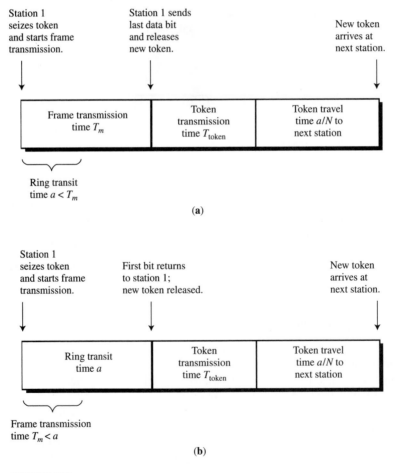

(a)

(b)

FIGURE 6.10
Timing diagram for the two cases $a < T_m$ and $a > T_m$.

duration T_m, then the total time spent transmitting messages is NT_m. From this we find that the efficiency is

$$\eta_{\text{TR}} = \frac{NT_m}{NT} = \frac{NT_m}{N(T_m + T_{\text{token}} + a/N)} \approx \frac{1}{1 + a/NT_m} \qquad (6.2)$$

The parameter a is the length of the ring divided by the signal propagation speed, which is 2.3×10^8 m/s in a coaxial cable. Thus for a 2300-m-long ring, $a = 0.01$ ms. With $T_m = 10$ ms and $N = 100$, the efficiency then is

$$\eta_{\text{TR}} = \frac{1}{1 + a/NT_m} = \frac{1}{1.00001} \approx 100\% \qquad (6.3)$$

This shows that the efficiency of the token ring is extremely close to 100 percent, which is quite typical.

When $a > T_m$, the station has to wait a time a after the start of transmission before sending out a token, as indicated by the timing diagram in Fig. 6.10b. Again after station 1 releases a token, the token takes a time T_{token} to transmit and a time a/N to arrive at the next station. Now the total time elapsed from the instant station 1 starts transmitting until the time station 2 can start sending its message is

$$T = a + T_{\text{token}} + \frac{a}{N} \approx a \left(1 + \frac{1}{N}\right) \qquad (6.4)$$

so that the efficiency becomes

$$\eta_{TR} = \frac{T_m}{T} \approx \frac{T_m/a}{\left(1 + \dfrac{1}{N}\right)} \qquad (6.5)$$

6.2 DEDICATED TOKEN RING

The *dedicated token ring* (DTR) is based on CTR specifications and was developed for high-speed, point-to-point data transfer. The IEEE has ratified it as the 802.5r Standard.[14] The DTR defines signaling protocols and attachment policies that provide a dedicated 16-Mbps bandwidth for each station, which greatly increases the transmission capacity of the attached stations.

Figure 6.11 shows a basic DTR network. The three main entities in the network are the DTR stations, the concentrator ports (C-ports), and the concentrator. Whereas CTR is based on a *shared media architecture,* DTR uses a *dedicated media architecture.* The C-port supplies an interface to the rest of the network once the station and the C-port complete a *join process.* The join process is done via an access protocol that does not require the use of a token to transmit. This DTR access protocol is called the *transmit intermediate* (TXI) access protocol. This environment also supports the classic token-ring access protocol, which is known as the *token-passing* (TKP) access protocol.

The DTR station has all the capabilities of a CTR station with the addition of the MAC Protocol that enables it to run in the TXI mode. In this mode of operation the station does not need a token to transmit data. When a message is ready to be sent out, the station simply transmits the data. The concept of the C-port is a new MAC Protocol entity introduced in the DTR Standard. Its function is to control network access of the

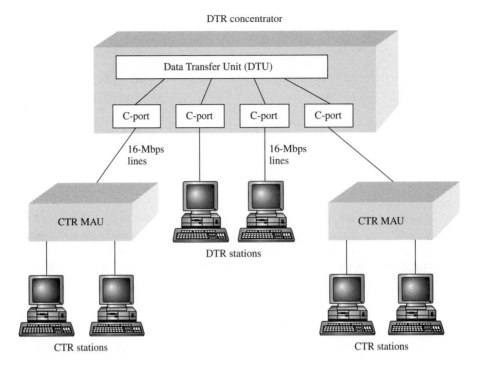

FIGURE 6.11
Fundamental concept of a dedicated token ring (DTR) architecture.

attached station. The C-port can operate in either a C-port mode or a station emulation mode. In the first case the C-port is directly attached to a station. In the second case the C-port is directly attached to a classic token-ring MAU.

The *concentrator* is a collection of C-ports that are interconnected by means of a *data transfer unit* (DTU). As Fig. 6.11 shows, DTR stations attach to the C-ports using the TXI access protocol. This offers 16-Mbps connectivity in both directions between a DTR station and the DTR concentrator. Communication between the stations takes place by means of the DTU, which can be a high-speed switching backplane. In addition, a classic token-ring concentrator (i.e., an MAU) can be connected to a C-port to provide 16-Mbps network access to a cluster of CTR stations.

6.3 HIGH-SPEED TOKEN RINGS

Beyond the DTR architecture there are several high-speed token-ring (HSTR) configurations. These include the 100-Mbps DTR described in the IEEE-802.5t Standard[15] and the Gigabit Token-Ring Operation specified in the IEEE-802.5v Standard.[16] These standards maintain the frame-based, native token-ring environment. This enables organizations to implement higher speeds seamlessly on the network backbone and at server connections. Another advantage to using the same basic Token-Ring Protocol for higher-speed implementations is that it does not place additional learning or training requirements on the management information systems (MIS) organization. In addition, migrating to higher-speed token rings does not require any additional cabling upgrades to the network since HSTR will run on standard Cat-5 UTP cable, STP Type-1 cable, and standard multimode optical fiber cables.

The High-Speed Token-Ring Alliance (HSTRA) provided a major impetus for developing these standards.[17] This organization was founded in 1997 by leading token-ring vendors. Its mission was to develop rapidly the technologies, standards, and products that are necessary to deliver 100-Mbps and 1-Gbps token-ring services. However, by early 2000 vendor support of these technologies declined dramatically in favor of other LAN technologies, in particular, Gigabit Ethernet.

6.4   FDDI AND CDDI

The *fiber distributed data interface* (FDDI) is an optical fiber-based 100-Mbps Token-Ring LAN Protocol that is similar to the IEEE-802.5 Standard.[18–20] It is implemented as dual self-healing counter-rotating rings, as shown in Fig. 6.12. Starting in 1985 the standards organization ANSI (ASC X3T9.5) and the ITU-T (ITU-T X.3) developed the specifications for this protocol. FDDI can connect up to 500 nodes over a maximum length of 200 km of optical fiber. The distance between nodes cannot be more than a few kilometers. FDDI is now an older technology and is mainly used for high-speed backbones. In 1994 a related copper-based specification called *copper distributed data interface* (CDDI) was created to provide 100-Mbps service over Cat-5 UTP wires.[18] CDDI distances are limited to 100 m from the wiring closet to the network node.

Figure 6.13 shows the four FDDI standards—MAC, PHY, PMD, and SMT—and their functions along with the IEEE-802.2 LLC Standard.

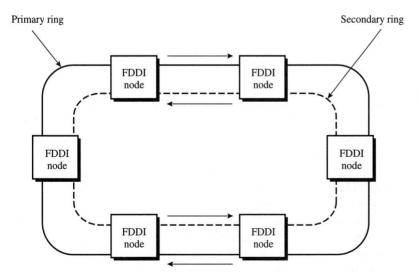

FIGURE 6.12
FDDI is implemented as dual self-healing counter-rotating rings.

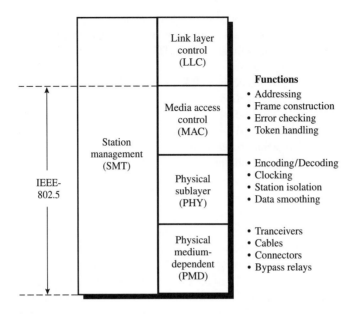

FIGURE 6.13
The four FDDI standards—MAC, PHY, PMD, and SMT—and their functions along with the IEEE-802.2 LLC Standard.

6.4.1 FDDI MAC Layer

The medium access control (MAC) layer defines rules for frame formats, medium access, addressing, error checking, and token management. As shown in Fig. 6.14, the data and token frame formats are similar to those of the IEEE 802.5 but with some differences. For example, note that there is no access control field. First each data or token frame is preceded by sixteen 4-bit idle symbols (1111), which forms a 64-bit (8-byte) *preamble*. This is used to initiate clock synchronization in the receiver. The eight fields of the FDDI data frame are as follows:

1. *Start delimiter (SD).* The 1-byte SD field indicates the start of a data frame. It uses the same J and K nondata symbols as in the token ring.
2. *Frame control (FC).* The 1-byte FC field has the format CLFFZZZZ. Here C indicates whether the frame arises from synchronous or asynchronous traffic (see Sec. 6.4.2), L identifies the address length (16 or 48 bits), and FF identifies whether this is an LLC, MAC control, or reserved frame. If it is a control frame, then the four ZZZZ bits indicate the type of control.
3. *Destination address (DA).* The 2- or 6-byte DA field contains the address of the station or stations for which the frame is intended. It could be a unique address, a multicast address to a group of stations, or a broadcast address to all the stations. The FDDI ring can contain a mixture of 16- and 48-bit addresses.
4. *Source address (SA).* Similarly, the SA is a 2- or 6-byte field that contains the address of the sending station.

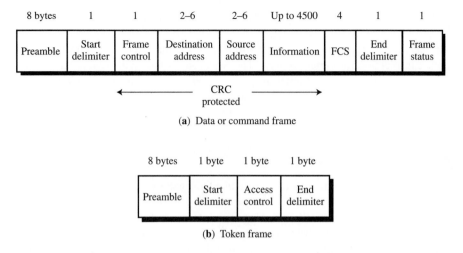

FIGURE 6.14
The data and token frame formats of FDDI are similar to those of the IEEE-802.5 Standard.

5. *Data field.* The data field contains the protocol data unit (PDU) and can be up to 4500 bytes long.
6. *Frame check sequence (FCS).* The 4-byte FCS field contains the same 32-bit cyclic redundancy check (CRC) as in the Token-Ring Standard. It is based on the FC, SA, DA, and information fields.
7. *End delimiter (ED).* Similar to the SD field, the 1-byte end delimiter (ED) field contains a pair of noncode symbols T to distinguish it from data. Its function is to indicate the end of the data or control information.
8. *Frame status (FS).* The FDDI frame status (FS) field is similar to that used in the Token-Ring Protocol.

The FDDI MAC Protocol is basically the same as that of the IEEE-802.5 Token-Ring Protocol, except for the following two fundamental differences:

- When an FDDI station has data to transmit, it seizes the token by not repeating it as soon as the token frame is recognized. After it completely receives the captured token, the station starts sending out one or more data frames within its allotted access period.
- As so on as an FDDI station completes transmitting its data frames, it releases a new token, even if the station has not started to receive the frames it sent out.

6.4.2 FDDI Access Method

Access is limited by time in an FDDI network. This allows a station to send out as many frames as it can within an allotted access period. The one condition with this is that real-time information must be sent first. Thus FDDI distinguishes between synchronous and asynchronous data frames. A *synchronous* frame contains real-time information, such as audio or video signals, which need to be transmitted within a short time period. An *asynchronous* frame contains non-real-time information, such as data traffic, which usually can tolerate large variable delays. The synchronous and asynchronous data frames are known as S-frames and A-frames, respectively. When a station seizes a token, it must send its S-frames first. If there is any allotted time remaining after all the S-frames are transmitted, it can transmit any A-frames that are waiting to be sent out.

6.4.3   FDDI Physical Layer

As shown in Fig. 6.13, the physical layer in FDDI has two sublayers. The physical (PHY) sublayer deals with issues such as the encoding and decoding scheme, clock synchronization, isolation of a malfunctioning station (see Sec. 6.4.4), and data smoothing, which prevents frames from being lost because of shortened preambles. The encoding scheme is the 4B5B method described in Sec. 5.3.3. For control words FDDI uses 8 of the 16 symbols that are not designated for encoding data.

The physical medium-dependent (PMD) sublayer specifies the optical fiber transmission medium, the optical transmitters and receivers, the optical connectors, and the optical bypass switches used for network reconfiguration. Although various types of fiber can be used, the basic specification is for a graded-index fiber with a 62.5-μm core diameter and an attenuation of at most 2.5 dB/km. This fiber can be up to 2 km in length. For longer connections a single-mode fiber with an 8-μm core diameter is specified. The transmitters are light-emitting diodes operating at 1300 nm and the receivers use *pin* photodiodes. FDDI also can operate over either Type-1 STP or Cat-5 UTP wire cables that are up to 100 m long. The bit error rate (BER) over any link must not exceed 4×10^{-11}.

6.4.4   Station Management

The *station management* (SMT) protocol provides the necessary services at the station level to monitor and control an FDDI station. The three major components of SMT are *connection management* (CMT), *ring management* (RMT), and SMT *frame services.* CMT performs physical layer insertion and removal of stations. Its functions include identifying and isolating faulty components, testing the quality of a link before establishing a connection, and monitoring error rates.

The function of the RMT portion of SMT is to ensure proper operation of the ring. In particular, it reconfigures the network to circumvent station failures or breaks in the ring. Since FDDI is based on dual counter-rotating rings, it uses the same self-healing techniques for fault isolation as described in Sec. 6.1.3 for token rings.

The SMT frame services deal with frame classes and types. The frame class identifies the function that the frame performs, such as determining the upstream and downstream neighbors of a station, exchanging information with other stations on the characteristics and configuration of a station, and managing an FDDI station. The frame type designates whether the frame is an announcement, a request, or a response to a request.

6.4.5 CDDI or TP-PMD

The *copper distributed data interface* (CDDI) is the implementation of FDDI protocols over twisted-pair copper wire. The ANSI X3T9.5 Committee has defined the specifications for CDDI, which officially is called the *Twisted-Pair Physical Medium-Dependent* (TP-PMD) Standard.[21] Similar to FDDI, TP-PMD provides data rates of 100 Mbps over distances of up to 100 m from the desktop to the MAU. Likewise, it is configured as a dual-ring architecture to provide redundancy for fault isolation. The ANSI Standard defines two types of twisted-pair cable for TP-PMD. These are a 150-Ω (ohm) STP cable, which adheres to EIA/TIA 568 (IBM Type-1) specifications, and the eight-pair Cat-5 UTP cable (EIA/TIA 568B specifications).

6.5 SUMMARY

The first token-ring product appeared in 1985 and operated at 4 Mbps. Later it was upgraded to 16 Mbps and is known as the *classical token ring* (CTR). Token rings resolve time-delay uncertainty by requiring that the attached stations take turns sending messages. The network allows only one device to transmit at a time. Depending on the particular token-passing method used, each station either transmits only one frame during its turn or sends as many frames as it can during an allotted access period.

The *dedicated token ring* (DTR) is based on CTR specifications and was developed for high-speed, point-to-point data transfer. The IEEE ratified it as the 802.5r Standard. The DTR defines signaling protocols and attachment policies that provide a dedicated 16-Mbps bandwidth for each station, which greatly increases the transmission capacity of the attached stations.

The *Fiber Distributed Data Interface* (FDDI) is an optical fiber-based 100-Mbps Token-Ring LAN Protocol, which is implemented as dual self-healing counter-rotating rings. FDDI can connect up to 500 nodes over a maximum length of 200 km of optical fiber. FDDI is now an older technology and is mainly used for high-speed backbones.

In the late 1990s a growing demand for greater backbone bandwidth to handle streaming video and other bandwidth-intensive applications led to concepts for 100- and 1000-Mbps token rings. However, support for this technology has virtually disappeared since it was surpassed by other more widely used technologies, such as Ethernet.

PROBLEMS

6.1. Consider a token-passing ring network that has N stations. On the same graph, make plots of the efficiency η_{TR} as a function of the parameter a/T_m for values of $N = 1$, 10, and 100. Let a/T_m range from 0.01 to 100.

6.2. Consider a token-passing ring network that has N stations. On the same graph, plot the efficiency η_{TR} as a function of the number of stations N for values of the parameter $a/T_m = 0.1$ and 1.0. Let N range from 1 to 25.

6.3. A token ring transmits at a rate of 16 Mbps. If the propagation speed on the medium is 2.0×10^8 m/s, to how many meters of cable is a 1-bit delay at a token-ring interface equivalent?

6.4. Assume we have a 2-km-long token ring with 50 stations operating at a 16-Mbps transmission rate. If the propagation delay is 5 μs/km, the header length is 24 bits, the delay per station is 1 bit, and the packets have a mean length of 1000 bits, what is the round-trip delay in the ring?

6.5. Using resources found on the Web, list some capabilities of available token-ring network interface cards. Consider parameters such as peak throughput, DTR capability, automatic ring speed detection, and Windows software diagnostic abilities.

REFERENCES

1. J. T. Carlo, R. D. Love, M. S. Siegel, and K. T. Wilson, *Understanding Token Ring Protocols and Standards,* Artech House, Boston, 1998.
2. H. J. Keller, H. Meyr, and H. R. Mueller, "Transmission design criteria for a synchronous token ring," *IEEE J. Select. Areas Commun.,* vol. SAC-1, pp. 721–733, Nov. 1983.
3. W. Bux, F. H. Closs, K. Kuemmerle, H. J. Keller, and H. R. Mueller, "Architecture and design of a reliable token-ring network," *IEEE J. Select. Areas Commun.,* vol. SAC-1, pp. 756–765, Nov. 1983.
4. N. C. Strole, "A local communications network based on interconnected token-access rings: A tutorial," *IBM J. Res. Develop.,* vol. 27, pp. 481–496, Sept. 1983.
5. IEEE Standard 802.5-1998, "Token ring access method," Revision 3 of the base standard, 1998.
6. ISO/IEC 8802-5:1998, "Token ring access method and physical layer specifications," 1998.
7. C. Smythe, "ISO 8802-5 token ring local-area networks," *Electronics and Commun. Engr. J.,* vol. 11, pp. 195–207, Aug. 1999.
8. R. J. Bates and D. W. Gregory, *Voice and Data Communications Handbook,* McGraw-Hill, New York, 3rd ed., 2000, Chap. 21.
9. As an example, the website for Madge Networks (http://www.madge.com) describes token-ring switching products.
10. B. Kumar, *Broadband Communications,* McGraw-Hill, New York, 2nd ed., 1998, Chap. 3.
11. W. Bux, "Local area subnetworks: A performance comparison," *IEEE Trans. Commun.,* vol. COM-29, pp. 1465–1473, Oct. 1981.
12. B. W. Stuck, "Calculating the maximum mean data rate in local area networks," *Computer,* vol. 16, pp. 72–76, May 1983.
13. G. Higginbottom, *Performance Evaluation of Communication Networks,* Artech House, Boston. 1998.
14. IEEE Standard 802.5r, "Dedicated Token Ring," 1998.
15. IEEE Standard 802.5t, "100-Mbps Dedicated Token Ring," 2000.
16. IEEE Standard 802.5v, "Gigabit Token Ring Operation," 2000.
17. High-Speed Token Ring Association (HSTRA) (http://www.hstra.com). This organization is involved with developing token-ring technology.
18. R. Jain, *FDDI Handbook: High-Speed Networking with Fiber and Other Media,* Addison-Wesley, Reading, MA, 1994.
19. R. J. Bates and D. W. Gregory, *Voice and Data Communications Handbook,* McGraw-Hill, New York, 3rd ed., 2000, Chap. 23.
20. J. Knapp, *Nortel Networks: The Complete Reference,* Osborne/McGraw-Hill, Berkeley, CA, 2000.
21. American National Standards Institute, Standard ANSI X3.263-1995, "Fiber Distributed Data Interface (FDDI)—Token Ring Twisted-Pair Physical Layer Medium Dependent (TP-PMD)," 1995.

CHAPTER

7

ATM LANS

Asynchronous transfer mode (ATM) is a high-performance switching and multiplexing technology that utilizes fixed-length packets to carry different types of traffic. A key attraction of ATM is that it enables carriers to offer multiple classes of service over wide area networks (WANs), to connect devices that operate at different speeds, and to mix a variety of traffic types having different transmission requirements, such as voice, video, and data traffic. In addition, ATM can serve as a backbone for high-speed LANs and can be used to interconnect widely separated high-capacity LANs.

In this chapter we first present some basics on ATM in Sec. 7.1. Next, in Secs. 7.2 through 7.4, respectively, we examine more details on the ATM cell structure, ATM service categories, and the ATM adaptation layer (AAL), which provides support for higher layer services. In Sec. 7.5 we look at how ATM can be used within a LAN (local area network) environment. Finally Sec. 7.6 addresses the concept of LAN emulation, which enables an ATM switch to behave like a LAN switch in order to connect remote Ethernet or token-ring LANs together over an ATM backbone.

7.1 ATM FUNDAMENTALS

Here we present highlights of the basic concepts of ATM in order to see how this technology applies in LANs. The literature contains more details on these topics and others, such as ATM-switching schemes and the ATM-multiplexing process.[1-4] In addition, the ATM Forum and the ITU-T have published a large number of specifications on ATM.[5-7]

7.1.1 Use of ATM Cells

The ATM scheme formats all information into fixed-length packets (called *cells*), which consist of 48 bytes of payload and 5 bytes of overhead, as Fig. 7.1 illustrates. The

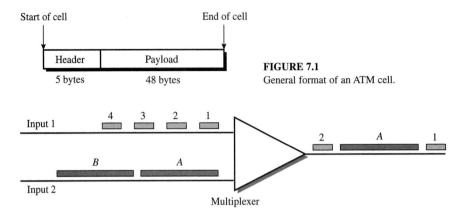

FIGURE 7.1
General format of an ATM cell.

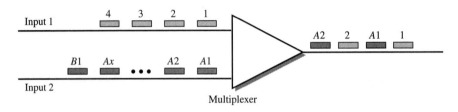

FIGURE 7.2
Multiplexing packets of different sizes can cause delay in small packets.

FIGURE 7.3
Multiplexing of ATM cells mitigates delays caused by long packets.

function of the header is to enable efficient high-speed switching. It contains payload-type information, virtual circuit identifiers, and header error check. Section 7.2 gives the details on the cell structure.

The advantage of using a fixed cell size is that it ensures that time-sensitive information, such as voice or video services, arrives at the destination in a timely fashion. Since voice and video packets normally are small compared to data packets, mixing the two types of traffic using ordinary multiplexing techniques can cause unacceptable delays in the time-sensitive traffic. Figure 7.2 gives an example of this for a stream of short voice packets (1, 2, 3, etc.) that are multiplexed with a string of long data packets (A, B, etc.). If the multiplexing occurs as shown, then there is a long delay between voice packets 1 and 2, for example.

When using ATM, both the voice and the data packets are divided into equal-length cells, as illustrated in Fig. 7.3. For simplicity of illustration we assume the voice packets are already of the appropriate ATM cell length and divide the data packets into x ATM cells. Now the cells from the voice and data streams are interleaved so that neither stream suffers a long delay. Furthermore since ATM uses high-speed transmission links, the small cells arrive at their respective destinations in the same continuous stream as they arrived at the multiplexer despite having been interleaved with cells from other traffic streams. This means that an ATM network can carry both time-sensitive traffic, such as real-time video, and nontime critical data traffic without any of the users being aware of the underlying segmentation and reassembly processes.

7.1.2 ATM Architecture

A cell-switched network, as shown in Fig. 7.4, describes the ATM architecture. The user access devices are called the *endpoints.* These endpoints are connected through a *user-to-network interface* (UNI) to the ATM switches residing inside of the network. A connection between switches is done through a *network-to-network interface* (NNI). To simplify the discussion of devices attached to a network, the depiction of an *ATM cloud,* which includes all the switching functions and transmission lines, often is used, as illustrated in Fig. 7.4.

An ATM network is a *virtual circuit network.* Here a connection between endpoints is made by means of a transmission path (TP), a virtual path (VP), and a virtual circuit (VC). A *transmission path* is the physical connection between an endpoint and a switch or between two switches. This could be a copper wire, an optical fiber, a satellite link, or other transmission media. As Fig. 7.5 shows, a TP is divided into several virtual paths. The function of a *virtual path* is to provide one or more connections between two switches. All cells belonging to a particular VP are routed the same way through an ATM network. This results in faster recovery in case of major equipment or line failures.

A *virtual circuit* is the basic unit that carries a single stream of cells from user to user. That is, all cells that belong to a single message follow the same VC and remain in their original order until they reach their destination. A collection of virtual circuits can be bundled together into a virtual path. For example, two ATM switches may have many

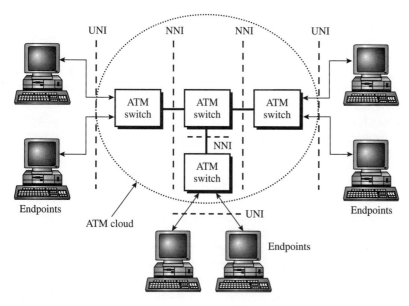

FIGURE 7.4
General architecture of an ATM network.

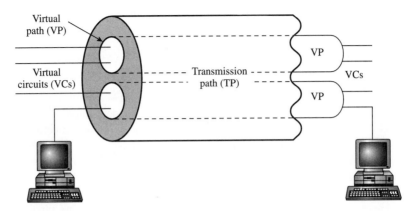

FIGURE 7.5
Relationships among transmission path (TP), virtual path (VP), and virtual circuit (VC).

different VC connections belonging to different users between them. When these are bundled into a VP, the VP can be handled as a single entity between two ATM switches.

To route information-bearing cells from one point to another in a virtual circuit network, the virtual connections need to be identified. For this ATM uses a two-level hierarchy consisting of a *virtual path identifier* (VPI) and a *virtual circuit identifier* (VCI). In both UNI and NNI headers the VCI is a 16-bit (2-byte) unit that identifies a single VC on a particular VP. In a UNI the VPI is an 8-bit unit, whereas in an NNI it is 12 bits long. The same VPI applies to all the VCs that are logically bundled into one VP. Switching at a VP connecting point is done based on the VPI; that is, the VCI is ignored at this point.

Connection setup between two ATM endpoints is done via either a *permanent virtual circuit* (PVC) or a *switched virtual circuit* (SVC). In a PVC connection the VPIs and VCIs are defined for the desired permanent connections and their values are entered into routing tables at each switch. In a SVC connection the network establishes a new VC each time an endpoint wants to connect to another endpoint. ATM does this with the assistance of network layer addresses and the services of another protocol such as IP. The signaling level of the assisting protocol makes a connection request using the network layer address of the two endpoints. The actual process depends on the type of network layer protocol that is used.

7.1.3 ATM Layers

The ATM Standard defines the three layers shown in Fig. 7.6. These layers are the physical (PHY) layer, the ATM layer where the cell structuring occurs, and the ATM adaptation layer (AAL), which provides support for higher layer services. These correspond to the two lower layers of the OSI (Open System Interconnection) model. Sections 7.2 and 7.4 give more information on the ATM and AAL layers, respectively.

The physical layer defines the transmission medium, the encoding required by a particular transmission link (e.g., SONET or SDH), the clocking of bit transmission over

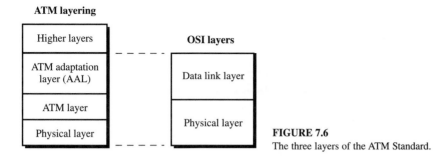

ATM layering

| Higher layers |
| ATM adaptation layer (AAL) |
| ATM layer |
| Physical layer |

OSI layers

| Data link layer |
| Physical layer |

FIGURE 7.6
The three layers of the ATM Standard.

the physical medium, and any electrical-to-optical transforming required to interface the ATM cell stream to the physical medium. In addition, it defines the mechanism for converting between the bit stream that is clocked to the physical medium and the flow of cells to and from the ATM layer. Another important physical layer function is to generate the header error check (HEC) when transmitting cells and to use it in order to detect and correct errors when receiving cells.

The ATM layer shown in Fig. 7.6 provides functions such as the following:

- Cell construction at the sender location (Sec. 7.2 shows the construction of the ATM cell header and describes the meaning of each field)
- Cell reception and header validation at the receiver end
- Cell relaying, forwarding, and copying using the VPI and VCI designators
- Support for multiple quality-of-service classes for various application requirements on cell delay and cell loss performance
- Generic flow control to regulate the cell flow at the local UNI
- Cell loss priority processing for identifying high-priority cells
- Connection assignment and removal

The function of the AAL is to allow various information transfer protocols that are not based on ATM, such as IP packets, to interface to ATM facilities. The ATM protocols at this layer accept information streams from upper layers and map them into ATM cells. This process is known as *segmentation*. The information streams can be of any type, including voice, data packets, and video, and they can arrive at variable or fixed rates. The reverse process takes place at the receiver; that is, the segments are reassembled into their original formats and are passed to the upper layer. The AAL services also are responsible for handling issues such as transmission errors, lost cells, flow control, and timing control.

7.2 ATM CELL STRUCTURE

ATM uses two different formats for the cell header, depending on whether the cell is used for a UNI or a NNI. Figure 7.7 shows the header format for a UNI cell. The NNI cell has almost the same format, except that the four GFC bits become VPI bits. Thus for the NNI header the VPI field is 12 bits long. The standard way of depicting the ATM

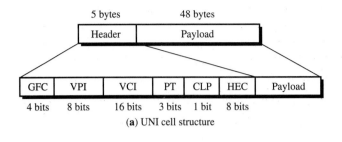

(a) UNI cell structure

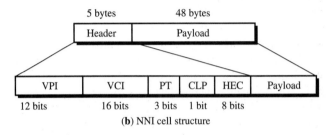

(b) NNI cell structure

FIGURE 7.7
Structure of the ATM cell header.

cell is on a byte-by-byte basis, as Fig. 7.7 illustrates. The functions of the various fields are as follows:

- *Generic flow control (GFC).* The 4-bit GFC field in a UNI cell allows a multiplexer to control the cell flow from an ATM terminal, that is, at the local network-user interface (UNI). Its basic function is to alleviate short-term overload conditions in the network. This flow control is not necessary at the NNI level, so the 4 GFC bits become VPI bits.
- *Virtual path identifier (VPI).* The VPI is an 8-bit field in a UNI cell and a 12-bit field in a NNI cell. The longer VPI field in a NNI cell allows more virtual paths to be defined at the interface between ATM switches.
- *Virtual channel identifier (VCI).* The VCI field for both UNI and NNI cells is 16 bits long. The VCI field is used for routing cells between end users.
- *Payload type (PT).* The 3-bit PT field indicates whether the cell contains user data, signaling data, or maintenance information.
- *Cell loss priority (CLP).* The 1-bit CLP field indicates the relative priority of the cell. This information is used for congestion control. When links become congested, low-priority cells may be discarded to maintain the quality of service expected from higher-priority cells. The value of the CLP bit notifies an ATM switch what cells may be dropped and which ones should be retained as long as there are low-priority cells. A CLP value of 0 designates a cell of relatively high priority, which generally should not be discarded. A value of 1 for the CLP bit indicates that the cell could be discarded within the network. Examples of low-priority cells are those generated when a user transmits at a higher data rate than allowed, that is, at a rate greater than that agreed upon between the user and the network.

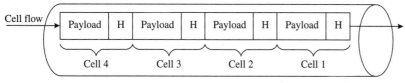

FIGURE 7.8
Flow of header and payload bits in a stream of ATM cells.

- *Header error check (HEC).* The 8-bit HEC field is calculated based on the other 4 bytes in the header. It employs a *cyclic redundancy check* (CRC) code of the form $x^8 + x^2 + x + 1$. Since in an ATM cell this code needs to examine only 32 bits, compared to 8 bits for the code itself, the relatively short input and the redundancy in the code allow it to detect errors as well as to correct certain error patterns. These include single-bit errors and a large class of multiple-bit errors.

All payload data is switched and multiplexed in an ATM network based on the information in these header fields. Figure 7.8 shows how a stream of UNI ATM cells flows along a transmission path.

7.3 ATM SERVICE CATEGORIES

A key characteristic of ATM is that it can transfer a diverse set of traffic types simultaneously, including both real-time and non-real-time traffic. *Real-time services* need to deliver information in a timely fashion and as a continuous, smooth flow. Examples of this are telephone conversations, videoconferencing, television, and distance learning. Any delay greater than a few tenths of a second or any loss-induced gaps in the information flow will cause a significant degradation in the quality of service. *Non-real-time services* are used for applications that do not have tight constraints on delay or delay variations. Examples of this are data transfers, airline reservations, and banking or investment transactions.

7.3.1 Service Classes

To enable the simultaneous transfer of diverse traffic types, the ATM Standard defines five classes or categories of service. Table 7.1 lists the service classes, the associated *quality-of-service* (QoS) parameters, and example applications. The real-time services include *constant bit rate* (CBR) and *real-time variable bit rate* (rt-VBR) services. Non-real-time services include *non-real-time variable bit rate* (nrt-VBR), *available bit rate* (ABR), and *unspecified bit rate* (UBR).

7.3.2 Quality-of-Service Parameters

The QoS defines a set of attributes that are associated with the performance of a network connection. Some of these attributes are user-oriented, whereas others are related to the network.

TABLE 7.1
Descriptions of the five ATM classes of service

Service class	Quality-of-service parameter	Example applications
Constant bit rate (CBR)	In CBR the cell rate is constant with time to satisfy those applications that are sensitive to cell-delay variations.	Telephone traffic, television, video-on-demand, and videoconferencing.
Variable bit rate—non-real-time (VBR-nrt)	This service class allows users to send traffic at a rate that may vary with time; that is, the traffic rate depends on the availability of user information. Statistical multiplexing may be provided to make optimum use of network resources.	Banking or investment transactions, airline reservations or process monitoring.
Variable bit rate—real-time (VBR-rt)	This service class is similar to VBR-nrt but is intended for applications that are sensitive to cell-delay variations.	Voice with speech activity detection and interactive compressed video.
Available bit rate (ABR)	This class provides rate-based flow control. Depending on congestion in the network, the source is required to control its rate. Users may declare a minimum cell rate, which is guaranteed by the network.	File transfers and e-mail.
Unspecified bit rate (UBR)	Cells are forwarded on a first-in first-out (FIFO) basis using the capacity not consumed by other services. Both delays and variable losses of cells are possible.	Transfer, messaging, distribution, or retrieval of text, data, or images.

The *user-oriented attributes* define the rate at which a user desires to send data. These rates are negotiated between a user and a network at the time of connection establishment. They include the following basic parameters:

- *Peak cell rate (PCR).* The PCR defines the maximum rate at which a user will transmit.
- *Sustained cell rate (SCR).* The SCR is the average cell rate measured over a long time period. The actual cell rate may be higher or lower than this value, and sometimes can reach the PCR.

The *network-related attributes* define the characteristics of the network. The key parameters include the following:

- *Cell loss ratio (CLR).* The CLR is the percentage of cells that are not delivered to their destination. These cells could be lost or delivered so late that they are considered lost. The loss in the network could be due to congestion or buffer overflow.

- *Cell error rate (CER).* The CER designates the fraction of cells that are delivered with errors.
- *Cell transfer delay (CTD).* The CTD is the delay experienced by a cell between the time it entered the network at the source and the time it exited at the destination. It includes propagation delays, queuing delays at various intermediate switches, and service times at queuing points.
- *Cell delay variation (CDV).* The CDV parameter measures the difference between the maximum and minimum CTD.

7.4 ATM ADAPTATION LAYER (AAL)

ATM defines four categories of protocols for the AAL to support the service categories that Table 7.1 lists.[8] These are types AAL 1, AAL 2, AAL 3/4, and AAL 5. Types 3 and 4 were originally separate but later were combined since their functions were very similar. As shown in Sec. 7.6, AAL 5 is the most important for LAN applications.

Each AAL layer is divided into a *convergence sublayer* (CS) and the *segmentation and reassembly* (SAR) sublayer. The basic function of the CS is to support the specific service applications that use a particular AAL type. The function of the SAR sublayer is to convert the information received from the CS into ATM cells for transmission and to reassemble received cells into the original format at the destination.

7.4.1 AAL 1

AAL 1 specifies how CBR applications, such as voice and video, transfer information over an ATM network.[9] In particular, it describes details of *circuit emulation,* which refers to the connection of existing digital telephone services (e.g., DS-1, E-1, or DS-3) over an ATM network. Other CBR services supported by AAL 1 include ISDN and voice-over-ATM.

Figure 7.9 shows the cell structure of an AAL-1 data unit at the SAR level. First the CS divides the information bit stream from higher layers into 47-byte segments and passes them to the SAR sublayer below it. The SAR sublayer adds a 1-byte header to

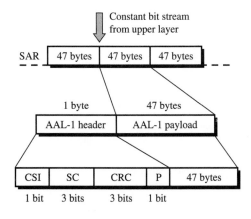

FIGURE 7.9
Cell structure of an AAL-1 data unit at the SAR (segmentation and reassembly) level.

form the 48-byte payload of an ATM cell. The SAR header contains the following four fields:

- *Convergence sublayer identifier (CSI).* This 1-bit field is reserved for signaling purposes.
- *Sequence count (SC).* This 3-bit field is used for ordering and identifying the cells for end-to-end error control and flow control.
- *Cyclic redundancy check (CRC).* This 3-bit field uses the 4-bit divisor $x^3 + x + 1$ to perform a cyclic redundancy check on the first 4 bits of the header. The use of 3 bits for the CRC process here is that it also allows for correction of single-bit errors. This is important for improving the QoS for the real-time applications supported by AAL 1 since in real-time information exchanges it is not possible to retransmit cells having errors.
- *Parity (P).* This 1-bit field is a standard parity check over the first 7 bits in the header.

7.4.2 AAL 2

AAL 2 supports real-time variable-bit-rate (rt-VBR) applications.[10] For example, the ATM loop-emulation service specifies the use of ATM virtual circuits with AAL 2 to transport narrowband information and signaling over a broadband subscriber line connection.[11] The services include voice, voice-band data, fax traffic, ISDN B-channels and D-channels. The virtual circuits used may be PVCs, SPVCs, or SVCs.

Figure 7.10 shows the cell structure of an AAL-2 data unit at the SAR level. The SAR sublayer accepts a 45-byte payload from the CS and adds a 1-byte header and a 2-byte trailer to form the 48-byte payload of an ATM cell. The SAR header contains the following five fields:

- *Convergence sublayer identifier (CSI).* This 1-bit field is reserved for signaling purposes.
- *Sequence count (SC).* This 3-bit field is used for ordering and identifying the cells for end-to-end error control and flow control.

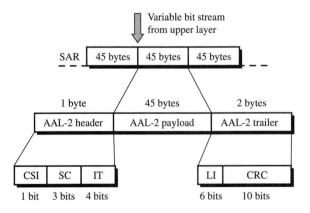

FIGURE 7.10
Cell structure of an AAL-2 data unit at the SAR level.

- *Information type (IT).* The 4 IT bits identify whether the data segment falls at the beginning, middle, or end of the message.
- *Length indicator (LI).* When the IT bits indicate the end of the message, the first 6 bits of the trailer indicate how much of the final cell is data and how much is padding. That is, since generally the original bit stream is not divisible by 45, padding bits are added to the last segment to complete a 48-byte ATM cell. The LI field thus indicates where those bits are.
- *CRC.* The final 10 bits of the trailer are a CRC for the entire data unit. These bits also can be used to correct single-bit errors in the SAR data unit, including the header, payload, and LI-field bits.

7.4.3 AAL 3/4

AAL 3/4 supports connectionless VBR data services, such as connectionless broadband data services (CBDS), that can tolerate varying delay requirements.[12] Figure 7.11 shows the process for forming ATM cells using AAL 3/4. First the CS accepts a data packet, which can be up to 65,535 ($2^{16} - 1$) bytes long, from an upper-layer service. The CS then adds a header, a trailer, and padding bits. The header and trailer are for reassembly purposes at the destination to indicate the beginning and end of the entire message. The padding bits are used to form a complete 44-byte final segment that will be passed to the SAR sublayer.

The SAR sublayer accepts 44-byte payload segments from the CS and adds a 2-byte header and a 2-byte trailer to form the 48-byte payload of an ATM cell. The SAR header and trailer contain the following six fields:

- *Segment type (ST).* The 2 ST bits identify whether the data segment falls at the beginning (ST = 10), middle (ST = 00), or end (ST = 01) of the message, or whether it is a single-segment message (ST = 11).
- *Convergence sublayer identifier (CSI).* This 1-bit field is reserved for signaling purposes.
- *Sequence count (SC).* This 3-bit field is used for ordering and identifying the cells for end-to-end error control and flow control.
- *Multiplexing identification (MID).* The 10-bit MID field (giving 1024 possible values) allows for the multiplexing of many cells coming from different data flows on the same virtual connection.
- *Length indicator (LI).* When the ST bits indicate the end of the message or when ST = 11, the 6 LI bits indicate how much of the final cell (or single cell) is data and how much is padding.
- *CRC.* The final 10 bits of the trailer are a CRC for the entire SAR data unit, including the header, payload, and LI-field bits.

7.4.4 AAL 5

AAL 5 is the most important AAL Protocol for LAN applications.[13] This protocol was established for connection-oriented services to reduce protocol-processing overhead, to reduce transmission overhead, and to simplify adaptation to other transport protocols.

AAL 5 dispenses with most connection-management issues, such as sequencing and integrity checking inherent in AAL 3/4, by shifting these functions to the end users of the ATM network. Thus most fields used in the SAR and CS PDUs of other AAL types are not needed for AAL 5. As shown in Fig. 7.12, AAL 5 only adds a short (8-byte)

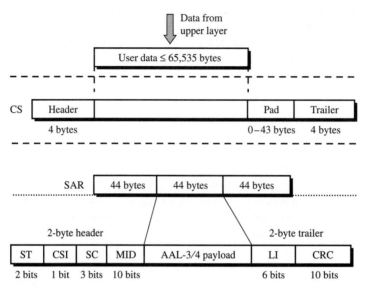

FIGURE 7.11
Process for forming ATM cells using AAL 3/4.

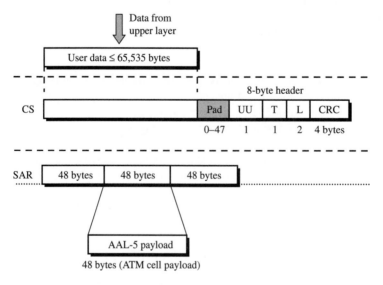

FIGURE 7.12
Cell structure of an AAL-5 data unit.

trailer to the higher layer PDU. The CS-PDU can range from 1 to 65,535 bytes in length. The SAR sublayer then divides this CS-PDU into 48-byte ATM cell-payload segments, which are passed to the ATM layer.

The CS trailer contains 0 to 47 padding bytes to form a complete 48-byte final segment and the following four fields:

- *User-to-user identification (UU).* The 1-byte UU field is for transferring user-to-user information transparently.
- *Common part indicator (CPI).* The 1-byte CPI field interprets the other fields of the CS-PDU trailer. One function of the CPI field is to align the CS-PDU trailer to 64 bits. Other functions are for further study. These may include identification of layer-management messages. When only the 64-bit alignment function is used, this field is coded as 0.
- *Length (L).* The 2-byte L field indicates the length of the CS-PDU payload field. As such, it also indicates how much of the final segment is data and how much is padding. In addition, the receiver uses the L field value to detect the loss or gain of information.
- *CRC.* The final 4 bytes of the trailer are a CRC for the entire CS protocol data unit, including the higher layer PDU, the padding, and the UU, CPI, and L fields. The CRC generator polynomial is

$$G(x) = x^{32}+x^{26}+x^{23}+x^{22}+x^{16}+x^{12}+x^{11}+x^{10}+x^8+x^7+x^5+x^4+x^2+x+1$$

7.5 ATM LANS

Originally the intent of ATM was for high-capacity use in wide area networks (WANs). However, two factors led network designers to consider the use of ATM in local area networks (LANs). First, as the amount of sophisticated computer-based equipment grew in an organization, there was a growing emphasis on client-server computing. Uses of this equipment for applications such as multimedia and high-resolution graphics increased the traffic demands in typical LANs. Secondly, the desire arose to connect LAN users seamlessly to other distantly located LAN entities across an ATM network and to have LAN stations interface with an application residing on a device attached to an ATM network. This section addresses the use of ATM within a LAN. Section 7.6 looks at the second factor, LAN-to-LAN communications and LAN host-to-ATM device interfaces across an ATM network.

ATM is a connection-oriented switched transmission technology that supports multiple guaranteed classes of service. Thus it is attractive for delivering real-time services, such as voice and video, in a LAN environment along with standard non-real-time data transfers. For example, a videoconference application may require guaranteed 2-Mbps connections among the participants, whereas simultaneously a file transfer application can utilize a less demanding class of service. Another attraction of ATM in a LAN environment is that it is readily scalable to larger configurations by activating more ATM nodes or by using different data rates for attached devices.

A variety of ATM LAN configurations may be constructed. First Fig. 7.13 depicts an ATM switch used as a hub to interconnect localized computing equipment. The utility of this configuration is the versatility of the ATM switch. As Fig. 7.13 illustrates, nominally an ATM switch contains a number of card slots. Each card slot can accept a different network interface card for handling a particular service, for example, different cards can interface to ATM, Ethernet, token ring, or DS-3 equipment. The interface cards contain the necessary conversion firmware to convert from the protocol of the end system to an ATM Protocol. Thereby each end system has a dedicated point-to-point link to the ATM hub. Connections then can be established to other entities on the same LAN or to another distant LAN over a wide area ATM network via LAN emulation, as Sec. 7.6 describes.

As another possible ATM LAN configuration, Fig. 7.14 illustrates an ATM backbone consisting of three large capacity ATM switches connecting various types of legacy LANs in a local environment. These backbone ATM switches might run at 622 Mbps or higher speeds and have 155-Mbps or faster interfaces to end equipment. Examples of the possible connections to the backbone include high-capacity corporate servers or workstations that have internal 622-Mbps ATM network interface cards, smaller 155-Mbps

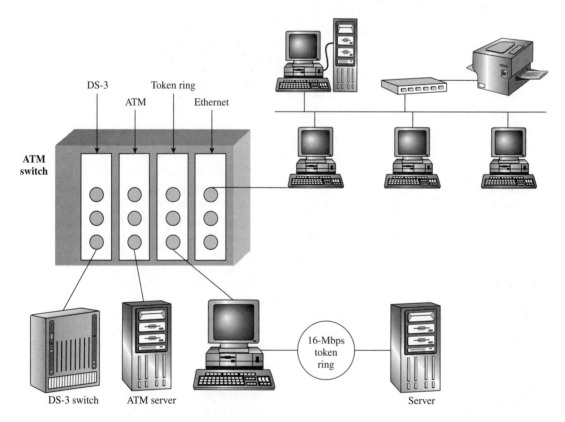

FIGURE 7.13
ATM switch used as a hub to interconnect localized computing equipment.

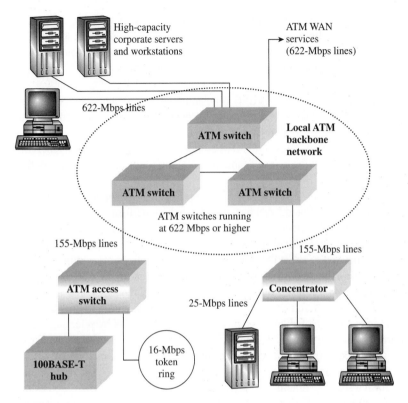

FIGURE 7.14
Example of an ATM backbone connecting various legacy LANs in a local environment.

ATM access switches such as those shown in Fig. 7.13, or concentrators that interface to a large number of lower-speed devices. In addition, there may be an access to wide area network (WAN) services.

7.6 LAN EMULATION

LAN emulation (LANE) makes an ATM interface look like one or more separate LAN interfaces, thereby allowing the interconnection of legacy LANs over an ATM backbone.[14–18] With LANE an ATM network basically serves as a transparent, high-speed transport network. Multiple-emulated LANs (ELANs), which are logically separated, may share the same physical ATM network. Thus the LANE specification allows users of LANs, such as Ethernet or token rings, to make use of the benefits of ATM without making modifications to end-station hardware or software. The LANE concept provides a connectionless service to LAN users, enables the stations to use their traditional LAN addresses instead of converting to VPI/VCI connection identifiers, and allows delivery of broadcast messages.

LANE is based on a client-server approach. To implement an ELAN, a set of four software components needs to be configured. These components can run on a number of different devices, such as an ATM router, an ATM switch, a LAN switch, or other ATM equipment, and they may be physically distributed. The motivation for these modules is for efficient operation and to minimize the communication burden. The nomenclature and characteristics of the client and server software modules are as follows:

- *LAN emulation client (LEC).*   A LEC is an endpoint entity such as a workstation, a LAN switch, or a router. Functions performed by this entity include setting up control connections to LANE servers, setting up data connections to other clients, mapping MAC addresses to ATM addresses, and forwarding and receiving data. The LANE client provides a standard LAN service to any higher layers that interface to it.
- *LAN emulation server (LES).*   The LES accepts clients that want to join the emulated LAN. Each emulated LAN has one LES, which performs ATM address-to-MAC address pairings. Once a client has joined an ELAN, it can exchange MAC frames with other clients over the ATM network, or it can communicate with an application attached to the ATM network. The MAC frames are segmented into ATM cells during their transmission over a virtual channel in the ATM network.
- *LAN emulation configuration server (LECS).*   Basically the LECS acts as a database of ELAN names and the LES addresses associated with each ELAN. The LECS assigns individual clients to a particular emulated LAN by selecting a LES that corresponds to that ELAN. The LECS gives the client the ATM address of the LES and sends the client information about the ELAN, such as the MAC Protocol, the maximum frame size, and the name of the ELAN. The LECS also can perform a security function by restricting access to a certain ELAN based on the MAC address of a client. Once the LEC has this information, it no longer needs to communicate with the LECS unless it needs to reinitialize.
- *Broadcast and unknown server (BUS).*   This server forwards multicast and broadcast traffic to clients within an emulated LAN. This is used when the sending client needs to send a frame to a group of clients or to every station on the ELAN. In this application the sending station directs the frame to the BUS, which has a permanent virtual connection to every station. The BUS then sends a copy of the frame to a group of stations or to all stations, thereby simulating a multicasting or broadcasting process. It also can be used when the sending client does not know the address of the receiving client. In this case the BUS sends the frame to every station. One BUS exists per emulated LAN.

Figure 7.15 shows the protocol architecture for carrying out ATM LAN emulation. The setup is for a station connected to an Ethernet or token-ring LAN (shown on the far right) interacting with an application residing on a computer attached to an ATM system (shown on the far left). The protocol stack on the right is that of a standard LAN. The end station employs the MAC protocol specific to the LAN to which it is connected and uses standard TCP/IP and LCC services. Thus the various applications used by the station are not aware that there is an underlying ATM network.

The next block from the right in Fig. 7.15 shows the bridging function used by an *ATM-capable LAN switch* to convert MAC frames to and from ATM cells. This is

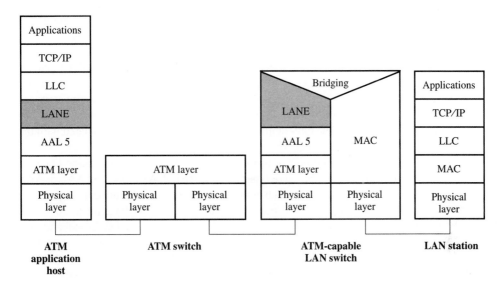

FIGURE 7.15
Protocol architecture involved in ATM LAN emulation.

one of the basic functions of the LAN emulation module, which uses AAL 5 for this process. The output of the LAN switch is connected to the ATM cloud through an ATM switch. The ATM-equipped workstation containing the desired application with which the LAN station wishes to communicate is attached either directly to this ATM switch or via another ATM connection through the ATM cloud.

Note that LANE does not emulate every particular physical or data link characteristic. For example, it does not support carrier sense multiple access collision detection (CSMA/CD) for Ethernet. LANE on the ATM switch supports only the IP (Internet Protocol).

7.7 SUMMARY

ATM is a high-performance switching and multiplexing technology that utilizes fixed-length 53-byte packets to carry different types of traffic. These packets, which are called *cells,* contain a 5-byte header and 48 bytes of payload. An attraction of ATM is that it enables carriers to offer multiple classes of service over a WAN, to connect devices that operate at different speeds, and to mix traffic types having different transmission requirements, such as voice, video, and data. In addition, ATM can serve as a backbone for high-speed LANs and can be used to interconnect geographically dispersed high-capacity LANs.

A key characteristic of ATM is that it can transfer both real-time and non-real-time traffic simultaneously. *Real-time services* need to deliver information in a timely fashion and as a continuous, smooth flow. Examples of this are telephone conversations, videoconferencing, television, and distance learning. Any delay greater than a few tenths of a second or any loss-induced gaps in the information flow will cause a significant degradation in the quality of service. *Non-real-time services* are used for applications that do not have tight constraints on delay or delay variations.

To enable the simultaneous transfer of diverse traffic types, the ATM Standard defines five *quality-of-service* (QoS) classes. The real-time services include *constant bit rate* (CBR) and *real-time variable-bit-rate* (rt-VBR) services. Non-real-time services include *non-real-time variable bit rate* (nrt-VBR), *available bit rate* (ABR), and *unspecified bit rate* (UBR). The QoS defines a set of attributes that are associated with the performance of a network connection.

ATM defines four categories of protocols for the AAL (ATM adaptation layer) to support the QoS categories. These are types AAL 1, AAL 2, AAL 3/4, and AAL 5. AAL 1 specifies how CBR applications, such as voice and video, transfer information over an ATM network. AAL 2 supports real-time variable-bit-rate (rt-VBR) applications. AAL 3/4 supports connectionless VBR data services, such as connectionless broadband data services, that can tolerate varying delay requirements. AAL 5 is the most important AAL Protocol for LAN applications. This protocol was established for connection-oriented services to reduce protocol-processing overhead, to reduce transmission overhead, and to simplify adaptation to other transport protocols.

ATM is a connection-oriented switched transmission technology that supports multiple guaranteed classes of service. Thus it is attractive for delivering real-time services, such as voice and video, in a LAN environment along with standard non-real-time data transfers. Another attraction of ATM in a LAN environment is that it is scalable to larger configurations by activating more ATM nodes or by using different data rates for attached devices.

LAN emulation (LANE) makes an ATM interface look like one or more separate LAN interfaces, thereby allowing the interconnection of legacy LANs over an ATM backbone. With LANE an ATM network serves as a transparent, high-speed transport network. Multiple-emulated LANs, which are logically separated, may share the same physical ATM network. Thus the LANE specification allows users of LANs to make use of the benefits of ATM without making modifications to end-station hardware or software.

PROBLEMS

7.1. The CRC used in the ATM header can correct all single errors and detect all double errors occurring in the header. If bit errors occur in the header (of length $L = 40$ bits) at random with an error rate p, then the probability $P(x)$ that x errors occur is given by

$$P(x) = \frac{L!}{x!(L-x)!}(1-p)^{L-x}p^x$$

Find the probability that the header has no errors, one error, and two errors for error rates of $p = 10^{-6}$ and 10^{-9}.

7.2. To what ATM service classes would the following applications belong:
  (a)   Downloading of a document from the Internet
  (b)   A telephone call between people in two different cities
  (c)   Online purchase of some stock
  (d)   Medical consultation via a telemedicine application
  (e)   Sending an e-mail message

7.3. A user needs an ATM service guarantee to send information at a rate of 200 kbps using an AAL-1 Protocol. The user occasionally may want to transmit at five times this rate for short periods of time. If the bit rate on the ATM link is 155 Mbps, what is the sustained cell rate (SCR)? What is the peak cell rate (PCR)?

7.4. Consider an ATM network in which 8 out of 10,000 cells are lost during transmission and 4 out of 10,000 contain errors.
  (a) What is the cell loss ratio (CLR)?
  (b) What is the cell error ratio (CER)?

7.5. Assume an AAL 1 receives data at a 4-Mbps rate.
  (a) How many cells are created per second by the ATM layer?
  (b) What is the efficiency (ratio of bits received by the AAL 1 to bits sent out over the link) of ATM when using AAL 1?

7.6. Assume an AAL 5 receives data at a 4-Mbps rate.
  (a) How many cells are created per second by the ATM layer?
  (b) What is the efficiency of ATM when using AAL 5?

7.7. How many bytes in a 53-byte ATM cell consist of actual data when using the following protocols: (a) AAL 1; (b) AAL 2; (c) AAL 3/4; (d) AAL 5? Assume there is no padding in the cells.

7.8. Discuss some advantages and limitations of using ATM versus Fast Ethernet for connecting LAN users residing in buildings that are 2 km apart.

7.9. Using web resources, describe the offerings of several ATM service providers. Consider factors such as classes of service offered, bandwidth options, security features, and subscription prices.

7.10. Using web resources, describe the features of switches that can be used for LAN emulation to send Ethernet traffic across an ATM campus network.

REFERENCES

1. R. H. Davis, *ATM for Public Networks,* McGraw-Hill, New York, 1999.
2. D. McDysan and D. L. Spohn, *ATM Theory and Applications,* McGraw-Hill, New York, 1998.
3. H. Brandt and C. Hapke, *ATM Signaling: Protocols and Practice,* Wiley, New York, 2001.
4. J. M. Pitts and J. A. Schormans, *Introduction to IP and ATM Design and Performance,* Wiley, New York, 2001.
5. The ATM Forum (http://www.atmforum.com).
6. Telecommunication Standardization Sector of the International Telecommunication Union (ITU-T), Place des nations, CH-1211 Geneva 20, Switzerland (http://www.itu.ch).
7. ITU-T Recommendation I.361, *B-ISDN ATM layer specification,* 1995.
8. ITU-T Recommendation I.363, *B-ISDN ATM adaptation layer specification,* Mar. 1993.
9. ITU-T Recommendation I.363.1, *B-ISDN ATM adaptation layer specification: Type 1 AAL,* Aug. 1997.
10. ITU-T Recommendation I.363.2, *B-ISDN ATM adaptation layer specification: Type 2 AAL,* Sept. 1997.
11. The ATM Forum, *Voice and Multimedia over ATM, Loop-Emulation Service Using AAL 2,* AF-VMOA-0145.000, July 2000.
12. ITU-T Recommendation I.363.3, *B-ISDN ATM adaptation layer specification: Type 3/4 AAL,* Aug. 1996.
13. ITU-T Recommendation I.363.5, *B-ISDN ATM adaptation layer specification: Type 5 AAL,* Aug. 1996.
14. The ATM Forum, *LAN Emulation over ATM, LANE User-Network Interface (LUNI) Specification,* version 2, AF-LANE-084.000, July 1997.
15. The ATM Forum, *LAN Emulation over ATM, LANE Network-Network Interface (LNNI) Specification,* version 2, AF-LANE-0112.000, Feb. 1999.
16. G. Held, *Internetworking LANs and WANs,* Wiley, New York, 2nd ed., 1998.
17. L. R. Rossi, L. D. Rossi, and T. Rossi, *Cisco Catalyst LAN Switching,* McGraw-Hill, New York, 2000, Chap. 10.
18. J. Knapp, *Nortel Networks,* McGraw-Hill/Osborne, Berkeley, CA, 2000, Chap. 13.

CHAPTER
8

WIRELESS
LANS

The rapid increase of Internet usage created new concepts and devices for mobile communications within a localized area. Examples of such an environment include a home, a school campus, a health care institute, an office suite, a manufacturing facility, a warehouse, or a retail store. A user might have a device such as a palmtop or laptop computer, a personal digital assistant (PDA), or a portable data collector, all of which may contain a wireless network interface card (NIC). In addition, a person might have a mobile phone with Internet access capabilities. Having this equipment is beneficial only if there is a local wireless network that is available to support its use. Looking at the wide range of applications, one can categorize the wireless LANs broadly into networks for enterprise, small business, home, and personal use.

This chapter describes the types of wireless LANs that are available and presents the standards on which they are based. Section 8.1 gives an overview of the concepts of what a wireless LAN is, what its limitations are, how it is configured, and what its applications are. In addition, Sec. 8.1 gives the basic ideas behind the IEEE-802.11 Standard for wireless LANs. Similar to other IEEE-802 standards, 802.11 addresses the data link and physical layer functions. Thus Sec. 8.2 describes the medium access control sublayer for wireless LANs. The next three sections discuss the various physical layer options. First Sec. 8.3 addresses wireless LANs that are based on spread-spectrum radio links, which operate in a radio-frequency band that does not require licensing from regulatory agencies. Wireless LANs that use infrared light signals as the transmission means are described next in Sec. 8.4. Thirdly, Sec. 8.5 discusses the IEEE-802.11a and 802.11b physical layer protocol extensions, which address higher transmission speeds. These higher-speed LANs allow the application of standard and Fast Ethernet over a wireless LAN. Another standardization effort has resulted in the IEEE-802.15 Standard for a wireless personal area network (PAN) for wire replacement in a limited area about the size of a room. As Sec. 8.6 describes, the IEEE-802.15 Standard for supporting such a network is based on the Bluetooth specification for short-range radio systems. The final topic concerns the applications of a wireless LAN for communication and automation technology in the home, which is discussed in Sec. 8.7.

8.1 WIRELESS LAN CONCEPTS

Basically a *wireless LAN* (WLAN) is a LAN that uses over-the-air infrared light waves or radio waves instead of copper wires or optical fibers as the transmission means.[1-5] Thus a wireless LAN provides the same features and benefits of a traditional LAN, such as Ethernet. This has the advantage of allowing a great deal of user mobility, but generally with a lower transmission rate than a wired LAN offers. Typical applications of a wireless LAN include inventory control or product retrieval in warehouses, data transfers between workstations in large open manufacturing areas, information exchanges between personnel in office buildings where installing cable upgrades may be difficult, communications among medical staff members in a health care facility, or voice and data transfer among computing and communication devices in a home.

Infrared-based wireless LANs use near-visible infrared light in the 800- to 950-nm range. Broadcast infrared LANs typically operate within a room or other enclosed area over maximum distances of 10 to 20 m at nominal data rates of 1 to 2 Mbps. Point-to-point infrared links can achieve longer distances and much higher data rates, as Sec. 8.4 describes. Radio-based LANs are more versatile and cover larger areas than infrared LANs. These nominally operate in unlicensed frequency bands centered at 900 MHz, 2.4 GHz, and 5.7 GHz. Although initially wireless LAN devices operated in the 900-MHz band, most major vendors have settled on the 2.4-GHz frequency band. This band is allocated in the United States, Europe, Japan, and elsewhere for unlicensed radio operation at low-power output. In addition, many products are emerging for operation in the 5.7-GHz band.

8.1.1 IEEE-802.11 Overview

To ensure product compatibility and reliability among the various wireless-LAN manufacturers, the IEEE in 1997 ratified the IEEE-802.11 Standard.[5-7] The initial 802.11 version specifies both medium access control (MAC) functions and three different physical layer (PHY) options for operation at 1 and 2 Mbps. It also provides a set of fundamental signaling methods and other services, such as asynchronous and time-bounded delivery, multicasting, network management, registration, and authentication. To satisfy the demand for higher data rates, the IEEE in 1999 ratified the 802.11b enhancement, which also is known as 802.11 *high rate*. This extension to the basic 802.11 Standard offers more physical layer options and provides for 11-Mbps and higher transmission rates in the 2.4-GHz band.[8] The IEEE-802.11a enhancement also was ratified in 1999 and supports substantially higher rates of at least 54 Mbps in the 5.7-GHz band.[9]

Figure 8.1 compares the 802.11 Standard with the ISO (International Standards Organization) model. Similar to other IEEE-802 standards, the 802.11 specification covers the physical and data link layers of the ISO model. The original 802.11 Standard defines the basic architecture, features, and services for the 802.11a and 802.11b enhancements, which are affected only at the physical layer with the addition of higher data rates and more robust connectivity.

8.1.2 Physical Layer Architecture

The 802.11 Standard defines several physical layers to operate with the MAC layer. As Fig. 8.1 illustrates, the physical layer is divided into the *physical layer convergence procedure* (PLCP) sublayer and the *physical medium-dependent* (PMD) sublayer.

The PLCP is the upper sublayer and communicates with the MAC layer by means of *service primitives* (see Sec. 2.1) through the physical layer *service access point* (SAP). Based on instructions from the MAC layer, the PLCP maps a LLC (logical link control) protocol data unit (PDU) into a format that is suitable for transmission over a given physical medium. The LLC PDU also is called a MAC *service data unit* (MSDU) since it is the data field at the MAC layer. As a reminder of the terminology definitions given in Chap. 2, a *protocol data unit* (PDU) consists of a header containing management information, a trailer field, and a block of user information called a *service data unit* (SDU).

At a receiving station the PLCP delivers incoming frames from the wireless medium to the MAC layer. As shown in Fig. 8.2, the MAC sublayer adds a header

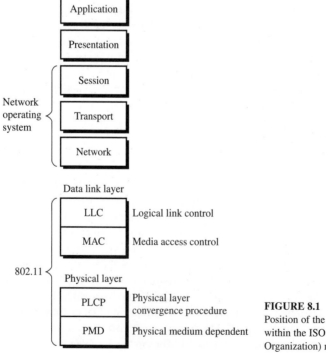

FIGURE 8.1
Position of the IEEE-802.11 Standard within the ISO (International Standards Organization) model.

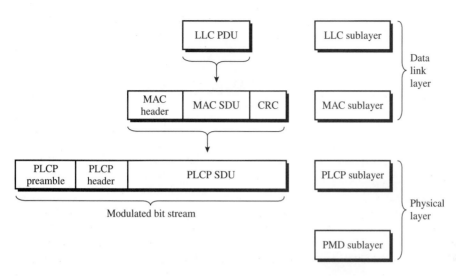

FIGURE 8.2
Formation of a PLCP (physical layer convergence procedure) frame from a LLC (logical link control) protocol data unit.

and trailer to the MSDU to form the PLCP SDU (PSDU). The header contains control information and the trailer consists of a CRC (cyclic redundancy check) field used by the receiver to verify the integrity of the incoming frames. The PLCP sublayer then adds two parts to form a PLCP frame or a PLCP PDU (PPDU). The first part is a preamble that contains synchronization and start-of-frame information. The second part provides transmission-related information. The specific structure of a PLCP frame depends on the particular physical layer with which it is associated, as described in Secs. 8.3 through 8.5.

The PMD sublayer is concerned with the characteristics of the physical medium and the specific transmission techniques used to send information over a particular medium. The PLCP and the PMD communicate by means of primitives in order to carry out the transmission and reception functions.

8.1.3 Wireless LAN Configurations

Figure 8.3 shows a simple example of a wireless LAN. Normally there is a backbone network that ties together various wired devices, such as workstations, printers, or servers. In Fig. 8.3 this is shown as an Ethernet LAN. Also attached to this LAN is a wireless interface device called an *access point* (AP), which acts as a central base station or a bridge between the wireless equipment and the wired network. An AP nominally consists of a radio with a wired interface to a network, such as an Ethernet LAN, and bridging software that conforms to the IEEE-802.1d bridging standard. The AP is the base station for a group of users within a basic geographic service area, which is called a *cell*. Variable power levels allow cells to be sized according to the number of subscribers in a given area and the demand for services within a particular region. Examples of the wireless

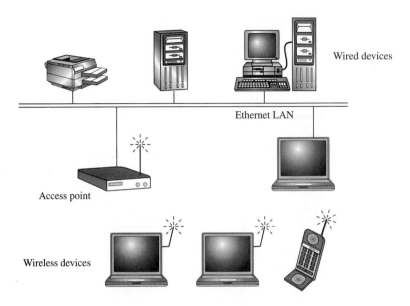

Wired devices

Ethernet LAN

Access point

Wireless devices

FIGURE 8.3
Signals sent from wireless devices to an access point on a LAN (local area network).

end stations include an embedded application in an IEEE-802.11-based device such as a telephone handset or an 802.11 NIC (network interface card) in a mobile platform, such as a laptop computer.

Other cells operating at different transmission frequencies can be added to areas outside of a particular cell to extend the network, or they can be overlaid on existing cells to increase the number of communicating users in a given location. As mobile users move or *roam* from cell to cell, their conversations are transferred from the frequency in one cell to that in the next one in order to maintain seamless service. The 802.11 Standard refers to the network architecture shown in Fig. 8.4 as an *infrastructure network*. The network configuration with one cell is called the *basic service set* (BSS), and the geographical area it covers is known as the *basic service area* (BSA). An *extended service set* (ESS) is a configuration that has more than one BSS forming a single subnetwork, as shown by the set of two BSS cells in Fig. 8.4.

The *ad hoc network* is another configuration for a wireless LAN.[10–13] This also is called a *peer-to-peer network* or an *independent basic service set* (IBSS). This is simply a set of 802.11 wireless stations that communicate directly with one another without using an AP or any connection to a wired network, as Fig. 8.5 illustrates. This mode is useful for quickly and easily setting up a temporary wireless network for satisfying some immediate short-term need. For example, such a network could be used by either staff members at a convention center to coordinate activities, people in a conference room to exchange data via personal computers during a business meeting, or students in a classroom setting for interactive participation among themselves and an instructor. Since there is no infrastructure for an ad hoc network, the participating stations dynamically set up a temporary network using a common software-based interconnection application. Thus they are referred to as *self-creating, self-organizing,* and *self-administering.*

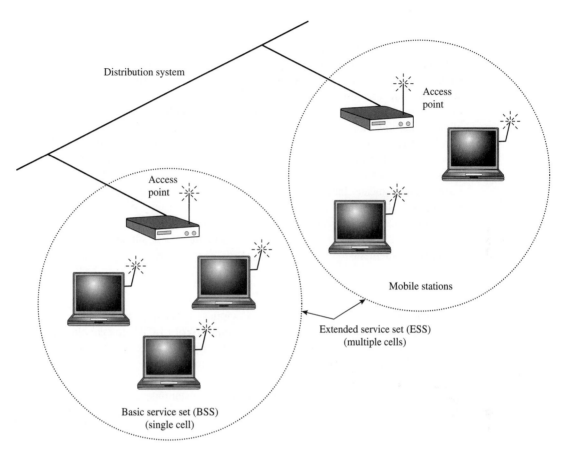

FIGURE 8.4
Example of a basic service set (BSS) and an extended service set (ESS).

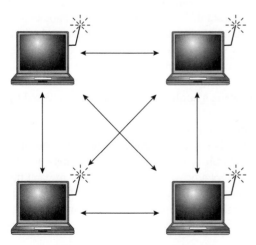

Independent basic service set (IBSS)
(ad hoc network)

FIGURE 8.5
Example of an ad hoc wireless LAN.

8.2 MAC LAYER

The purpose of the MAC layer is to support the LLC layer in providing access control functions for the various shared physical media.[14,15] This includes offering functions such as addressing, access coordination, generation and verification of frame check sequences, and frame fragmentation and reassembly in support of the LLC. Other optional services include information security through authentication and privacy mechanisms, roaming support, and power management. The dynamic nature of users in a wireless LAN requires the MAC protocols to be somewhat different from those of wired LANs. The main difference is that in a wireless LAN the MAC address identifies the station but not the location since the station can be portable or mobile. The term *portable* means that the station may move from one location to another, but it remains in a fixed place when in use. A *mobile* station may move during operation. Since the 802.11-MAC sublayer is required to present the same set of standard services to the LLC as other IEEE-802 LANs do, the MAC sublayer needs to handle mobility requirements.

8.2.1 IEEE-802.11 MAC Services

Each station and AP on an IEEE-802.11 wireless LAN implements the MAC layer service. These services allow peer-to-peer exchanges of MSDUs to take place between LLC entities, which could reside on either a wired or a wireless LAN. To achieve this functionality, the MAC layer implements two categories of service, one relating to the station and the other to the distribution system.

The *station services* provide functions among stations and APs. These functions include sending and receiving MSDUs and providing adequate levels of information security. These services include the following:

- *Authentication.* Since basically any station having a properly tuned antenna can achieve connectivity in a wireless LAN, IEEE 802.11 defines an *authentication service* to control LAN access. All 802.11 stations must use the authentication service to identify themselves prior to establishing a connection with another station. The 802.11 Standard does not require any specific authentication method, so depending on the application this may vary from a simple nonsecure handshaking scheme to a highly secure public-key encryption procedure.
- *Deauthentication.* A station uses the *deauthentication service* to end a connection with one or more stations. This service is a notification and cannot be refused by the addressed station.
- *MSDU delivery.* Section 8.2.2 addresses this service.
- *Privacy.* An issue with wireless LANs is that any station, whether or not it is part of the network, can listen to data traffic if it is within range of the network. To counter this problem, IEEE 802.11 offers a *privacy service* option to prevent the contents of messages from being read by stations other than the intended recipient. This service applies to all data frames and some authentication management frames. It is based on the *wired equivalent privacy* (WEP) algorithm, which performs encryption of messages.[16]

Access points provide *distribution system services,* which include the following:

- *Association.* Before a station can send or receive information through a wireless LAN distribution system, it must make its identity and address known to an AP. The *association service* maps the identity of a station to the LAN distribution system via a single AP within a particular BSS. This AP then can send the association information to other APs within its affiliated ESS in order to allow the station to roam from one BSS to another.
- *Disassociation.* A station or an AP may use the *disassociation service* to terminate an existing association. Normally a station should invoke this notification when leaving an ESS or when shutting down. As another example, an AP uses this service to disassociate itself from all its stations before it is removed for maintenance.
- *Reassociation.* A mobile station can initiate the *reassociation service* to transition from one AP to another. This allows the station to move from one BSS to another within an ESS.
- *Distribution.* A station applies the *distribution service* whenever it sends MAC frames across a distribution system. The specific method for doing this is flexible since the distribution system only gets enough information to identify the destination BSS.

8.2.2 MAC Layer Operation

The MAC sublayer uses one of two methods to gain access to the network. The protocol for these is specified in terms of *coordination functions* that determine when a station within a BSS may transmit and when it may receive a PDU. The first method is the *distributed coordination function* (DCF), which supports asynchronous data transfer on a best-effort basis.[17] Using the DCF, all the stations contend for the channels for each packet transmission. IEEE 802.11 also defines an optional *point coordination function* (PCF), which uses a centralized decision maker, such as an AP, to regulate transmissions and to provide contention-free frame transfers.

Figure 8.6 illustrates the architecture of these two coordination functions within the MAC sublayer. The DCF resides directly on top of the physical layer and the PCF is implemented on top of the DCF. The five physical layer protocols shown in Fig. 8.6 are described in Secs. 8.3 through 8.5. Both the DCF and the PCF can operate concurrently in the same BSS to provide alternating contention and contention-free transmission periods. All stations are required to support the distributed coordination function. In an ad hoc network the stations use only the DCF. In other networks the stations can operate using just the DCF or a coexisting combination of the DCF and PCF. Let us now look at some highlights of these functions.

Distributed Coordination Function (DCF)

The DCF is based on a *carrier sense multiple access with collision avoidance* (CSMA/CA) method, which is similar to the 802.3 Ethernet Standard for a wired LAN. However, there is no collision detection function because this is not practical in a wireless network. This

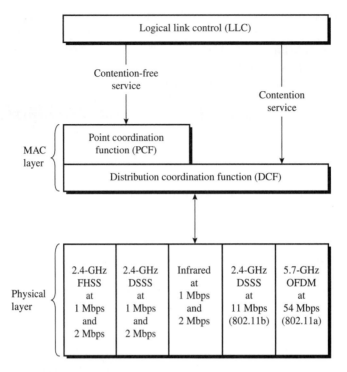

FIGURE 8.6
IEEE-802.11 MAC architecture.

is due to the large dynamic range of signals on the medium, which makes it difficult to distinguish weak incoming signals from noise. Obviously a station must wait for the channel to be idle before transmitting. Once the channel becomes idle, a smooth and fair mechanism must be used to gain access to the channel since other stations also may be waiting to transmit. Otherwise all waiting stations would transmit at once and collisions would occur, thereby wasting transmission time. To solve this, the CSMA/CA Protocol uses a random set of delays to allow stations to transmit.

Figure 8.7 illustrates the operation of the CSMA/CA Protocol. All stations are required to remain silent for a certain minimum period after the channel becomes idle. This basic time delay is called the *interframe space* (IFS). The IFS can take on one of three different length values, depending on the type of frame that the station is about to transmit. Each interval defines the time from the end of the last symbol of the previous frame to the beginning of the first symbol of the next frame. The following are the three types of IFS intervals:

1. *Short IFS.* The *short IFS* (SIFS) is the shortest IFS. High-priority frames only need to wait the SIFS period before they contend for the channel. Frames that use the SIFS include acknowledgment (ACK) frames, *clear-to-send* (CTS) frames, frames that are responding to a poll from the AP, and data frames that are the second or subsequent part of a segmented MAC service data unit.

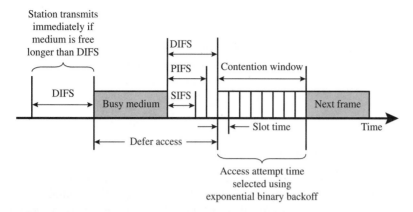

FIGURE 8.7
Basic operation of the access method for the CSMA/CA Protocol.

2. *Point coordination function IFS.* The *point coordination function IFS* (PIFS) is intermediate in duration and used by the PCF to gain priority access to the medium. Stations using the PCF have priority over stations using DCF and can transmit contention-free traffic once they sense that the channel is idle after the PIFS interval.

3. *Distributed coordination function IFS.* The *distributed coordination function IFS* (DIFS) is the longest IFS. All stations operating under the DCF use the DIFS interval for transmitting data and management frames. Since the DIFS is longer than the PIFS, a DCF-based frame has a lower priority than a PCF-based frame.

As Fig. 8.7 illustrates, if the medium is free for a time period longer than the DIFS, the station can transmit immediately. Now suppose the medium is busy and one or more stations operating under the DCF protocol have information to send. In this case the station calculates a random backoff period using a *binary exponential backoff scheme* (see Sec. 4.5) to schedule an attempt at gaining access to the channel.[18] As noted previously, this scheduling is done so that all waiting stations have a fair chance of transmitting. The time period during which stations attempt to gain access is called the *contention window.* This window is segmented into *slots* of time.

Using this calculated backoff period, the station sets an internal timer to an integer number of slot times and waits for the medium to become idle. When the current transmission ends, the station waits for a DIFS interval and then senses the medium again. If the medium is still idle after the DIFS interval, then during the following contention-window interval the station waits for a period equal to the delay time it calculated. When the backoff timer expires and the medium is still idle, the station may transmit. In case the medium becomes busy during the contention-window interval the backoff procedure is suspended and resumed the next time a contention period takes place. Analogous to Ethernet, the binary exponential backoff scheme introduces a degree of fairness in accessing the channel and supports transmission stability under heavy load conditions.

The DCF includes a means for handling lost or corrupted frames. Receiver stations return an ACK (acknowledgment) frame if a data frame is received and its CRC is correct.

If the sending station fails to receive such a frame within a specified time period, it will take this as an indication that the frame is corrupted or lost. The time period for each data frame is equal to an ACK frame time plus a SIFS. When an ACK is not received, the sender executes the backoff procedure to schedule another transmission attempt. In case the sender does not receive an ACK frame because the ACK itself was lost, a receiver may get duplicate frames. Receiver stations use the sequence numbers in the frame to detect such duplicates.

Point Coordination Function (PCF)

In normal operation all 802.11-compliant stations use the DCF. As an option the priority-based PCF may be used to provide contention-free frame transfers. For example, this may be activated to support time-sensitive information such as audio or video. The price for using the PCF is a greater overhead on the network since the PCF needs to send out polling frames that grant a station permission to send a frame to any destination. The *point coordinator* (PC) that performs the PCF resides in the AP within a BSS. When the PC wants to gain control of the medium, it sends out a beacon at the end of the PIFS interval. The information in the beacon communicates the length of the contention-free period to all stations and prevents them from taking control of the medium until the end of this period. The exact methods for carrying this out are somewhat involved and can be found in the literature and the standards.[6,19]

8.2.3 MAC Frame Formats

The IEEE-802.11 Standard supports management, control, and data frames. A station uses *management frames* for functions such as association and disassociation with an AP, timing and synchronization, and authentication to establish the identity of other stations. *Control frames* provide functionality to assist in the delivery of data frames. The general frame format is shown in Fig. 8.8, where the first seven fields constitute the

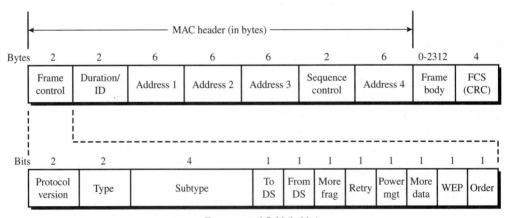

FIGURE 8.8
General IEEE-802.11 frame format.

MAC header. All frames, regardless of their type, use this structure. However, a specific frame type does not need to use all the fields. The various MAC frame fields have the following sizes and functions:

- *Frame control.*   The 2-byte *frame control field* carries control information from station to station and indicates the frame type. The following discussion relating to the lower part of Fig. 8.8 gives more details.
- *Duration/ID.*   The 2-byte *duration/ID (identification) field* has two purposes. Usually it contains a duration value, which indicates the time that the station will be allocated for transmitting the next data and acknowledgment frames. In some types of control frames this field carries the identification (ID) of the station that transmitted the frame.
- *Address 1, 2, 3, and 4.*   Each of the four *address fields* is 6 bytes long. The fields contain different address formats, depending on the type of frame being sent. The formats include source, destination, transmitting-station, and receiving-station addresses. They can be either individual or group addresses, such as multicast or broadcast addresses. A *multicast address* is associated with a group of logically related stations, whereas a *broadcast address* refers to all stations on a particular LAN.
- *Sequence control.*   The 2-byte *sequence control field* contains a 4-bit *fragment number* subfield used for fragmentation and reassembly of an MSDU. The number starts with 0 for the first fragment and increments by 1 for each successive fragment. The next 12 bits are a *sequence number* subfield for numbering frames sent between a given transmitter and receiver. The numbering starts at 0 and increments by 1 for each subsequent MSDU, up to a maximum of 4096. Note that each fragment of a specific MSDU will have the same sequence number.
- *Frame body.*   The *frame body field* has a variable-length payload, which can range from 0 to 2312 bytes. The payload can be either an MSDU or MAC management or control information.
- *Frame check sequence (FCS).*   The *frame check sequence field* contains a 4-byte (32-bit) *cyclic redundancy check* (CRC), which is calculated over the MAC header and the frame body field. This CRC uses the generator polynomial

$$G(x) = x^{32}+x^{26}+x^{23}+x^{22}+x^{16}+x^{12}+x^{11}+x^{10}+x^8+x^7+x^5+x^4+x^2+x+1$$

The frame control field shown in Fig. 8.8 specifies the following items:

- *Protocol version.*   This 2-bit field denotes the 802.11 version.
- *Type.*   This is a 2-bit field denoting the frame as a management (00), control (01), or data (10) frame.
- *Subtype.*   This 4-bit field further defines the function of the frame. For example, for a control type frame the subtype might be ACK.
- *To DS.*   This single-bit field is set to 1 for data frames that are destined for the distribution system to which the station belongs. It is set to 0 for all other destinations, for example, if the frame is destined for a BSS belonging to a different AP.
- *From DS.*   The MAC coordination sets this single-bit field to 1 in any frame leaving the distribution system. Both the "To DS" and the "From DS" fields are set to 1 if the frame is sent from one AP through the distribution system to another AP.

- *More fragments.* This 1-bit field is set to 1 if more fragments of the same MSDU follow in a subsequent frame.
- *Retry.* This single-bit field is set to 1 if the frame is a retransmission of a previous one. This helps the receiver to deal with duplicate frames.
- *Power management.* This bit indicates the power-management mode in which the sending station will be after transmitting. The MAC layer sets the bit to 1 if the station will be in a sleep mode, which 802.11 calls a *power-saver mode.* For example, most battery-powered devices should be kept in the power-saver mode to conserve battery power. When the bit is set to 0, it indicates the station will be in a fully active mode. To support clients that periodically enter the sleep mode, the 802.11 specifies that an AP includes buffers to queue waiting messages. Sleeping clients must awaken periodically and retrieve any messages. An AP may dump unread messages after a specified time passes and the messages are not retrieved.
- *More data.* If the sending station has additional MSDUs for a station that is in the power-saver mode, it sets this bit to 1. This alerts the receiving station to be ready for more frames.
- *Wired equivalent privacy (WEP).* This 1-bit field is set to 1 if a secret key has encrypted the data bits in the frame body. The WEP field bit is set to 0 for all other types of transmissions.
- *Order.* This field is set to 1 in any data frame that is sent using the "strictly ordered" service class. This setting tells the receiving station that the incoming frames must be processed in the order they arrived.

8.3 SPREAD-SPECTRUM WIRELESS LANS

Radio-based wireless LANs specified by 802.11 and 802.11b use spread-spectrum modulation techniques and operate in the 900-MHz, 2.4-GHz, and 5.8-GHz bands. Figure 8.9 compares the frequency ranges for these bands, which are 902 to 928 MHz, 2.400 to 2.4835 GHz, and 5.725 to 5.850 GHz, respectively. These are known as the *industrial, scientific, and medical* (ISM) *bands.* International regulatory agencies, such as the FCC (Federal Communications Commission) in the United States, the ETSI (European Telecommunications Standardization Institute) in Europe, and the MPT (Ministry of Posts and Telecommunications) in Japan recognize these bands for unlicensed radio operation. Therefore 802.11-based products do not require user licensing or special training of the equipment operators.

Analogous to cellular telephone and personal communication system (PCS) applications, a wireless LAN must have a *multiple access capability* wherein many users share a band of frequencies. This sharing is needed since not enough bandwidth is available to assign a permanent frequency channel to each user. The multiple access technique must be jam-proof, be robust against interference, and have a low probability of signal interception by others in order to maintain privacy between communicating users. Spread-spectrum techniques offer such features.[20-22] These techniques provide simultaneous access by many clients to a wide frequency band through the use of *code division multiple access* (CDMA) methods. Section 8.5 addresses CDMA in more detail. Here we look at the operation of spread-spectrum systems.

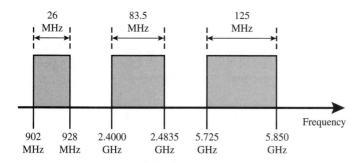

FIGURE 8.9
Comparison of the three ISM (industrial, scientific, and medical) spectral bands used for wireless LANs.

8.3.1   Overview of Spread-Spectrum Systems

The basic concept of *spread spectrum* is to distribute the power of the information signal over a bandwidth W, which is much greater than the information rate R in bits per second. This means that the bandwidth expansion factor W/R for a spread-spectrum signal is much larger than unity. By introducing coded waveforms to exploit the redundancy inherent in such an expanded bandwidth, spread-spectrum communication systems overcome the high levels of interference that may occur in wireless channels. The use of pseudorandom sequences is a second important factor in spread-spectrum systems since it makes the signals appear similar to random noise. This makes it difficult for an unauthorized receiver to intercept and demodulate a signal that is not intended for it.

Figure 8.10*a* shows the key elements of a digital spread-spectrum communication system. At the transmitting end information at a rate of R bps enters an encoder that produces an analog signal with a relatively narrow bandwidth around some center frequency. A pattern generator produces a *pseudorandom* or *pseudonoise* (PN) binary-valued sequence that is impressed on the transmitted signal in a modulator. The binary PN sequence is a random series of digits, which repeats after a certain period. The effect of modulating the signal with the PN sequence is to increase significantly the bandwidth (spread the spectrum) of the transmitted signal, as shown in Fig. 8.10*b*. At the receiving end an identical PN pattern generator is used to demodulate the spread-spectrum signal. Finally the channel decoder recovers the original data stream.

The two basic spread-spectrum methods used in a wireless LAN are frequency-hopping spread spectrum and direct sequence spread spectrum. An important point is that although both concepts are used for wireless LANs, they are fundamentally different signaling techniques and will not operate with one another. Consequently either one or the other must be used in order for a group of devices to communicate.

8.3.2   Frequency-Hopping Spread Spectrum

Frequency-hopping spread spectrum[23–24] (FHSS) does exactly what its name implies. It uses the data signal to modulate a carrier that hops from one frequency to another at fixed time intervals over a wide frequency band. The pseudorandom sequence selects the frequency of the transmitted signal. FCC regulations require using 75 or more

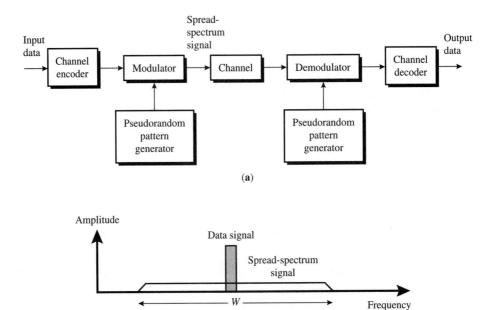

FIGURE 8.10

The concept of spread spectrum is to spread the power of the information signal over a wider band of frequencies.

frequencies per transmission channel, with a maximum time spent at a particular frequency of 400 ms, which is known as the *dwell time*. The IEEE-802.11 Standard specifies a set of 79 nonoverlapping 1-MHz frequency channels and a 300-ms dwell time in the 2.400- to 2.4835-GHz ISM band. This is used in the Americas and in Europe. For Japan the 802.11 Standard supports a set of 23 channels in the 2.473- to 2.495-GHz band. Figure 8.11 shows an example of frequency hopping over this carrier frequency range. Information exchange in an 802.11 network occurs over a specific hopping pattern in order to minimize interference with other neighboring networks. The possible hopping patterns allow up to 26 networks to be collocated and to operate simultaneously.

When using FHSS, the sender and receiver agree upon a hopping pattern, which is established by means of a PN code. Data is then sent over the carrier frequencies using either two-level or four-level *gaussian-filtered frequency-shift-keyed* (GFSK) modulation for 1- or 2-Mbps data rates, respectively. As Sec. 3.2 describes, the concept of FSK is to use different frequencies of the carrier wave to represent different binary symbols. Thus two-level GFSK uses two frequencies (one for a logic 0 and the other for a logic 1) and four-level GFSK uses four frequencies, one for each of the four possible 2-bit combinations of a logic 0 and a logic 1. The 802.11 specification for GFSK recommends filtering the NRZ data with a BT (bandwidth × symbol interval) product = 0.5 low-pass gaussian filter and using a low modulation index of 0.35 at 1-Mbps and 0.15 at 2-Mbps data rates. This gives a relatively narrow spectrum, thereby allowing 1- and 2-Mbps rates in the narrow 1-MHz hop channels.

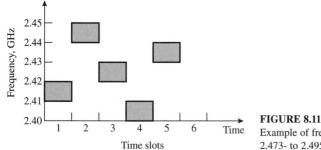

FIGURE 8.11
Example of frequency hopping over the
2.473- to 2.495-GHz carrier frequency range.

The nature of FHSS allows for a fairly simple radio design but limits the transmission speeds to 2 Mbps. This is because the GFSK modulation scheme increases the sensitivity to noise and other signal impairments, such as fading from multipath propagation, at higher data rates. Thus higher transmission rates are susceptible to a large number of errors. Using direct sequence spread-spectrum techniques solves this, as Sec. 8.3.3 describes.

8.3.3 Direct Sequence Spread Spectrum

In the *direct sequence spread spectrum*[25–27] (DSSS) technique each bit in the original signal is transformed into multiple bits in the DSSS signal, which is sent using PSK modulation. To utilize the entire available channel bandwidth, the phase of the carrier is shifted at a pseudorandom rate of W times per second according to the pattern from the PN generator. The reciprocal of W, which is denoted by T_c, defines the duration of a DSSS pulse. The pulse, which is a basic element in a DSSS signal, is called a *chip* and the parameter T_c is called the *chip interval*. If $T_b = 1/R$ is the duration of a rectangular pulse corresponding to the transmission time of an information bit, then the bandwidth expansion factor B_e can be expressed as

$$B_e = \frac{W}{R} = \frac{T_b}{T_c} = L_c \tag{8.1}$$

In actual systems this ratio is an integer L_c, which is the number of chips per information bit. That is, L_c is the number of carrier phase shifts that can occur in the transmitted signal during the information bit duration T_b.

The binary pattern of L_c chips per information bit is known as a *pseudorandom number* (PN) *code,* and also is referred to as a *chip sequence* or *spreading sequence.* Thus the multiplication process transforms the bit sequence of the original signal into a higher data rate bit sequence, thereby adding *processing gain.* The processing gain is equal to the data rate of the spread DSSS signal divided by the rate of the original signal. A high processing gain increases the resistance of a signal to interference and noise, as well as offering some protection against multipath propagation.

The 802.11 specification sets the processing gain for DSSS to 11. For example, a 1-Mbps input signal is converted into an 11-Mbps spread-spectrum output signal using *differential binary phase-shift-keyed* (DBPSK) modulation. The specific PN code

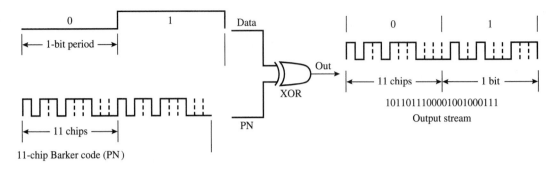

FIGURE 8.12
The 11-chip Barker sequences and the XOR function used to transmit a 1 and a 0 in DSSS.

for 802.11 DSSS is the following 11-chip *Barker sequence,* where the leftmost bit is applied first:

$$Barker\ sequence = 10110111000$$

Figure 8.12 shows the resulting 11-Mbps output pulse patterns when an exclusive-OR (XOR) function combines 0 and 1 input bits arriving at 1 Mbps with the 11-chip Barker sequence.

8.4 INFRARED WIRELESS LANS

The physical layer for infrared wireless LANs in IEEE 802.11 operates in the near-visible infrared light range of 800 to 950 nm.[28–31] Two alternative transmission concepts are *direct beams* for point-to-point links and *diffused-light operation,* wherein a transmitted light beam is aimed at a diffusing surface such as a ceiling. As Fig. 8.13 illustrates for the latter case, when the infrared beam strikes the ceiling, it is diffusely reflected in all directions so that any receiver in the vicinity can pick up the signal. The diagram in Fig. 8.13 shows the diffusely reflected infrared (IR) light from a single point on the ceiling. Transmission rates for diffused infrared LANs are 1 or 2 Mbps over distances limited to 10 to 20 m, depending on the ceiling height. Point-to-point links can accommodate much higher rates over greater distances because of the highly collimated nature of the transmitted beam. For example, available laser-based products can support 100BASE-T (100-Mbps Ethernet) or 155-Mbps ATM rates over distances ranging up to 3.5 km.

Within the localized areas in which an infrared LAN operates, IR light offers higher performance and is more secure than radio waves since it does not pass through opaque objects such as walls. Thus the signals are confined within the room or building area in which the LAN operates. Higher performance comes about since common noise sources such as radio transmitters and microwave ovens do not interfere with IR light but can affect radio waves.

Infrared wireless transmission uses a *pulse position modulation* (PPM) scheme, which maps the digital data bits into symbols that consist of a larger group of bits. For operation at 1 Mbps the infrared PMD uses 16-PPM. As Table 8.1 shows, this scheme maps each possible group of 4 bits (in the PPDU) to a unique group of 16 bits. For a

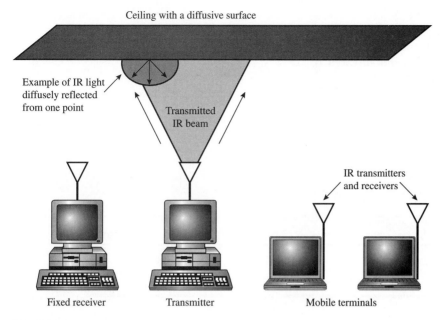

FIGURE 8.13
Operational concept of a diffused-light infrared wireless LAN.

TABLE 8.1

Bit mappings for the 16-PPM modulation scheme used in infrared wireless LANs

Data bits	16-PPM symbol
0000	0000000000000001
0001	0000000000000010
0011	0000000000000100
0010	0000000000001000
0110	0000000000010000
0111	0000000000100000
0101	0000000001000000
0100	0000000010000000
1100	0000000100000000
1101	0000001000000000
1111	0000010000000000
1110	0000100000000000
1010	0001000000000000
1011	0010000000000000
1001	0100000000000000
1000	1000000000000000

TABLE 8.2

Bit mappings for the 4-PPM modulation scheme used in infrared wireless LANs

Data bits	4-PPM symbol
00	0001
01	0010
11	0100
10	1000

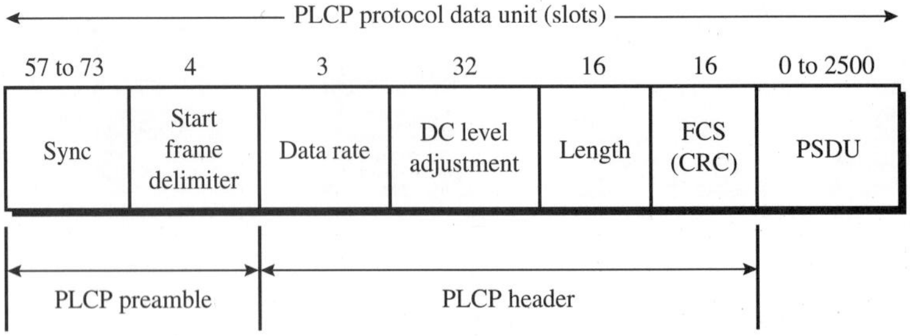

57 to 73	4	3	32	16	16	0 to 2500
Sync	Start frame delimiter	Data rate	DC level adjustment	Length	FCS (CRC)	PSDU

PLCP protocol data unit (slots)

PLCP preamble | PLCP header

FIGURE 8.14
The PLCP frame format that IEEE 802.11 specifies for infrared physical media.

2-Mbps operation the infrared PMD uses 4-PPM, which maps each possible combination of 2 bits into a unique group of 4 bits, as Table 8.2 shows. Each of the newly formed bit times is referred to as a *slot,* where a slot is 250 ns in duration.

Figure 8.14 shows the PLCP frame format that IEEE 802.11 specifies for infrared physical media. The frame consists of three basic parts. The *preamble* enables the receiver to synchronize on the incoming signal before the payload arrives. This consists of a synchronization field and a start frame delimiter. The second part is the four-field *header,* which provides information about the frame. The last part is the *PLCP service data unit* (PSDU), which is a variable-length field containing the payload data. The various fields have the following sizes and functions:

- *Sync.* IEEE 802.11 specifies the *sync field* in the PLCP preamble to vary between 57 and 73 time slots. The field consists of an alternating presence and absence of pulses in consecutive time slots. The field must end with the absence of a pulse. A receiver starts to synchronize with the incoming signal after first detecting the sync.
- *Start frame delimiter.* The PLCP preamble ends with a four-slot *start frame delimiter* (SFD), which is indicated by the bit pattern 1001. This pattern indicates the start of a frame and notifies the receiver to perform bit and symbol synchronization.
- *Data rate.* This first field in the PLCP header consists of three slots that identify the data rate. The value is 000 for 1 Mbps and 001 for a 2-Mbps rate.

- *DC level adjustment.*   This 32-slot field contains a sequence of pulses that enable the receiver to stabilize the dc level of the received signal. The bit patterns for the two supported data rates are
  00000000100000000000000010000000 for 1 Mbps, and
  00100010001000100010001000100010 for a 2 Mbps rate.
- *Length.*   The value of the *length field* is an unassigned 16-bit integer (i.e., it is not one of the 16-PPM patterns listed in Table 8.2) that indicates the length of the PSDU. The receiver will use this information to determine the end of the frame.
- *Frame check sequence.*   The last field of the PLCP frame header is a frame check sequence, which is based on the 16-bit CRC given by $G(x) = x^{16} + x^{12} + x^5 + 1$. The CRC is calculated over the length field before frame transmission. The physical layer does not check for errors in the PSDU since the MAC layer performs this function.
- *PSDU.*   The PSDU field contains the MAC PDU that is sent by the MAC layer. This field can range from 0 to a maximum of 2500 bytes.

8.5   OTHER PHYSICAL LAYER PROTOCOLS

To enhance the performance of the basic IEEE-802.11 Protocol, the wireless LAN industry and the IEEE Standards Committee are working continually on methods for both increasing the transmission speed and widening the application scope of wireless LANs. For example, for higher speeds the IEEE-802.11b enhancement was ratified in 1999 for operation at 5.5 and 11 Mbps in the 2.4-GHz band, and the IEEE 802.11a amendment describes a further increase in transmission speed to 54 Mbps in the 5.7-GHz band. The following subsections describe these enhancements.

8.5.1   IEEE 802.11b

Data sent using the IEEE-802.11b Standard is encoded by means of DSSS technology in the 2.4-GHz ISM (industrial, scientific, and medical) band at signaling rates of 11 Mbps. The standard provides for an automatic fallback to lower rates of 5.5, 2, or 1 Mbps under adverse channel conditions. For the user the 11-Mbps rate is essentially equivalent to a conventional 10-Mbps wireless shared half-duplex Ethernet. To achieve the 11-Mbps rate, a modulation method called *complementary code keying* (CCK) is used.[8,32–34] With the CCK method, the input data is grouped into blocks of 6 and 2 bits. The 6-bit blocks are used to select one of $2^6 = 64$ unique 8-chip spreading-code symbols. The other 2 bits are used for differential QPSK (DQPSK) modulation of the entire symbol. Overall the symbol rate (code word rate) for CCK is 1.375 Mbps with a chipping rate of 11×10^6 chips per second. Since each symbol is a 6-bit block, this translates into an 11-Mbps data rate. Multiplying this by 2 MHz (the null-to-null bandwidth of a chip) for QPSK encoding yields a 22-MHz-frequency spectrum in the 2.4-GHz band.

To support data rates of 1, 2, 5.5, and 11 Mbps, the IEEE-802.11b Protocol uses two PHY preamble header structures. These structures include a long and short preamble, as shown in Fig. 8.15. The *long preamble* uses the standard 1- and 2-Mbps IEEE-802.11 DSSS header to allow interoperability with other legacy systems. The preamble consists of a 16-byte sync field containing a string of scrambled logic 1 bits followed by a

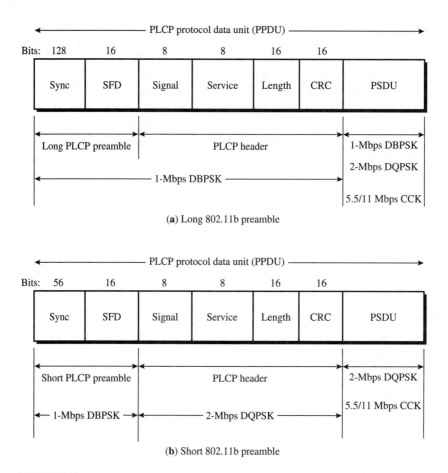

FIGURE 8.15
IEEE-802.11b frame structure for (*a*) long preambles supporting 1-Mbps DBPSK and 2-Mbps DQPSK Barker-coded data, and 5.5- or 11-Mbps CCK-formatted data, and (*b*) short preambles for 2-Mbps DQPSK Barker-coded data and 5.5- or 11-Mbps CCK-formatted data.

2-byte SFD field. Acquisition of the received signal for long preambles and headers are processed at 1 Mbps. Data packets contained in the PSDU can be received at 1-Mbps DBPSK, 2-Mbps DQPSK, and 5.5- and 11-Mbps CCK. The rate at which the PSDU is received is determined by the value stored in the signal field. To ensure interoperability with legacy systems, all 802.11b-compliant systems must support the long preamble.

The function of the *short preamble* option is to improve the efficiency of network throughput. The short preamble uses a 7-byte sync field, which is scrambled with logic 0s, followed by a 2-byte SFD field. The acquisition of the preamble signal is processed at a 1-Mbps rate. Header processing is done at 2 Mbps and the payload in the PSDU can be processed at 2, 5.5, or 11 Mbps. Processing time takes a maximum of 192 ms for the long preamble and 96 ms for the short preamble. The short preamble yields a 50 percent savings in overhead in a PPDU frame on a per packet basis. This can improve the throughput of a network when transmitting control frames and fragmented data packets carrying time-sensitive information, such as voice and real-time video.

8.5.2 IEEE 802.11a

The IEEE has issued specification 802.11a for equipment operating in the 5.7-GHz band that supports data rates up to 54 Mbps. Several vendors are producing chip sets that started appearing on the market in 2001. A further increase in the data rate to 100 Mbps allows full-duplex Fast Ethernet operation. Table 8.3 lists some basic parameters of the IEEE-802.11a Standard.[9,34,35]

When going to higher data rates, one needs to consider various multipath impairments. Figure 8.16 illustrates the *multipath* phenomenon. Here the signal from a transmitter radiates in all directions. The signal travels not only directly to the receiver, but part of it also is reflected off nearby surfaces, thereby arriving at the receiver somewhat later than the direct signal. This causes a spread in the received signal and is the main degradation mechanism for indoor wireless systems. Note that since the signal decays exponentially with distance traveled, the signal spread exhibits an exponentially decaying characteristic, as shown in Fig. 8.16. The root-mean-squared (rms) delay spread can

TABLE 8.3
Basic parameters of the IEEE-802.11a Standard

Parameter	Value
Data rates	6, 9, 12, 18, 24, 36, 48, 54 Mbps
Modulation	BPSK, QPSK, 16-QAM, 64-QAM
Number of subcarriers	52 (48 for data; 4 for pilots)
Subcarrier spacing	312.5 kHz
OFDM symbol duration	4 μs
Guard interval (GI)	800 ns
Channel spacing	20 MHz

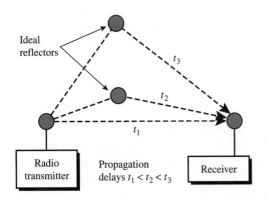

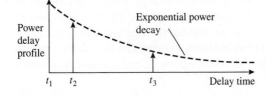

FIGURE 8.16
Multipath phenomenon in a wireless LAN.

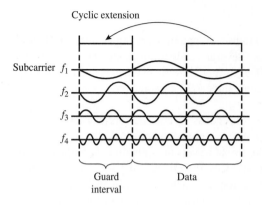

Cyclic extension

Subcarrier f_1

f_2

f_3

f_4

Guard
interval

Data

FIGURE 8.17
Examples of OFDM (orthogonal frequency
divison multiplexing) symbols with cyclic
extensions at four frequencies.

vary from 20 to 50 ns for a *small office/home office* environment (the so-called *SOHO environment*) to a range of 100 to 200 ns in a large factory.

Equipment operating under IEEE 802.11a uses *orthogonal frequency division multiplexing* (OFDM), as opposed to the spread-spectrum techniques used for other 802.11 physical layers.[36–38] The basic principle of OFDM is to divide a high-rate data stream into several lower-rate streams, which then are transmitted simultaneously on multiple subcarriers. There are 52 subcarriers available; 48 of these are data subcarriers and four are *pilot subcarriers* that can be used to track residual carrier frequency offsets. The OFDM symbol duration is 4 μs, so that the relative symbol-spreading effect caused by multipath delay is negligible. IEEE 802.11a also mitigates the effect of intersymbol interference (ISI) by having an 800-ns *guard interval* (GI) in every OFDM symbol. This guard time consists of a cyclic extension of the OFDM symbol, as Fig. 8.17 illustrates for four different carrier frequencies. The subcarrier spacing is 312.5 kHz, which is the inverse of the symbol duration minus the guard time. OFDM offers data rates ranging from 6 to 54 Mbps, depending on the modulation format and forward error correction (FEC), as shown in Table 8.3. The possible modulation formats are BPSK (binary phase-shift keying), QPSK (quadrature PSK), 16-QAM (quadrature amplitude modulation), and 64-QAM.

8.6 WIRELESS PANS

The IEEE-802.15 Standard addresses a wireless *personal area network* (PAN) for wire replacement in a limited area about the size of a room.[39–45] This standard is based on the *Bluetooth* specification, which was initiated by Ericsson Mobile Communications in 1994 for short-range radio systems.[41–46] Its key characteristics include a short transmission range within a personal operating space (10 m or less), low power consumption (battery life of months to forever), low cost, small network size (8 to 16 nodes), and communication between devices at data rates up to 20 Mbps. Applications of PAN equipment include computer peripherals, sensors and actuators, toys, smart badges, health-monitoring devices, remote controls, home automation devices, and automatic meter readers. As an example, mobile workers and business travelers can download e-mail to a laptop via a cellular telephone, synchronize palmtop devices, and access local printers.

IEEE-802.15-enabled devices operate in the same 2.4-GHz ISM band as IEEE-802.11 equipment so that there is the potential of some interference.

8.6.1 Bluetooth Technology

In order to be used in a PAN environment, Bluetooth-compatible communication products have inexpensive short-range radio transceivers built into them. When operating in a Bluetooth network, a device is categorized as either a master or a slave for transmission purposes. The *master* is the device whose clock and hopping sequence are used to synchronize all the other devices, called *slaves,* with which it communicates.

Owing to the small area in which Bluetooth operates, the networks are referred to as *piconets.* Up to seven slaves can be active in a piconet although many more slaves can remain locked to the master in a so-called *parked state.* These parked slaves cannot be active on the channel but remain synchronized to the master. A piconet can consist of a point-to-point connection in which only two Bluetooth units are involved, or it could be a point-to-multipoint connection, as shown in Fig. 8.18. In addition, several piconets can be established and linked together in a topology called a *scatternet.* Each piconet in a scatternet is identified by a different frequency-hopping sequence. All users belonging to a specific piconet are synchronized to its hopping sequence. Since each piconet can have only a single master in a scatternet, a master in one piconet can be a slave in another piconet.

8.6.2 Bluetooth Packets

The data on the piconet channel is conveyed in packets. Figure 8.19 shows the general packet format, which consists of three parts: an access code, a header, and the payload. Sixteen different packet types exist, all of which have an access code. However, in some cases a packet may not have a payload, and other packets may have neither a header nor a payload. The access code and header sizes are 72 or 68 bits and 54 bits, respectively.

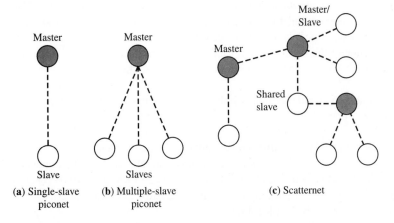

(a) Single-slave piconet **(b)** Multiple-slave piconet **(c)** Scatternet

FIGURE 8.18
Master/slave relationships for Bluetooth network topologies.

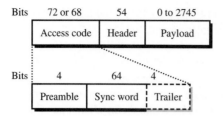

Bits   72 or 68   54   0 to 2745

| Access code | Header | Payload |

Bits   4   64   4

| Preamble | Sync word | Trailer |

FIGURE 8.19
General Bluetooth packet format and its access code format.

The payload can range from 0 to a maximum of 2745 bits. The access code is used for signaling functions and consists of a preamble, a sync word, and possibly a trailer, as shown in Fig. 8.19. If the packet contains a header, the access code is 72 bits long; otherwise it is only 68 bits. The 4-bit preamble indicates the arrival of a packet to the receiver. The 64-bit sync word is used for timing synchronization with the receiver. When it is used, the trailer is a fixed 4-bit zero-one (either 1010 or 0101) pattern.

Bluetooth uses the following three types of access codes:

- *Channel access code (CAC).* The CAC identifies a piconet and is included in all packets exchanged on that piconet. All packets sent on a given piconet have the same CAC. The CAC is 72 bits long and consists of a preamble, sync word, and trailer.
- *Device access code (DAC).* The DAC is used for special signaling procedures, such as paging and responses to paging. The *paging* process involves transmitting a series of messages with the objective of establishing a communication link to an active Bluetooth device that is within the coverage area. When that device responds to the page, the communication link can be set up. As noted earlier, the Bluetooth unit that sent out the page then is the master and the responding unit is the slave. When used as a self-contained message without a header, the DAC does not include the trailer bits and is 68 bits long.
- *Inquiry access code (IAC).* The IAC includes two variations that are termed *general* and *dedicated.* The general IAC, which is common to all devices, is used to discover other Bluetooth units that are within the range of the sender. The dedicated IAC is common to a specific group of Bluetooth units that share a common characteristic. It is used to discover only these dedicated units that are within the range of the sender. When used as a self-contained message without a header, the IAC does not include the trailer bits and is 68 bits long.

When it is used, the header contains link control information and consists of the following six fields:

- A 3-bit *address* that is used to distinguish between the active member devices on a piconet. With this 3-bit address, up to seven slaves are allowed on a piconet. The addresses are assigned temporarily to slave units when they are active. When a slave gets disconnected or parked, it gives up its address and must be assigned a new one when it reenters the piconet.
- A 4-bit packet *type indicator* that specifies which of the 16 possible packet types is being sent.

- A 1-bit field used for *flow control* of the packets.
- A 1-bit *automatic repeat request* (ARQ) field that is used to inform the transmitting device of a successful transfer of payload data.
- A 1-bit *sequence number* field that provides a method for putting the data packet stream in the proper order when it reaches the receiving Bluetooth device.
- An 8-bit *header error check* (HEC) field that is used for verifying the integrity of the header.

The total header length from these six fields is 18 bits. These bits get encoded with a rate one-third forward error-correcting (FEC) code, thereby resulting in a 54-bit header.

8.7 WIRELESS HOME NETWORKING

The widespread use of personal computers and the Internet in homes created a demand for applying networking technology in the home. In addition to personal use of these assets, telecommuters who work at their homes must be able to access files and information stored at corporate facilities through their home network connections and must have a high-quality voice connection over the same network. Basically *home networking* can be defined as the collection of elements that process, manage, transport, and store information to allow the connection of multiple computing, control, and communication devices in the home or in a small office environment. To a large extent this home networking is based on wireless technology since in most cases it is difficult to rewire existing homes with the necessary cabling system for high-speed interconnections. Figure 8.20 gives an example of such a wireless network. Nominally the wireless transmissions distances are less than 50 m, which permits full coverage within most homes (unless one lives in a mansion or a castle).

The basis for wireless home networking is the *Shared Wireless Access Protocol* (SWAP) developed by the HomeRF Networking Group.[47–50] HomeRF products use the 2.4-GHz ISM band, which allows signal transmissions through most basic home structures, such as conventional walls and floors. SWAP uses frequency-hopping spread-spectrum with a hopping rate of 50 hops per second. The transmitted power level is 100 mW and the initial data rates were specified as either 0.8 or 1.6 Mbps. In 2001 the FCC approved operation at 5 Mbps. The eventual goal is to operate at 10 Mbps in order to be compatible with 10BASE-T Ethernet.

Some examples of what users can do with products that adhere to the SWAP specification include:

- Set up a wireless home network to share voice and data among PCs, peripherals, PC-enhanced cordless phones, and other portable devices.
- Access the Internet from anywhere inside and outside of the home from portable display devices that are within transmission reach of the controller.
- Share equipment such as files, modems, and printers in multi-PC homes.
- Intelligently forward incoming telephone calls to multiple cordless handsets, fax machines, and voice mailboxes.
- Review incoming voice, fax, and e-mail messages from a small PC-enhanced cordless telephone handset.

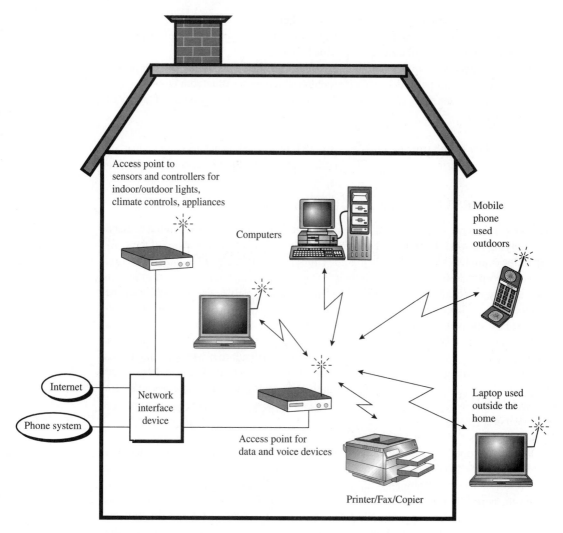

FIGURE 8.20
Example of a wireless network in a home environment.

- Activate home electronic systems by simply speaking a command into a PC-enhanced cordless handset.
- Enjoy multiplayer games that are based on PC or Internet resources.

The HomeRF products must be simple to install and use since most home users do not want to engineer and administer a complex network. Normally a controller containing a microprocessor-based switch acts as the communication server to address and route voice and data traffic throughout the home. Network devices require only a wireless

NIC and no other wires or connectors. Furthermore the system also allows wireless connectivity outside of the house. Up to 127 devices can be supported on a standard HomeRF network.

8.8 SUMMARY

Growing Internet usage has created new concepts and devices for mobile communications within a localized area, such as a home, a school campus, a health care institute, an office suite, a manufacturing facility, a warehouse, or a retail store. A user might have a device such as a palmtop or laptop computer, a personal digital assistant (PDA), or a portable data collector, which all may contain a wireless network interface card (NIC). In addition, a person might have a mobile phone with Internet access capabilities. Looking at the wide range of applications, one can broadly categorize the wireless LANs into networks for enterprise, small business, home, and personal use.

To ensure product compatibility and reliability among the various wireless LAN manufacturers, the IEEE in 1997 ratified the IEEE-802.11 Standard for operation at 1 and 2 Mbps. This provides a set of fundamental signaling methods and other services, such as asynchronous and time-bounded delivery, multicasting, network management, registration, and authentication. To satisfy the demand for higher data rates, the IEEE in 1999 ratified the 802.11b enhancement. This extension offers more physical layer options and provides for 11 Mbps and higher transmission rates in the 2.4-GHz band. The IEEE-802.11a enhancement was ratified in 1999 and supports substantially higher rates of at least 54 Mbps in the 5.7-GHz band.

Radio-based wireless LANs specified by 802.11 and 802.11b use spread-spectrum modulation techniques and operate in the 900-MHz, 2.4-GHz, and 5.8-GHz bands. Analogous to cellular telephone and personal communication system applications, a wireless LAN must have a *multiple access capability* wherein many users share a band of frequencies. This sharing is needed since not enough bandwidth is available to assign a permanent frequency channel to each user. The multiple access technique must be jam-proof, be robust against interference, and have a low probability of signal interception by others in order to maintain privacy between communicating users. Spread-spectrum techniques offer such features.

To address the growing need of communications among devices within a room-sized area, the IEEE-802.15 Standard for a wireless *personal area network* (PAN) was developed. This standard is based on the *Bluetooth* specification, which was initiated by Ericsson Mobile Communications for short-range radio systems. Its key characteristics include a short transmission range within an operating space of 10 m or less; low power consumption; low cost, small network size (8 to 16 nodes); and communication between devices at data rates up to 20 Mbps. Applications of PAN equipment include computer peripherals, sensors and actuators, toys, smart badges, health-monitoring devices, remote controls, home automation devices, and automatic meter readers.

The widespread use of personal computers (PCs) and the Internet in homes created a demand for applying networking technology in the home. *Home networking* can be defined as the collection of elements that process, manage, transport, and store information in order to allow the connection of multiple computing, control, and communication devices in the home or in a small office environment. The basis for wireless home networking is the *Shared Wireless Access Protocol* (SWAP) developed by the HomeRF Networking Group. These products use the 2.4-GHz ISM band, which allows signal transmissions through most basic home structures, such as conventional walls and floors. The initial data rates were specified as either 0.8 or 1.6 Mbps. In 2001 the FCC approved operation at 5 Mbps. The eventual goal is to operate at 10 Mbps in order to be compatible with the 10BASE-T Ethernet.

PROBLEMS

8.1. When setting up a wireless LAN, consider the following factors in order to meet user needs and system requirements: user profile and interface, function of the network, applications, information flow in the network, mobility needs, performance (e.g., reliability, availability, access delay), security, and network interfaces. For each of these factors, discuss the attributes, requirements, implementation strategies, or operational issues that may need to be considered.

8.2. A network designer wishes to link 10 mobile laptop computers to a 10BASE-T network. Assume the wireless links run at 2 Mbps over distances up to 200 m. Using web resources, list the hardware and software components needed to achieve this and determine their costs. For example, the components could include access points (APs), a wireless NIC for each laptop, and application software.

8.3. Draw a timing diagram for the successful transmission of a data frame between two mobile stations residing in the same BSS when using the CSMA/CA Protocol.

8.4. Consider an IEEE-802.11 infrastructure network. Suppose a station sends a frame to a recipient in a different BSS but within the same ESS. Draw the various data frames and ACK frames that are exchanged. Include the contents in the relevant fields in the headers.

8.5. Suppose two stations in an ad hoc IEEE-802.11 network send frames to each other. Draw the data frames and the ACK frames that are exchanged.

8.6. As a research topic, consider several of the quality-of-service (QoS) issues for ad hoc wireless networks described in Ref. 13.
 (a) Write a one-page summary of the key QoS factors that need to be addressed in such networks.
 (b) Examine the recent literature to determine what further resolutions have been proposed to guarantee QoS in an ad hoc wireless network.

8.7. What is the resulting output pulse pattern when the circuit shown in Fig. 8.12 combines the input bits 1101 with the 11-bit Barker sequence?

8.8. Suppose an infrared transmitter which emits 1.0 W of optical power illuminates a circular area on a diffusely reflecting ceiling. If the ceiling is 10 m from the transmitter:
 (a) What is the power level falling on a photodetector having a 2-cm diameter lens? Assume the receiver is at the same height off the floor as the transmitter.
 (b) What is the power level falling on such a photodetector for this same transmitter if the ceiling is 5 m from the transmitter?

8.9. Using web resources, describe the characteristics of several IR (infrared) transceivers that can be used for an indoors 802.11 LAN. Consider parameters such as the wavelength used, transmitted IR power level, data rate, and interface options.

8.10. Using web resources, describe the characteristics of several IR transceivers that can be used for a point-to-point outdoors IR link. Consider parameters such as the wavelength used, transmitted IR power level, transmission distance, data rate, and interface options.

8.11. Consider an indoors 802.11a LAN that operates in a small office environment. Suppose the transmitter and receiver are located 6 m apart and there is a reflection point on the ceiling that contributes to multipath effects.

  (a) If the ceiling height is 4 m relative to the transceiver levels, what is the time delay between signals going directly from the transmitter to the receiver and those bouncing off the reflection point?

  (b) If the system operates at 54 Mbps, what is the effect of the delay on the signal spread?

  (c) If the signal attenuates as r^2 in propagating through the air, what is the strength of the reflected signal relative to the direct-path signal? Assume an ideal reflecting surface.

8.12. Make a list of at least 10 devices that could be connected with Bluetooth and show how they might be networked. Consider the possibility that some of these devices may be in a parked mode.

8.13. Using web resources, examine the characteristics and functions of at least two Bluetooth PC adapter cards that are commercially available. Consider parameters such as support of the operating system, device interfaces, size, and power consumption.

8.14. Make a list of at least 10 devices that could be used with a HomeRF network and describe their data rate requirements.

8.15. Using web resources, examine the characteristics of some commercially available wireless networking controllers for home use. Consider factors such as data rates, transmission distances, installation complexity, and cost.

8.16. Design a wireless HomeRF network that can be used to monitor and control home equipment such as the heating systems, air-conditioning, fire and smoke alarms, window and door security controls, and kitchen appliances.

8.17. Design a wireless HomeRF network that can be used to share voice and data between PCs, peripherals (e.g., printers and fax machines), PC-enhanced cordless phones, and other portable devices and that allows Internet access from anywhere inside and outside of the home.

8.18. As a research topic, consider several of the performance issues described in Ref. 51 for using the TCP/IP Protocol to provide Internet connectivity over wireless LANs.

  (a) Write a one-page summary of the key performance factors that need to be addressed in such networks.

  (b) Examine the recent literature to determine what further resolutions have been proposed or implemented in this area.

REFERENCES

1. J. Geier, *Wireless LANs—Implementing Interoperable Networks,* Macmillan Technical Publishing, New York, 1999.
2. B. Bing, *High-Speed ATM and Wireless LANs,* Artech House, Boston, 2000.
3. W. Stallings, *Local and Metropolitan Area Networks,* Prentice-Hall, Upper Saddle River, NJ, 6th ed., 2000.
4. The website (http://www.ieee.org) leads to the home page of the Institute of Electrical and Electronics Engineers (IEEE), which will have the latest information on wireless LAN standards.
5. The website (http://www.wlana.com) describes the activities of the Wireless LAN Association (WLANA), which is a nonprofit consortium of wireless LAN vendors established to help educate the marketplace about wireless LANs and their uses.
6. IEEE Standard 802.11-1999, *Wireless LAN Medium Access Control (MAC) and Physical Layer (PHY) Specifications,* 1999 ed.
7. B. O'Hara and A. Petrick, *The IEEE-802.11 Handbook: A Designer's Companion,* IEEE Press, New York, 2000.
8. IEEE Standard 802.11b, *Higher Speed Physical Layer (PHY) Extension in the 2.4-GHz Band,* 1999.

9. IEEE Standard 802.11a, *High Speed Physical Layer (PHY) in the 5-GHz Band,* 1999.

10. J. L. Sobrinho and A. S. Krishnakumar, "Quality-of-service in ad hoc carrier sense multiple access wireless networks," *IEEE J. Select. Areas Commun.,* vol. 17, pp. 1353–1368, Aug. 1999.

11. L. Sanjay and E. S. Sousa, "Distributed resource allocation for DS-CDMA-based multimedia ad hoc wireless LANs," *IEEE J. Select. Areas Commun.,* vol. 17, pp. 947–967, May 1999.

12. C. Tschudin, H. Lundgren, and H. Gulbrandsen, "Active routing for ad hoc networks," *IEEE Commun. Mag.,* vol. 36, pp. 122–127, Apr. 2000.

13. S. Chakrabarti and A. Mishra, "QoS issues in ad hoc wireless networks," *IEEE Commun. Mag.,* vol. 39, pp. 142–148, Feb. 2001.

14. F. D. Priscoli, "Design and implementation of a simple and efficient medium access control for high-speed wireless local area networks," *IEEE J. Select. Areas Commun.,* vol. 17, pp. 2052–2064, Nov. 1999.

15. H. Woesner, J.-P. Ebert, M. Schlager, and A. Wolisz, "Power-saving mechanisms in emerging standards for wireless LANs: The MAC level perspective," *IEEE Personal Commun.,* vol. 5, pp. 40–48, June 1998.

16. S. Weatherspoon, "Overview of IEEE 802.11b security," *Intel Tech. J.,* Q2, 2000 (see http://developer.intel.com/technology/itj/q22000.htm).

17. G. Bianchi, "Performance analysis of the IEEE-802.11 distributed coordination function," *IEEE J. Select. Areas Commun.,* vol. 18, pp. 535–547, Mar. 2000.

18. F. Cali, M. Conti, and E. Gregori, "IEEE-802.11 Protocol: Design and performance evaluation of an adaptive backoff mechanism," *IEEE J. Select. Areas Commun.,* vol. 18, pp. 1774–1786, Sept. 2000.

19. B. P. Crow, I. Widjaja, L. G. Kim, and P. T. Sakai, "IEEE-802.11 wireless local area networks," *IEEE Commun. Mag.,* vol. 35, pp. 116–126, Sept. 1997.

20. L. W. Couch II, *Digital and Analog Communication Systems,* Prentice-Hall, Upper Saddle River, NJ, 6th ed., 2001.

21. J. Proakis, *Digital Communications,* McGraw-Hill, New York, 4th ed., 2001.

22. A. Leon-Garcia and I. Widjaja, *Communication Networks,* McGraw-Hill, Burr Ridge, IL, 2000.

23. S. Glisic, Z. Nikolic, N. Milosevic, and A. Pouttu, "Advanced frequency hopping modulation for spread spectrum WLAN," *IEEE J. Select. Areas Commun.,* vol. 18, pp. 16–29, Jan. 2000.

24. M. Shimizu, N. Aoki, K. Shirakawa, Y. Tozawa, N. Okubo, and Y. Daido, "New method of analyzing BER performance of GFSK with postdetection filtering," *IEEE Trans. Commun.,* vol. 45, pp. 429–436, Apr. 1997.

25. A. Kamerman and L. Monteban, "WaveLAN-II: A high-performance wireless LAN for the unlicensed band," *Bell Labs Tech. J.,* vol. 2, pp. 118–133, Summer 1997.

26. B. Razavi, "A 2.4-GHz CMOS receiver for IEEE-802.11 wireless LANs," *IEEE J. Solid-State Circuits,* vol. 34, pp. 1382–1385, Oct. 1999.

27. H. Samavati, H. R. Rategh, and T. H. Lee, "A 5-GHz CMOS wireless LAN receiver front end," *IEEE J. Solid-State Circuits,* vol. 35, pp. 765–772, May 2000.

28. J. Kahn and J. Barry, "Wireless infrared communications," *Proc. IEEE,* vol. 85, pp. 265–298, Feb. 1997.

29. R. T. Valadas, A. R. Tavares, A. M. de Oliveira Duarte, A. C. Moreire, and C. T. Lomba, "The infrared physical layer of the IEEE-802.11 Standard for wireless local area networks," *IEEE Commun. Mag.,* vol. 36, pp. 107–112, Dec. 1998.

30. P. Theodorou, J. M. H. Elmirghani, and R. A. Cryan, "ATM infrared wireless LANs: A proposed architecture," *IEEE Commun. Mag.,* vol. 36, pp. 118–123, Dec. 1998.

31. H. Yang and C. Lu, "Infrared wireless LAN using multiple optical sources," *IEEE Proc.—Optoelectronics,* vol. 147, pp. 301–307, Aug. 2000.

32. K. Halford, S. Halford, M. Webster, and C. Andren, "Complementary code keying for RAKE-based indoor wireless communication," *Proc. IEEE International Symp. on Circuits and Systems,* vol. 4, pp. 427–430, 30 May–2 June 1999.

33. M. Avery, "Putting 802.11b to the test," *Network World,* vol. 18, pp. 50–58, Feb. 5, 2001.

34. R. van Nee, G. Awater, M. Morikura, H. Takanashi, M. Webster, and K. W. Halford, "New high-rate wireless LAN Standard," *IEEE Commun. Mag.,* vol. 37, pp. 82–88, Dec. 1999.

35. C. Fisher, "Wireless home nets need 802.11a," *EE Times,* July 28, 2000.

36. R. D. J. van Nee and R. Prasad, *OFDM for Wireless Multimedia Communication,* Artech House, Boston, 2000.

37. L. Hanzo, W. Webb, and T. Keller, *Single- and Multi-Carrier Quadrature Amplitude Modulation: Principles and Applications for Personal Communications, WLANs and Broadcasting,* Wiley, New York, 2000.

38. J. Cimini and Ye Li, *Orthogonal Frequency Division Multiplexing for Wireless Communications,* Prentice-Hall, Upper Saddle River, NJ, 2001.

39. IEEE Standard 802.15, *Wireless Personal Area Networks,* 2001.

40. T. M. Siep, I. C. Gifford, R. C. Braley, and R. F. Heile, "Paving the way for personal area network standards: An overview of the IEEE P802.15 Working Group for Personal Area Networks," *IEEE Personal Commun.,* vol. 7, pp. 37–43, Feb. 2000.

41. J. C. Haartsen, "The Bluetooth radio system," *IEEE Personal Commun.,* vol. 7, pp. 28–36, Feb. 2000.

42. N. J. Muller, *Bluetooth Demystified,* McGraw-Hill, New York, 2001.

43. B. A. Miller and C. Bisdikian, *Bluetooth Revealed,* Prentice-Hall, Upper Saddle River, NJ, 2000.

44. G. Held, *Data over Wireless Networks: Bluetooth, WAP, and Wireless LANs,* McGraw-Hill, New York, 2001.

45. J. Bray and C. Sturman, *Bluetooth: Connect Without Cables,* Prentice-Hall, Upper Saddle River, NJ, 2001.

46. *Bluetooth Specification,* version 1.1, Feb. 2001. (See http://www.bluetooth.com.)

47. Information about the HomeRF Working Group, product vendors, and related resources can be found at the website (http://www.homerf.org).

48. J. Lansford and P. Bahl, "The design and implementation of HomeRF," *Proc. IEEE,* vol. 88, pp. 1662–1676, Oct. 2000.

49. K. J. Negus, A. P Stephens, and J. Lansford, "HomeRF: Wireless networking for the connected home," *IEEE Personal Commun.,* vol. 7, pp. 20–27, Feb. 2000.

50. L. D. Paulson, "Exploring the wireless LANscape," *Computer,* vol. 33, pp. 12–16, Oct. 2000.

51. G. Xylomenos, G. C. Polyzos, P. Mähönen, and M. Saaranen, "TCP performance issues over wireless links," *IEEE Commun. Mag.,* vol. 39, pp. 52–58, Apr. 2001.

CHAPTER
9

FIBRE CHANNEL AND SANS

Fibre Channel was designed and developed in 1988 as a means for connecting high-speed peripherals, such as a cluster of high-performance computers or supercomputers, to a storage device. Point-to-point and switched configurations were the first topologies developed for Fibre Channel. The capability to support loop topologies was added later in order to make Fibre Channel economically attractive for the networking of information-generating-and-processing equipment with a common set of mass storage devices. The result is that Fibre Channel has a generic architecture that blends gigabit-networking technology and input/output (I/O) channel connection technology, which offers high-speed transmission and guaranteed delivery of data. Consequently Fibre Channel is suitable for connecting peripheral storage equipment to host computers, as well as for network connectivity in a local environment, such as a workgroup or a campus setting.[1-6]

One of the most valuable assets of any corporation is its stored information. New computer applications and new business models are generating vast amounts of information that not only need to be stored somewhere, but also need to be shared internal to the organization and with corporate partners and customers. The information could include accounting records, customer information, engineering drawings, inventory status, and presentation material. A major challenge in corporate information technology (IT) networks is how to move, manage, utilize, store, and back up this information in a timely and cost-effective manner. Fibre Channel has become the principal interconnection and networking technology for specialized networks that are used for these information storage functions.

This chapter first defines the concepts of storage area networks in Sec. 9.1 and illustrates how Fibre Channel is used to realize such a network. Next Sec. 9.2 describes the concept of an I/O channel, the physical structure of Fibre Channel, and the transmission media that are commonly used. In Fibre Channel the traditional physical and media access control (MAC) protocol layers are divided into six hierarchical protocol levels. Each level defines a function or set of related functions, such as physical, transmission, signaling, or frame protocol characteristics. These levels and their functions are described in Sec. 9.3. Next Sec. 9.4 examines the services offered by Fibre Channel to achieve specific types of flow control and message acknowledgment for different categories of traffic. Finally Sec. 9.5 gives an overview of storage over IP (Internet Protocol).

9.1 STORAGE AREA NETWORKS (SANS)

The need to network storage devices to computing and communication resources in order to manage huge quantities of new and existing information gave rise to the concept of a storage area network[7–12] (SAN). A *storage area network* is a dedicated network that connects one or more computing systems to a collection of storage devices, as shown in Fig. 9.1. A storage system could include high-end disk arrays, a collection of individual disk drives (nicknamed JBOD for *just a bunch of disks*), a *redundant array of inexpensive disks* (RAID) system, or tape-drive libraries. Tape drives are used primarily for backup and recovery schemes because they are relatively slow compared to disk drives. Since continuing advances in storage technology are greatly reducing the cost of storing data, the main challenge to IT personnel is how to manage and to provide access to the vast amounts of stored information cost effectively.

The flexible, high-speed, and scalable networking characteristics of Fibre Channel have made it the prime networking technology for SANs. Figure 9.2 shows typical storage applications using a Fibre Channel network. The basic network topologies are point-to-point links with dedicated bandwidth, loop configurations with shared bandwidth, and switched architectures with scaled bandwidth. The point-to-point topology is a very elementary Fibre Channel implementation that directly connects servers to storage devices. Of greater interest are the loop and switch topologies, which are used in SAN applications.

Examples of the equipment that may be connected to a SAN with a Fibre Channel network include computers, workstations, servers, and printers. Connections between this equipment and storage devices or subsystems are made by using elements such as switches, hubs, and bridges. The switches could be stackable Fibre Channel switches, LAN switches that interface Fibre Channel with legacy LANs, and externally controlled link switches that provide point-to-point connections. Fibre Channel delivers gigabit-per-second connections over distances up to 10 km in a campus environment. Link extenders may be used to provide longer cable distances of up to 100 km to remote locations.

In addition to providing the network infrastructure for storing and retrieving information, the underlying network must offer the ability to back up and recover information in case of any type of disaster.[13,14] These could include hurricanes, floods, fires, extended power outages, or sabotage. In these events the back-up data must be current and stored in a safe location. Depending on the severity of the disaster, the data processing center at a primary corporate facility may be out of commission for days, weeks, or months. Thus

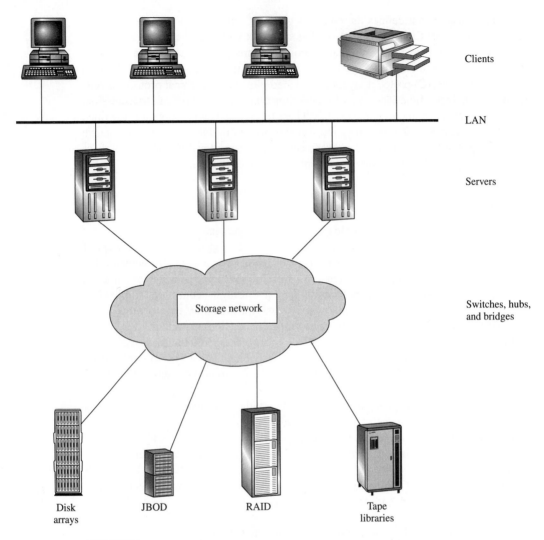

FIGURE 9.1

A storage area network (SAN) connects various computing entities to a collection of storage devices.

the goal of disaster recovery is to store critical information safely in a remote location so that it can be retrieved easily in the wake of an emergency. The remote storage site must be outside of any perceived threat radius, which is the maximum distance from the data center that a disaster may cover. Figure 9.3 illustrates this scenario. For example, a major corporation in Manhattan may locate its recovery facilities in New Jersey, in Brooklyn, or on Long Island. Since single-mode Fibre Channel links can span distances up to 100 km, this is a reasonable scenario. Other possibilities are to use a high-speed SONET (Synchronous Optical Network) link to transport critical data to more distant locations. For example, a corporation in Los Angeles may decide to store its information in facilities in Arizona or New Mexico.

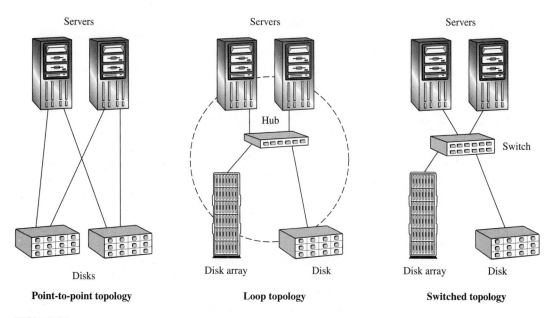

FIGURE 9.2
Typical storage applications using a Fibre Channel network.

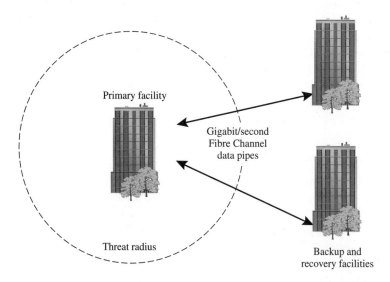

FIGURE 9.3
Data backup and recovery facilities must be outside of any perceived threat radius.

The other factors to consider are the bandwidth requirements of the transmission channel between a data center and the remote recovery facility. These requirements include a very short-time window within which to back up the data, an ability to collect and send real-time data updates, and a rapid retrieval time of the data from the remote facility following recovery from a disaster. A gigabit Fibre Channel network offers the speed, scalability, flexibility, and reliability to realize an effective system of backup and recovery. At a 100-Mbps rate each Fibre Channel link has the capability to move a gigabyte of data every 80 seconds. At a 10-Gbps rate a Fibre Channel link can transfer a terabyte of data in less than 15 minutes.

9.2 THE STRUCTURE OF FIBRE CHANNEL

Fibre Channel has features of both a channel and a network. Let us look at the contrasts between these two technologies. A *channel connection* provides either a direct or a switched point-to-point linkage between communicating devices. Its function is simply to transmit data as fast as possible from one location to another with a predetermined address and very limited data processing demands. In contrast, *network connections* are multipoint connections that depend on addressing and routing mechanisms to ensure that the data goes to the appropriate destination. In addition, network connections nominally have fairly sophisticated error detection and correction capabilities.

The combination of these two technologies enables Fibre Channel to function as a simple high-speed channel that has the flexibility of protocol-based communication capabilities for connecting computing equipment to a network fabric. The *network fabric* is the ensemble of connections and switches in the network. The fabric size can range from two pieces of equipment with a single cable between them to a large mesh network consisting of the connections between many devices and numerous switches.

Fibre Channel is highly flexible and protocol-independent because it is a generic transport mechanism. Thus it can support command sets from a variety of other standard protocols, such as the Small Computer Systems Interface (SCSI), the Internet Protocol (IP), the IEEE-802.2 logical link control (LLC) protocol, or the asynchronous transfer mode (ATM) protocol. The speed and guaranteed delivery features of Fibre Channel make it an attractive protocol for connecting network devices arranged in point-to-point, loop, or switched topologies in a relatively local environment.

9.2.1 Concept of I/O Channels

In terms of channel characteristics an important concept in storage technology is that of an I/O channel. An *I/O channel* is a direct high-speed link between a processor and some device where data is stored. For example, the bus in a workstation to which the network interface card (NIC) is attached generally is known as the I/O bus or the data bus. This I/O bus is the main data transfer channel between the central processing unit (CPU) and the random-access memory (RAM) in the workstation. Figure 9.4 shows a simple example of an I/O channel. Storage networks can be viewed as a subset or an extension to the basic idea of an I/O channel.

A key I/O technology is SCSI.[15–17] SCSI is a high-speed interface that traditionally has been implemented on personal computers, workstations, and servers. In that application it is used to support data transfers between processors and high-capacity devices, such as storage disks, CD-ROM drives, graphics displays, and video equipment. Although SCSI interfaces function well in a direct, one-to-one interconnection between servers and storage, they are unable to support the levels of performance, manageability,

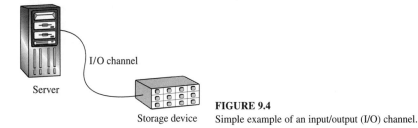

FIGURE 9.4

Server   I/O channel   Storage device   Simple example of an input/output (I/O) channel.

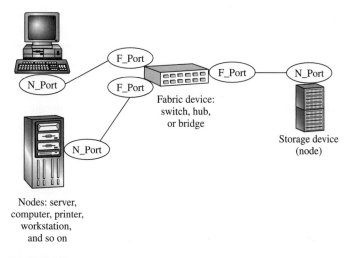

Nodes: server,
computer, printer,
workstation,
and so on

FIGURE 9.5
Basic architecture of a Fibre Channel network fabric showing the concept of N_Ports and F_Ports.

and scalability required by networked massive storage environments. In addition, SCSI interfaces have a distance limitation of 25 m between servers and storage devices. Fibre Channel combines the best of both SCSI and networking in that it implements the SCSI common command set over the Fibre Channel network protocol layer. Thus Fibre Channel extends the highly reliable I/O channel of SCSI to link computing elements to storage devices over significantly longer distances.

9.2.2 Physical Architecture

Figure 9.5 illustrates the basic architecture of a Fibre Channel network fabric. The key elements are nodes and the network itself. A *node* is any hardware entity that can send or receive information. Thus a node can be a computer, a server, a storage device or subsystem, a printer, or a scanner. The term *node* does not refer to network equipment such as switches, hubs, or bridges, which connect nodes to storage devices and do not initiate or receive data transmissions.

Each node has one or more ports called *network ports* or N_Ports. The responsibility of N_Ports is to initiate and conclude transmission of frames at the two ends of a communication link. Similarly, each switching element in the fabric has one or more *fabric ports* called F_Ports that are access points to the fabric. The N_Ports are linked either directly with a bidirectional point-to-point link or through an F_Port into a switching network. The F_Ports provide management and connection services to handle all transmission of frames between N_Ports. For example, if an initiating N_Port wants to connect to a recipient N_Port that is busy or unavailable, the F_Port associated with the initiating N_Port can queue the connection request in a buffer until the path to the destination N_Port clears. If the path remains blocked after a specific time, the F_Port notifies the initiating N_Port of this condition.

The fabric may buffer frames at switching elements so that various N_Ports may connect to the fabric at different speeds. However, since the transmission mechanism is isolated from the control protocol, Fibre Channel switches read a minimal amount of information in the transmissions and have optimized hardware for very fast data transfers. Thus the switches are able to forward data packets very quickly without needing large amounts of buffer resources. This means that a switch normally starts forwarding frames to the destination node while they still are coming from the source node.

Point-to-point and switched configurations were the first topologies developed for Fibre Channel. Loop topologies were devised later in order to make Fibre Channel economically attractive as an I/O channel for connecting storage devices. In contrast to the dedicated links on point-to-point and switched networks, nodes on a loop network share a common cabling system. Thus the concept of a *loop port* or L_Port arose. Whereas N_Ports were designed to interact with F_Ports in fabrics, L_Ports are designed to communicate directly with any other L_Port on a loop, even when there are intermediate nodes on the loop. Since there is no switch in a loop to control the access of the node to the network, loops use an arbitration access scheme to avoid or manage potential collisions during the time that nodes contend for loop access. Therefore a loop topology in SAN applications is referred to as an *arbitrated loop.*

When an L_Port wants to establish communications with another L_Port, it waits until the loop is available. At that time it sends an *arbitration frame* to identify itself as an arbitration participant. This frame is passed from node to node around the loop. When it reads the frame, each successive node decides if it also wants to arbitrate for loop access. If it has a higher priority than the initiating node, the downstream node replaces the address in the arbitration field of the frame with its own address. When it does not have a higher priority, it passes the arbitration frame unchanged to the next node. When the initiating node recognizes its own address after the arbitration frame completes a trip around the loop, the node knows that it successfully has gained access to the loop and can start a login procedure. If the initiating node sees an address with a higher priority in the frame, it passes the frame to the next node. The arbitration frame then continues around the loop until it arrives at the arbitrating node with the highest priority.

With the addition of a loop to the family of Fibre Channel topologies, two other port definitions were formed in order to allow N_Ports in fabrics to communicate with L_Ports in loops. As Fig. 9.6 shows, these are FL_Ports and NL_Ports. FL_Ports enable a switch to participate as a special node on a Fibre Channel loop. The loop network reserves an address for only one FL_Port, so there can only be one active switch at a time communicating on any specific loop. An NL_Port resides in a loop and has both N_Port and L_Port capabilities. This means it can support both fabric login as well as loop arbitration procedures. This allows network elements in fabrics and loops to communicate across the boundary between them. For example, a server system in a loop may wish to communicate with a large storage subsystem in a fabric, as shown in Fig. 9.7.

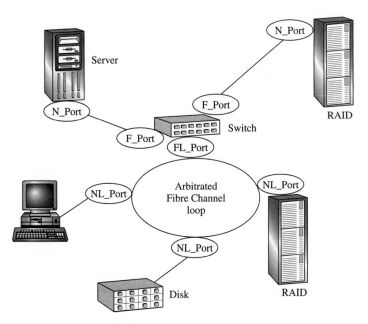

FIGURE 9.6
Illustration of the concept of FL_Ports and NL_Ports in a Fibre Channel loop topology.

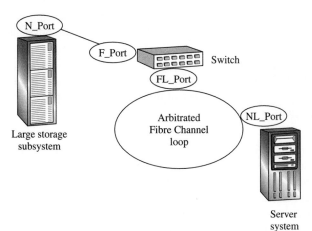

FIGURE 9.7
Server system in a Fibre Channel loop communicating with a large storage subsystem in a fabric.

9.2.3 Transmission Media

Although the networking technology is called Fibre Channel, the transmission media can be either copper wires or optical fibers. Transmission rates of up to 100 Mbps can use either copper or fiber media, whereas higher speeds normally need to be sent over optical fibers. Copper-based cables can include video cable, miniature cable, and shielded twisted-pair wires. For lightwave links, the choices are 62.5-μm multimode, 50-μm multimode, and single-mode fiber. The standard specifies both long-wavelength (1310- and 1550-nm) and short-wavelength (850-nm) semiconductor laser diode transmitters. The 850-nm transmitters are used for short distances. The long-wavelength systems are used for distances up to 10 km in a campus environment.[18] Link extenders may be used to provide longer cable distances of up to 100 km to remote locations.[19]

The optical links have the option to implement the *open fiber control* (OFC) protection scheme. This scheme is designed as an eye safety precaution to prevent disconnected fiber ends or open fibers in a severed cable from continuously transmitting light. OFC uses a simple protocol whereby each transmitter on a link periodically transmits short pulses of light to the other receiver. When the receivers detect these pulses, the transmitters can operate normally. The transmitters turn off when no monitoring signal is received.

9.3 PROTOCOL LAYERS

In traditional networking schemes the first two modular levels in the TCP/IP and the OSI protocol stacks are the physical layer and the medium access control (MAC) layers. These two layers implement the algorithms that determine what system may communicate over the network. For example, Ethernet uses the CSMA/CD (or IEEE 802.3) Protocol and wireless LANs use the IEEE-802.11 Protocol. The Fibre Channel Standard expands on the two-layer concept by defining six modular protocol levels that provide the same functionality but greater flexibility, as shown in Fig. 9.8. These are designated as Fibre Channel layer 0 (FC-0) through Fibre Channel layer 4 (FC-4), and FC-AL for the arbitrated loop topology. Each level defines a function or a set of related functions. Layers FC-0 through FC-2 are part of the basic *Fibre Channel Physical and Signaling Interface* Standard,[3] which is abbreviated FC-PH. The FC-PH Standard defines physical layer, transmission, signaling, and framing protocols. The FC-AL Standard augments FC-PH to define transmission and signaling functions for loop topologies that do not require a fabric.[12,20] The FC-3 Protocol describes common services. The FC-4 standards, which are above the FC-PH and FC-AL layers, consist of functions that map application protocols to Fibre Channel services.

1. *Layer FC-0* is called the *physical interface*. This defines the physical and media interfaces, such as the transmitters, receivers, connectors, and cables used by Fibre Channel. In addition, it describes the electrical or optical characteristics of the transmission media. The physical media may be optical fibers, coaxial cables, or shielded twisted-pair (STP) wires. Data rates on these media range from 100 Mbps to 10 Gbps. Depending on the data rate and the medium used, the point-to-point distances for a link can range from 50 m to 100 km.

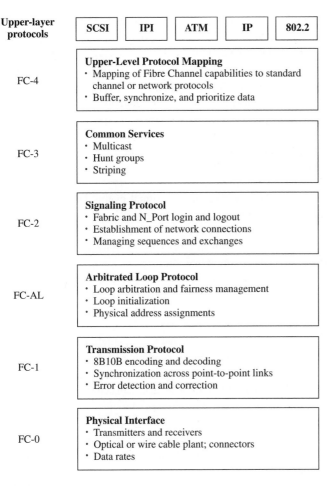

Upper-layer protocols

| SCSI | IPI | ATM | IP | 802.2 |

FC-4

Upper-Level Protocol Mapping
· Mapping of Fibre Channel capabilities to standard channel or network protocols
· Buffer, synchronize, and prioritize data

FC-3

Common Services
· Multicast
· Hunt groups
· Striping

FC-2

Signaling Protocol
· Fabric and N_Port login and logout
· Establishment of network connections
· Managing sequences and exchanges

FC-AL

Arbitrated Loop Protocol
· Loop arbitration and fairness management
· Loop initialization
· Physical address assignments

FC-1

Transmission Protocol
· 8B10B encoding and decoding
· Synchronization across point-to-point links
· Error detection and correction

FC-0

Physical Interface
· Transmitters and receivers
· Optical or wire cable plant; connectors
· Data rates

FIGURE 9.8
Fibre Channel expands on the two-layer PHY and MAC concept by defining six protocol levels that provide the same functionality.

2. *Layer FC-1* is called the *Transmission Protocol.* This is responsible for synchronization across the point-to-point links and for establishing the signal encoding rules for transmitting data packets. The encoding mechanism is the 8B10B scheme described in Chap. 5 for Gigabit Ethernet. Recall that this means that eight consecutive bits of data from a higher-protocol level are converted into 10 bits for transmission. These uniformly sized 10-bit code units enable the protocol to synchronize data transmission, and provide an error recovery and retransmission mechanism.

3. *Layer FC-AL* is the *Fibre Channel Arbitrated Loop Protocol.* Here point-to-point unidirectional serial links interconnect neighboring ports to form a loop. The protocol allows up to 126 devices, plus one optional fabric element, such as a switch, to attach to a loop. As described in Sec. 9.2, the FC-AL Protocol defines the procedures for acquiring loop access and for establishing a connection with the receiving port. Once a point-to-point connection exists between the sender and the receiver, the framing protocol defined in the FC-PH Standard governs the transfer of data frames. The FC-AL Standard supports multiple loops, with dual-loop topologies being typical in FC-AL storage networks.

4. *Layer FC-2* is the *Signaling Protocol*. This level is the most complex part of Fibre Channel and includes most of the constructs, procedures, and operations that are specific to Fibre Channel. Basically it defines the frame format and specifies how data bits are transferred between N_Ports through the F_Ports of the Fibre Channel switching device. The N_Ports have a management system called the Link_Control_Facility, which manages the physical and logical links between them through objects called ordered set, frame, sequence, and exchange.

   (a) An *ordered set* is a delimiter or flag used to signal events in low-level link functions. This signaling helps Fibre Channel to establish a network connection when devices are first turned on and also helps with some basic recovery actions.

   (b) A *sequence* is the unit of data transfer in Fibre Channel and consists of a frame or group of frames describing a single operation.

   (c) *Frames* are the smallest communication unit in Fibre Channel. As shown in Fig. 9.9, they are similar to frames in other network implementations. They have start- and stop-delimiters, headers, payload, and CRC fields. Each frame belongs to a sequence.

   (d) An *exchange* is a group of sequences that make up a single operation, which usually involves several tasks. For example, sending a packet of data includes connection initiation, connection acknowledgment, packet transmission, and packet-receipt acknowledgment. Each of these tasks is a separate sequence, but together they constitute a single exchange.

   Other concepts defined by FC-2 include segmentation and reassembly of data frames, class of service designations, sequencing of frames, flow control (i.e., congestion management), and error control.

5. *Layer FC-3* provides a set of services that are common across multiple N_Ports of a node. The three main functions are multicast, hunt groups, and striping:

   (a) *Multicast* delivers a single transmission to multiple destination ports by means of a group address. This could be a broadcast to all N_Ports on a particular network fabric or to a subset of these ports.

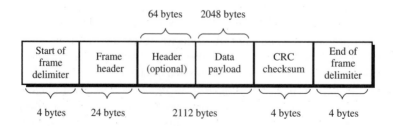

FIGURE 9.9
The composition of a Fibre Channel frame.

(*b*) A *hunt group* in Fibre Channel is similar to a telephone hunt group in which an incoming call can be answered by any one of a predefined group of phones. In Fibre Channel a hunt group is a predefined set of associated N_Ports at a single node, such as ports belonging to a mass storage device. Frames addressed to a hunt group are delivered to any available port within this group. This may reduce latency by decreasing the chance of waiting for a busy N_Port to become free.

(*c*) *Striping* is a parallel transmission method that uses multiple N_Ports in parallel to send a single information unit. For example, it may divide an information unit into *M* parts and send these simultaneously across *M* links connecting N_Ports. Thus the information unit is sent as *M* parallel "stripes" from one location to another. This results in a higher aggregate information throughput.

6. The *FC-4 layer* is the application layer, which provides buffering, synchronization, and prioritization of data. It also provides mapping of Fibre Channel capabilities to various standard channel or network protocols. Examples of these are the SCSI and Intelligent Peripheral Interface-3 (IPI-3), which are channel interfaces, and the IP, the IEEE-802.2 LLC Protocol, or the asynchronous transfer mode (ATM) protocol, all of which are network interfaces.

9.4 FIBRE CHANNEL SERVICE CLASSES

The types of flow control and acknowledgment of message delivery offered by Fibre Channel depend on the class of service (CoS) that is designated for the particular network traffic that is sent. These service classes are defined within the FC-2 layer and range from Class 1 through Class 6. No Class 5 is defined. The CoS is determined during the login procedures for the fabric and the nodes. All participating ports are required to support the same CoS. Unrelated communications among another set of ports on the same network may implement a different CoS.

9.4.1 Class 1 Service

Class 1 service is an acknowledged service that guarantees a specific data rate between two communicating ports and guarantees delivery of frames. This service provides a dedicated path through the fabric, which is established before data transfer can take place. The two ports reserve the path through the fabric for as long as they need to complete their information exchange. This could be for seconds, minutes, hours, or permanently.

Class 1 service delivers data frames in the same order in which they are transmitted since they are sent over a dedicated connection. Eliminating the need to reorder frames at the receiving node can reduce significantly the burden of protocol processing. Class 1 confirms the delivery of each frame by means of an acknowledgment from the receiving port. If congestion causes a frame to be dropped, a busy signal is returned to the sending port, which then retransmits the frame. Class 1 service is well suited to applications in which large blocks of data must be transmitted or if high-speed guaranteed information delivery is required, such as full-motion video.

9.4.2 Class 2 Service

In *Class 2 service* the link between N_Ports is shared with other users. This allows a more efficient use of network capacity since data frames from a number of sources can be multiplexed over the same link within the network fabric.

The frames are not necessarily received in the same order as they were sent. Since the reordering of the frames is done at the receiving port, a Class 2 switch can balance internal and network resources efficiently to provide the highest possible aggregate bandwidth for the entire network fabric. However, the reordering at the recipient port needs to be done within a certain time period. If there is a long latency in a particular switch, the frames may arrive too late for the recipient port to reorder them. In that case error recovery will take place and the sending port will retransmit the information.

Class 2 guarantees delivery of frames by means of an acknowledgment from the receiving port. Analogous to Class 1 service, the sending port will receive a busy signal from the receiving port if congestion causes a frame to be dropped. Thus the sender knows to retransmit the missing frame. Class 2 service therefore is well suited for networks that are not sending time-sensitive information, such as storage area networks (SANs).

9.4.3 Class 3 Service

Class 3 service is a connectionless packet-switched service that does not offer guaranteed frame delivery, gives no acknowledgment of frame receipt, and does not provide reordering of frames by the recipient port. To reduce the number of lost packets due to congestion, buffers are required on both the transmitting and receiving ports. Since Class 3 service does not have the overhead associated with message acknowledgment and frame reordering features, it offers lower port latency. Thus the transmitted information can be exchanged more rapidly with higher layer functions.

In data storage applications the upper-layer protocols normally include message acknowledgment and frame-reordering functions so that not having them in Class 3 service is not a problem. Thus some storage applications, in particular, data back-up systems, may use Class 3 service to benefit from its larger bandwidth and higher efficiency.

9.4.4 Class 4 Service

In Class 4 a connection between two N_Ports consists of two unidirectional virtual circuits (VCs) between them, which do not need to run at the same speed. Class 4 circuits will guarantee that frames arrive in the order that they were transmitted and will provide acknowledgment of delivered frames. An N_Port may have more than one Class 4 circuit at the same time. These connections may be with one or more other N_Ports. Since the bandwidth resources in Class 4 may be divided into potentially many circuits, it is known as a *fractional bandwidth service.*

Class 4 enables the virtual circuit that is established between two N_Ports to have a reserved bandwidth with a predictable quality of service (QoS). The QoS is established independently for each direction of the VC and includes parameters such as guaranteed throughput and bounded end-to-end delay. Thus Class 4 service is a good candidate for time-sensitive and real-time applications, such as audio, videoconferencing, and remote training.

9.4.5 Class 6 Service

Class 6 service is known as a *Simplex* or *Unidirectional Connection Service*. It is similar to Class 1 service, and, in addition, it offers multicast functionality through a fabric and frame preemption. Basically when a station wants to transmit frames to more than one N_Port at a time, it sets up a Class 1 dedicated connection with the multicast server within the fabric. The multicast server sets up individual dedicated connections between the original N_Port and each of the desired destination N_Ports. The multicast server is responsible for replicating and forwarding the frame to all other N_Ports in the multicast group. End-to-end flow control is used between the N_Ports and the multicast server. Class 6 service generally is used for video broadcast applications and for real-time systems that transfer large amounts of data.

9.5 OTHER STORAGE METHODS

9.5.1 Storage over Internet Links

The widespread use of the Internet and the desire to store data in distant locations gave rise to an interest in sending block-level storage data over IP networks.[21,22] To achieve this, the Internet Engineering Task Force (IETF) is looking at two approaches. The first is a *tunneling* method in which Fibre Channel control codes and data are translated into IP packets for transport over the Internet between two geographically separated Fibre Channel SANs. In the second approach native block-level SCSI data is encapsulated in an IP packet, as shown in Fig. 9.10, and then tunneled through the TCP/IP stack. After

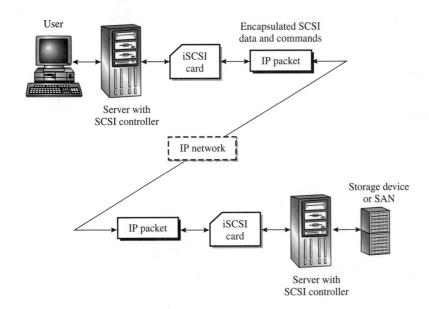

FIGURE 9.10
Transmission of block-level SCSI (Small Computer Systems Interface) data over an IP (Internet Protocol) network.

passing through the IP network, at the receiving end the IP packet is unwrapped by an external router and converted back to SCSI data. This type of storage network scheme is referred to as an IP SAN, which is known popularly as *iSCSI*. To ensure reliability, an IP SAN can use standard network management tools and utilities that have been developed for IP networks.

9.5.2 Storage over Ethernet Links

Owing to the large base of installed Ethernet equipment, SANs based on switched Ethernet are another alternative to Fibre Channel implementations.[23] The attractive point of this is that since the storage data runs over the existing Ethernet infrastructure, this storage technique retains all the existing networking, interoperability, manageability, compatibility, and cost advantages of Ethernet. This scheme is particularly useful for building smaller localized SANs that use the same Ethernet infrastructure as the LAN with which they are associated within an enterprise facility. As shown in Fig. 9.11, the SCSI data is encapsulated in an IP packet which then gets sent over an Ethernet link to a storage area.

9.6 SUMMARY

Fibre Channel has a generic architecture that blends gigabit-networking technology and input/output (I/O) channel connection technology, which offers high-speed transmission and guaranteed delivery of data. As a result, Fibre Channel has become the principal interconnection and networking technology for specialized information storage networks, which are known as storage area networks or SANs. A SAN is a dedicated network that connects one or more computing systems to a collection of storage devices. These could

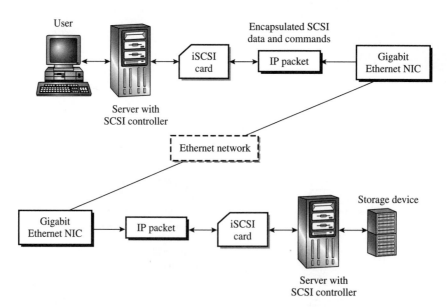

FIGURE 9.11
Transmission of block-level SCSI data over an Ethernet network.

include high-end disk arrays, a collection of individual disk drives (nicknamed JBOD for *just a bunch of disks*), a *redundant array of inexpensive disks* (RAID) system, or tape-drive libraries.

Examples of the equipment that may be connected to a SAN with a Fibre Channel network include computers, workstations, servers, and printers. Connections between this equipment and storage devices or subsystems are made using elements such as switches, hubs, and bridges. The switches could be stackable Fibre Channel switches, LAN switches that interface Fibre Channel with legacy LANs, and externally controlled link switches that provide point-to-point connections. Fibre Channel delivers gigabit-per-second connections over distances up to 10 km in a campus environment. Link extenders may be used to provide longer cable distances of up to 100 km to remote locations.

Although the networking technology is called Fibre Channel, the transmission media can be either copper wires or optical fibers. Transmission rates of up to 100 Mbps can use either copper or fiber media, whereas higher speeds normally need to be sent over optical fibers. Copper-based cables can include video cable, miniature cable, and shielded twisted-pair wires.

Alternatives to using only Fibre Channel for SAN purposes include methods of sending block-level storage data over IP networks and Ethernet links. In these methods either the Fibre Channel control codes and data or the native SCSI data is translated into IP packets. These packets then are sent over IP or Ethernet links.

PROBLEMS

9.1. List and discuss five reasons for the growth of Internet storage.

9.2. Using web resources, describe the features of a commercially available JBOD (just a bunch of disks) storage array.

9.3. A RAID (redundant array of inexpensive disks) system is an important component for SANs (storage area networks). Using web resources, describe the features and capabilities of at least two different commercially available RAID systems.

9.4. Vendors have agreed upon six RAID levels that have different characteristics and protocols. Using web resources that show vendor offerings, describe each of these six levels in a few sentences.

9.5. Discuss some factors to consider for implementing data backup and recover strategies.

9.6. Describe at least three reasons why Fibre Channel is more advantageous for SAN applications than a protocol such as Ethernet.

9.7. Why is Fibre Channel more advantageous for SAN applications than a protocol such as ATM?

9.8. List some features of SCSI (Small Computer Systems Interface). What are some of its limitations for transferring data between processors and high-capacity storage devices? Some resources concerning SCSI can be found at website (www.scsilibrary.org).

9.9. Using web resources, examine the characteristics of some commercially available Fibre Channel switches. Consider factors such as the number of ports, port speeds, service classes that are supported, switch latency, and management protocols that are supported.

9.10. Discuss the impact on the initial selection of products and their deployment for the following storage network design considerations:
- Application requirements
- Protocol support
- Cable plant and distances between nodes

- Number of current devices and anticipated growth
- Accommodation of legacy equipment
- Traffic volumes
- Departmental segregation
- Redundancy, backup, and disaster recovery

9.11. Using information available on the Web, research the resources you need and the procedures you have to follow in order to store data on a FTP (File Transfer Protocol) site. Consider both secure and anonymous FTP sites.

9.12. Using web resources, compare the operational characteristics of disks versus tape drives. Consider factors such as speed, capacity, and cost.

9.13. Striping is a parallel transmission method that uses multiple N_Ports in parallel to send a single information unit. List and discuss some examples of striping applications.

9.14. Using web resources, research what type of transceivers and transmission media are best suited for transmission distances ranging from 50 m to 10 km and speeds ranging from 100 Mbps to 1 Gbps.

9.15. Using web resources, research the latest status concerning the two approaches to the iSCSI specification described in Sec. 9.5.1.

9.16. Draw a diagram showing the main physical devices (e.g., computer, circuit card, switch, and storage element) that are needed in the path between the data source and the storage equipment when implementing a storage-over-Ethernet system. Give a one-sentence description of the purpose of each device.

REFERENCES

1. A. F. Benner, *Fibre Channel,* McGraw-Hill, New York, 1996.
2. The American National Standards Institute (ANSI) is the main organization that is setting Fibre Channel standards (http://www.ansi.org).
3. ANSI, *Fibre Channel Physical and Signaling Interface-3 (FC-PH-3),* ANSI X3.303-1998. This document recommends the development of a third generation physical interface for Fibre Channel. This interface is fully backward compatible with the architecture defined in the earlier FC-PH and FC-PH-2 versions, but it also incorporates significant new technologies and functionality.
4. The Fibre Channel Industry Association (FCIA) is an international organization of manufacturers, systems integrators, developers, systems vendors, industry professionals, and end users of Fibre Channel products (*see* http://www.fibrechannel.org).
5. T. Parnell, *Building High-Speed Networks,* McGraw-Hill/Osborne, Berkeley, CA, 1999, Chap. 11.
6. The Fibre Channel Conference is devoted to Fibre Channel and its applications (*see* http://www.fibreconference.com).
7. M. Farley, *Building Storage Networks,* McGraw-Hill/Osborne, Berkeley, CA, 2000.
8. T. Clark, *Designing Storage Area Networks: A Practical Reference for Implementing Fibre Channel SANs,* Addison-Wesley, Reading, MA, 1999.
9. The Storage Network Industry Association (SNIA) (http://www.snia.org).
10. R. H. Thornburgh and B. J. Schoenborn, *Storage Area Networks: Designing and Implementing a Mass Storage System,* Prentice-Hall, Upper Saddle River, NJ, 2001.
11. B. Phillips, "Have storage area networks come of age?" *Computer,* vol. 31, pp. 10–12, July 1998.
12. J. R. Heath and P. J. Yakutis, "High-speed storage area networks using a Fibre Channel arbitrated loop interconnect," *IEEE Network,* vol. 14, pp. 51–56, Mar.–Apr. 2000.
13. J. W. Toigo, *Disaster Recovery Planning: Strategies for Protecting Critical Information,* Prentice-Hall, Upper Saddle River, NJ, 2nd ed., 2000.
14. E. Marcus and H. Stern, *Blueprints for High Availability: Designing Resilient Distributed Systems,* Wiley, New York, 2000.
15. W. Stallings, *Computer Organization and Architecture,* Prentice-Hall, Upper Saddle River, NJ, 5th ed., 2000.

16. F. Schmidt, *The SCSI Bus and IDE Interface: Protocols, Applications and Programming,* Addison-Wesley, Reading, MA, 2nd ed., 1998.

17. ANSI, *SCSI Fibre Channel Protocol,* X3.269-1996.

18. ANSI, *Fibre Channel: Low-Cost 10-km Optical 1063-MBaud Interface (100-SM-LC-L),* ANSI NCITS 326-1999.

19. ANSI, *Fibre Channel: Very Long-Length Optical Interface (SM-LL-V),* ANSI NCITS 339-2000.

20. ANSI, *Fibre Channel Arbitrated Loop (FC-AL-2),* ANSI NCITS 332-1999.

21. B. Ross, "Storage over the Internet—iSCSI emerges," *Network World,* vol. 17, p. 59, Dec. 4, 2000.

22. C. Clark, "SAN meets WAN," *Network World,* vol. 18, pp. 56–58, Mar. 19, 2001.

23. R. Horst, "Gigabit Ethernet storage networks," *Network World,* vol. 18, p. 55, Mar. 26, 2001.

CHAPTER
10

INTERNETWORKING

The phenomenal growth in the use of the Internet has resulted in services that millions of people now take for granted, such as e-mail, web browsing, and electronic exchange of business transactions. More and more Internet services and applications are appearing constantly as the power and versatility of networks, protocols, and computing hardware and software increase. As a result, the concept of a local area network (LAN) as an isolated entity has become obsolete. No matter whether the LAN is used in a large business, in a small office, at home, or within our personal spaces, it is now imperative that LAN users have the capability to share not only resources that belong to their own LAN, but also to interact with other users, to access corporate databases (if authorized), and to retrieve marketing and product information from other businesses, all of which may be located anywhere in the world.

The concept for achieving this is known as *internetworking* and effectively creates a single large, loosely coupled network from many different local, metropolitan, and wide area networks. The large network is known generally as an *internet*. Internetworking essentially provides the electronic highway that is needed to link separate communities of connectivity. By means of this highway a larger network is created from a collection of smaller networks. For example, a corporate site may have different types of LANs that handle a variety of needs or that are segregated for security reasons. An organization may have LANs at different locations, which need to be interconnected. As computing devices have become more sophisticated and widely used, a particular LAN may have grown to the point where it must be divided into multiple LANs in order to maintain a proper performance level for all users. Furthermore users attached to a LAN may need to have access to web resources or data storage devices in distant locations. In all these cases some type of communication mechanism is necessary for users on different networks to exchange messages.

In this chapter Sec. 10.1 first points out some basic business drivers for internetworking. Section 10.2 presents some basic concepts of internetworking. The two main topics are an overview of how LANs are interconnected to each other and to other networks, and what the standard, global addressing procedure is for uniquely identifying any node on the Internet. We then examine the characteristics of the key communications equipment used for internetworking and the types of networks that may be formed with them. Included in this equipment are bridges, routers, and switches, which are discussed in Secs. 10.3 through 10.5, respectively. Section 10.6 addresses the concept of a virtual LAN. This is a limited broadcast domain in which only a certain number of specific stations receive the information sent by the members assigned to the virtual LAN. For example, finance, marketing, and engineering development departments in a corporation all may want to restrict communications over a common LAN to members of their individual organizations.

10.1 BUSINESS DRIVERS

To offer the capabilities for interconnecting computers all over the world obviously requires network providers to make major investments in the underlying network infrastructure, the protocols needed to enable internetworking, and the management of the communications assets. A major economic incentive for the investing organizations to pursue internetworking is the revenue they can collect from corporations that use the network and the applications running on it for electronic business purposes. This section examines the basic business drivers for internetworking. These include the function of the Internet, the software applications that are transported over the Internet, the concepts of intranets and extranets, and applications such as electronic commerce, e-mail, and World Wide Web services.

10.1.1 The Internet

The *Internet* is a worldwide computer network made up of thousands of networks that enables communications among 10s of millions of computers.[1,2] What is amazing from the point of view of internetworking is that no one is in overall charge of the Internet. Although various standards organizations have developed technical aspects of this network, no governing body has global control. The Internet backbone is owned by many companies that are located in all corners of the world.

An important distinction to keep in mind between the Internet and the applications running on it is that the Internet is a network medium and not a service. This means that the Internet is an information highway that enables software applications to run over it. The Internet can be accessed by entities ranging from large organizations (e.g., corporations, research institutes, universities, and governments) to home users. Larger organizations normally access the Internet through a router that interconnects their internal LAN with leased high-capacity transmission lines. Section 10.4 presents the operational details of routers. Small businesses and home users access the Internet via a dial-up modem that connects to an *Internet service provider* (ISP) through standard local telephone lines. The ISP then provides the interconnection to the Internet through high-capacity transmission lines that it either owns or leases.

The various networks that make up the Internet itself are run by *network service providers* (NSPs). An NSP leases or buys transmission facilities consisting of copper wires, optical fiber cables, wireless links, or satellite links from organizations such as telecommunications companies, wireless communications service providers, and cable plant operators that own transmission facilities. NSPs offer high-speed Internet access by selling bandwidth and network connectivity to ISPs. NSPs commonly are referred to as *backbone providers* because they offer direct access to the Internet backbone and the network access points (NAPs).

Figure 10.1 gives an example of the internetwork path that a message might follow in a user-to-user message exchange. Suppose the sender is located in a small business. Therefore at that end the user connection is made through a modem to a local ISP via standard telephone lines. The ISP connects to a network service provider through leased wire or wireless lines from local telephone companies. The NSP inserts the message onto the Internet, where it may traverse numerous links and routers before reaching another NSP at the receiving end. If the message recipient is located in a large organization, the message will travel from the NSP to an external router and then go through the LAN of the organization to the recipient.

Internet users have access to a wide variety of services by means of the *World Wide Web* (WWW), which popularly is referred to as the *Web*. The Web is a software application that easily enables almost anyone to publish and browse hypertext documents on the Internet. *Hypertext* are web pages that have hyperlinks which, when selected,

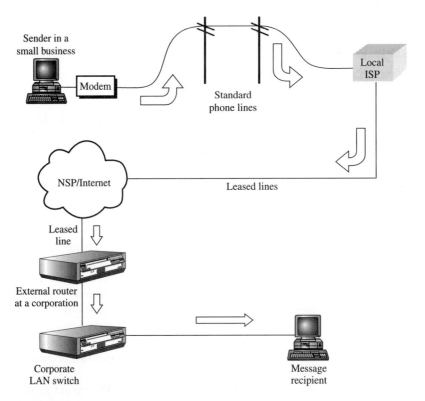

FIGURE 10.1
Example of the path that a message might follow through an Internet.

will cause the web browser to retrieve and display another web page or graphic. Among the web-based services are chat sessions between interest-group members, web-based electronic learning, interactive collaboration between widely dispersed research organizations, multimedia entertainment, and shopping opportunities. Other applications that use the Internet as a transport mechanism are electronic mail (e-mail) and file transfer capabilities via the *File Transfer Protocol* (FTP).

10.1.2 Intranets

An intranet is a private web-based collaborative computing network within an organization.[3–5] Thus an intranet is a LAN configuration that provides the same capabilities and features for electronic information access and delivery inside an organization as the Internet does on the outside. To implement this intranet, corporate databases are placed on internal servers that are accessible only by authorized users belonging to the organization. The individual users access these databases through the standard web browsers with which they are familiar for viewing web pages on the Internet. In addition, this enables users to link to other intranets within the corporation and to external information by means of the Internet.

Figure 10.2 illustrates an integration scenario between an intranet and the Internet. The top of the figure shows the corporate LAN, which is depicted as being based on Ethernet. This LAN links various servers, which handle services such as file storage, fax transmission and receipt, or departmental database deposition. These general purpose LAN servers normally are accessible by all corporate users. The mail server provides the entire enterprise with e-mail services. The intranet servers can be accessed by members from various departments, provided they have been assigned the rights to view the information. Users access the information from their computer after logging in their user name and password. Once they find the content for which they are looking, they either can view it, print it, download it into a spreadsheet if they need to analyze the data further, or even update the content if this option is available. Note that both the mail server and the LAN itself are attached through a high-speed Ethernet router to a security firewall.

There are many corporate information resources and transactions that are potential candidates for an intranet. Among these are the following:

- Information in databases
- Manuals on policies and procedures, quality control, work procedures, and so on
- Company newsletters and special public relations announcements
- Software user guides and hardware manuals
- Questions concerning employee medical and other benefits programs
- Job postings and opportunities
- Expense report submission and printing

10.1.3 Extranets

The same benefits that web technologies brought to corporate intranets also have driven the move to electronic business-to-business transactions (popularly known as *B2B transactions*). This has led to the concept of an *extranet,* which is a private network that uses

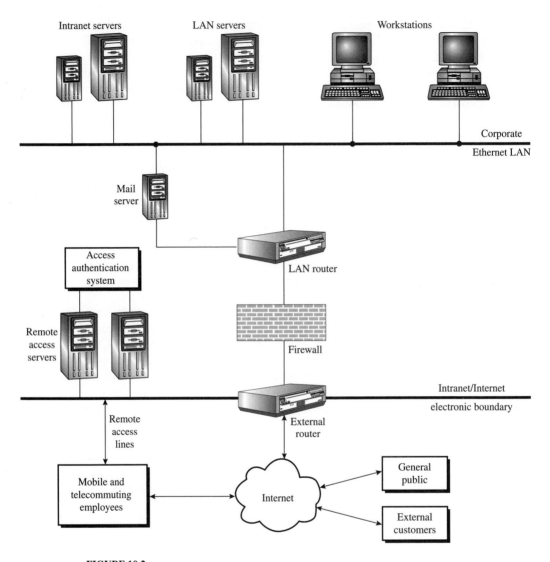

FIGURE 10.2
An integration scenario between an intranet and the Internet.

Internet protocols and the public telecommunication system to share securely part of the proprietary information or operations of the host organization with suppliers, vendors, partners, customers, or other businesses. Figure 10.3 shows a basic relationship among intranets, extranets, and the Internet. An extranet can be considered as part of an intranet that is extended to users outside of the company. Extranets can be used to exchange large volumes of data, to share product catalogs, to share news with trading partners, to collaborate with other companies on joint development efforts, to develop and share

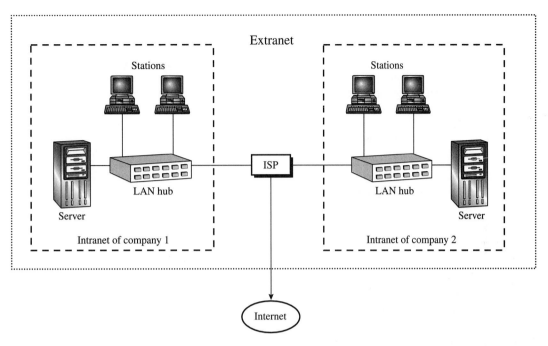

FIGURE 10.3
Illustration of a basic relationship among intranets, extranets, and the Internet.

training programs with other companies, and to provide or access applications between companies. An extranet has restricted (password-protected) access so that it may be connected directly to the internal systems of the participating parties.

The benefits of extranets include reduced time to market, a lower cost of doing business, and faster access to partner information. In addition, compared to other business-to-business communications, such as *electronic data interchange* (EDI), an extranet is more user-friendly because of its web interface and the fact that it allows for less regimented and more ad hoc inquiries. However, a number of security precautions must be exercised with extranets to prevent company-sensitive or mission-critical information from inadvertently falling into the wrong hands. Chapter 12 addresses the security issues of extranets in more detail.

10.2 INTERNETWORKING PERSPECTIVE

This section gives some basic concepts in order to understand internetworking better. First we look at some methodologies for interconnecting networks. Next we examine what the addressing scheme is for identifying nodes on the Internet. From this we will see that every device on a LAN or any other network has a unique IP address associated with it.

10.2.1 Interconnection Methodologies

The three main data communication devices used for setting up internetwork connections are bridges, routers, and switches.[6–9] Bridges work at layer 2 (the link layer) of the OSI (Open System Interconnection) model, whereas routing occurs at layer 3 (the network layer). Bridges normally connect similar LAN segments. Switches can operate at layers 2 or 3, depending on their built-in capabilities. Routers and switches are viewed as general purpose devices that interconnect either similar or dissimilar networks.

The three basic interconnection methodologies are:

1. Connections between homogeneous LANs
2. Connections between heterogeneous LANs
3. Connections of a LAN to other types of networks

The reasons for creating an internetwork between homogeneous LANs include breaking a large overburdened LAN into several segments, isolating one or more servers for a select group of users, and interconnecting geographically dispersed segments of the same network. A physical *segment* is defined as all stations that are connected to the same medium. As shown in Fig. 10.4a, if stations of a particular group mainly communicate with each other, then *segmentation* reduces congestion and improves network performance on this particular LAN since there will be less contention for the LAN resources on each segment. In this example 80 percent of the traffic originating in either LAN segment 1 or LAN segment 2 stays within the respective segments, and only 20 percent of the traffic is exchanged between the two segments. Segmentation will not improve performance if the stations on different segments send a high percentage of their traffic to the outside.

The linkage of LAN segments is done at the data link layer by means of a bridge or a switch. Similarly, a switch can be used for *server isolation.* In this case, as shown in Fig. 10.4b, a switch can connect individual LAN segments to high-performance servers that are isolated to a separate LAN segment in order to improve access to network resources. Finally, as shown in Fig. 10.4c, a simple *LAN extender* or *repeater* can be used to connect remote LAN segments directly to each other by means of terrestrial telecommunication lines, microwave links, satellite links, or a combination thereof. LAN extenders and repeaters operate at layer 1 of the OSI model (the physical layer) and merely repeat whatever they receive in order to extend the distance that a signal can be transported over a given medium.

Interconnections among heterogeneous LANs are needed when users or devices in different organizations or in different departments in the same organization are required to communicate with one another. Figure 10.5 shows an example of this. Here users attached to an Ethernet LAN have access to devices connected to a Fibre Channel storage area network (SAN) or to an ATM network. A router or a switch with appropriate adapter cards operating at the network layer (layer 3) may act as the internetworking device. LAN switches also can be used to interconnect different types of Ethernet LANs, such as 10- and 100-Mbps segments, as shown in Fig. 10.6.

The third interconnection, that is, between a local area network (LAN) and a metropolitan area network or a wide area network, provides a user with access to other

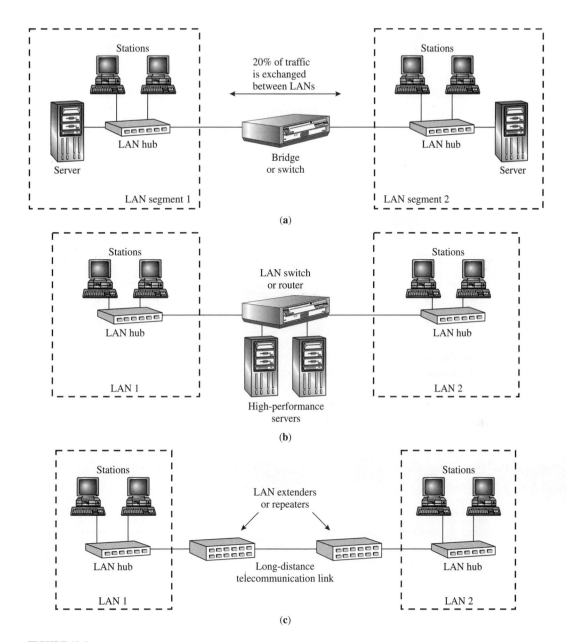

FIGURE 10.4

Network interconnection devices can be used for (*a*) segmentation of a large network, (*b*) server isolation, and (*c*) extension of a local area network (LAN).

communication elements or information resources all over the world. Examples of this are LAN connections to the Web. Again either a router or a switch acts as the internetworking device.

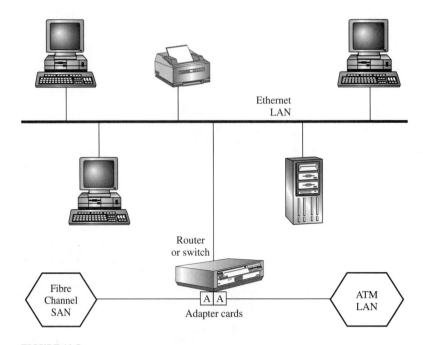

FIGURE 10.5
Switches or routers can be used to interconnect heterogeneous LANs.

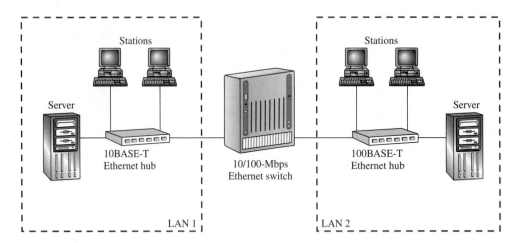

FIGURE 10.6
Use of a switch to interconnect different types of Ethernet LANs.

10.2.2 Internet Addressing Scheme

To identify any node uniquely on the Internet, TCP/IP uses a standard, global addressing procedure.[10–12] The identifier is called an *IP address*. Recall that the points where devices connect to the network are referred to as *nodes* and that a particular device such as a switch or a router may have more than one network connection. In this situation an IP address is associated with a network connection rather than with the network device. However, for a computer with a single network interface the IP address identifies the computer itself.

As shown in Fig. 10.7, based on version 4 of the Internet Protocol (IPv4), an IP address consists of four 1-byte fields (32 bits) of binary values separated by decimal points. This allows for 2^{32} unique addresses, which is somewhat over four billion. The emerging version 6 of the Internet Protocol (IPv6) advocates the use of 128-bit addresses. This yields $2^{128} = 3.4 \times 10^{38}$ unique addresses. Since the largest 8-bit number is 255, for IPv4 the allowed address numbers can range from 0.0.0.0 to 255.255.255.255. For example, it might be the number 133.175.6.87, which is shown in Fig. 10.7 along with its binary equivalent. There are two major parts to the address, a network identifier or a number, and a host or a machine number. The *network number* defines the network to which a particular user belongs. The *host number* uniquely identifies a specific user node within the network. All hosts on the same network have identical network numbers but different host numbers. Note that historically several network sizes were established so that the network number can range from 1 byte for a large network with many users to 3 bytes for many networks with a small number of users. The corresponding host numbers therefore are 3 bytes for a many-user network to 1 byte for a small network. Addresses are no longer given out according to these classifications. Instead, blocks of IP addresses are assigned to organizations based on their address needs.

Figure 10.8 shows an example of IP address assignments for two Ethernet LANs connected by switches and routers through the Internet. The network addresses of the two LANs are 142.8.0.0 and 135.6.0.0. The latter LAN is segmented into two subnets designated by 135.6.8.0 and 135.6.28.0 in order to organize the attached users into two groups. When a packet is sent from a user on LAN 2 to node 142.8.32.1 on LAN 1, two steps are needed for the packet to reach its destination. First the packet is delivered to the network site based on the network address 142.8.0.0 and then it is delivered to the host at 142.8.32.1. If a host on LAN 1 wants to correspond with user 135.6.28.3 on LAN 2, the routing process of the packet involves the following three steps: First it is delivered to the network, then to the subnet, and finally to the host.

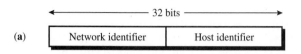

(a)

(b)   Example decimal IP address: 133.175.6.87

FIGURE 10.7
(*a*) Simple representation of an IPv4 address; (*b*) example of an IP address using decimal numbers; (*c*) binary equivalent of the IP address in part (*b*).

(c)   Binary equivalent IP address:

        10000101 10101111 00000110 01010111

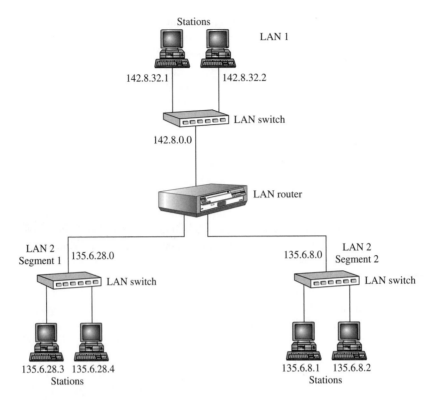

FIGURE 10.8
Example of IP address assignments for two Ethernet LANs connected by routers through the Internet.

10.2.3   Domain Name System

Instead of using an IP address, which is cumbersome to remember, people prefer to use a name as the address for a host. This led to the creation of the *domain name system* (DNS) protocol, which maps a name to an address and vice versa.[12–14] In modern jargon DNS maps user-friendly names into router-friendly addresses. As Fig. 10.9 illustrates, DNS uses a hierarchical naming structure in which the components or domains are separated by dots and processed from right to left.

A *domain* refers to a subdivision of a wide area network. A major subdivision is the *top-level domain,* which is broken into organizational and geographic domains. The geographic or country domains use two letters to identify a country. Table 10.1 shows some of the 225 country domain labels that are available. Example country domain labels are *.cn* for China, *.de* for Germany, *.jp* for Japan, and *.ve* for Venezuela. The organizational domain designations are intended to define registered hosts according to their generic behavior. Table 10.2 lists some commonly used organizational domains and their generic descriptions. The first seven labels were the ones defined originally. In 2001 more labels were added to handle an ever-increasing demand for domain names and to broaden the generic descriptions. For example, it is common to use *.com* for commercial organizations, *.edu* for educational institutes, and *.gov* for government groups in the United States. Note that these generic descriptions do not need to be followed strictly.

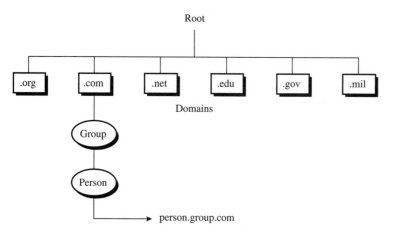

FIGURE 10.9
Example of the hierarchical naming structure used by the DNS (Domain Name System) Protocol.

TABLE 10.1
Examples of country domain labels

Domain name	Country
au	Australia
ca	Canada
cn	China
de	Germany
eg	Egypt
fr	France
il	Israel
in	India
jp	Japan
tr	Turkey
uk	United Kingdom
ve	Venezuela

TABLE 10.2
Some common organizational domains and their generic descriptions

Label	Generic description (traditional)	Label	Generic description (new labels in 2001)
com	Commercial organizations	biz	For businesses
edu	Educational institutes	info	Information service providers
gov	U.S. government institutions	museum	Museums
int	International organizations	name	For registration by individuals
mil	U.S. Department of Defense	pro	Professional: for example, accountants, lawyers, physicians
net	Networking organizations	ws	Website
org	Nonprofit organizations		

Address at local site	@	Destination domain name

FIGURE 10.10
Construction of an e-mail address.

The domains under the top-level domain are the path designators that are used to map an address to a name. These paths can consist of several levels or *zones*. To send e-mail to a user mailbox, one simply connects the mailbox name and the domain name with an @ sign, as shown in Fig. 10.10.

EXAMPLE 10.1

1. A user called *hammer* who is within the zone called *tool* within the commercial organization *hardware* can be located by the e-mail address (hammer@tool.hardware.com).
2. A user called *daffodil* who is within the nonprofit organization *happiness* can be located by the e-mail address (daffodil@happiness.org).
3. The educational and consulting firm PhotonicsComm Solutions, Inc. has the domain name (photonicscomm.com). The mailbox name of the sales department at this firm is *sales*. Thus the e-mail address of this department is (sales@photonicscomm.com).

10.3   BRIDGES

Bridges were used widely in the mid-1980s to interconnect multiple LAN segments in a corporation. As networks evolved since then, switches now are used more widely than bridges. This is due to the superior performance, higher port density, lower-per-port costs, and greater implementation flexibility that switches offer compared to bridges. However, since LAN switches evolved from bridging concepts, we will look at the basic functions of bridges and their limitations compared to switches.[9,15–17]

Bridges work at the MAC level in the data link layer, which controls data flow, handles transmission errors, provides physical addressing, and manages access to the physical medium. The three basic functions of bridges are forwarding, filtering, and learning.

- *Forwarding* involves passing a frame toward its ultimate destination. Bridges are fairly simple devices that analyze incoming frames, use the information in the MAC address of the frame to make forwarding decisions based on a bridging table, and direct the frames toward their destination. For example, consider LAN 1 and LAN 2, which are connected by a bridge as shown in Fig. 10.11. Suppose Cindy (known to the LAN by the IP address 132.78.8.10) wants to send a message to Rocky on LAN 2 (who has an IP address 132.78.9.3). The addresses indicate that Cindy and Rocky are on the same company network (132.78.0.0) but on different LAN segments (132.78.8.0 and 132.78.9.0, respectively). Upon analyzing the incoming frame from Cindy, the bridge sees from the IP address that it needs to be forwarded to LAN 2 based on the information in its bridge table.
- *Filtering* relates to discarding frames that are headed in a direction where they do not need to go. This means that a bridge can be programmed to filter out all frames

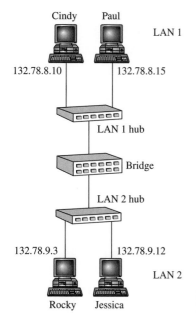

Cindy Paul

LAN 1

132.78.8.10 132.78.8.15

LAN 1 hub

Bridge

LAN 2 hub

132.78.9.3 132.78.9.12

LAN 2

Rocky Jessica

FIGURE 10.11
Frame forwarding function of a bridge.

from a particular network and not to forward them. Again the bridge carries this out by comparing the address of an incoming frame with that contained in a bridge table. This function can be useful in reducing traffic by eliminating those broadcast and multicast messages that do not need to be sent to a particular group of users.

* *Learning* is the function that a bridge performs when it receives a frame from a device for which it has no address in its bridge table. In this case the bridge dynamically updates its table and then is aware of the device; that is, the bridge has learned the host and network address of the new device.

The IEEE-802.1D specification defines the protocol architecture that was developed to ensure that LANs which are extended by bridges exhibit consistent characteristics.[18] The latest version of 802.1D augments the concept of MAC bridging to support both the transmission of time-critical information and the dynamic use of group MAC addresses in a LAN environment. Several basic algorithms are used for the bridging of LANs. The more common algorithm is called *transparent bridging* and has been standardized for extended LAN configurations by the IEEE-802.1D specification. Another is called *source route bridging* and is used on IEEE-802.5 Token-Ring LANs. The IEEE has combined these two methods into a device called a *source routing transparent* (SRT) *bridge*. This configuration concurrently provides both source route and transparent bridging. A third bridging method uses *translating bridges* to connect dissimilar LANs.

Bridges that interconnect 802-type LANs directly are called *local bridges*. This category of bridges can permit segmentation and connectivity of LANs at the same time, as shown in Fig. 10.12. Here each of the engineering, marketing, and manufacturing departments has its own LAN. The LANs are connected through bridges, thereby

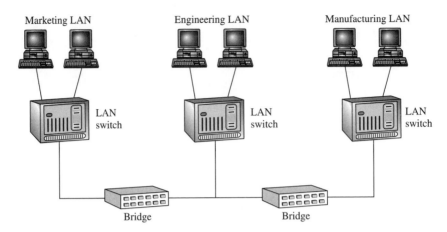

FIGURE 10.12
A local bridge permits both segmentation and connectivity of LANs.

allowing isolation of departmental computing on the individual LANs and yet maintaining a communications capability between users in different departments.

Bridges in which one or more ports interface to metropolitan area (MAN) or wide area (WAN) networks are known as *remote bridges.* Remote bridges incorporate MAN and WAN interfaces that are designed to provide an internetworking capability between two or more geographically dispersed LANs linked by a MAN or a WAN.

10.3.1   Transparent Bridges

A *transparent bridge* is the simplest type of bridge. It is used to provide a connection between two LANs that employ the same data link protocol, as Fig. 10.13 illustrates. Here a station on the left-hand LAN sends a message through a transparent bridge to a user station in the right-hand LAN. The symbols t_i are used to indicate what the frame looks like at successive time periods (t_1 through t_8) as the message flows through the link. The term "transparent" means that when the bridge is placed in the network, it does not change any of the MAC addresses in frames that flow through it, as shown by the frame formats at times t_4 and t_5 in Fig. 10.13. Therefore a frame will pass through a bridge when going from one LAN segment to another without the bridge identifying itself as the device that sent the frame to the next segment. When the frame arrives at its destination, the receiving device will be able to determine the MAC address of the originating station.

A transparent bridge operates by first reading the source address contained in each incoming frame, as shown in Fig. 10.14. From these addresses the bridge uses its internal learning logic to assemble a *forwarding table* of local addresses for each network. In practice, such a table can have a few thousand entries to handle an interconnected network of multiple LANs. Normally a row in a forwarding table will contain the mapping from a network address to an outgoing interface port. The table also may contain some MAC information, such as the Ethernet address of the next hop. The bridge reads the destination address (the MAC layer address of the NIC at the destination) of each incoming data frame. Using its forwarding lookup logic, it decides whether the destination is local (on

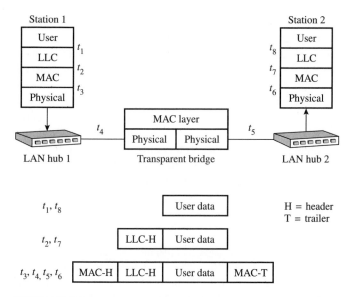

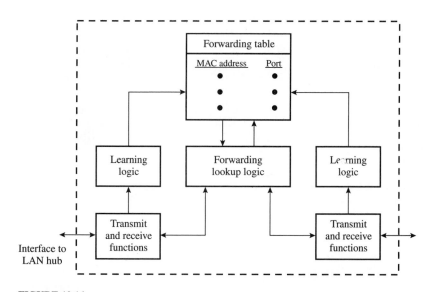

FIGURE 10.13

A transparent bridge provides a connection between two LANs that employ the same data link protocol.

FIGURE 10.14

Operational concept of a transparent bridge.

the same LAN as the originating station) or remote (on the other side of the bridge). If the destination address is not contained in the local address table of the bridge, this indicates that the destination of the frame is not on the current LAN or LAN segment. In this case the bridge transmits the frame onto the other segment.

Since the number of entries in the forwarding table is large and needs to be updated *dynamically*, the simplest and most elegant way is to have the bridge build the table automatically. The bridge does this by inspecting the *source address* of all frames it receives and then builds or updates its forwarding table as follows. When a bridge receives a frame, it first compares the source address of the frame with each entry in the forwarding table. If it does not find a match, the bridge adds the source address to the table together with the port number on which the frame was received. Next the bridge compares the *destination address* of the frame with each entry in the forwarding table. When there is a match, the bridge sends the frame out on the port indicated in the entry. In case the port is the one on which the frame was received, the bridge discards the frame since the destination address is local so that no forwarding is required. If there is no match of the destination address, the bridge sends the frame out on all ports except the one on which it arrived. This latter process is known as *flooding*.

EXAMPLE 10.2

To see how a transparent bridge builds a forwarding table, consider the network consisting of three LANs interconnected by two bridges shown in Fig. 10.15. The forwarding table for each bridge is shown below it in Fig. 10.15. Suppose initially the table is empty and station S1 (which has an IP address 195.100.3.31) on LAN 1 decides to send a frame to station S5 (which has an IP address 195.100.8.10) on LAN 3. Thus the MAC address of this frame designates S1 as the source address

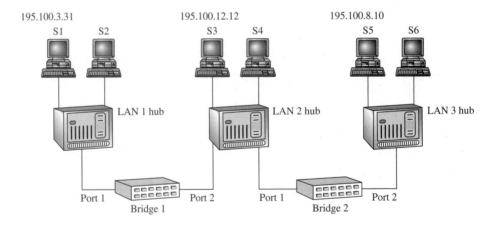

	Address	Port		Address	Port	
Step 1	195.100.3.31	1		195.100.3.31	1	Step 2
Step 3	195.100.12.12	2		195.100.12.12	1	Step 3

FIGURE 10.15
Creation of forwarding tables for two transparent bridges.

and S5 as the destination address. When bridge 1 receives the frame, it finds the table empty and therefore adds the source address of S1 and its corresponding port number (in this case port 1) to the table, as indicated by step 1 in Fig. 10.15. Since the destination address also is not in the forwarding table, bridge 1 forwards the frame to port 2. The frame thus is transmitted to LAN 2 and consequently arrives at bridge 2. When bridge 2 receives the frame, it performs the same table-updating process as bridge 1 just had gone through. That is, bridge 2 adds the source address and corresponding port number to its forwarding table as indicated in step 2 in Fig. 10.15. Bridge 2 also forwards the frame out of its port 2 to LAN 3 so that the frame then arrives at station S5. By means of this frame both bridges have learned about the location of S1.

Next suppose station S3 (which has an IP address 195.100.12.12) on LAN 2 sends a frame to S2. Since both bridges are connected to LAN 2, and since neither bridge has the address of S3 in their tables, each one will forward the frame. Bridge 1 sends the frame out of its port 1 and bridge 2 forwards it out of its port 2. As a result, the forwarding tables of both bridges are updated as shown by step 3 in Fig. 10.15. If this learning process continues for a long period of time, then eventually both forwarding tables will contain the address of each station in this bridged LAN.

To allow for the possibility of adding stations or moving stations to another LAN, a timing mechanism is used so that the bridge can adapt to the dynamic nature of a network. When the bridge adds an address to its forwarding table, it sets a *timer* for that address. The timer value is usually on the order of a few minutes. When this value reaches zero, the address entry in the table is erased. Thus if a station is removed from a LAN, its address will soon be removed from a forwarding table.

One limitation of bridges is that frames which are addressed improperly or destined for addresses that do not exist can be flooded indefinitely onto all bridged connections. This condition is known as a *broadcast storm* and can affect network performance dramatically. In addition, bridges generally cannot support networks that have redundant paths since broadcast storms can arise when there are multiple active loops between LANs.

10.3.2 Source Routing Bridge

A second type of bridge, which is used mainly in token-ring networks, is the *source routing bridge*. In source routing the transmitter, or source, of the frame specifies which route the frame is to follow, hence the term *source routing*. The source routing algorithm operates dynamically. To find a route to a given destination, the source sends out a *discovery frame* or *explorer packet* which is broadcast over the entire bridged LAN. These frames will travel through all possible paths between the source and the destination stations. Along the way each frame records the route it takes. Upon reaching the destination all the route discovery frames will be returned to the source along the recorded path. The source then can choose which route to use.

Whereas transparent bridges do not modify a frame, each source routing bridge between the source and the destination adds a *route-designator field* to the discovery frame as shown in Fig. 10.16. The *routing information field* (RIF) can be up to 18 bytes in length. It consists of a 2-byte *routing control field* and up to eight route-designator fields, each of which is 2 bytes long and contains a LAN segment number and a bridge number. The route-designator fields indicate the path between nodes on different physical rings. When the discovery frame reaches the destination, the end station sends the completed

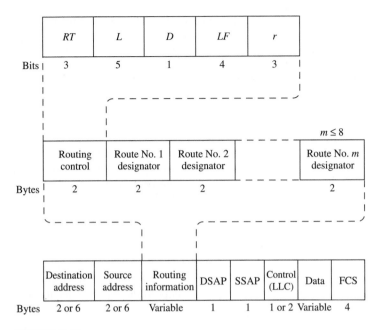

FIGURE 10.16
Format of a route discovery frame.

RIF back to the source station. This field then is included immediately after the source address in every token-ring data frame that is sent to the destination station.

A limitation of a source routing bridge is that discovery packets add to the traffic flow and thus can affect network performance negatively. In addition, the paths between the source and the destination stations cannot have more than seven intermediate bridges, which limits the flexibility and size of a network.

10.3.3   Translating Bridge

A *translating bridge* connects two LANs that employ different protocols at the data link layer. Since LANs that use different data link protocols may not use the same type of transmission media, a translating bridge also provides support for different physical layer connections. An example of a translating bridge is a device that connects an Ethernet LAN to a token-ring network, as shown in Fig. 10.17. When frames pass from one network to another, the bridge will perform functions such as frame and transmission rate conversion. This is where problems can arise in network performance. For example, the information field in Ethernet can vary from 64 to 1500 bytes, whereas a token ring may have a frame size of up to 18,000 bytes at a ring rate of 16 Mbps. Since there is no provision for frame fragmentation within either the Ethernet or the token-ring data link protocol, a token-ring station would not be allowed to transmit frames having information fields that are greater than 1500 bytes.

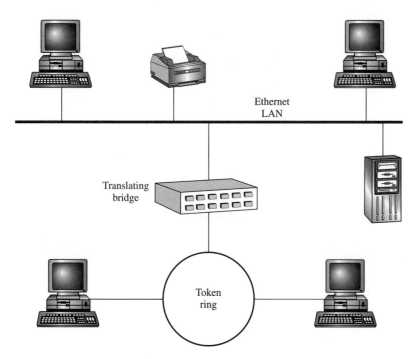

FIGURE 10.17
A translating bridge connects two LANs that use different link layer protocols.

10.4 ROUTERS

Routers are found throughout the global Internet for tying together its individual constituent networks.[9,19–21] In this section we use the terms *enterprise, access,* and *dial-up routers.* Basically they provide routing capabilities for large, medium, and small organizations, respectively. There is nothing magic about these terms and, depending on what product or technical literature one reads, they may be used slightly differently. For example, one reference may use the word *backbone* to describe the routers used for global Internet connections, whereas elsewhere an enterprise router might be referred to as a corporate backbone router. Here we use these terms for convenience in describing the functions of routers at different network levels. The following subsections first examine the functions that enterprise, access, and dial-up routers perform. Next we describe how they interface to intranets, extranets, and the Internet, and then we give an overview of how routers operate.

10.4.1 Router Types

Figure 10.18 shows a generic implementation of various types of routers used to support work at the main facility of large corporations or campus-level organizations. First *enterprise routers* connect to multiple dedicated-leased communication lines to enable

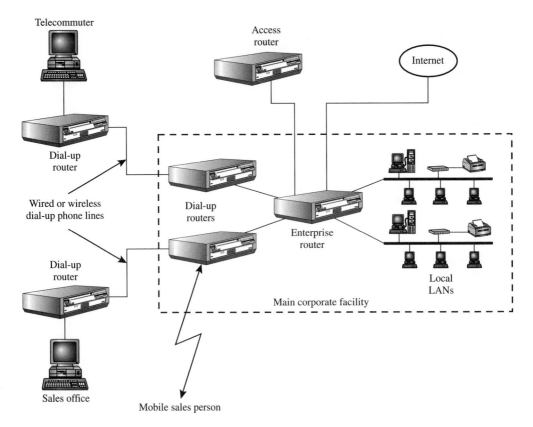

FIGURE 10.18
Implementation of various types of routers at the main facility of a large organization.

many LAN users of these enterprises to share information with users on other internal LANs, to connect to remote locations, and to access the Internet for e-mail, e-commerce, file transfers, and other applications. The majority of these enterprise networks are built from Ethernet segments that are connected by Ethernet switches or bridges. Some internetworking design requirements for routers at this level include support of security firewalls, traffic filters, and virtual LANs (see Sec. 10.6).

For medium-sized businesses and branch offices *access routers* offer flexible Internet, intranet, and extranet access that can be tailored to the needs of the organization. These smaller routers normally provide multiple LAN users with simultaneous shared Internet access over a single high-speed link. *Dial-up routers* offer a cost-effective solution in order to connect users in small businesses, sales personnel who are on the road or in branch offices, or telecommuters in their home offices with the main corporate facility. In this case there is usually not enough traffic leaving the LAN or an individual computer to justify the expense of a dedicated leased line so that a dial-up connection is more economical.

For an idea of what functions the routers shown in Fig. 10.18 support the following examples give some generic characteristics of three sizes of routers and illustrate their roles in typical network configurations.

EXAMPLE 10.3

Generic characteristics of dial-up routers for SOHO (small office/home office) applications include the following:

1. An IP router plus TCP/IP server software needed for WAN connectivity to an IP network via a 56-kbps analog phone line. All users share access to this line.
2. One or two V.90 analog interfaces. Two V.90 interfaces would allow the accommodation of simultaneous dial-in and dial-out connections.
3. A four-port Ethernet hub for setting up a LAN that allows up to nominally 25 users to share printers, fax machines, and servers and to exchange files and information.
4. One or two voice ports for fax machines or other analog devices.
5. The capability to act as a dial-in host for remote users.

EXAMPLE 10.4

Generic characteristics of access routers for medium-sized businesses include the following:

1. Ethernet ports that can sense automatically whether the input is 10 or 100 Mbps to simplify implementation in mixed Ethernet environments.
2. A console port for assisting with a network setup configuration, performance monitoring, and diagnostics.
3. Security features such as firewall, encryption, and authentication services (see Chap. 12).
4. Allocation of WAN bandwidth to allow a better *quality of service* (QoS) to higher-priority applications. QoS refers to the different levels of prioritization offered by a network. In a prioritization scheme time-critical messages that have a higher need to be transferred with low latency are given a higher priority (a better QoS) than non-time-critical messages that can tolerate more latency.
5. Support of virtual private network (VPN) services. As Chap. 12 describes, VPNs enable companies to reduce recurring WAN costs, to improve data security, to increase network performance and availability, and to simplify network operations by taking advantage of the shared communications infrastructure of the Internet.

EXAMPLE 10.5

In addition to the features listed in Example 10.4, the characteristics of enterprise routers for large businesses include the following:

1. Multiple LAN, WAN, and ATM connections; for example, 15 to 50 LAN interfaces, 30 to 100 WAN interfaces, and 4 to 12 ATM connections.
2. Data compression to increase the amount of data that can be sent over WAN links, thereby reducing WAN costs.
3. Fault resilience (self-healing capabilities) to provide continuous network availability.
4. VPN connectivity support up to 50 Mbps.
5. Support of hundreds of simultaneous users with strong 128-bit encryption.

10.4.2 Interface to the Internet

Figure 10.19 shows a high-level concept of an external router acting as the interface among a corporate intranet, an extranet, and the Internet. The router can access the outside world over standard copper phone lines or through high-speed digital lines. Many different organizational departments can be attached to the local corporate network through various departmental LAN servers interconnected by a high-speed LAN switch. The *intranet servers* function like data warehouses that workstations from the various departments may access for stored corporate information. In addition, there is a mail server that supplies e-mail services to the entire enterprise internally and also provides e-mail access to the external world. This mail server and the LAN itself (through the LAN switch) interface to a firewall and then to a router for connection to the Internet.

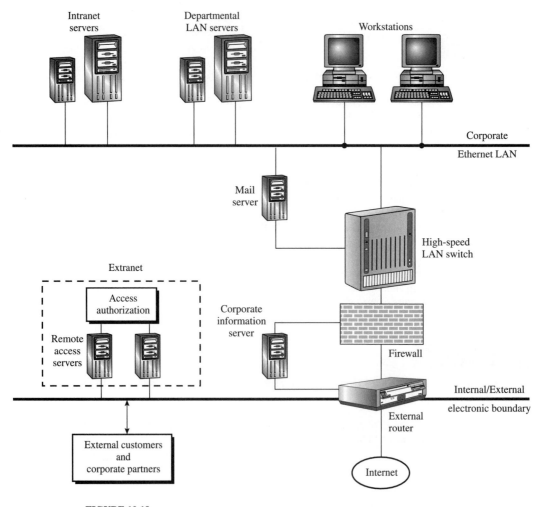

FIGURE 10.19

High-level concept of a router acting as the interface among a corporate intranet, an extranet, and the Internet.

The extranet or remote-access servers are internal to the organization but are outside of the firewall since their function is to allow external customers to have EDI (electronic data interchange) access to electronic documents such as purchase orders, inventory status, or invoices. These extranet servers require the customer to have a password or logon capabilities in order to protect the information. Also shown between the firewall and the router is a corporate information server that allows the general public to have access to items such as marketing brochures, product descriptions, or corporate news.

10.4.3 Router Operations

Routers operate at the network layer of the OSI model, as Fig 10.20 illustrates. In contrast to bridges that make routing decisions based on the MAC layer address (i.e., the physical address) contained in the header of each incoming data link layer frame, routers examine the network layer address (i.e., the logical address) embedded within the data field of these frames. This means that a bridge needs to read every frame on the LAN to which it is attached. Unlike a bridge, a router examines only those frames that are addressed to it at the network level. The process of monitoring all incoming frames is referred to as a *promiscuous mode of operation,* whereas the selective examination of frames is called a *nonpromiscuous mode of operation.*

The two basic functions of routing are (1) determining optimal paths from the source to the destination and (2) transporting packets through an internetwork. The transporting function is referred to as *switching.* Although switching is relatively straightforward, path determination can be quite complex. A common routing algorithm for finding the best path through the internetwork is the *Open Shortest Path First* (OSPF) Protocol.[12,13,21,22] With this protocol routers use a short message to check for the presence of other devices on the network. The responses enable each router to discover its neighbors and the number of hops to the destination. From the received information the router creates a *routing table,* which contains path and router information about the entire network. These tables are updated every 30 minutes or when there is a network change, such as a failed router. In that case the routing tables are updated immediately. One important item is the MAC address of the next router in the path, which is referred to as the *next hop,* that will establish an optimal path to a particular destination. When

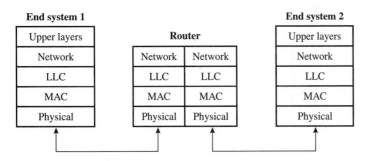

FIGURE 10.20
Routers operate at the network layer of the OSI (Open System Interconnecting) model.

a router receives an incoming packet, it checks the destination address and then consults its routing table to associate this address with a next hop on which to forward this data packet.

10.5   INTERNETWORKING WITH SWITCHES

Another means of internetworking is to use switches.[23-27] The word *switch* is a broadly used (or misused) term for various types of networking devices since it has been applied to everything from a simple bridge to a sophisticated routing device. For LAN applications we look at layer-2 and layer-3 switching functions. These are known as LAN switches (or layer-2 switches) and layer-3 switches, respectively. The basic role of a *LAN switch* is to forward frames based on layer-2 MAC addresses. A primary reason for using LAN switches is that they can isolate communications between a pair of stations from other users on the network, as shown in Fig. 10.21, for three pairs of stations that are communicating independently at the same time. This is in contrast to a broadcast LAN architecture in which numerous users contend for the transmission medium. This isolation process is known as *microsegmentation,* which allows the creation of a dedicated segment per user. Thereby each user has full access to the available bandwidth and does not have to contend with others for these resources.

To increase performance and to allow greater scalability in the interconnection of LANs with other networks, network providers devised a *layer-3 switch*. This is an extension of a layer-2 LAN switch that has extensive layer-3 routing capabilities.

Unless otherwise stated, this section describes only Ethernet switches since they are used widely in both the LAN environment itself and for interconnecting LANs with other networks.

10.5.1   Generic Switch Characteristics

Figure 10.22 shows the basic concept of a generic switch. The major constituents are the input/output (I/O) ports, line cards, interconnection circuitry (which is referred to as a *switch fabric*), and a switch controller. A *line card* or an *interface card* normally

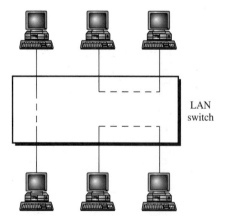

FIGURE 10.21
LAN switches can isolate communications between two stations from other network users.

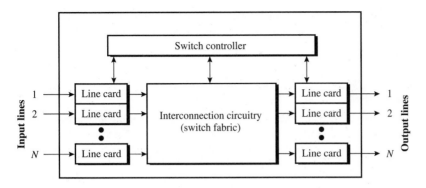

FIGURE 10.22
Basic concept of a generic switch.

handles several I/O ports and is responsible for physical and data link layer functions. These functions include media access control, symbol timing, line coding, data framing, physical layer addressing, and error checking. In addition, the line cards contain buffers to handle any speed mismatches between the transmission line and the switch fabric. The *switch controller* carries out functions such as directing the incoming frames to the appropriate output ports, filtering frames, managing connection bandwidth, handling prioritized frames, and controlling congestion.

The role of the *switch fabric* is to transfer frames between the line cards. This fabric can function in either a blocking or a nonblocking manner, depending on the fabric architecture. Certain fabric types utilize an architecture in which a group of input lines share several possible paths to the output, thereby reducing the internal size of the switch. However, in this case as soon as one of the input lines has established a connection to the output port, all the other input lines sharing that switch link are *blocked*. In a *nonblocking fabric* the connection requests are never denied because of lack of connectivity resources within the fabric. They are denied only when the requested output line is occupied already with another connection.

10.5.2 LAN Switches

LAN switches or *layer-2 switches* are operationally equivalent to transparent bridges through functions such as forwarding and filtering of frames and learning the network topology. However, they have some additional features, such as a higher port density, dedicated communications between network devices, the ability to support multiple simultaneous connections, full-duplex communications, and adaptation to different media rates. The higher port density allows multiple groups of users to have simultaneous information exchanges by forwarding or switching several frames at the same time on different links, as shown before in Fig. 10.21. The feature of dedicated collision-free communications between devices increases the information throughput, and full-duplex communications effectively double the throughput. By automatically adapting to different media rates, an Ethernet LAN switch can translate between input and output rates of 10 and 100 Mbps, for example, or between 100 and 1000 Mbps, thereby allowing bandwidth to be allocated as needed. This function is known as *autosensing* or *auto-negotiating*.

EXAMPLE 10.6

As an example of some Ethernet switches, compare the following generic characteristics of a low-end and a medium-sized switch. In most cases these switches can be *stacked* so that several interconnected switches act as a single device. This allows for easy expansion and performance enhancement of a network.

1. Small Ethernet switch:
   (*a*)   8 to 12 autosensing 10/100-Mbps ports
   (*b*)   Use 1: stand-alone switch for server farms or workgroups
   (*c*)   Use 2: LAN backbone switch for small offices
   (*d*)   Use 3: connection switch to a higher-performance switch for making a larger network
2. Medium-sized Ethernet switch:
   (*a*)   12 to 24 autosensing 10/100-Mbps ports
   (*b*)   2 to 6 Gigabit Ethernet ports
   (*c*)   Ports can be load-shared to match network bandwidth with server performance
   (*d*)   Fully operational with routers using IP routing protocols
   (*e*)   Used to meet the intranet and Internet demands of medium-sized businesses

---

LAN switches support three types of forwarding methods: the store-and-forward scheme and two types of cut-through methods. In the *store-and-forward switching* method the LAN switch will copy the entire frame into its buffer and compute the cyclic redundancy check (CRC) before forwarding the frame to its destination. The switch will discard the frame if it contains a CRC error. It also will discard the frame if it is either a *runt* (shorter than 64 bytes including the CRC) or a *giant* (longer than 1518 bytes including the CRC). If the frame has no errors, the LAN switch will look up the destination address in its forwarding table, determine the outgoing port, and forward the frame to its destination. By buffering the entire frame, the store-and-forward method also can convert the frame to another MAC layer format.

In the *cut-through switching* method the LAN switch will copy only the destination address into its buffer. At this point the switch looks up the destination address in its forwarding table, determines the outgoing port, and forwards the frame to its destination without performing any error checking. This process reduces transmission delay since the switch starts to forward a frame as soon as it has read the destination address and has determined the output port. However, since there is no error checking, the cut-through switch is generally not used in networks that require fault tolerance and high reliability. In addition, since cut-through switches cannot be used between different types of LANs and also do not support different bandwidths, they are mainly used in small workgroup environments where no connection to other networks is required.

In the *error-free, cut-through switching* method the LAN switch reads both the address and the CRC of every frame. Similar to the standard cut-through method, the switch also forwards all frames immediately. Now, however, when the switch senses that a particular port is producing corrupted frames, it can reconfigure that port to use store-and-forward switching. When the errors decrease to some tolerable preset threshold, the port is changed back to the cut-through method to enable a higher-performance throughput.

10.5.3 Layer-3 Switching

Recall that network characteristics at layer 3, the routing layer, include logical partitioning of subnets, scalability, security, and quality of service (QoS). The basic structure of the Internet and the backbones of many large organizations is built on a layer-3 foundation. The fundamental protocol at this layer is IP. For routing purposes, in addition to layer-2 MAC addresses, an IP packet contains the source and the destination addresses.

In the evolution of Ethernet LANs from a shared medium to a switched architecture the use of Ethernet LAN switches operating at layer 2 worked well as long as most of the traffic stayed within the subnet that was served by the LAN switch. As the local network usage expanded extensively beyond its boundary to include the deployment of intranets based on web technology and access to remotely located server farms, the routers needed to enable these external information flows became a bottleneck in the larger enterprise network. The solution was the development of a layer-3 switch, which integrates layer-2 switching and layer-3 routing functions.

In contrast to general purpose routers in which packet switching typically is performed by microprocessor-based engines, a layer-3 switch uses *application-specific integrated circuit* (ASIC) hardware to perform all its packet-forwarding functions, whether it is unicast, multicast, or broadcast at either layer 2 or layer 3. This allows higher switching speeds, thereby providing greater raw throughput. Software is deployed to handle network administration, routing table updates, and policy implementations. A *policy* provides a means to alter the normal forwarding procedure of a packet. Policy examples include security functions, load balancing, and QoS processes, such as bandwidth allocation, packet prioritization management, and congestion control. Packet prioritization management also is known as a *class of service* (CoS) function. Together QoS and CoS enable multimedia applications, such as LAN telephony and the integration of voice, video, and data onto the same infrastructure.

A layer-3 switch does everything to a packet that a traditional router does. This includes determining the path on which to forward a packet, updating forwarding statistics in the routing table, allocating bandwidth to satisfy the QoS requirements of higher-priority users, and applying any required security controls. However, since it also has inherent layer-2 switching capabilities, it can simplify network configuration. For example, as shown in Fig. 10.23, the combination of two layer-2 LAN switches plus a router can be replaced with a single layer-3 switch. In terms of network management a layer-3 switch possesses the same capabilities as LAN switches and traditional routers. Chapter 11 gives more details on these management functions.

An important point to keep in mind is that layer-3 switches are optimized for high-performance LAN support, which increases their performance to as much as 10 times that of a legacy router. Layer-3 switches can have packet throughputs of over 50 million packets per second (pps), whereas the throughput of traditional general purpose routers ranges from 100,000 to over one million pps. Since they are not intended to service WAN connections, layer-3 switches interface to a WAN through a standard wide area router.

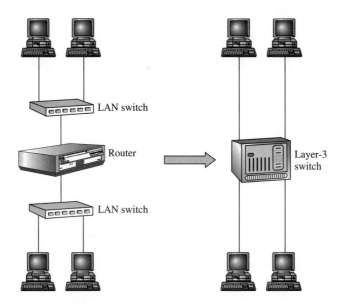

FIGURE 10.23
Two layer-2 LAN switches plus a router can be replaced with a single layer-3 switch.

Within most enterprise networks numerous routing protocols are used to optimize network connectivity. Layer-3 switches need to offer sophisticated translation or redistribution support among these routing protocols since this is an important function for ensuring stable, resilient, and high-performance networks. The ability to redistribute routing protocols allows network designers to configure the network architecture and operational characteristics to meet the needs and to support the desired applications of the enterprise. Among the TCP/IP protocols that layer-3 switches nominally support are the following:

1. *Internet Protocol (IP).* IP is the most commonly used network layer protocol for the Internet. All web browsing, e-mail exchanges, and media streaming on the Internet is carried by IP.

2. *Internet Packet Exchange (IPX).* Note that the "I" in IPX stands for "internet" and is not to be confused with the "Internet." IPX is a fairly small, easily configured protocol that was primarily developed to support LAN configurations.[20] Although it has been implemented widely, its usage is declining.

3. *Routing Information Protocol (RIP).* A router implementing RIP broadcasts its routing table to its neighbors every 30 seconds.[25,28] If the router does not receive an update message from a particular neighbor within 180 seconds, it assumes the direct link to that neighbor has failed and updates its routing table accordingly. A limitation of RIP is that its *convergence,* the process by which all routers agree upon optimal routes, is slow, which makes the protocol inefficient. RIP still exists in many systems, but new implementations have been superseded by OSPF.

4. *Open Shortest Path First (OSPF).* As noted in Sec. 10.4.2, OSPF is a unicast routing protocol that offers very fast convergence with fewer updates in stable topologies.

It operates by exchanging link status information with its neighbors and floods this information around the network so that each device has an identical map of the network topology.

5. *Interior Gateway Routing Protocol (IGRP).* IGRP is a unicast routing protocol which was developed to provide greater flexibility in determining the path that a packet takes through the network by considering link speeds, link quality, delay, and other metrics when making the intelligent forwarding decision.[12] Consequently IGRP was adopted widely as a standard routing protocol in numerous enterprise networks because of its flexibility, robustness, and ease of use.

6. *Protocol-Independent Multicast (PIM).* PIM is a multicast protocol that operates independently of the underlying unicast protocol (such as IGRP or OSPF).[13] It supports applications that operate with fewer servers transmitting to multiple destinations (called the *dense mode*) or numerous small workgroups operating in different multicast groups (called the *sparse mode*).

In addition to providing high-speed routing, layer-3 switches also offer a set of *intelligent network services.*[26,27] These services permit critical applications such as enterprise resource planning, databases, and financial systems to run optimally on the network, and they enable network managers to carry out cost-effectively daily network operations and management. Among the key intelligent network services are the following:

1. *Resilience.* Layer-3 switches offer a resilient (quick recovery) design for maximum availability of communications among intelligent network elements. One of the available tools is the *Hot Standby Router Protocol* (HSRP) that allows users to route transparently around failed layer-3 switches with minimal downtime of an application and no impact on the end-user workstation.

2. *Security.* Security is a major concern of network managers. Common security functions in a network include encrypted passwords and configuration files, access control lists, and authentication systems that authenticate user logons and record login attempts. This operational infrastructure does not change when using layer-3 switches.

3. *Remote management.* Remote access to a layer-3 switch or any other device is a necessary capability for making configuration changes. Layer-3 switches reconfigure without requiring a reboot.

4. *Network reconfigurations.* Layer-3 switches support the use of tools such as the *Dynamic Host Configuration Protocol* (DHCP), which automatically configures hosts that want to connect to a TCP/IP network.[13,25]

5. *Troubleshooting.* Layer-3 switches nominally provide a suite of online debugging capabilities that enable network managers to troubleshoot network problems remotely.[29]

EXAMPLE 10.7

The typical nonblocking layer-3 switch can be controlled through web-based management interfaces.[26,27,30] These switches can provide switched 10/100 Mbps auto-negotiating Ethernet ports for linking to multiple desktop computers, various types of local servers, server farms, metropolitan area networks, and other local assets. They enable policy-based QoS, such as bandwidth management, packet prioritization management, and congestion control. In addition, they may provide fault tolerance through multiple load-sharing trunks and redundant power supplies.

EXAMPLE 10.8

Figure 10.24 shows a policy-based enterprise backbone network that incorporates Ethernet LAN and layer-3 switches. Here Gigabit Ethernet links connect layer-2 and layer-3 switches to form the basic backbone. Fast Ethernet connections between the backbone switches and layer-2 LAN

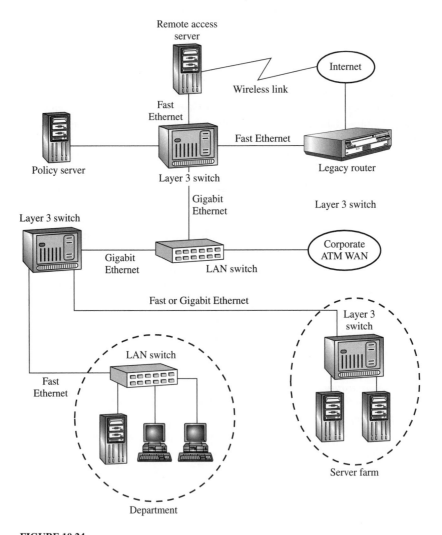

FIGURE 10.24
Example of a policy-based enterprise backbone network that incorporates Ethernet LAN and layer-3 switches.

switches provide connectivity among departments, server farms located at data centers, and a corporatewide ATM-based network. Links between the backbone switches and traditional routers provide users with access to Internet resources. A remote access server connected to a layer-3 switch allows remotely located employees to connect to the network. A network manager may administer policy services through a policy server connected to a layer-3 switch. This administration can extend as far as devices located on the desktop, thereby enabling network access and signaling mechanisms for both CoS and QoS across the entire network.

10.6 VIRTUAL LANS

Virtual networking refers to the ability of routers and switches to configure logical topologies on top of the physical network infrastructure.[8,9,15,31,32] Thereby a single extended LAN may be partitioned into several independent LANs. To see how virtual networking functions, consider the network shown in Fig. 10.25. Here several physical LANs are connected through an ATM backbone via either a LAN switch or a router. Each physical LAN is segmented logically into different *broadcast domains* or *virtual LANs* (VLANs). Thus in this example VLAN 1 is dedicated to message exchanges among users in an engineering organization, VLAN 2 is used by marketing personnel, and VLAN 3 handles

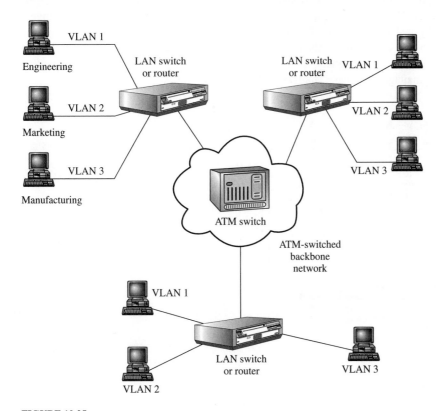

FIGURE 10.25
Virtual LANs (VLANs) created for three separate departmental communications across an ATM backbone.

traffic related to manufacturing functions. Packets originating on a particular VLAN are switched only between ports that are designated for that VLAN. For example, suppose station *A* on VLAN 1 wants to send a message to station *B*, which is on the same virtual LAN. When the packet from station *A* arrives at LAN switch 1, the switch will forward the message only on an egress port that is configured as being in VLAN 1.

10.6.1 Types of Virtual LANs

There are a number of different ways that a VLAN can be implemented. The selection of a particular solution depends on factors such as the simplicity of implementation, the need of network reconfiguration, the ease of this reconfiguration, and the ability to extend the LAN across multiple switches in a LAN or across a wide area network. Some general categories of virtual LANs are described next.

Port-based VLAN. The simplest form of a virtual LAN is based on port grouping, which is a popular method of defining membership in a VLAN. This is called a *port-based virtual LAN* or a *port-grouped VLAN*. For example, suppose a network manager wants to form two VLANs using the eight-port switch shown in Fig. 10.26. Here VLAN 1 consists of ports 1, 2, 6, and 7. The other four ports make up VLAN 2. Although setting up the configuration of a port-based VLAN is relatively easy, reconfiguring it can be time-consuming. For example, if a user moves to another port, the network manager must physically reconfigure the membership. In addition, since a particular port can belong to only one virtual LAN, multiple VLANs cannot use the same physical segment or switch port. An advantage of a port-based VLAN is that it is secure since only a network manager can make changes to the configuration.

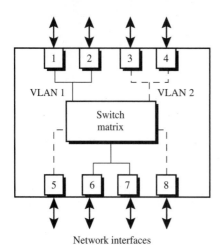

Network interfaces

n = Port n

VLAN 1 = Ports 1, 2, 6, 7
VLAN 2 = Ports 3, 4, 5, 8

FIGURE 10.26
Formation of two port-grouped VLANs in an eight-port switch.

Protocol-based VLAN. Another simple method of configuring a VLAN is to group users according to protocol. This type of virtual LAN works at layer 3. For example, all users defined by their MAC address can form one VLAN and other users defined by their IP address might form another VLAN grouping. However, normally this is not done alone; rather, it is used in conjunction with another VLAN configuration method, such as an IP-based scheme.

MAC-based VLAN. In a *MAC-based virtual LAN* the MAC addresses are associated with the creation of a VLAN. This configuration scheme also is known as a *layer-2 virtual LAN.* Since MAC layer addresses are hardwired into the network interface card of the end user, this method allows for more sophisticated VLAN management. For example, if two users with network node addresses 4 and 5 on VLAN 1 needed to be moved to VLAN 2, a network manager simply could delete addresses 4 and 5 from VLAN 1 and move them to VLAN 2. This procedure might be as elementary as dragging a MAC address icon from one VLAN to another using a graphical user interface (GUI) on a network management display screen. In contrast, with a port-based VLAN nodes 4 and 5 would need to be rewired physically from one VLAN to the other. A limitation of the MAC-based VLAN method is that the entry of MAC addresses into switch tables can be a very time-consuming task.

Layer-3 grouping. A *layer-3-based virtual LAN* is configured using information that is contained in the network layer header of packets. Thus this type of VLAN is restricted to routers and LAN switches that have a layer-3 routing capability. Depending on the capability of the routers and switches, a number of different layer-3 VLANs can be created. A common configuration is an *IP-based virtual LAN.* This type of VLAN uses layer-3 information and IP network addresses.

Figure 10.27 illustrates how two IP-based virtual LANs are established in a layer-3 LAN switch using Class C IP network addresses. In this case one IP-based VLAN is associated with the subnet 256.82.54 and the other IP-based VLAN is associated with the subnet 256.82.65. Users on these subnets will have an address of the form 256.82.54.xxx or 256.82.65.xxx. The configuration shown in Fig. 10.27 also assumes the LAN switch can support the assignment of more than one subnet per port. Here stations on port 1 may be assigned to either subnet. Note that not all LAN switches have this capability.

The three main advantages of layer-3 VLANs are the station attachment flexibility, the ease of configuration, and the capability to communicate between VLANs. *Station attachment* is flexible since when a user moves to another segment of a VLAN but retains the same subnet number, the switch may have the capability to sense this move automatically and not to require reconfiguration. *VLAN configuration* is easy since a network manager can allocate a subnet to a particular virtual LAN with a simple drag-and-drop process on the VLAN management display screen. Thirdly, the fact that a layer-3 virtual LAN supports routing eliminates the need for a separate router to enable inter-VLAN communications.

Precautions that need to be observed when implementing a layer-3 VLAN include a careful check that the network stations are using the correct protocol and network address and that the correct switch is selected for support of multiple subnets on a port.

Policy-based VLAN. A LAN switch used in a *policy-based* or *rule-based virtual LAN* needs to have the ability to examine the contents of a packet and to use predefined fields, portions of fields, or individual bit settings to create a virtual LAN. Policy-based

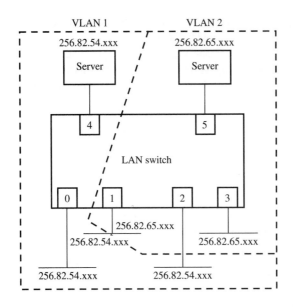

FIGURE 10.27

Formation of two IP-based VLANs in a six-port switch.

VLAN 1 = Network 256.82.54.xxx
VLAN 2 = Network 256.82.65.xxx

virtual LANs have been used mainly for network management functions, such as fault, performance, security, configuration, and accounting management. This type of VLAN application provides network managers with a great flexibility to create VLANs that meet a wide range of communication management needs. It is especially useful for reducing administrative costs, strengthening network security, and assisting with troubleshooting. This is done by setting standards for handling a wide possibility of situations ranging from adding new users to the network to reacting to system faults. For example, a security policy might be implemented which specifies that any communications between nonsecure and secure VLANs must pass through a router in order to filter messages appropriately between these two VLAN types.

10.6.2 The IEEE-802.1Q Standard

The accepted standard for virtual LANs is IEEE 802.1Q, entitled *Virtual Bridged Local Area Networks.*[32] This standard defines an architecture for virtual bridged LANs, the services provided in virtual bridged LANs, and the protocols and algorithms involved in the provision of those services. A limitation of the standard is that it is concerned only with virtual LANs that are configured as logical bridged networks contained in selected switch ports. As such, it addresses only a small subset of the features that virtual LAN vendors have deployed during the years prior to the ratification of the standard.

The IEEE-802.1Q Standard is based on other IEEE-802.1 standards, such as transparent bridging and spanning tree algorithms. What is added is the concept of a virtual bridged network or VLAN. LAN switches that operate based on 802.1Q are basically just IEEE-802.1D-compatible bridges with a modified set of ingress and egress rules, an additional protocol for identifying the VLAN capabilities of end systems, and a VLAN transport mechanism based on a *frame-tagging* implementation. A *tagged frame* is a MAC frame that contains a tag header. The frame tag indicates the VLAN identifier of the frame, as well as other information related to the priority of the frame and the addressing format.

10.7 SUMMARY

Internetworking provides the means to create a larger network from a collection of smaller networks. A major economic incentive for the investing organizations to pursue internetworking is the revenue they can collect from corporations that use the network and the applications running on it for electronic business purposes. The basic business drivers for internetworking include the sale and use of software applications that are transported over the Internet, the implementations of intranets and extranets, and applications such as electronic commerce, e-mail, and World Wide Web (WWW) services.

Large organizations access the Internet through a router that interconnects their internal LAN with leased high-capacity transmission lines. Small businesses and home users access the Internet via a dial-up modem that connects to an *Internet service provider* (ISP) through standard local telephone lines. The ISP connects to the Internet through high-capacity transmission lines that it either owns or leases. Internet users have access to a wide variety of services by means of the WWW which popularly is referred to as the *Web.* Among the web-based services are chat sessions between interest-group members, web-based electronic learning, interactive collaborations, multimedia entertainment, and shopping opportunities. Other applications that use the Internet are electronic mail (e-mail) and file transfer capabilities.

An intranet is a private web-based collaborative computing network within an organization. Thus an intranet is a LAN configuration that provides the same capabilities and features for electronic information access and delivery inside an organization as the Internet does on the outside. The same benefits that web technologies brought to corporate intranets also have driven the move to electronic business-to-business transactions. This has led to the concept of an *extranet,* which is a private network that uses Internet protocols and the public telecommunication system to share securely part of the proprietary information or operations of the host organization with suppliers, vendors, partners, customers, or other businesses.

The three main data communication devices used for setting up internetwork connections are bridges, routers, and switches. Bridges work at layer 2 (the link layer) of the OSI model and normally connect similar LAN segments. The three basic functions of bridges are forwarding, filtering, and learning.

Routers are found throughout the global Internet. They are general purpose devices that offer a variety of capabilities for interconnecting either similar or dissimilar networks at layer 3 (the network layer). *Enterprise routers* are used in large organizations to exchange information on internal LANs, to connect to remote locations, and to access the Internet for e-mail, e-commerce, file transfers, and other applications. The majority of these enterprise networks are built from Ethernet segments that are connected by Ethernet switches or bridges. For medium-sized businesses and branch offices *access routers* offer flexible Internet, intranet, and extranet access. *Dial-up routers* offer a cost-effective solution to connect users in small businesses, sales personnel who are on the road or in branch offices, or telecommuters in their home offices with the main corporate facility.

Switches can operate at layers 2 or 3 depending on their built-in capabilities. These are known as LAN switches (or layer-2 switches) and layer-3 switches, respectively. The basic role of a *LAN switch* is to forward frames based on layer-2 MAC addresses. A primary reason for using LAN switches is that they can isolate communications between a pair of stations from other users on the network. A *layer-3 switch* is an extension of a layer-2 LAN switch that has extensive layer-3 routing capabilities. It does everything to a packet that a traditional router does. This includes determining the path on which to forward a packet, updating forwarding statistics in the routing table, allocating bandwidth to satisfy the QoS requirements of higher-priority users, and applying any required security controls. However, since it also has inherent layer-2 switching capabilities, it can simplify network configuration.

Virtual networking refers to the ability of routers and switches to configure logical topologies on top of the physical network infrastructure. Thereby a single-extended LAN may be partitioned into several independent LANs. The way a VLAN is implemented depends on factors such as the simplicity of implementation, the need of network reconfiguration, the ease of this reconfiguration, and the ability to extend the LAN across multiple switches in a LAN or across a wide area network.

PROBLEMS

10.1. Find out what Internet service providers are available in your area. Describe some of the features that an ISP might provide. For example, consider questions such as: What connection options do they offer? What is the highest connection rate that is available? What equipment do you need to access the Internet at these speeds?

10.2. What are five potential benefits of e-commerce for businesses? What are five potential benefits of e-commerce for customers?

10.3. List some competitive business intelligence information that should be included on an Intranet? Consider factors such as competitor, financial, technology, product, supplier, and customer information. Why should access to such information be restricted to specific intranet users?

10.4. Consider the network shown in Fig. 10.2. Where would the network manager place a marketing server that would provide the general public with catalog information about company products?

10.5. Discuss the following two issues that might arise when creating and using an extranet: (1) restricted access to company information by external vendors, and (2) maintaining confidentiality of sensitive data.

10.6. Using web resources, research the capabilities of various types of LAN extenders for Ethernet applications. Consider capabilities such as transmission medium, extension distance, transmission speed, and manageability.

10.7. What are the binary forms of the following IP addresses: (a) 128.11.3.31, (b) 129.14.6.8, (c) 114.34.7.10, and (d) 238.34.2.5?

10.8. Version 6 of the Internet Protocol (IPv6) offers a 128-bit address space, which is much larger than the 32-bit address length of IPv4. How might the larger address capability of IPv6 be useful in a home network that includes various sensors, controls, communications equipment, and entertainment devices?

10.9. Two important bridging functions are filtering and forwarding. What are the differences between these functions and how would each be used?

10.10. From the bridged LAN diagram shown in Fig. 10.28, describe how a broadcast storm might originate. Which lines should be blocked so that this can be prevented?

10.11. Consider the network consisting of six stations on three LANs that are interconnected by transparent bridges, as shown in Fig. 10.29. Suppose initially the two forwarding tables

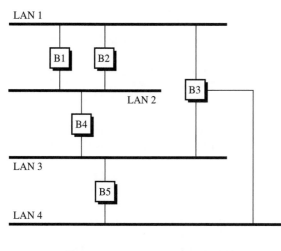

FIGURE 10.28
Bridged LAN diagram for Prob. 10.10.

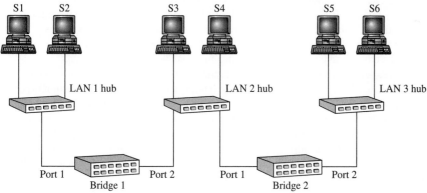

Address	Port

Address	Port

FIGURE 10.29
Network configuration for Prob. 10.11.

are empty and the following sequence of transmissions then takes place: S1 to S2; S4 to S5; S3 to S6; S2 to S1; and S5 to S6. Fill in the entries of the forwarding tables after each of the frames has been completely transmitted.

10.12. Suppose four transparent learning bridges (B1 through B4) and three stations (S1, S2, and S3) are arranged as shown in Fig. 10.30. If all the forwarding tables are initially empty, what are the table entries for each bridge after the following three transmissions: S1 sends to S2; S2 sends to S1; S3 sends to S2?

10.13. When using a bridge between Ethernet and token-ring LANs, discuss interconnection issues such as different data rates and frame sizes. How can these be resolved?

10.14. From information available on the Web, list some features of a moderate-sized Ethernet router that can be used for LAN applications. Consider factors such as the number of 10/100-Mbps Ethernet ports, the number and types of WAN interfaces, equipment size and power requirements, QoS capabilities, and security features.

10.15. Discuss the issues involved when interconnecting Ethernet and ATM LANs with a router or a switch. Consider factors such as different data rates and frame sizes.

10.16. Discuss the issues involved when connecting an Ethernet LAN and a Fibre Channel storage network with a switch. Consider factors such as different data rates and frame sizes.

10.17. Consider an Ethernet LAN that has 60 engineering workstations, 5 management workstations, and 2 workstations for administrative assistants. Suppose the estimated traffic loads for each workstation are those given in Table 10.3.
(a)   Calculate the bit rate for each activity and list it in Table 10.3.
(b)   Using these results, calculate the total network activity in kbps (kilobits per second).

10.18. Consider two Fast Ethernet LANs, each of which has a traffic load of 40 Mbps. Suppose these two LANs are to be connected by an Ethernet switch, which also provides a connection to an Internet router. If 30 percent of the traffic from each LAN passes from one LAN to the other and if 20 percent of the traffic from each LAN goes to the Internet, what is the traffic load that the Ethernet switch must handle?

10.19. A message consisting of 1600 bits of data and 160 bits of header is to be transmitted across two networks to a third network. The two intermediate networks have a maximum packet size of 1024 bits which includes a 24-bit header on each packet. If the final network has a maximum packet size of 800 bits, how many bits (including headers) are delivered at the destination? Into how many packets is the original message fragmented?

10.20. From information available on the Web, check out the differences between RFC 1723 (RIP) and RFC 2328 (OSPF). Why do people now tend to use OSPF instead of RIP?

10.21. Assuming the LAN switches shown in Fig. 10.25 are eight-port devices, show how three separate port-based virtual LANs might be implemented. How difficult would it be to change this configuration if a fourth VLAN needed to be added?

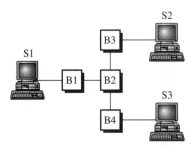

FIGURE 10.30
Network configuration for Prob. 10.12.

TABLE 10.3
Estimated traffic loads for the workstations discussed in Problem 10.17

Activity per workstation	Message size, kbytes	Frequency, per hour	Bit rate, bps
Engineering workstation			
Download Internet document	150	1	
Access file server	120	2	
Save files	100	2	
Send and receive e-mail	2	5	
Manager workstation			
Download Internet document	150	2	
Access file server	120	2	
Save files	40	2	
Send and receive e-mail	4	10	
Administrator workstation			
Download Internet document	150	1	
Access file server	120	2	
Save files	20	5	
Send and receive e-mail	3	10	

REFERENCES

1. R. Greenlaw and E. Hepp, *Fundamentals of the Internet and the World Wide Web,* McGraw-Hill, New York, 2nd ed., 2002.
2. D. E. Comer, *The Internet Book,* Prentice-Hall, Upper Saddle River, NJ, 3rd ed., 2000.
3. J. Rayport and B. J. Jaworski, *E-commerce,* McGraw-Hill, Burr Ridge, IL, 2001.
4. M. Greenstein and T. M. Feinman, *Electronic Commerce,* McGraw-Hill/Irwin, New York, 2000.
5. R. J. Bates and D. W. Gregory, *Voice and Data Communications Handbook,* McGraw-Hill, New York, 3rd ed., 2000, Chap. 17.
6. P. J. Louis, *Telecommunications Internetworking,* McGraw-Hill, Burr Ridge, IL, 2000.
7. G. Held, *Internetworking LANs and WANs,* Wiley, Chichester, England, 1998.
8. L. R. Rossi, L. D. Rossi, and T. Rossi, *Cisco Catalyst LAN Switching,* McGraw-Hill, New York, 2000.
9. R. Perlman, *Interconnections: Bridges, Routers, Switches, and Internetworking Protocols,* Addison-Wesley, Reading, MA, 2nd ed., 2000.
10. M. Goncalves and K. Niles, *IPv6 Networks,* McGraw-Hill, New York, 1998.
11. S. Feit, *TCP/IP,* McGraw-Hill, New York, 1999.
12. C. Lewis, *Cisco TCP/IP: Routing Professional Reference,* McGraw-Hill, New York, 2nd ed., 1998.
13. L. L. Peterson and B. S. Davie, *Computer Networks,* Morgan-Kaufmann, San Francisco, 2nd ed., 2000.
14. B. A. Forouzan, *Introduction to Data Communications and Networking,* McGraw-Hill, Burr Ridge, IL, 2nd ed., 2001.
15. R. Seifert, *The Switch Book: The Complete Guide to LAN Switching Technology,* Wiley, New York, 2000.
16. W. Stallings, *Local and Metropolitan Area Networks,* Prentice-Hall, Upper Saddle River, NJ, 6th ed., 2000, Chap. 12.
17. Ed Taylor, *The Network Architecture Design Handbook,* McGraw-Hill, New York, 1998.
18. IEEE 802.1D-1998, *Local Area Network MAC (Media Access Control) Bridges,* May 25, 1998.
19. S. Keshav and R. Sharma, "Issues and trends in router design," *IEEE Commun. Mag.,* vol. 36, pp. 144–151, May 1998.
20. J. Goldman and P. Rawles, *Local Area Networks: A Business-Oriented Approach,* Wiley, New York, 2nd ed., 2000.

21. J. Knapp, *Nortel Networks: The Complete Reference,* McGraw-Hill/Osborne, Berkeley, CA, 2000.

22. RFC 2328, *Open Shortest Path First (OSPF) Protocol,* Internet Engineering Task Force (IETF), Apr. 1998 (http://www.ietf.org).

23. J. J. Roese, *Switched LANs,* McGraw-Hill, New York, 1998.

24. C. Lewis, *Cisco Switched Internetworks,* McGraw-Hill, New York, 1999.

25. A. Leon-Garcia and I. Widjaja, *Communication Networks,* McGraw-Hill, Burr Ridge, IL, 2000.

26. The website for 3Com Corporation has a number of informative tutorials (http://www.3com.com).

27. The website for Cisco Systems, Inc has a number of informative tutorials (http://www.cisco.com).

28. RFC 1723, *Routing Information Protocol (RIP),* Internet Engineering Task Force (IETF), Nov. 1994 (http://www.ietf.org).

29. T. M. Thomas II, M. J. Newcomb, and A. G. Mason, *Cisco Internetwork Troubleshooting,* McGraw-Hill, New York, 2000.

30. Extreme Networks, Inc. (http://www.extremenetworks.com).

31. M. Smith, *Virtual LANs,* McGraw-Hill, New York, 1998.

32. IEEE 802.1Q-1998, *IEEE Standards for Local and Metropolitan Area Networks: Virtual Bridged Local Area Networks,* Mar. 8, 1999.

CHAPTER
11

NETWORK
MANAGEMENT

O nce the hardware and software elements of a local area network (LAN) have been properly installed and successfully integrated, they need to be managed to ensure that the required level of network performance is met. In addition, the network devices must be monitored to verify that they are configured properly and to ensure that corporate policies regarding network use and security procedures are followed. This is carried out through *network management,* which is a service that uses a variety of hardware and software tools, applications, and devices to assist human network managers in monitoring and maintaining networks. The International Standards Organization (ISO) has defined five primary conceptual areas of management for networks. These functional areas are performance, configuration, accounting, fault, and security management.

In an actual system different groups of network operations personnel normally take separate responsibilities for issues such as administration aspects, performance monitoring, network integrity, access control, and security. There is no special method of allocating the various management functions to particular groups of people since each organization may take a different approach to fit its own needs. Here we use the two generic categories of *LAN element management* and *LAN operations management.* The first deals with administrative and performance aspects of individual network components, whereas the second category is concerned with the operation of the LAN as a whole and its interaction with other networks.

As the first topic Sec. 11.1 describes the constituents of a network management architecture and outlines their purposes. Section 11.2 presents the basic concepts of the five generic network management areas outlined by the ISO. Section 11.3 gives details on functions that are specific to LAN elements directly, such as desktop, configuration, server, and application management. Included in this discussion are examples of the functions performed by software-based desktop, server, and network-monitoring tools from Novell and HP.

The gathering of status information from network devices is done via some type of network management protocol. The *Simple Network Management Protocol* (SNMP) is one example of this, as Sec. 11.4 shows. This section also addresses the *Remote Monitoring* (RMON) set of standards that extends and improves on the SNMP framework, and the *Switch Monitoring* (SMON) Protocol, which serves as an extension to RMON for monitoring switched networks. Using these concepts as a background, Sec. 11.5 discusses the methods and tools used for monitoring and control of elements used within a LAN, for the performance and operational integrity of the LAN as a whole, and for the management issues related to interfacing to other networks. Many of these management tools are web browser-enabled software applications that allow control from a central workstation. Examples are given of such tools from Agilent, Cisco, HP, and Novell.

Section 11.6 describes how software-based network planning and simulation tools can be used to estimate proactively the current use and future capacity needs of a network. Examples are given for such tools from VPIsystems and OPNET Technologies. The CD-ROM packaged with the book contains an introductory program from the tool suite that allows users to estimate network capacity needs based on the traffic generation behavior of various network elements.

11.1   NETWORK MANAGEMENT ARCHITECTURE

Figure 11.1 shows the components of a typical network management system and their relationships.[1–4] The *network management console* is a specialized workstation that serves as the interface for the human network manager. Several of these workstations can perform different functions in a network. From such a console a network manager can view the health and status of the network to verify that all devices are functioning properly, that they are configured correctly, and that their application software is up-to-date. A network manager also can see how the network is performing, for example, in terms of traffic loads and fault conditions. In addition, the console allows the network manager to control the resources of the LAN.

The *managed devices* are network components, such as workstations, servers, switches, and routers. Management software modules or *agents* that reside within these components continuously gather and compile information on the status and performance of the managed devices. The agents store this information in a *management information base* (MIB) and then provide this information to *management entities* within a *network management system* (NMS) that resides in the management workstation. A MIB is a logical base of information that defines data elements and their appropriate syntax and identifier, such as the fields in a database. This information may be stored in tables, counters, or switch settings. The MIB does not define how to collect or use data elements, but only specifies what the agent should collect and how to organize these data elements so that other systems can use them. The information transfer from the MIB to the NMS is done via a *network management protocol,* such as SNMP.

When agents notice problems in the device they are monitoring (e.g., link or component faults, traffic overloads, or excessive error rates), they send alerts to the management entities. Upon receiving an alert, the management entities can initiate one or more actions, such as operator notification, event logging, system shutdown, or automatic attempts at fault isolation or repair. Management entities also can query or poll the

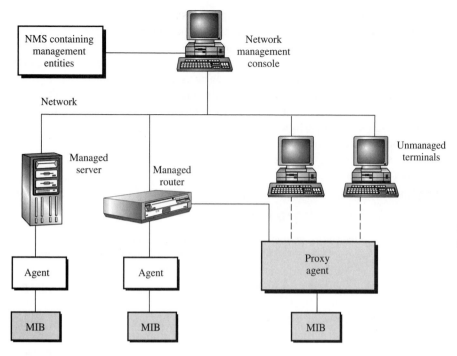

FIGURE 11.1
Components of a typical network management system (NMS) and their relationships.

agents in end stations to check the status of certain conditions or variables. This polling can be automatic or initiated by an operator. In addition, *management proxies* provide management information on behalf of devices that are not able to host an agent, such as the terminals shown in the right-hand side of Fig. 11.1.

11.2 BASIC NETWORK MANAGEMENT FUNCTIONS

The ISO has grouped network management functions into five generic categories.[5] These are performance, configuration, accounting, fault, and security management. The principles for applying these functions to managing networks in general are described in the ITU-T Recommendation X.701, *System Management Overview.*[6] This section defines each of these categories and shows how they relate to managing LANs.

11.2.1 Performance Management

In carrying out *performance management* a system will monitor parameters such as network throughput, user response times, line utilization, the number of seconds during which errors occur, and the number of bad messages delivered. This function also is responsible for collecting traffic statistics and applying controls to prevent traffic congestion. Another performance management function is to monitor and control the quality of service continually. This may include assigning threshold values to performance or resource parameters and informing the management system or generating alarms when these thresholds are exceeded. Examples of resource parameters include memory usage, free disk space, and the number of concurrent logins or sessions.

Performance management also permits proactive performance planning. For example, a software-based *capacity-planning* tool can be used to predict how network growth will affect performance metrics. Capacity planning involves forecasting network utilization and workloads and then developing plans to ensure that the network will be able to support the anticipated performance demands. Based on such predictions, network administrators can take proactive countermeasures to prevent impending overload problems. Section 11.6 gives examples of such commercially available capacity-planning and network simulation tools.

11.2.2 Configuration Management

The goal of *configuration management* is to monitor both network setup information and network device configurations in order to track and manage the effects on network operation of the various constituent hardware and software elements. Configuration management allows a system to provide network resources and services, to monitor and control their state, and to collect status information. This provisioning may include reserving bandwidth for a user when setting up a connection, assigning special features requested by a user, distributing software to computers, scheduling jobs, and updating applications and corporate information to mobile platforms that are only occasionally linked to corporate computers. In addition, information technology (IT) support personnel need to know what hardware, operating system, and application software resources are installed on both fixed and mobile computers. Configuration management stores all this information in a readily accessible database so that when a problem occurs the database can be searched for assistance in solving the problem.

11.2.3 Accounting Management

The purpose of *accounting management* is to measure network utilization parameters so that individuals or groups of users on the network can be regulated and billed for services appropriately. This regulation maximizes the fairness of network access across all users since network resources can be allocated based on their capacities. Thus accounting management is responsible for measuring, collecting, and recording statistics on resource and network usage. In addition, accounting management also may examine current usage patterns in order to allocate network usage quotas. From the gathered statistics the service provider then can generate a bill or a tariff for the usage of the service, as well as assure continued fair and optimal resource utilization.

11.2.4 Fault Management

Faults in a network, such as physical cuts in a communication line or failure of a circuit card, can cause portions of a network to be inoperable. Since network faults can result in system downtime or unacceptable network degradation, *fault management* is one of the most widely implemented and important network management functions.[7–9] With the growing dependence of people on network resources for carrying out their work and

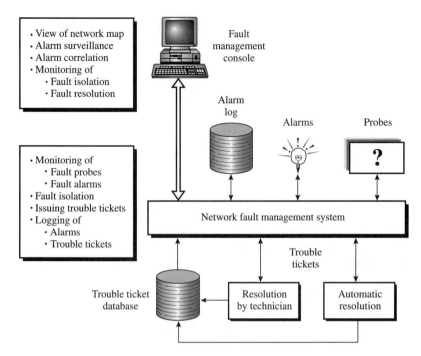

FIGURE 11.2

Functions and interactions of a network fault management system.

communications, users expect rapid and reliable resolutions of network fault conditions. As Fig. 11.2 illustrates, fault management involves the following processes:

- Detecting fault or degradation symptoms, which usually is done through alarm surveillance. *Alarm surveillance* involves reporting alarms that may have different levels of severity and indicating possible causes of these alarms. Fault management also provides a summary of unresolved alarms and allows the network manager to retrieve and view the alarm information from an alarm log.
- Determining the origin and possible cause of faults either automatically or through the intervention of a network manager. To determine the location or origin of faults, the management system might use *fault isolation* techniques, such as alarm correlation from different parts of the network and diagnostic testing.
- Once the faults are isolated, the system issues *trouble tickets* that indicate what the problem is and possible means of how to resolve the fault. These tickets go to either a technician for manual intervention or an automatic fault correction mechanism. When the fault or degradation is corrected, this fact and the resolution method is indicated on the trouble ticket, which is then stored in a database.
- Once the problem has been fixed, the repair is operationally tested on all major subsystems of the network. *Operational testing* involves requesting performance tests, tracking the progress of these tests, and recording the results. The classes of tests that might be performed include echo tests and connectivity examinations.

An important factor in troubleshooting faults in a LAN is to have a comprehensive physical and logical map of the network. Ideally this map should be part of a software-based management system that can show the network connectivity and the operational status of the constituent elements of the network on a display screen. With such a map, failed or degraded devices can be viewed easily and corrective action can be taken immediately.

11.2.5   Security Management

The ability of users to gain worldwide access to information resources easily and rapidly has made network security a major concern among network administrators. In addition, the need of remote users and personnel who telecommute to access corporate data from outside of the corporation presents another dimension to network security. Figure 11.3 shows some points in a network and at its external interfaces where security may be an issue. As Chap. 12 describes in more detail, the topic of LAN security covers a number of disciplines, including:[10–16]

- Developing security policies and principles
- Creating a security architecture for the network
- Implementing special firewall software to prevent unauthorized access of corporate information from the Internet
- Applying encryption techniques to certain types of traffic
- Setting up virus protection software
- Establishing access authentication procedures
- Enforcing network security

The principal goal of network *security management* is to establish and enforce guidelines to control access to network resources. This control is needed to prevent intentional or unintentional sabotage of network capabilities and to prevent viewing or modification of sensitive information by people who do not have appropriate access

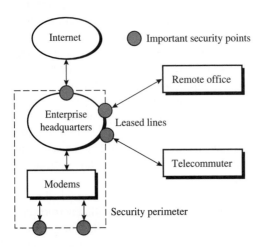

FIGURE 11.3
Network points where security may be an issue.

authorization. For example, a security management system can monitor users attempting to log on to a particular network resource and can prevent access to those who do not have an authorized password.

11.3 LAN ELEMENT MANAGEMENT

Maintaining and managing LAN elements such as desktops and servers have become key functions in running a LAN as network administration has shifted from a device-centric to a user-centric approach, which deals with content-aware information systems that transport both data and voice traffic. To address this issue, directory-based management software tools that can be administered from a centralized workstation have been devised to automate these functions. This section addresses some concepts and functions that are associated with LAN element management and then gives examples of commercially available management software from Multima, Novell, and HP.

11.3.1 Concepts and Functions

An important aspect of LAN element management is the storage of information about people, applications, and resources that are scattered throughout an entire enterprise. This can be provided through a *directory service,* which provides a common location within a network to store, access, and manage such data. A directory service includes not only the storage location, but also the services that make the information available to other users and computers on the network. By using a central repository, the information can be kept up-to-date easily instead of having to modify it in many individual storage locations. As an example, the Microsoft Windows 2000 operating system has an integrated active directory service that uses standard Internet technologies.[16,17] These directory services provide a consistent way to name, describe, locate, access, and manage information about these resources. In addition, this directory service has the ability to set and enforce the security of the information and the service administration, as well as the ability to partition, distribute, and replicate the information.

To maintain effective and orderly control over its network, an enterprise needs to establish and enforce policies and standards for *change and configuration management* of desktops, laptops, and servers. For example, the policies may prevent users from installing programs without authorization; they can specify procedures for adding devices to the network or they can give a user access rights to specific files, applications, and servers. The implementation and monitoring of these policies are done through software-based configuration management tools. These tools contain *policy-based applications* that enable centralized change and configuration management of network devices based on the policies and standards specified by the enterprise. For example, in Windows 2000 this application is called Group Policy, which can provide functions such as software installation services, configuring and locking down user desktops, configuring computers, and specifying a wide range of security settings. The policies can be implemented locally for individual users, at the site level, or at the global enterprise level.

Since a LAN typically supports a substantial amount of equipment, an *inventory management* system is needed. As a LAN evolves and grows, new hardware resources must get installed, old equipment must be upgraded or replaced, new software applications need to be added, and existing software has to be updated. An example of LAN inventory software is NetKeeper Express[TM] from Multima Corporation, which automatically audits hardware and software across a LAN or WAN (wide area network) and interfaces to the help desk in real time.[18] Such inventory software can keep a record of all the operating systems and versions on the network, and can track other data such as vendor names and addresses, maintenance records, and barcode data. In addition, it may keep a list of users, their locations, and their telephone numbers and e-mail addresses.

11.3.2 Novell ZENworks[TM]

ZENworks[TM] from Novell is an integrated set of technologies that enables a remotely located network manager to deliver and manage applications, to configure Windows-based desktops, to repair workstation problems using a single management utility, and to manage servers. Two subsets of this tool suite are ZENworks for Desktops and ZENworks for Servers.[19–20]

ZENworks for Desktops is a directory-enabled, policy-based desktop management application. This tool can be used for automatically installing software and efficiently managing Windows-based workstations in a network. Imaging features are included to install operating systems automatically and to rebuild workstations from the management console, thereby eliminating time-consuming installation trips to every company desktop. All applications delivered through ZENworks for Desktops are linked to the login ID of a user. This enables users to access their applications from any workstation on the network, thus allowing them to reach quickly the tools they need. A network manager can gather information on the amount of RAM that a workstation has, the devices and services it is running, and the interrupts and I/O ports in use, as well as which applications are installed.

ZENworks for Servers is a directory-integrated application that provides automatic distribution, configuration, and management of files and software to multiple servers. It also encompasses sophisticated network traffic monitoring and analysis software. ZENworks for Servers can be implemented from a single point of administration through centrally administered policies. Policies can be scheduled to run daily, weekly, monthly, or yearly, at a specific time, at intervals of time, when certain events occur, or at a time relative to when the policy was last refreshed. The policies can be associated with individual servers, server groups, or organizational units, according to the needs of the enterprise. This enables a network to have one set of policies for database servers, another set for web servers, one for file and print servers, and so on. The ZENworks for Servers tool allows the network administrator to use a web browser to manage and configure all server policies and software distribution services over the Internet. The tool also allows the network manager to monitor and analyze any traffic, whether it is generated by network segments, nodes, switches, or protocols. In addition, it enables the collection of current and historical statistics on the network components and can display that data in tables, graphs, charts, or reports.

11.3.3 HP OpenView Express[TM]

HP OpenView encompasses a wide range of network management tools that are implemented extensively throughout many networks.[21] One of the subsets is OpenView

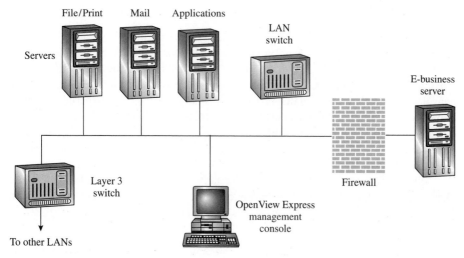

FIGURE 11.4
Example of devices controlled by HP OpenView Express.

Express, which was designed to help administrators manage Windows NT/2000 networks, servers, applications, and data environments, as shown in Fig. 11.4.

OpenView Express provides the following features and capabilities:

- Automatic discovery of the network configuration together with its related environment. It provides graphical displays for easy monitoring and administration.
- Remote user access to reports and messages anywhere Internet access is available. The network manager also can change passwords, restart servers, and perform other administrative tasks for multiple systems from a central location.
- Tightly integrated application, server, network, and storage management functions. Its integrated event correlation, threshold specifications, alarming, and reporting capabilities allow rapid pinpointing of problems.
- The ability to manage a corporate e-business server that is outside of a firewall.
- Automatic backup of key applications and databases.
- Central management of remote backup and recovery needs.
- Ability to restore single files, databases, or complete systems with a few mouse clicks.
- Real-time monitoring and full data protection of the Active Directory Service (ADS) database for Microsoft Windows 2000 management.
- Management of more than 30 applications and utilities from numerous vendors.

11.4 NETWORK MANAGEMENT PROTOCOLS

A number of communication protocols exist for gathering information from network devices. This section describes the widely used Simple Network Management Protocol, which is known as SNMP and some enhancements and extensions that have been added to increase its scope and flexibility.

11.4.1 SNMP

SNMP originally was developed for interconnected devices operating under TCP/IP, but since then it has undergone several revisions and is now applicable in all types of networking environments.[22–25] As shown in Fig 11.5, each network device hosts an agent that gathers information about the status of that device and sends it to the management console. SNMP is the protocol that provides the query language for gathering the information and for sending it to the console. In general the SNMP management system will discover the topology of the network automatically and will display it on the management console in the form of a graph. From this display the human network manager can select a particular segment of the network to view its status in greater detail.

SNMP defines five message types for accessing management information in a client-server relationship. Here the manager is the client and the agent is the server. Figure 11.6 shows the flow of the messages, which are defined as follows:

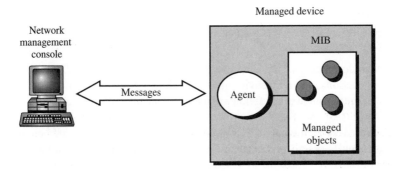

FIGURE 11.5
Basic SNMP (Simple Network Management Protocol) architecture.

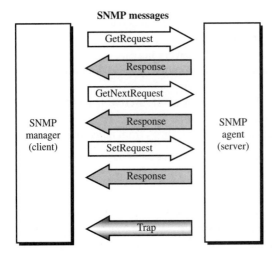

FIGURE 11.6
SNMP message types and their flows.

- *GetRequest.*   This is the most commonly used message and is sent from the manager to the agent to retrieve the value of a specific management variable. The NMS must send out one SNMP GetRequest for each value of a variable that needs to be retrieved.
- *GetNextRequest.*   The GetNextRequest message goes from the manager to the agent for requesting the next set of information. This is used mostly to retrieve the values of entries in a management information table if the network manager does not know how many variables there are in the MIB for a certain event.
- *Response.*   An agent sends this message to a manager in response to GetRequest and GetNextRequest messages. It contains the value of the variable requested by the manager.
- *SetRequest.*   The manager sends the SetRequest message to an agent to create, store, or modify an information variable. The agent must reply using a Response message.
- *Trap.*   An agent sends a Trap message to the manager to report an event when a certain set of circumstances arises. This is done without any request from the manager. For example, if the agent resides in a router that gets rebooted, it informs the manager of this event and reports the time of the rebooting. Table 11.1 lists some typical Trap message types.

SNMP was designed as an application layer protocol in the TCP/IP scheme and is intended to operate over the user datagram protocol (UDP). Thus, as Fig. 11.7 shows, SNMP operates above UDP, IP, and the network-dependent protocols, such as Ethernet. Both the manager and the agent must implement SNMP, UDP, and IP. Note that SNMP is connectionless since it relies on UDP, which is a connectionless protocol. Therefore no continuous connections exist between a management station and its agents so that each message exchange between them is a separate transaction.

Enhanced versions of SNMP, such as SNMPv2 and SNMPv3, have additional message types and allow the establishment of multiple manager entities within a single network. This enables the network to have distributed instead of only centralized

TABLE 11.1
Examples of SNMP Trap message types

Trap type	Message meaning
Cold start	The managed device has undergone a complete reboot, which may result in a reconfiguration.
Warm start	The device has performed a warm reboot, which does not change the existing configuration.
Link down	A link connected to the device is not operational.
Link up	A previously failed link has been restored.
Authentication failure	A workstation that is trying to communicate with the device has failed to authenticate itself properly.
EGP neighbor loss	Communication with a neighboring device linked through the Exterior Gateway Protocol (EGP) has been lost.

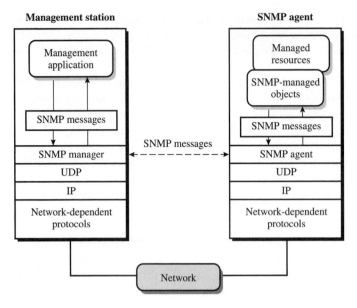

FIGURE 11.7
Operation of SNMP in the protocol hierarchy.

management. This reduces overall traffic since most network management information can remain confined to smaller management domains controlled by individual network segment managers. Information is passed from these segments to a centralized management console via manager-to-manager communications only when requested by the central manager or if certain predefined error conditions occur on a network segment.

11.4.2 RMON

Although SNMP is a simple and robust protocol, the information-gathering procedures increase network traffic and put a large management burden on the central network management console. To alleviate some of this stress, the Internet Engineering Task Force (IETF) developed the RMON scheme.

The RMON set of standards extends and improves the SNMP framework.[22, 26–28] The main document is the RFC 1757 Ethernet RMON MIB, which describes the framework for remote monitoring of a MIB.[29] The basic purpose of the RMON MIB specification is to implement readily a distributed management system consisting of a *RMON manager* and a *RMON probe,* as shown in Fig. 11.8. The probe is responsible for collection of management data. It may be a stand-alone piece of equipment or it could be a software application that is embedded within the managed device. It is now common for RMON probe functions to be part of a LAN switch. The function of the manager is to retrieve the RMON information, process it, and then present it to the system administrator. Representative LAN management platforms that incorporate RMON functions include

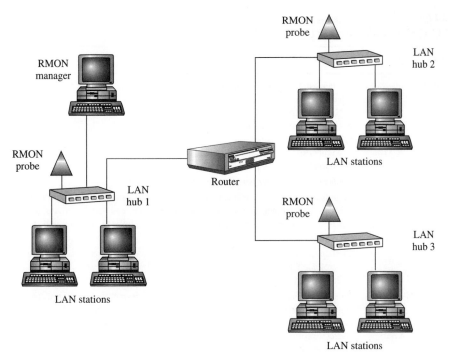

FIGURE 11.8
Placement of RMON (remote monitoring) probes and a RMON manager.

OpenView[TM] from HP, LAN Management Solution[TM] from Cisco, and NetView[TM] from Tivoli.[21,30,31]

The RMON specifications give network administrators more freedom to select network-monitoring probes and consoles that meet the needs of a particular network. By defining a set of statistics and functions that can be exchanged between RMON-compliant consoles and network probes, the specifications provide the administrators with comprehensive fault diagnosis, planning, and performance-tuning information.

Management applications do not communicate directly with the managed device itself, but instead go through a RMON agent in the probe by using SNMP. This setup makes it easier to share information among multiple management stations. The RMON MIB specifications define how the information should be categorized in a common format so that the manager and the probe can exchange data. They do not explicitly define how the probe should collect the data or how the manager should format the data for presentation.

As described in RFC 1757, RMON delivers information in nine *Ethernet RMON groups* of monitoring elements. Table 11.2 summarizes the basic functions and elements of these nine groups. Each group provides specific sets of data to meet common network-monitoring requirements. To be RMON-compliant, a manager or probe can implement any combination of the nine groups, as long as they are implemented fully. For example,

TABLE 11.2
RFC 1757 remote monitoring (RMON) groups

RMON group	Function
1. Statistics	Contains statistics such as the following measured by the probe for each device interface: • Number of packets dropped and sent • Number of broadcast and multicast packets • CRC errors, collisions • Number of runts, giants, fragments, jabbers • Counters for various ranges of packet sizes
2. History	Records and stores periodic samples from a network.
3. Alarm	Periodically compares statistical samples from probe variables with previously configured thresholds. Generates an event if the monitored variable crosses a threshold. Elements in the group include alarm type, interval, and start-and-stop thresholds.
4. Host	Contains statistics associated with each host detected on the network. Elements in the group include host addresses, packets, and bytes received, as well as broadcast, multicast, and error packets.
5. HostTopN	This enhancement to the host group lists the top N devices that generate a specific statistic. The main purpose is to add some time reference to the statistics in the host group. For example, a HostTopN configuration could be to find the top 10 addresses for the broadcast-out statistic during the next 60 minutes. Thus these statistics are rate-based.
6. Matrix	Stores statistics for message exchanges between sets of two addresses. The table entries include source and destination address pairs and packets, bytes, and errors for each pair.
7. Filters	Allows the RMON probe to look for packets that match any user-defined filter. If the packets match, they may be counted and optionally captured in a buffer for further analysis.
8. Packet capture	Enables packets to be captured after they flow through a channel. Table entries include size of buffer for captured packets, full status alarm, and number of captured packets.
9. Events	Controls the generation and notification of events from the device. Table entries include event type, description, and last time event was sent.

on simple RMON probes it is common to see only groups 1, 2, 3, and 9. On more complex probes groups 7 and 8, plus some vendor-specific groups, may be added.

11.4.3   SMON

In June 1999 the IETF defined the SMON MIB in the RFC 2613 document.[32,33] The purpose of this document was to provide monitoring capabilities for modern switched LANs. When the RMON Standard was formulated, LANs nominally consisted of a few LAN segments that were interconnected with bridges or routers. A network administrator could monitor such a network by placing only several dedicated probes on the main segments. Usually these probes had a small number of interfaces through which multiple LAN segments could be monitored simultaneously. Since there was no inherent logical connection between the segments, RMON was able to deal independently with each probe interface. Thus this type of configuration allowed for a reasonable number of interfaces to be monitored.

Once inexpensive LAN switches were introduced, the number of segments increased dramatically since switched networks differ from standard shared media architectures. This is because each user can have a dedicated switch port, thereby becoming an individual LAN segment. If RMON is used in this situation, the network administrator can see only a small portion of the network since a dedicated RMON probe can monitor only a few segments at any one time. Monitoring the multiple entry and exit points from a switching device with RMON thus would require a vast amount of memory and CPU resources. Furthermore switches can create logical segmentation of a network into smaller independent networks, such as *virtual LANs* (VLANs). Because a VLAN exists only within the switch, a traditional RMON probe connected to one of the switch ports would not be able to view all the traffic within that VLAN.

SMON serves as an extension to RMON by allowing remote views of traffic flowing through a switch, views of specific switch-related entities such as VLANs, and control of monitoring-related switch functions. The major addition provided by SMON to the RMON Standard is the ability to define physical entities (such as an entire switch or switching fabric module) and logical entities (such as VLANs) as valid data sources for other RMON groups. That is, SMON treats a switch as a monitored entity rather than as a disconnected collection of LAN segments. The SMON MIB provides an information entry structure that lists the available data sources on the switch and their capabilities. There are also SMON MIB groups that can collect VLAN traffic statistics and traffic in different priority levels since switching incorporates packet prioritization. These two categories of statistics are important to managers of switched networks.

11.5 LAN OPERATIONS MANAGEMENT

The performance and operations management of a LAN requires the ability to configure and monitor network devices quickly and easily so that connections and services are always available. Early detection of changes in network status is critical in avoiding potential problems. This requires the use of sophisticated instruments and software-based diagnostic tools. This section addresses some concepts, functions, and examples of commercially available equipment and software from Agilent, Cisco, HP, and Novell related to LAN operations management.

11.5.1 Concepts and Functions

LAN operations management is concerned with issues such as network performance monitoring, fault detection and isolation, network configuration management, device location processes, remote-access management, and capacity planning. Performance monitoring is carried out with the assistance of agents using the network management protocols, such as SNMP, RMON, and SMON, described in Sec. 11.4. Capacity planning is the topic of Sec. 11.6. The other topics are discussed in this section after descriptions of a few basic concepts.

Testing and diagnostic equipment or software is essential for enabling network managers to observe network performance in real time, to localize problems, and to perform detailed analyses of trouble spots. The two basic categories of network diagnostic tools are *physical layer analyzers* that check transmission line integrity and higher layer *protocol analyzers,* which also are known as *network analyzers.* Protocol analyzers are of particular interest to LAN managers. They can examine frames, packets, data transfer integrity, and session connections. These analyzers also can monitor application performance, which involves measuring parameters such as throughput, error rates, and delay by using software agents that stimulate network use of typical applications. In addition, they can collate, analyze, and format statistics for archiving and distribution. The protocol analyzers can be either a software-based application that runs on a customer-supplied PC or they can be fully integrated portable instruments.

Major network management products contain *device discovery* applications. These applications will examine the network topology, determine actual connectivity at the physical layer, and create a graphical representation showing what devices are attached to the network. More sophisticated discovery routines will try to pinpoint to which hub port an interface is connected. These discovery programs usually run in the background and consume low system resources. They have filters to limit the number of packets they are putting on the network.

Network management tools based on using *web browser* methodologies are now quite prevalent. These are known alternatively as *web-based, web-enabled,* or *browser-based tools.* The basis of using web technologies is the *client/server interaction* (see Chap. 1). A common client interface is the *graphical user interface* (GUI) that supports an application tailored to access web information. This GUI is the web browser, which is used to address a server, to retrieve the web page, and then to display it on the client monitor screen. Browser technology is constantly advancing and enhancing its widely used audio, video, animation, and other hypermedia formats. The popularity of web browsers arises from the fact that they are relatively intuitive and their graphical nature makes them easy to use.

11.5.2 Agilent Advisor LAN™

A widely used piece of equipment for diagnosing problems with network performance is a LAN *network analyzer.* This instrument is able to characterize data packets without interrupting normal network operation. Some of its functions include decoding the packets, monitoring packet traffic statistics, and simulating network traffic by means of an internal generator of traffic test patterns. In some cases the instruments operate at a specific protocol layer. For example, testers that examine the characteristics of the physical level often are referred to as *cable scanners* or *cable testers.* Table 11.3 lists some physical layer parameters that may be examined with a cable tester. Instruments that evaluate performance of layers 2 through 7 frequently are called *protocol analyzers.* An example of this is the Advisor LAN™ from Agilent, which has extensive measurement capabilities on Ethernet, Fast Ethernet, Gigabit Ethernet, token-ring, and FDDI networks.[34]

These software-based fault and performance management tools run on a standard PC for collecting current and historical network segment statistics. These statistics can be displayed in real time for an instant snapshot of network activity, stored for later display, or transferred to a database, spreadsheet, or management reporting program. The systems also include the ability to generate management reports in either predefined or custom formats. Table 11.4 lists some capabilities of such software-based LAN analyzers.

TABLE 11.3
Some physical parameters that may be measured with a cable tester

Parameter	Features
Attenuation	Loss of signal strength as a function of distance.
Ambient noise	Level of electrical noise coupled into the cable from external sources such as fluorescent lights or electrical equipment.
Continuity	Check of an uninterrupted electrical or optical path in the cable.
Loop back	Ability of the tester to send a signal out through the medium and back into itself for link performance checks.
Signal-to-noise ratio (SNR)	Comparison of the signal strength to background noise, usually measured in decibels (dB).
TDR function	For electrical cables a time domain reflectometer (TDR) that measures the time it takes for an electric signal to travel down a wire and back after being reflected at discontinuities (e.g., endpoints, connectors, and breaks). This allows measures of cable length, distance to breaks, and attenuation.
OTDR function	For optical cables, an optical time domain reflectometer (OTDR) that measures the time it takes for light to travel down a fiber and back from reflection points. This allows attenuation measurements of the fiber, splices, and connectors, as well as provides checks for cable fault locations.
Near-end crosstalk (NeXT)	This is a measure of the degree of interference between strong signals that are transmitted on one end of a line and the receipt of weaker ones at the same end.
Wire map	This is a check of factors such as pin-to-pin continuity, polarity reversal, short circuits, and open circuits. Usually it is displayed graphically on a screen.

TABLE 11.4
Representative capabilities of software-based protocol and analyzers

Performance characteristic	Values measured/recorded
Network statistics monitored	• Percent utilization • Frames monitored • Frame size distribution • Number of stations
Error statistics	• Number of run errors • Number of CRC errors • Number of collisions • Total frame errors
Protocol statistics	• Percent network utilization by protocol • Number of frames by protocol • Number of bytes by protocol
Frame size statistics	• Percent of frames by frame size • Number of frames by frame size
Statistics for each active station	• Traffic received and transmitted • Percent utilization (average and current)
Network alarms	• Rate of error threshold • Network idle time threshold • Oversize frame alarm

11.5.3 Cisco LAN Management Solution™

The web-based LAN Management Solution (LMS) is a part of the CiscoWorks2000 family of products for configuration, fault monitoring, and troubleshooting of campus networks. The LMS addresses these needs by incorporating advanced network element discovery technologies, port assignment tools, sophisticated connectivity analysis, configuration management tools, and device and network diagnostic capabilities. In addition, it includes fault management and RMON traffic-monitoring functions. Specific probes are available for enhanced LAN, switch, ATM, and Fast and Gigabit Ethernet RMON hardware. A browser interface allows network administrators to access topology maps, configuration services, and system, device, and performance information from anywhere within the network.

Table 11.5 highlights some capabilities of LMS. Note that these features may change if the software undergoes modifications in the future.

TABLE 11.5
Capability highlights of the LAN Management Solution™ from Cisco

LMS applications	Functions
*n*Genius Real-Time Monitor	This is a web-enabled system for multiuser access to networkwide, real-time RMON information for monitoring, troubleshooting, and maintaining network availability. It can graphically report and analyze device, link, and port-level RMON-collected traffic data from Cisco switches, internal network analysis modules, and external WAN/LAN switch probes.
Device Fault Manager (DFM)	This application provides real-time fault analysis for Cisco devices. Through a variety of data collection and analysis techniques, DFM generates "intelligent Cisco traps," which can be forwarded to other multidevice, multivendor event management systems installed in the network, sent to e-mail or pager gateways, or displayed in the DFM alarm window.
Campus Manager	This application provides layer-2 tools for configuring, managing, and understanding complex physical and logical infrastructures. Campus Manager enables administrators to change, monitor, and control network relationships, making them more effective in delivering business-critical and advanced networking services to their users and customers.
Resource Manager Essentials	This suite of web-based applications offers network management solutions for Cisco switches, access servers, and routers. Its browser interface allows easy access to information critical to network uptime and simplifies time-consuming administrative tasks.
Content Flow Monitor	This application provides real-time load-balancing and performance monitoring of servers. It provides vital load-balancing statistics so that decisions affecting router configuration changes can be made accurately and rapidly to meet changing flow or usage patterns.
CiscoView 5.3	This application provides dynamic status, monitoring, and configuration information for Cisco internetworking products. It displays a physical view of a device chassis, with color coding of modules and ports for at-a-glance status.

11.5.4   HP OpenView™ NNM

The HP OpenView Network Node Manager (NNM) is a comprehensive network management program, which provides concise and in-depth views of network devices and connections in an intuitive graphical format.[21,35] Network managers can easily and quickly evaluate network performance and health and determine where attention may be needed. A further application called Customer Views™ extends these capabilities by providing multiple, hierarchical views of network resources and their relationships. This enables network managers to associate customers with the network resources they use, such as Internet access links and servers and the network events affecting those customers.

Figure 11.9 shows the mapping of three of the views. These are opened by clicking on an icon displayed on a management screen and then using a pull-down menu to access the desired information. The *Customers* object contains information about organizations and the network resources they use. The *Sites* object categorizes network resources by location, such as by geography or by locations in a service provider network. The *Devices* object enables direct management of important network equipment.

The NNM application provides the following features:

- *Automated device discovery* features enable the locating of TCP/IP, IPX, and level-2 devices on both LANs and WANs. NNM presents this information in a graphical format, monitors the network for new devices, and examines the status of previously discovered equipment.
- *Event correlation technology* pinpoints the cause of network problems by letting the administrator examine all events that contributed to an alarm.
- *User interface based on Java*™ provides easy access to network maps and enables management of data from anywhere on the Web.
- *Proactive management through reporting and data warehousing* enables historical data analysis using preconfigured web-based reports. This provides a view of the network devices and helps administrators to take actions that prevent problems from occurring. Topology, event, and SNMP-collected data are exported to the NNM data warehouse, where they are collected and summarized.

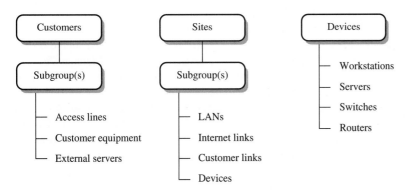

FIGURE 11.9
Mapping of three functions provided by the HP OpenView Network Node Manager.

- *Fault tolerance capabilities* allow network managers to schedule backups of business-critical network management information. NNM management stations can be configured to take over the functions of the collection stations if one or more collection stations fail.
- *Scalability* features enable Windows NT/2000 and UNIX collection stations to be distributed throughout the environment to collect data locally and to forward the data to management stations.

11.5.5 Novell ManageWise™

Using the SNMP-based ManageWise software tool from Novell,[19] a network manager can monitor and remotely control all devices on a network from a single point of administration. These functions include monitoring directories, managing servers, analyzing network traffic, and keeping track of network inventory and health. ManageWise also contains early warning alarms to help prevent downtime by alerting the manager to problems before they impact network performance.

ManageWise provides integrated graphical maps of a network, which allow a network administrator to create customized displays of networked devices that show the actual geographic organization of the enterprise. It is able to locate every device on the network using an auto-discovery feature, and it can create an automated inventory of all network software and hardware (including workstations) simply by double-clicking on appropriate icons. The tool can be integrated with ZENworks™, which is Novell's directory-enabled management program described in Sec. 11.2, thereby allowing ManageWise to manage and remotely control ZENworks clients.

The ManageWise application provides the additional following features:

- The ability to analyze LAN traffic, to identify trends through network usage statistics, and to monitor performance with an extensive server performance summary. It can display any network bottlenecks, identify the users responsible for the overloads, show what they are doing to cause overloading, and segment network traffic to achieve better load-balancing. ManageWise can provide alerts to more than 650 problems through alarms and threshold settings.
- The ability to manage LAN environments from any SNMP-based console and to control networks and workstations from a remote location.
- The capability to monitor hundreds of conditions on each server, including directory structure, disk drive, volume, and memory. In addition, ManageWise can monitor the performance trends of each server, such as file activity, volume data, disk-drive configuration, and adapter card and CPU utilization.
- The capability to monitor, diagnose, fix, and control a wide variety of workstations across the network quickly and efficiently. This includes editing files or demonstrating to users how to navigate an application, communicating with users in real time through their monitors, and selectively transferring files to their local hard disks.

11.6 NETWORK PLANNING AND SIMULATION TOOLS

The large collection of diverse equipment as well as the applications, protocols, and different communication links that make up a typical LAN require the assistance of *network modeling and simulation tools* to predict how the network will function and perform.[36,37] A number of such software-based simulation tools are available. These tools typically include library modules that contain the operational characteristics of devices, such as routers, switches, workstations, and servers, plus the transfer characteristics of communication channels, including various wire lines, optical fiber cables, and wireless links. To check the performance of the network or the capacity that devices such as switches and servers need to handle, network designers invoke different traffic loads, routing protocols, and applications in the simulation programs. This section describes the characteristics of two of these commercially available tools.

11.6.1 VPIsystems, Inc.

One example of a program for network capacity planning is included in the suite of software-based modeling tools from VPIsystems, Inc.[38,39] These design and planning tools are intended for use across all levels of network analyses, performance evaluations, and technology comparisons ranging from components to modules, to entire networks. They are currently in use by component and system manufacturers, system integrators, network operators, and access service providers for carrying out capacity planning, comparative assessments of various technologies, optimization of transport and service networks, syntheses and analyses of WDM (wavelength division multiplexing) system and link designs, and component designs.

The VPIsystems tools encompass five hierarchical modules which can be linked; that is, values of parameters calculated with one tool can be transported to another tool for further detailed analyses. The modules include the following:

- *VPIaccessMaker^{TM}* allows modeling of geographical regions in terms of the density of customer categories (e.g., industrial facility, office park, campus environment, or residential area) and the anticipated evolution of their service requirements. From these inputs the evolution of network capacity and performance characteristics can be predicted and displayed as charts or graphs. These values then can be transported to the VPIserviceMaker^{TM} module.
- *VPIserviceMaker^{TM}* can be used to generate detailed point-to-point traffic matrices from basic forecasts of traffic volume by location, community of interest, and other user-specified attributes. Once the statistics for bandwidth demand are determined, the information may be ported to the VPItransportMaker^{TM} module.
- *VPItransportMaker^{TM}* enables network designers to determine what physical network is required to support this traffic currently and in the future. This includes optimizations for any routing, multiplexing, or restoration requirements.
- *VPItransmissionMaker^{TM}* automatically synthesizes and analyzes the physical aspects of the selected cable system design. This module imports designs from

VPIcomponentMaker to investigate their performance and what effects they have on systems and links.

- *VPIcomponentMaker^{TM}* contains accurate performance characterizations of devices and circuits, which allows a designer to investigate their effects when incorporated into a system.

One particular program from this suite is the VPIserviceMakerIP, which is a capacity planning tool that can help to design networks of any size. This tool can be used by either an equipment vendor or an Internet service provider in network capacity estimation. The VPIserviceMakerIP tool allows IP network capacity design for best-effort services [e.g., web browsing, file transfers (using FTP), e-mail, and news services], voice-over-IP (VoIP), and other services in an access IP network. It deploys traffic characterization models that include self-similarity and statistical multiplexing. The modeling program provides many functions, such as a routing topology check, an effective bandwidth calculation, automatic calculations of interface costs and the number of links needed, networkwide or individual computer group overloads, bottleneck identifications, failure simulations, export and import of user-definable access profiles and device libraries, and detailed reports of all planning data.

The CD-ROM in the back of this book contains an introductory version of the VPIserviceMakerIP program, which is based on a Microsoft Windows operating system.

11.6.2 OPNET Technologies, Inc.

OPNET Technologies, Inc. offers a modeling and simulation tool called OPNET Modeler^{TM} that is applicable to a wide variety of network types, including Ethernet, ATM, VLANs, and wireless LANs.[40] The tool is based on the following three hierarchically related editors that directly parallel the structure of actual networks:

- The *Network Editor* graphically shows the topology of a communications network. The network is built from drag-and-drop node and link objects from the object palette of the editor. The physical characteristics of these objects are configurable by means of dialog boxes.
- The *Node Editor* specifies the flow of data between functional elements or modules. Modules typically represent applications, protocol layers, and physical entities, such as buffers, ports, and buses. Each module can generate, transmit, and receive packets. The behavior of the modules is specified through assigned process models.
- The *Process Editor* uses a finite-state-machine approach that enables the network designer to specify the attributes of the protocols, resources, applications, and algorithms used in the simulation.

The standard model library of this OPNET tool contains hundreds of models of both vendor-specific and generic devices, including routers, switches, workstations, and packet generators. The network designer also can assemble custom devices. The analysis capabilities of the tool allows the user to plot and analyze time series, histograms, probability functions, parametric curves, and confidence intervals, all of which may be exported to spreadsheets.

11.7 SUMMARY

Network management is a service that uses a variety of hardware and software tools, applications, and devices to assist human network managers in monitoring and maintaining networks. In this chapter we use the two generic categories of *LAN element management* and *LAN operations management.* The first deals with administrative and performance aspects of individual network components, whereas the second category is concerned with the operation of the LAN as a whole and its interaction with other networks. Through the use of a *network management console,* a network manager can view the health and status of the network to verify that all devices are functioning properly, that they are configured correctly, and that their application software is up-to-date. A network manager also can see how the network is performing, for example, in terms of traffic loads and fault conditions. In addition, the console allows the network manager to control the resources of the LAN.

Maintaining and managing LAN elements such as desktops and servers have become key functions in running a LAN. To address this issue, directory-based management software tools, which can be administered from a centralized workstation, have been devised to automate these functions. These tools contain *policy-based applications* that enable centralized change and configuration management of network devices based on the policies and standards specified by the enterprise. The policies carry out functions such as preventing users from installing programs without authorization, specifying procedures for adding devices to the network, or giving a user access rights to specific files, applications, and servers.

The performance and operations management of a LAN requires the ability to configure and monitor network devices quickly and easily so that connections and services are always available. The gathering of status information from network devices is done via some type of network management protocol. The *Simple Network Management Protocol,* or SNMP, is one example of this. The *Remote Monitoring,* or RMON, set of standards extends and improves on the SNMP framework, and the *Switch Monitoring,* or SMON Protocol, serves as an extension to RMON for monitoring switched networks. These protocols are implemented for LAN operations management through the use of sophisticated instruments and software-based diagnostic tools, which are commercially available from numerous vendors.

PROBLEMS

11.1. List and discuss the importance of at least four parameters of a LAN switch that a software agent might monitor and store in a MIB (management information base). Include several that are routine status parameters and several that would trigger an alarm if they change significantly.

11.2. Many types of portable cable-testing instruments are available on the market. Using web resources, examine the capabilities and use of one such instrument for troubleshooting Ethernet LAN connections. Consider factors such as the ability to generate and edit test packets, the ability to capture and display real-time data, and what other LAN protocols it supports.

11.3. Figure 11.3 shows some external interface points at the edges of an enterprise network where security concerns may be an issue. List and discuss five points within an enterprise network where proprietary information might be compromised and where security measures should be considered.

11.4. Using web resources, describe and compare the capabilities of at least two commercially available LAN protocol analyzers. Consider parameters such as data rates that it supports, what protocols it supports, error detection features, and recording options.

11.5. A number of Bluetooth wireless protocol analyzers are commercially available. Using web resources, list the details and features of one such instrument and describe how it can be used in a Bluetooth application environment.

11.6. Using web resources, describe the need and functions of a directory service, for example, the Active Directory provided by Microsoft Windows 2000. Consider issues such as simplification of network management, enhanced security, and extended interoperability.

11.7. List and briefly describe some policies and standards that an enterprise might specify, implement, and monitor through software-based configuration management tools. Consider enterprises such as a large manufacturing corporation, a medical research facility, a financial organization, and a government agency.

11.8. Using web resources, list and discuss the functions of a typical inventory management software tool. Include factors such as platforms that are supported, data collection methods, report generation, and query capabilities.

11.9. Using web resources, write a one-page summary of a software-based desktop management tool, such as ZENworks for Desktops from Novell (Ref. 19).

11.10. Using web resources, write a one-page summary of a software-based server management tool, such as ZENworks for Servers from Novell (Ref. 19).

11.11. Using web resources, write a one-page summary about the capabilities and use of a threshold management tool, such as the ThresholdManager from Cisco (Ref. 31).

11.12. Using resources from the Novell website (Ref. 19), write a one-page summary on how the ManageWise software tool, or an equivalent application, handles either (*a*) the discovery process or (*b*) the response to alarms.

11.13. Using resources found either in the literature, on the IETF (Internet Engineering Task Force) website, or at (http://www.snmplink.org), describe some enhancements offered by RFC (request for comment) 2021, which is version 2 of the RMON MIB. Why are these enhancements useful?

11.14. Compare the LAN-monitoring capabilities of HP OpenView, LAN Management Solution, and NetView. Consider factors such as support of RMON, device-discovery capabilities, report generation, and fault tolerance capabilities.

11.15. Examine the capabilities of a RMON probe for switched networks, such as the Switch-Probe from Cisco (Ref. 31). Describe when and where to use such a probe in a network.

11.16. Using resources from the VPIsystems website (Ref. 38), write a one-page summary on the capabilities of their suite of software-based modeling tools. Examine how they can be used to plan network capacity, to predict network usage, and to determine what physical network is required for anticipated traffic loads.

REFERENCES

1. T. L. Case and L. D. Smith, *Managing Local Area Networks,* McGraw-Hill, New York, 1995.
2. R. Boutaba, K. El Guemhioui, and P. Dini, "An outlook on intranet management," *IEEE Commun. Mag.,* vol. 35, pp. 92–99, Oct. 1997.
3. T. Parnell, *Building High-Speed Networks,* McGraw-Hill/Osborne, New York, 1999, Chap. 19.
4. J. Goldman and P. Rawles, *Local Area Networks: A Business-Oriented Approach,* Wiley, New York, 2nd ed., 2000.

5. L. Raman, "OSI systems and network management," *IEEE Commun. Mag.,* vol. 36, pp. 46–53, Mar. 1998.

6. ITU-T Recommendation X.701, *Information Technology—Open Systems Interconnection—Systems Management Overview,* Aug. 1997.

7. J. Trulove, *LAN Wiring,* McGraw-Hill, New York, 2nd ed., 2001.

8. ITU-T Recommendation X.733, *Systems Management—Alarm Reporting Functions,* Feb. 1992.

9. ITU-T Recommendation X.734, *Systems Management—Event Report Management Functions,* Sept. 1992.

10. W. Stallings, *Cryptography and Network Security,* Prentice-Hall, Upper Saddle River, NJ, 1999.

11. M. J. Moyer, J. R. Rao, and P. Rohatgi, "A survey of security issues in multicast communications," *IEEE Network,* vol. 13, pp. 12–23, Nov./Dec. 1999.

12. L. Zhou and Z. J. Haas, "Securing ad hoc networks," *IEEE Network,* vol. 13, pp. 24–30, Nov./Dec. 1999.

13. R. K. Nichols, D. J. Ryan, and J. J. C. H. Ryan, *Defending Your Digital Assets,* McGraw-Hill, New York, 2000.

14. J. E. Canavan, *The Fundamentals of Network Security,* Artech House, Boston, 2001.

15. M. Goncalves, *Firewalls,* McGraw-Hill, New York, 2000.

16. P. Cox and T. Sheldon, *Windows 2000 Security Handbook,* McGraw-Hill/Osborne, New York, 2001.

17. J. Casad, *Windows 2000 Active Directory,* McGraw-Hill/Osborne, New York, 2000.

18. Details of this or equivalent LAN inventory software can be found on the Multima Corporation website (http://www.multima-corporation.com).

19. See the Novell website (http://www.novell.com).

20. G. Foster, *Desktop Management with Novell ZENworks,* O'Reilly, Sebastopol, CA, 2000.

21. Details of HP OpenView™ can be found on the Hewlett Packard website (http://www.hp.com).

22. W. Stallings, *SNMP, SNMPv2, SNMPv3, and RMON 1 and 2,* Addison-Wesley, Reading, MA, 3rd ed., 1999.

23. Useful links and information on topics such as SNMP, MIB, and RMON can be found at the website (http://www.snmplink.org).

24. IETF RFC 2571, *An Architecture for Describing SNMP Management Frameworks,* Apr. 1999 (http://www.ietf.org).

25. IETF RFC 2576, *Coexistence Between SNMP Versions,* Mar. 2000 (http://www.ietf.org).

26. D. T. Perkins, *RMON: Remote Monitoring of SNMP-Managed LANs,* Prentice-Hall, Upper Saddle River, NJ, 1999.

27. J. J. Roese, *Switched LANs,* McGraw-Hill, New York, 1998, Chap. 10.

28. E. E. Stelzer and T. A. Gonsalves, "Embedding RMON in large LAN switches," *IEEE Network,* vol. 13, pp. 63–72, Jan./Feb. 1999.

29. (*a*) IETF RFC 1757, *Remote Network Monitoring Management Information Base,* Feb. 1995; (*b*) RFC 2021, *Remote Network Monitoring MIB—Version 2,* Jan. 1997 (http://www.ietf.org).

30. Details of NetView™ can be found on the Tivoli website (http://www.tivoli.com).

31. Details of the LAN Management Solution™ can be found on the Cisco website (http://www.cisco.com).

32. IETF RFC 2613, *Remote Network Monitoring MIB Extensions for Switched Networks,* June 1999 (http://www.ietf.org).

33. D. Romascanu and I. E. Zilbershtein, "Switch monitoring—The new generation of monitoring for local area networks," *Bell Labs Tech. J.,* vol. 4, pp. 42–54, Oct.–Dec. 1999.

34. Details of the Advisor LAN™ and other protocol analyzers can be found on the Agilent website (http://www.agilent.com).

35. J. Blommers, *OpenView Network Node Manager: Designing and Implementing an Enterprise Solution,* Prentice-Hall, Upper Saddle River, NJ, 2001.

36. G. Kaplan, "Simulating networks," *IEEE Spectrum,* vol. 38, pp. 74–76, Jan. 2001.

37. M. A. Olabe and J. C. Olabe, "Telecommunications network design using modeling and simulation," *IEEE Trans. Education,* vol. 41, pp. 37–44, Feb. 1998.

38. Details on these and related design tools can be found on the VPIsystems, Inc. website (http://www.vpisystems.com).

39. A. Lowery and D. Hewitt, "Network architectures combine broadband, data, and voice services," *Lightwave,* vol. 18, pp. 160–164, Jan. 2001.

40. Details on these and related design tools can be found on the OPNET Technologies, Inc. website (http://www.opnet.com).

CHAPTER
12

NETWORK
SECURITY

A s the previous chapters illustrate, local area networks (LANs) are used extensively in environments ranging from large enterprises to personal applications in homes and small offices. Numerous computer systems are easily accessible, and tremendous amounts of data are transmitted in ever-greater quantities at high speeds over longer distances. This has resulted in higher productivity in enterprises through rapid access and exchange of information and increased convenience of personal activities, such as accessing data concerning bank records and investment portfolios, shopping on the Web, paying bills, and obtaining medical advice and care.

Unfortunately because most of this information has value, it has become a lucrative target for criminals. The content they are seeking in the data includes financial information of an enterprise, competitive marketing information, business secrets and intellectual property, personal investment records, and classified government plans and strategies. Besides obtaining illegal access to information, these intruders also can launch both internal and external attacks against a computer network in order to modify information maliciously, to damage the system, or to prevent the network from being used.

To protect both equipment and information, network managers must consider security measures for a wide range of administrative, physical, and technical issues. To select an appropriate set of network security measures, one first needs to evaluate the threat environment and to assess the security risks to that environment. For example, the threat environment determines whether the main concern is to protect the hardware physically from accidental or intentional damage, to ensure that only trustworthy people are operating and using the network, or to protect programs and data from accidental or malicious modification, disclosure, and destruction. Once the threat has been established, appropriate security techniques can be selected and applied.

This chapter first addresses in Sec. 12.1 some general issues concerning LAN security. Section 12.2 then describes methods to develop and implement comprehensive security management policies. An important element in ensuring the integrity of information is to encrypt the information so that it looks meaningless to anyone trying to intercept it. Three different encryption technologies are described in Sec. 12.3. Firewalls are an important security solution for protecting a network since they police the traffic that enters and leaves a network, as Sec. 12.4 discusses. When many people have access to a communication network, it is important to identify unambiguously the individuals who are trying to use the system. Section 12.5 addresses three basic categories of access control methods, which involve the use of passwords, tokens, and biometrics. The widespread use of public-key cryptography requires a means to distribute secret keys, which is the function of the public-key infrastructure that is described in Sec. 12.6. The goal of Internet Protocol security is to provide secure communications across a LAN, across private and public wide area networks, and across the Internet, which is the topic of Sec. 12.7. Making use of all these techniques is the concept of a virtual private network (VPN), which is a mechanism for simulating a private network over a public network such as the Internet, as Sec. 12.8 describes.

12.1 BASIC SECURITY ISSUES

The realm of network security encompasses many interrelated aspects. These security aspects often are divided into the two broad categories of determining what attacks might (and will!) be launched on a computer system or network and of using various protection mechanisms against these attacks to ensure the validity of information. This section gives an overview of these aspects.[1–7]

12.1.1 Security Attacks

Figure 12.1 shows a simple diagram of an enterprise network that is connected to the Internet. As discussed in earlier chapters, this connection is normally done through some type of router. Threats to the computers and servers on the enterprise network could come either from intentional, malicious external attacks or from internal sources, such as inadvertent or deliberate employee actions. External threats include an intruder who could be located anywhere on the globe attempting to break into servers, transmitting an e-mail message to a user that contains an executable virus, reading or modifying messages that have left the enterprise network, and launching *denial-of-service attacks* that transmit a continuous stream of useless messages which tie up the network.

Potential threats to a network from sources internal to an enterprise include attempts by curious or malicious employees to access and possibly alter confidential personnel information, to spy on business strategies, to read classified documents illegally, or to insert a virus into an internal e-mail message. The degree of importance of each type of threat must be considered and acted on by enterprise network managers.

12.1.2 Information Security Services

Before the widespread use of computers for information exchange, typically physical paper documents were employed in activities such as commercial transactions, personal financial or legal interactions, or foreign policy agreements. Numerous methods,

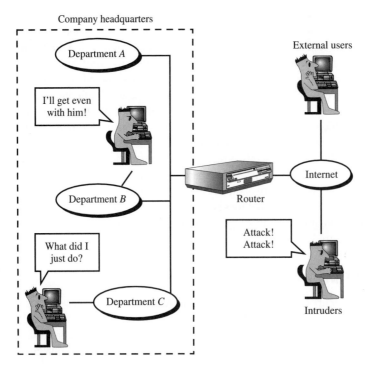

FIGURE 12.1
Some security threats in an enterprise network that is connected to the Internet.

including signatures, notarization, dating, or watermarking, normally are used to give the parties involved confidence about the integrity and authenticity of these documents. Likewise, documents that exist in electronic form need to possess the same degree of validity as paper documents. To achieve this, the following classifications of information security services are traditionally used:

- *Integrity.*   Information that cannot be trusted is worthless since it could be misleading, create havoc, or cause financial or legal damage. Therefore mechanisms must be in place to ensure that only authorized people can modify or transmit information and to detect if there has been any modification, insertion, deletion, or repetition of transmitted data. A common way of ensuring information integrity is through the use of cryptographic algorithms.
- *Authentication.*   The origin of the electronic data, message, or document must be correctly identified as coming from the source from which it claims to orignate. Several methods are available for user authentication. These include passwords and secret-key-based schemes that are administered by trusted third parties.
- *Privacy.*   This service prevents the disclosure of transmitted data to unauthorized parties either unintentionally or through eavesdropping.
- *Nonrepudiation.*   Users should not be able to deny falsely later that they sent a message or carried out particular transactions.

- *Access control.*   Network security administrators need to ensure that even if users are authenticated, they can access only those information and network resources to which they are allowed. Some methods for restricting access include passwords, firewalls, biometric identification schemes, and cryptography.
- *Availability.*   Information that is not available when it is needed is not very useful, even if its privacy is secure and its integrity is intact. If a network is vulnerable to denial-of-service attacks, individuals, organizations, or operations that depend on the inaccessible data may lose revenue, experience reputation damage, or incur operational slowdowns or even shutdowns.

12.2 SECURITY POLICIES

This section lists some issues related to the management of security services.[1,8] The basic steps to develop and implement a comprehensive security management policy are as follows:

- *Identify corporate security issues.*   Before establishing a security policy and creating a security architecture, it is important to identify the scope of the security needs and risks of an organization. An important consideration in doing this is to balance security measures properly and cost-effectively against productivity. For example, if the security access to corporate resources is too strict, then productivity may suffer if users cannot have timely access to needed information. Among the security factors to consider are determining what assets need to be protected, accurately identifying network users, allowing only authorized users to access specific resources, assuring that network-based communications are private, and assuring the integrity of the data on the network.
- *Establish a security policy.*   Security policies must be established to have users follow correct procedures and rules for protecting vital corporate intellectual resources. Among the policy factors are managing and protecting passwords, adhering to software license agreements, using up-to-date virus protection, following acceptable corporate-approved use of the Internet, using correct remote-access procedures, following guidelines for using e-mail, properly securing sensitive computer or telecommunication rooms and logging off computers when leaving the office, and observing policies regarding physical access by visitors and unauthorized personnel to confidential work areas.
- *Create a security architecture.*   After the security policy has been established, the security manager needs to create a security architecture by implementing the appropriate technology and associated processes in order to execute the policy. In addition to issuing security policy guidelines, this includes installing virus protection software on computers that have external access, creating password-issuing procedures, deploying special firewall software to both internal and external sensitive network interfaces, setting up access control to specific network resources, installing encryption equipment where needed for transfer of highly sensitive data, and providing authentication technology, such as smart cards or biometric devices that can authenticate users based on fingerprints, palm prints, retinal patterns, or voice recognition.

- *Monitor the effectiveness of network security.* To evaluate the effectiveness of a corporate security policy, one needs to audit and monitor network security on a continual basis. The audits may be done manually or automatically. Manual audits involve security personnel checking to see that employees are properly following security procedures, such as logging off when leaving work. The sophistication of automatic audits depends on the software used for security monitoring. For example, the audit software may gather large amounts of event data and then apply a filtering technique to look for exceptional or unusual events or patterns. These event data could be telephone calls, login attempts, access to specific Internet news groups or websites, or remote access attempts. From the event reports any security loopholes or weaknesses can be corrected or strengthened.

12.3 CRYPTOGRAPHY

Cryptography, which comes from the Greek words *kryptos* or "hidden" and *graphein* or "to write," is the science of secret communication.[9-12] It is a methodology for transforming the representation or appearance of a message through either a position-scrambling process or some method of transformation of letters or characters without changing its information content. The original message is called *plaintext* or *cleartext* and the transformed message is known as *ciphertext,* which also is called a *cryptogram.*

The process of changing plaintext to ciphertext is called *enciphering* or *encryption.* The inverse operation that changes ciphertext to plaintext is called *deciphering* or *decryption.* Encryption and decryption require the use of either a *key* or a *hash* function, which also is known as a *message digest* function. Using these methodologies, the three broad categories of encryption techniques employ secret-key algorithms, public-key algorithms, and message digest algorithms. As shown in Fig. 12.2, *secret-key* algorithms are *symmetric* in the sense that both the sender and the recipient share the same secret key, which is used for both encryption and decryption. Two examples of this type of algorithm are the Digital Encryption Standard (DES) and the Advanced Encryption Standard (AES), which are described in Secs. 12.3.2 and 12.3.3, respectively.

When using *public-key cryptography,* each participant in a message exchange has a *private key* that is shared with no one else and has a different *public key,* which is published so that everyone knows it. As shown in Fig. 12.3, to transmit a message, a

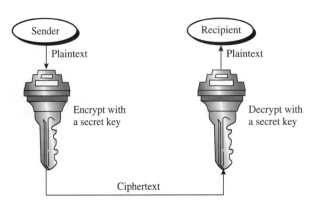

FIGURE 12.2
Secret-key encryption and decryption process.

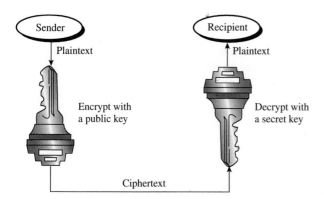

FIGURE 12.3
Public-key encryption and decryption process.

sender encrypts the message using the public key. At the destination the recipient decrypts the message using a private key. One might envision this as a process in which the public key is an open safe into which the sender can put a message. Upon closing the door of the safe, the message is locked inside. Only the recipient holds the private key to open the safe. The best-known public-key encryption technique is the RSA algorithm, which is described in Secs. 12.3.4 and 12.3.5. Since different keys are used to encrypt and decrypt messages, public-key systems are referred to as being *asymmetric*.

A *hash* or *message digest* function does not involve the use of keys. The fundamental concept is to map a large message into a smaller fixed-length number of bits. Two common hashing techniques are the Message Digest version 5 and the Secure Hash Algorithm, which are described in Sec. 12.3.6. A key feature of these algorithms is their faster computation compared to the DES and RSA algorithms, which speeds up the transmission process.

12.3.1 Basic Enciphering Concepts

Two fundamental encryption techniques used by key algorithms are transposition ciphers and substitution ciphers. *Transposition ciphers* are based on the rearrangement of each character in the plaintext message to produce a ciphertext. Some simple techniques include reversing the entire message, reforming the message into a geometrical shape, and rearranging the plaintext by scrambling a sequence of columns of characters. A more secure and efficient method is one which permutes the characters of the plaintext with a *fixed period d*. If the function f is a permutation of a block of d characters, then the encryption key is represented by $K(d, f)$. Thus a plaintext message of the form

$$M = m_1 m_2 \cdots m_d m_{d+1} \cdots m_{2d} \cdots \tag{12.1}$$

where the m_j are the individual characters, is encrypted as

$$E_K(M) = m_{f(1)} m_{f(2)} \cdots m_{f(d)} m_{d+f(1)} \cdots m_{d+f(d)} \cdots \tag{12.2}$$

Here E_K is the encryption function and $m_{f(1)} m_{f(2)} \cdots m_{f(d)}$ is a permutation of $m_1 m_2 \cdots m_d$.

EXAMPLE 12.1

Assume $d = 5$ and suppose f permutes the sequence $j = 1\ 2\ 3\ 4\ 5$ into $f(j) = 3\ 5\ 1\ 4\ 2$. As shown in Table 12.1, this means that the first entry in a block of five characters is moved to the third position, the second character moves to the fifth position, and so on. The plaintext word GROUP, for example, becomes OPGUR. As a longer example, using Table 12.1 the plaintext message

I LOVE BEETHOVENS MUSIC

is encrypted as

OEIVL EHBTE ESONV SCMIU

where we have left spaces in the ciphertext for clarity for the reader.

TABLE 12.1

Example of a permutation transposition with a period $d = 5$

Starting position	Permutation position	Example letter	Result
1	3	G	O
2	5	R	P
3	1	O	G
4	4	U	U
5	2	P	R

Substitution enciphering involves the replacement of each character by some other character. This can be either a letter, a number, or a symbol. The four basic classes of substitution ciphers are as follows:

- *Simple substitution* in which each character of plaintext is replaced by a corresponding character of ciphertext. Therefore a single one-to-one mapping from plaintext to ciphertext is used to encrypt an entire message.
- *Homophonic substitution* in which each character of plaintext is encrypted with a variety of ciphertext characters. The mapping from plaintext to ciphertext thus is a one-to-many mapping.
- *Polyalphabet substitution* in which multiple cipher alphabets are used to change plaintext to ciphertext. The mappings are usually one-to-one as in simple substitution but can change within a single message.
- *Polygram substitution* belongs to the most general ciphers. These permit arbitrary substitutions for groups of plaintext characters.

First let us look at some notation. Suppose B is a *plaintext n-character alphabet* ordered as $\{b_0, b_1, b_2, \ldots, b_{n-1}\}$. A simple substitution cipher then replaces each character of B by a corresponding character from an ordered *cipher alphabet* C denoted by $\{f(b_0), f(b_1), \ldots, f(b_{n-1})\}$. Here the function f represents a one-to-one mapping of each character of B to the corresponding character of C. A plaintext message $M = m_1 m_2, \ldots,$ then is written in ciphertext as

$$E_K(M) = f(m_1)f(m_2)\cdots \qquad (12.3)$$

where m_j is a character of B. Typically C is simply a rearrangement of B.

A historic simple substitution cipher is a *shifted alphabet*. In this scheme the letters of the alphabet are shifted to the right by k positions, modulo the size of the alphabet. That is, if b represents both a letter of B and its position in the alphabet, then

$$f(b) = (b + k) \bmod n \qquad (12.4)$$

where n is 26 for the standard English alphabet. This type of cipher also is known as a *Caesar cipher* since Julius Caesar used it with $k = 3$ to send messages to his general.

EXAMPLE 12.2

If $k = 3$, then we have

Plaintext alphabet: A B C D E F G H I J K L M N O P Q R S T U V W X Y Z

Ciphertext alphabet: D E F G H I J K L M N O P Q R S T U V W X Y Z A B C

Using this Caesar cipher, the plaintext word

LIECHTENSTEINER

becomes

OLHFKWHQVWHLQHU

in ciphertext.

12.3.2 Digital Encryption Standard

The *Digital Encryption Standard* (DES) first divides the original message into blocks of 64 bits.[13] It then separately encrypts each 64-bit block of plaintext using a 64-bit key. Within this key 56 of the bits are used directly by the encryption algorithm and the last bit in each of the 8 bytes is a parity bit for that byte. A 64-bit block of data to be encrypted first is permuted (shuffled) and then undergoes a complex key-dependent computation involving 16 identical iterations of a function that combines substitution and transposition ciphers. Finally after these 16 iterations are completed, the inverse of the original permutation is applied to the result.

Figure 12.4 shows the steps for the DES encryption process. The decryption basically carries out the same process, but in the reverse order. Each step takes a 64-bit block from the preceding step and produces another 64-bit block for the next step. The first step involves transposing the 64 input bits according to the *initial permutation* shown in Table 12.2. This table should be read from left to right and from top to bottom. This means that the permuted block has bit 58 as its first bit, bit 50 as the second bit, and so on with bit 7 as the last bit. This permuted block is the input to the iterative enciphering process.

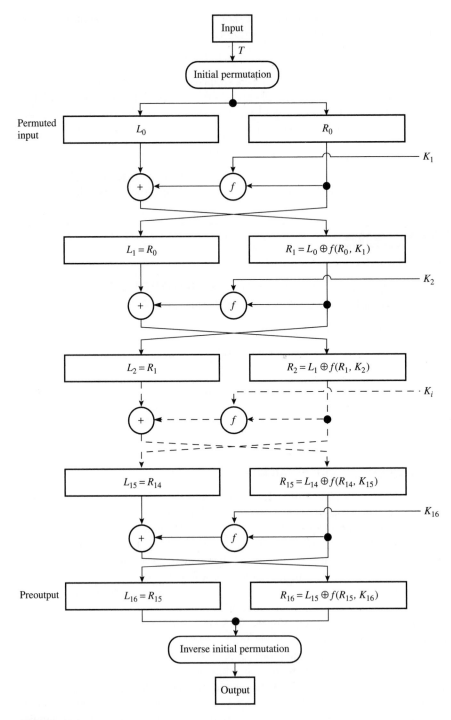

FIGURE 12.4
DES (Digital Encryption Standard) enciphering algorithm flowchart.

TABLE 12.2
Initial permutation IP

Original bit position	New positions of bits resulting from the initial permutation IP							
1–8	58	50	42	34	26	18	10	2
9–16	60	52	44	36	28	20	12	4
17–24	62	54	46	38	30	22	14	6
25–32	64	56	48	40	32	24	16	8
33–40	57	49	41	33	25	17	9	1
41–48	59	51	43	35	27	19	11	3
49–56	61	53	45	37	29	21	13	5
57–64	63	55	47	39	31	23	15	7

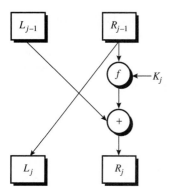

FIGURE 12.5
Data block manipulation at each round of the DES algorithm.

During each round j of the iteration the 64-bit block is broken into two 32-bit halves, denoted as a left block L_{j-1} and a right block R_{j-1}. A different set of 48 bits is selected from the 56-bit key for each iteration. The output of iteration j is two 32-bit blocks denoted by L_j and R_j. As shown in Fig. 12.5, the left half of the output is simply equal to the right half of the input. The right half is derived from a *bit-wise exclusive-OR* (XOR) addition of the left input half L_{j-1} and a function f of the right input half R_{j-1} and the 48-bit key K_j at the given iteration. That is, denoting the XOR operation by $\oplus$, then

$$L_j = R_{j-1}$$
$$R_j = L_{j-1} \oplus f(R_{j-1}, K_j) \tag{12.5}$$

After the 16 iterations the combined 64-bit block consisting of L_{16} and R_{16} is transposed by the *inverse initial permutation* IP^{-1} according to the bit position reordering shown in Table 12.3 to yield the final 64-bit encrypted output. As an example, the output of the IP^{-1} algorithm has bit 40 of the $L_{16}R_{16}$ block as its first bit, bit 8 as its second bit, and so on until bit 25 of $L_{16}R_{16}$ is the last bit of the ciphertext output.

With the emergence of faster computers having tremendous processing power, the simple DES algorithm became vulnerable to a brute-force deciphering attack. This concern led to the *Triple DES algorithm,* which simply performs the DES algorithm three

TABLE 12.3
Final permutation IP^{-1}

Original bit position	Inverse initial permutation IP^{-1}							
1–8	40	8	48	16	56	24	64	32
9–16	39	7	47	15	55	23	63	31
17–24	38	6	46	14	54	22	62	30
25–32	37	5	45	13	53	21	61	29
33–40	36	4	44	12	52	20	60	28
41–48	35	3	43	11	51	19	59	27
49–56	34	2	42	10	50	18	58	26
57–64	33	1	41	9	49	17	57	25

times.[13] With this method a sender runs a block of data through the DES algorithm using a key, then encrypts the result again using another key, and repeats the process a third time using a third key. This is essentially the same thing as using a 168-bit key, which is extremely more difficult to break by an intruder than a 56-bit key. One drawback of the Triple DES method is that it takes three times as long to encrypt data as the simple DES algorithm.

12.3.3 Advanced Encryption Standard

As a result of potential weaknesses in the DES algorithm, in 1997 the National Institute of Standards and Technology (NIST) initiated a search for a stronger encryption algorithm. The result was the *Advanced Encryption Standard* (AES), which is based on the *Rijndael algorithm* that was invented by the Belgium researchers Joan Daemen and Vincent Rijmen.[14,15] This algorithm is a symmetric block cipher that can encrypt and decrypt data blocks of 128 bits using cipher keys with lengths of 128, 192, and 256 bits. The notation AES-128, AES-192, and AES-256 are used to distinguish between the implementations of the three different key lengths, respectively.

The AES document includes the following:

- Definitions of terms, acronyms, and algorithm parameters, symbols, and functions.
- Notation and conventions used in the algorithm specification, including the ordering and numbering of bits, bytes, and words.
- Mathematical properties that are useful in understanding the algorithm.
- Algorithm specification, covering the key schedule, encryption, and decryption routines.
- Implementation issues, such as key length support, keying restrictions, and additional block and key sizes.

12.3.4 Mathematical Concepts for RSA

The RSA public-key encryption algorithm gets its name from its inventors, Rivest, Shamir, and Adleman.[16] This algorithm is based on the use of modular arithmetic and the factorization of large numbers. Before describing the RSA algorithm, let us look at some mathematical concepts related to it. These include prime numbers, modular arithmetic, the Euler function, and multiplicative inverses.[17,18]

12.3.4.1 PRIME NUMBERS. An integer $p > 1$ is defined to be a *prime number* (or a *prime*) if it is divisible only by 1 and itself. If an integer is not a prime, it is a *composite number* that can be expressed as a product of primes.

12.3.4.2 MODULAR ARITHMETIC. The advantage of using modular arithmetic is that it restricts the size of the numbers occurring at intermediate steps when carrying out an arithmetic operation. A key point is the concept of *congruence*. Given the integers a, b, and $n \neq 0$, then the statement *a is congruent to b modulo n* means that the difference $(a - b)$ is an *integer multiple of n*. This relationship is written as

$$a = b \bmod n \tag{12.6}$$

The notion of congruence can be easily understood by considering a 12-hour clock. In giving the time of day with such a clock, one counts only up to 12 and then begins over again. Two integers are defined to be congruent modulo 12 if they differ only by an integer multiple of 12. As an example, the numbers 7 and 19 are congruent modulo 12, which is written as $7 = 19 \bmod 12$.

12.3.4.3 EULER FUNCTION. The *Euler function* $\phi(m)$ denotes the number of positive integers less than or equal to m that are relatively prime to m, that is, having no common factor with m. For a prime p the Euler function states that the number of integers less than p that are *relatively prime* to p is simply given by

$$\phi(p) = p - 1 \tag{12.7}$$

As an example, for $p = 31$ we have $\phi(31) = 31 - 1 = 30$ since every integer less than 31 is relatively prime to 31.

Now let us consider composite numbers. Given the two prime numbers p and q, then for their product $n = pq$ the number of integers less than n that are relatively prime to n is

$$\phi(n) = \phi(p)\phi(q) = (p - 1) \times (q - 1) \tag{12.8}$$

EXAMPLE 12.3

If $p = 3$ and $q = 5$, then

$$\phi(15) = \phi(3)\phi(5) = (3 - 1) \times (5 - 1) = 8$$

Thus there are eight numbers that are relatively prime to 15. These are the set $\{1, 2, 4, 7, 8, 11, 13, 14\}$.

12.3.4.4 MULTIPLICATIVE INVERSES. For certain cases in modular arithmetic it is possible to compute *multiplicative inverses*. The case in point is, given an integer a in the range $[0, n - 1]$, it may be possible to find a unique integer x in the range $[0, n - 1]$ such that

$$ax \bmod n = 1 \tag{12.9}$$

For example, 3 and 11 are multiplicative inverses mod 8 since 33 mod 8 = 1. This characteristic makes modular arithmetic very useful in cryptographic applications. When a and n are relatively prime, then the solution to Eq. (12.9) for the integer x is

$$x = a^{\phi(n)-1} \bmod n \qquad (12.10)$$

where $\phi(n)$ is the Euler function.

Solutions also can be found to the general equation

$$ax \bmod n = b \qquad (12.11)$$

when the largest number that divides both a and n is 1. The solution is

$$x = bx_0 \bmod n \qquad (12.12)$$

where x_0 is the solution to

$$ax_0 \bmod n = 1 \qquad (12.13)$$

12.3.5 The RSA Algorithm

The RSA algorithm makes use of the fact that it is easy to generate two large prime numbers and to multiply them, but it is extremely difficult to factor the product. The product of two large secretly kept numbers thus can be made public without giving a clue to the factors, which effectively constitute the deciphering key.

Figure 12.6 shows the procedures for selecting the keys and performing the encryption and decryption steps in the RSA algorithm. The steps are as follows:

- First one needs to generate a public and a private key. This is done by choosing two large prime numbers p and q, and multiplying them together to get $n = pq$. Both p and q are typically 512 bits long in order to offer a high level of security.
- Next choose an encryption key e, such that e and $\phi(n) = (p - 1) \times (q - 1)$ are relatively prime; that is, they have no common factors except 1. The public key then consists of the set $\{e, n\}$.
- Compute the decryption key d, such that

$$d = e^{-1} \bmod [(p - 1) \times (q - 1)] \qquad (12.14)$$

This means that d and e are multiplicative inverses of each other mod $\phi(n)$. The private key is given by the set $\{d, n\}$. At this point the original prime numbers p and q are no longer needed. They may be discarded but should not be disclosed.

Once the public and private keys are established, one can carry out the encryption and decryption processes. Suppose P is an integer less than n that corresponds to a block of plaintext. This is encrypted into ciphertext C by raising P to the power of e mod n; that is,

$$C = P^e \bmod n \qquad (12.15)$$

To recover the plaintext at the receiving end, the parameters d and n are used as the decryption key via the relationship

$$C^d \bmod n = (P^e)^d \bmod n = P^{de} \bmod n = P \bmod n = P \qquad (12.16)$$

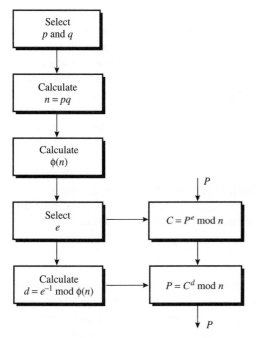

FIGURE 12.6
Various steps in the RSA algorithm.

EXAMPLE 12.4

Let us consider an example of the RSA process using small numbers for simplicity of illustration.

Step 1. Choose $p = 5$ and $q = 7$.
Step 2. Calculate $n = pq = 35$.
Step 3. Calculate $\phi(n) = (p - 1) \times (q - 1) = 24$.
Step 4. Select the encryption key $e = 5$.
Step 5. Then $d = e^{-1} \bmod 24 = 5$ since $ed \bmod \phi(n) = 5 \times 5 \bmod 24 = 1$.
Step 6. Supposing we have a plaintext $P = 2$, calculate the ciphertext C:

$$C = P^e \bmod n = 2^5 \bmod 35 = 32$$

Step 7. Use Eq. (12.16) to recover the plaintext P from C:

$$P = C^d \bmod n = 32^5 \bmod 35 = 2$$

which is the original message.

12.3.6 Message Digest Method

A *message digest* or a *fingerprint* is produced by means of a cryptographic hash function or algorithm that takes an arbitrarily long input message and produces a fixed-length, pseudorandom output. Two examples of hash functions are the *Message Digest 5* (MD5) algorithm[19] and the *Secure Hash Algorithm* (SHA-1).[20] These algorithms may be used in electronic mail, electronic funds transfer, software distribution, data storage, and other applications that require assurance of data integrity and authentication of the data origin.

A *hash function* is basically a *cryptographic checksum* over an arbitrarily long input message, which protects against malicious modification of the information content. The MD5 algorithm produces a 128-bit-long output, whereas the SHA-1 algorithm yields a message digest of 160 bits. The security of these algorithms arises from the conjecture that, given the hash, it is computationally impossible to find a message which produced that hash. Thus if a hash algorithm is used to encrypt a digital signature in a message, then any change to the message in transit will, with very high probability, result in a different message digest and the signature will fail to verify.

Since the Advanced Encryption Standard offers three key sizes of 128, 192, and 256 bits, a need arose for companion hash algorithms that provide similar levels of enhanced security. Thus new hash algorithms (called SHA-256, SHA-384, and SHA-512) have been developed and were issued by NIST in a draft standard in 2001.

12.4 FIREWALLS

A *firewall* is a specially programmed device that nominally is located between an enterprise network and the rest of the Internet, as illustrated in Fig. 12.7. Firewalls often are the most important security solution for protecting a network since they police the traffic that enters and leaves a network.[21,22] The firewall may disallow some traffic to enter or exit and can verify certain characteristics of other traffic. For example, it may discard rather than forward all incoming packets that are destined for a particular IP address or to a certain TCP port. The firewall also can protect hosts within the enterprise network from a flood of messages originating from a specific external source, thereby circumventing a denial-of-service attack. A well-configured firewall is capable of stopping the majority of attacks on a network.

The International Computer Security Association (ICSA) classifies firewalls into the following three categories: packet-filtering firewalls, application-level proxy servers, and stateful inspection firewalls, as the next three sections describe.

12.4.1 Packet-Filtering Firewalls

Many firewall systems are deployed using only a *packet-filtering router.* This is because a packet-filtering feature is included as part of standard router software releases so that no major software development is needed. The firewall router makes an entry or exit permit or deny decision by examining each packet to determine whether it matches one of its filtering rules. The *filtering rules* are based on the packet header-forwarding information, which consists of parameters, such as the IP source address, the IP destination address, the encapsulated protocol, the TCP source port, and the TCP destination port.

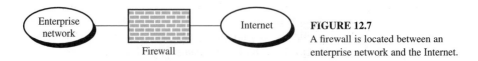

Firewall

FIGURE 12.7
A firewall is located between an enterprise network and the Internet.

If a match is found and the rule permits the packet, the packet is forwarded according to the information in the routing table. If a match is found but the rule denies the packet, the packet is discarded. If there is no matching rule, a user-configurable default parameter determines whether the packet is forwarded or discarded.

Even when a packet-filtering firewall feature is included in a commercially available router, implementing a filter-based firewall is not a trivial task. This arises from the need for network administrators to have a detailed understanding of the various Internet services, packet header formats, and the specific values they expect to find in each field. If complex filtering requirements must be supported, the filtering rule set can become lengthy and complicated, making it difficult to test, manage, and comprehend.

12.4.2 Application-Level Proxy Servers

To mitigate some weaknesses of filter-based firewalls, certain software applications in a firewall can be implemented to forward and filter connections for services such as Telnet and FTP (File Transfer Protocol). These applications are referred to as a *proxy service*. A *proxy* is a process that resides between client and server processes. The host device that runs the proxy service is referred to as a *proxy server* or an *application gateway*. Combining a proxy service with packet filtering provides a more robust level of protection and more flexible access control. Firewalls with both application gateway and packet-filtering capabilities are known as *hybrid gateways.*

Whereas filter-based firewalls determine the *legitimacy* of the client who is requesting information, the application-level proxy function ensures the *validity* of what the client is requesting. This is done by examining the entire request for information rather than just looking at the source and the destination addresses. Connections between the requesting clients and the server that contains the desired information are established only after the application gateway has validated the legitimacy of the request. If an application gateway contains proxies for FTP and Telenet, then only these two services are allowed into the protected subnet and all others are blocked. For example, certain application-level protocol commands that typically are used for probing or hacking into a computer system can be identified, halted, and removed. Proxies also can approve or deny connections based on the *direction of the request.* For example, users may be allowed to upload files but not to download them. Proxies thus offer an important degree of security since they ensure that only trusted services are allowed through the firewall.

Two disadvantages of proxy-based firewalls are the increased latency compared with filter-based firewalls and the inability to detect malicious codes such as macro viruses that might be embedded in an e-mail message. Once such a malicious program enters the system and starts running locally, it has virtually unlimited access to all local hosts.

12.4.3 Stateful Inspection Firewalls

A *stateful inspection firewall* is more advanced and secure than packet-filtering or proxy-based firewalls because it examines all parts of an IP packet when making the decision to accept or reject it. This type of firewall keeps track of all information requests coming from a network, and then scans each incoming communication to see if it was requested. If it was not requested, it gets rejected. After it is accepted, the requested data packet proceeds to the next level of screening software that determines its state. This is the origin of the term *stateful packet inspection.*

12.5   ACCESS CONTROL METHODS

When many people have access to a communication network, it is important to identify unambiguously the individuals trying to use the system. The three basic categories of access control methods are passwords, tokens, and biometrics. This means that the access control scheme makes use of something that the individual either knows (passwords), has (tokens), or is (biometrics).[23–26]

12.5.1   Passwords

A common method of system access is through the use of a *password.* The network administrator can assign either this password or users may be allowed to select their own password. Some security risks may arise when persons choose their own password since they naturally tend to find a word that is easy to remember. Unfortunately this means that a potential intruder has an easier time at guessing what the password is. If users are required to select a more sophisticated password, for example, one that contains letters and symbols or numbers, then they may decide to write it down and to keep it handy near the computer. Obviously this normally is against security policies since an intruder can hunt around a computer desk and find it.

Methods for making a password-based system more secure include assigning passwords instead of letting users select them, requiring that passwords be at least six characters in length and contain at least two numerals, requiring users to change their password periodically, denying or restricting multiple simultaneous logins, and allowing a password to be used only once (which no one likes to do!).

12.5.2   Tokens

A *token* is a small hardware device that fits inside a pocket or a wallet. It could be a plastic smart card, a plastic key, a small USB port attachment that fits on a key chain, or a ring that the user wears. Generally a token contains a small chip with a processor that performs security-related functions, such as retrieving stored keys, when a correct password or a *personal identification number* (PIN) activates it. If someone tries physically to get to the storage space in the device, the token will erase itself. This process is popularly referred to as a *scorched earth* policy.

A *smart card* is a piece of plastic the size of a credit card that has a small microprocessor with memory embedded in it. To transfer the key between the card and a computer, a smart card reader is needed. Smart cards conform to a set of standards, such as the ISO 7816 specification, which define the shape, thickness, electrical signals, protocols, and operating functions that the cards need to support.[26]

Since the Universal Serial Bus (USB) is an industry standard for attaching devices to a computer, one type of available token is a small cryptographic device that attaches to a USB port. These devices are approximately 2.5×0.5 inches (6×1 cm) and have more computing power and storage space, and therefore operate faster than a smart card.

12.5.3 Biometric Techniques

A *biometric device* measures some characteristic of the user for authentication purposes. This can be based on fingerprints, palm prints, retinal patterns, voice recognition, facial geometry, or other physical features that are unique to an individual. To use such a system, a master template of the biometric characteristic is created first and stored in the computer. Then when attempting to gain access to the computer or network, the user will be asked to present the biometric, for example, a fingerprint.

12.6 PUBLIC-KEY INFRASTRUCTURE

The widespread use of public-key cryptography brought forth the need to have mechanisms that manage and distribute public keys. The collection of hardware, software, personnel, policies, and procedures that are needed to create, manage, store, distribute, and revoke public keys is known as the *public-key infrastructure* (PKI).[27,28]

12.6.1 Technology Overview

The principal role of PKI is to establish digital identities that can be trusted. Once they are established, these identities can be used in conjunction with cryptographic mechanisms for security services, such as authentication, authorization, or validation of a digital signature. When using a public-key system, encrypting a plaintext message with a private key and decrypting it with the public key of the supposed sender creates a *digital signature.* Since the encryption key is private, only the holder of the key can encrypt the message. At the destination anyone can verify that the message (or an accompanying encrypted electronic document) came from the person who claims to have sent it since the decryption key is publicly known.

A basic concept in PKI is the *digital certificate* or *public-key certificate* (PKC), which is a tamper-proof set of data that binds a public key to an individual, organization, or system. To provide this binding, a set of trusted third parties vouches for the identity of the user. Such a trusted third party is known as a *certification authority* (CA). The CA implements procedures that verify the identity of an applicant requesting a certificate and then issues a digital certificate which can be used as proof of that identity. The identities are issued for a specific period of time, and the CA has the authority to revoke the certificate and to notify the user of this action.

12.6.2 X.509 Digital Certificates

Two standard digital certificate formats are X.509 and Pretty Good Privacy. The widely used X.509 Standard issued by the ITU defines the information and its format that can

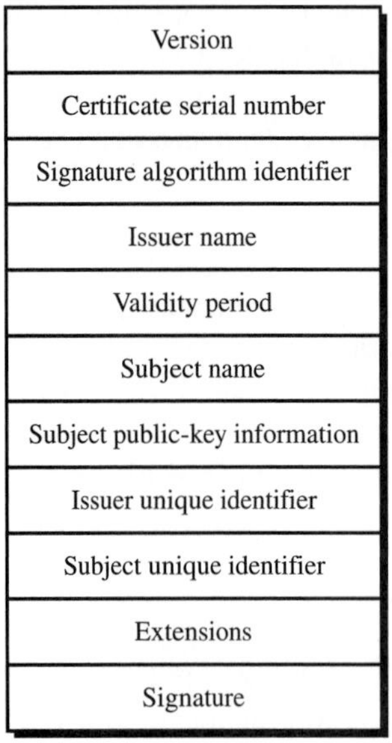

Version
Certificate serial number
Signature algorithm identifier
Issuer name
Validity period
Subject name
Subject public-key information
Issuer unique identifier
Subject unique identifier
Extensions
Signature

FIGURE 12.8
Structure of an X.509 certificate.

go into a certificate.[29] This standard can be applied in both the Internet community and enterprise environments. Figure 12.8 illustrates the structure of an X.509 certificate, which contains the following fields:

- *Version.* This field denotes which version of X.509 applies to the certificate. Version 3 was released in 1995.
- *Certificate serial number.* The serial number is a unique number that is assigned to a digital certificate by a CA.
- *Signature algorithm identifier.* This field contains the identifier for the digital signature algorithm that the CA uses to sign the certificate.
- *Issuer.* This field identifies the unique name, referred to as the *distinguished name* (DN), of the CA that created and signed the certificate.
- *Validity period.* Since a digital certificate is valid for only a limited period of time, this field contains two date and time values. These are the times and dates on which the certificate validity period begins and when it ends.
- *Subject name.* This field identifies the DN of the entity associated with the public key that is stored in the following field of the certificate, that is, in the *subject public-key information* field.
- *Subject public-key information.* This field contains the value of the subject's public key. It also contains the algorithm identifier and any associated parameters of the algorithm for which the key is used.
- *Issuer unique identifier.* This optional field contains a unique identifier of the issuer, which usually is the CA. It is included to handle the possibility of reusing an issuer name over time, although this is not a recommended practice.
- *Subject unique identifier.* Similarly, this optional field contains a unique identifier of the subject. Again it is included to handle the possibility of reusing a subject name over time, although this also is not a recommended practice.

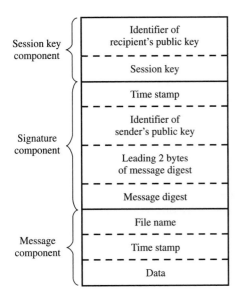

FIGURE 12.9

General format of a PGP (Pretty Good Privacy) message.

- *Extensions.* Extensions provide a means for associating additional attributes with users or public keys.
- *Signature.* This field contains the digital signature of the CA that issued the digital certificate.

12.6.3 PGP Certificates

Pretty Good Privacy (PGP) is an encryption application for e-mail transmission and file storage. Phil Zimmermann created this and published it in 1991 as free software.[30] As a result of the widespread use of PGP, the IETF developed an open specification called *OpenPGP*. This specification is given by RFC 2440, which outlines the message format, standards, cryptographic algorithms, and other issues.[31] The PGP software is available free worldwide in versions that are compatible with various operating systems, including Windows, UNIX, Macintosh, and others. There also is a commercial version for users who desire a product that has vendor support.[32] The software package includes algorithms for public-key encryption, private-key encryption, and hash coding.

Figure 12.9 shows the general format of a PGP message, which consists of a message component, a signature component, and a session key component. These have the following characteristics:

1. *Message component.* This field contains the actual data that is to be stored or transmitted, a file name, and a time stamp that denotes when the message was created.
2. *Signature component.* This field contains the following subfields:
   - Time stamps that designate when the signature was made.
   - The 160-bit SHA message digest that is encrypted with the private signature key of the sender.

- The leading 2 bytes of the message digest, which enable the recipient to determine if the correct public key was used to decrypt the message digest.
- The identification of the sender's public key that should be used to decrypt the message digest.

3. *Session key component.*   This includes the session key and the identifier of the recipient's public key that the sender used to encrypt the session key.

12.7   IP SECURITY

The *IP Security (IPSec) architecture* is designed to provide high-quality, interoperable cryptographic-based security for IPv4 and IPv6 packets since they are inherently not secure.[33] This architecture can provide secure communications across a LAN, private and public wide area networks, and the Internet. IPSec offers the following three broad features:

- Since it is highly modular, users or system administrators can choose from a variety of encryption algorithms and specialized security protocols.
- Users can select from a long list of security services, including access control, integrity, authentication, protection against messages that are replayed into the network, and privacy. A *replay attack* is one in which an intruder obtains a copy of an authenticated packet and later sends it once or many times to disrupt service in some way or to jam up the network.
- Users have control over the granularity of the services, which can range from a narrow stream of packets for individual TCP connections to a wide packet stream flowing between routers.

The two fundamental pieces of IPSec are a pair of protocols that implement the security services and support for key management. The two protocols are the Authentication Header and the Encapsulating Security Payload. These protocols may be applied alone or together to offer exactly the mix of security services that the user wants. The key management part is called the *Internet Security Association and Key Management Protocol* (ISAKMP), which we will not discuss here.[34] The abstraction that ties these two pieces together is the *security association* (SA). This is a one-way relationship that offers security services to the traffic flowing between a sender and a receiver.

An important point in IPSec is the use of a tunneling mechanism. *Tunneling,* which also is known as *packet encapsulation,* is a method of encapsulating a packet in a new packet with a new header. Therefore the whole original packet becomes the payload for the new packet. The new header is added at the tunnel starting point and removed at the tunnel endpoint, where the original packet is recovered. For example, these may be the Internet entrance and exit points along the path that a packet takes.

12.7.1   Authentication Header

The *authentication header* (AH) provides access control, message integrity, data-origin authentication, and protection against message replays. The message integrity feature ensures that there was no undetected modification to the contents of the packet during its transit from a sender to a receiver. The data-origin authentication feature enables an end system or device to verify the authenticity of the data sender or application and to filter the traffic accordingly.

Figure 12.10 shows the fields contained in the AH. Their functions are described in the AH specification RFC 2402 and are as follows:[35]

- *Next header.* This 8-bit field uniquely identifies the type of the next payload that immediately follows the AH.
- *Payload length.* The 8-bit payload length field indicates the length of the authentication data in multiples of 4-byte (32-bit) words minus two. For example, the default length of the authentication data field is 96 bits or three 4-byte words. Including a three-word fixed header, there are then a total of six 32-bit words in the header, so the payload length field has a value of $6 - 2 = 4$.
- *Reserved.* The 16-bit reserved field is for future use.
- *Security parameters index (SPI).* This 32-bit field uniquely identifies the security association for the traffic to which the packet belongs.
- *Sequence number.* The value of this 32-bit field is given by a monotonically increasing counter. The value is incremented by 1 for each packet sent in order to protect against replay attacks.
- *Authentication data.* This field holds a value referred to as the *integrity check value* (ICV). The ICV is the authentication data for the packet and is produced by a *message authentication code* or *message authentication checksum* (MAC) produced by an algorithm that is specified by the SA. When a MAC is produced by a hash function, it is called a *hash MAC* or HMAC. Its length is variable but must be an integral number of 32-bit words. The AH specification RFC 2402 mandates that at least the HMAC-MD5 and HMAC-SHA-1 be implemented in all IPSec applications.

A MAC authentication algorithm takes an arbitrarily long input message and combines it with a cryptographic key to produce a fixed-length output, which, analogous to hash functions, is called a *message digest* or a *fingerprint.* In contrast to hash functions, a MAC requires the use of a cryptographic key to generate the message digest. Typically a MAC is used to validate information transmitted between two parties that share a secret key.

The AH Protocol can operate in either a transport mode or a tunnel mode. Figure 12.11 illustrates these two concepts. The *transport mode* refers to direct connections between a server and a client workstation. The workstation can be on either the same network as the server or an external network. Provided the workstation and the server share a protected secure key, the authentication process in this transport mode SA is

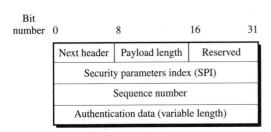

FIGURE 12.10
The fields contained in the AH.

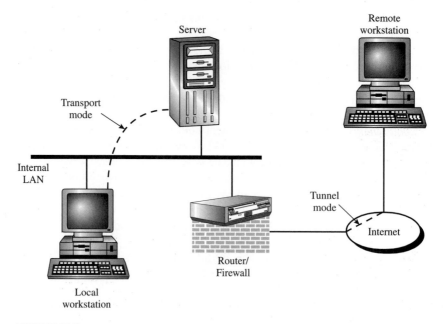

FIGURE 12.11
The AH (Authentication Header) Protocol can operate in either a transport mode or a tunnel mode.

IPv4 AH in transport mode

Original IP header	AH	TCP	Data

IPv6 AH in transport mode

Original IP header	Hop/hop, destination, routing, fragmentation	AH	Destination options	TCP	Data

FIGURE 12.12
Position of the AH relative to other headers in IPv4 and IPv6 packets for the transport mode.

secure. In the *tunnel mode* SA, a remote workstation authenticates itself to the enterprise firewall, which then communicates with the server. The tunnel mode is more useful when employed with the Encapsulating Security Payload Protocol.

Figure 12.12 illustrates the position of the AH relative to other headers in IPv4 and IPv6 packets for the transport mode. Here the AH is inserted after the original IP header and before the IP payload. Authentication covers the entire packet, excluding mutable fields in the IPv4 and IPv6 headers that are set to zero for MAC calculations. Figure 12.13 illustrates the position of the AH relative to other headers in IPv4 and IPv6 packets for the tunnel mode. Again, analogous to the transport mode, authentication covers the entire packet.

IPv4 AH in tunnel mode

New IP header	AH	Original IP header	TCP	Data

IPv6 AH in tunnel mode

New IP header	Extension headers	AH	Original IP header	Extension headers	TCP	Data

FIGURE 12.13
AH position relative to other headers in IPv4 and IPv6 packets for the tunnel mode.

12.7.2   Encapsulating Security Payload

The *Encapsulating Security Payload* (ESP) offers privacy, including confidentiality of message contents and limited traffic flow confidentiality.[36] As an optional feature it also supports the same services as those provided by the AH. The ESP consists of four fixed-length fields and three variable-length fields, as shown in Fig. 12.14. Their functions are as follows:

- *Security parameters index (SPI).*   This 32-bit field is similar to the SPI field of the AH in that it uniquely identifies the security association for the traffic to which the packet belongs.
- *Sequence number.*   This 32-bit field has the same function as in the AH.
- *Payload data.*   This variable-length field contains the actual payload data, which is the ciphertext for the encrypted portion of the packet. This field is mandatory so that it is present whether or not the SA requires the confidentiality service.
- *Padding.*   The length of this field can range from 0 to 255 padding bytes. Its purpose is to conform to a particular encryption algorithm that requires the plaintext to be an integral multiple of some number of bytes.
- *Pad length.*   This 8-bit field indicates the number of padding bytes in the padding field.
- *Next header.*   This is an 8-bit field that identifies the type of data that is encapsulated in the payload.
- *Authentication data.*   This variable-length field contains the ICV, which is calculated over the length of the ESP packet minus the authentication data field. Its length must be an integral number of 32-bit words.

Analogous to the AH Protocol, the IPSec ESP service can operate in either a transport mode or a tunnel mode. In the *transport mode* the ESP service provides encryption and, optionally, authentication for a SA between two directly connected hosts. The tunnel mode can be used to set up a virtual private network (VPN), which is a method of using the Internet as though it were a private network. Section 12.8 describes this type of network. Basically hosts on remotely located segments of an enterprise network interconnect across the Internet but do not interact with other Internet-based hosts. In this

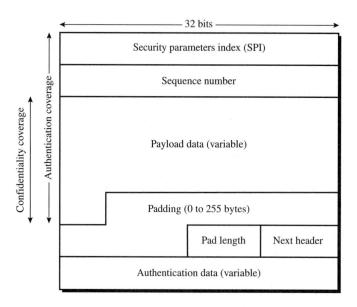

FIGURE 12.14

The ESP (Encapsulating Security Payload) consists of four fixed-length fields and three variable-length fields.

IPv4 ESP in transport mode

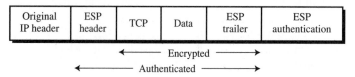

IPv6 ESP in transport mode

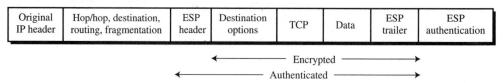

FIGURE 12.15

ESP header position in IPv4 and IPv6 packets for the transport mode.

case the ESP header is attached to the packet and then the entire IP packet plus the header are encrypted. This method can be used to guard against *traffic analysis attacks,* wherein an intruder attempts to discover the traffic pattern between communicating parties.

Figure 12.15 shows the position of the ESP relative to other headers in IPv4 and IPv6 packets for the transport mode. Using IPv4, the ESP header is inserted into the IP packet after the original header and before the IP payload. An ESP trailer is placed after the IP packet. The optional ESP authentication field follows the ESP trailer. The portions

IPv4 ESP in tunnel mode

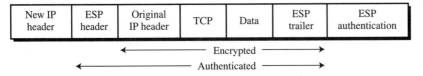

IPv6 ESP in tunnel mode

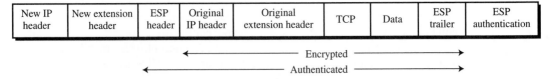

FIGURE 12.16
In the tunnel mode the ESP header comes before the original IP header and a new IP header is added in front.

of the new packet that are encrypted or authenticated are indicated in the diagram. When using IPv6, ESP is viewed as an end-to-end payload, which is not examined or processed by intermediate routers. Therefore the ESP header is inserted after the extension headers. As with IPv4, an ESP trailer is placed after the IP packet. The portions of the new packet that are encrypted or authenticated are indicated in the diagram.

In the *tunnel mode* the ESP header is inserted before the original IP header, and a new IP header is placed in front of the ESP header, as illustrated in Fig. 12.16. This new IP header is needed since the original IP header that contains the destination address and routing directives has become encrypted and intermediate routers in the Internet are not unable to process such a packet. The new IP header will contain enough information for routing purposes but not for traffic analysis.

12.8 VIRTUAL PRIVATE NETWORKS

A *virtual private network* (VPN) is a mechanism for *simulating* a private network over a public network such as the Internet.[37–39] It is *virtual* because it depends on the use of virtual or *temporary* secure connections that traverse public lines between users in geographically dispersed LANs belonging to the same enterprise. Packets then are routed over these connections on an ad hoc basis. The two fundamental security features of a VPN are to keep intruders out of a private computer network and to encrypt all information leaving a LAN so that unauthorized users are unable to read or modify it. A VPN can dramatically reduce telecommunication expenses by making use of Internet connectivity, which tends to be much lower in cost relative to the use of leased communication lines. The main operational concepts for VPNs are IPSec, encryption, packet tunneling, and firewalls.

VPN deployments can be implemented in a wide range of scenarios, each with its own specific set of technology requirements. However, the three main VPN categories are for intranet, remote-access, and extranet utilizations. An *intranet VPN* facilitates secure communications between the internal departments of a company and its branch offices. The primary technology requirements for this scenario are strong data encryption to protect sensitive information, reliability to ensure the prioritization of mission-critical applications (e.g., sales database management and document exchange), and scalable management to accommodate new users, branch offices, and applications. As Fig. 12.17 illustrates, this is achieved through a firewall/router combination, which is referred to as a *security gateway,* that provides an interface between the Internet and the various company intranets (e.g., sales and marketing, finance, engineering, and branch offices). These security gateways are configured to enforce the access control policies of the enterprise. A typical end-to-end connection uses a tunneling mechanism across the Internet. A new header that contains the tunnel endpoint is added to the original packet at the starting point of the tunnel and is removed at the tunnel end.

Figure 12.18 shows the *remote-access VPN* concept. Here mobile and remote workers of an enterprise are connected by means of a VPN using the Internet as a backbone. In this case authentication is critical to verify identities of the users in the most accurate and efficient manner possible. Since the remote or mobile workers could come from different organizations within the company, each separate department subnetwork might have its own firewall for further protection of confidential information.

Extranet VPNs are used between a corporation and its strategic partners, customers, and suppliers. This type of VPN implementation requires an open, standards-based approach to ensure interoperability with the various applications that the business partners might implement.

The accepted standard for Internet-based VPNs is the IPSec architecture described in Sec. 12.7. Other factors of concern when implementing a VPN are bandwidth management and quality-of-service mechanisms to guarantee the reliability and performance of the VPN.[39]

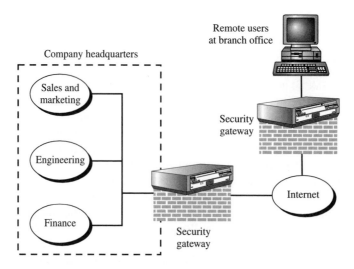

FIGURE 12.17
A security gateway provides an interface between the Internet and various intranets.

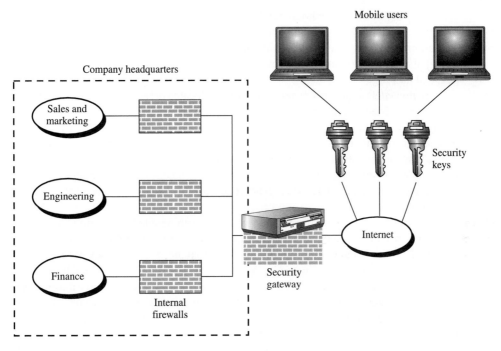

FIGURE 12.18
The remote-access VPN (virtual private network) concept.

12.9 SUMMARY

The growing use of local area networks (LANs) is generating tremendous amounts of data that are transmitted at high speeds over long distances. Unfortunately since this information has value, it has become a lucrative target for criminals and therefore must be protected. The realm of network security encompasses many interrelated aspects. These security aspects include determining what attacks might be launched on a computer system or network and using various protection mechanisms against these attacks to ensure the validity of information.

Threats to the computers and servers on an enterprise network could come from either intentional, malicious external attacks or internal sources, such as inadvertent or deliberate employee actions. External threats include an intruder attempting to break into servers, transmitting an e-mail message that contains an executable virus, reading or modifying messages leaving the enterprise network, and launching denial-of-service attacks which tie up the network. Potential threats from sources internal to an enterprise include attempts by curious or malicious employees to access and possibly alter confidential personnel information, to spy on business strategies, to read classified documents illegally, or to insert a virus into an internal e-mail message. The degree of importance of each of these types of threats must be considered and countered by enterprise network managers, and appropriate security policies must be put in place for employees to follow.

Cryptography is a methodology for transforming the representation or appearance of a message through a position-scrambling process or through some method of transformation of letters or characters without changing its information content. The three principal categories of encryption are public-key cryptography, private-key cryptography, and hashing.

A *firewall* is a specially programmed device located between an enterprise network and the rest of the Internet. Firewalls are an important security solution for protecting a network since they police the traffic that enters and leaves a network. The firewall may disallow some traffic to enter or exit and can verify certain characteristics of other traffic. The firewall also can protect hosts within the enterprise network from a flood of messages originating from a specific external source, thereby circumventing a denial-of-service attack. A well-configured firewall is capable of stopping the majority of attacks on a network.

An important security aspect is to identify unambiguously the individuals trying to use the system. Three basic categories of access control methods involve the use of passwords, tokens, and biometrics. A *password* contains a string of several letters and digits, which can be either assigned by the network administrator or selected by a user. A *token* is a small hardware device that fits inside a pocket or a wallet, such as a plastic smart card, a plastic key, or a small USB port attachment that fits on a key chain. Generally a token contains a small processor chip that performs security-related functions when a correct password or personal identification number activates it. A *biometric device* measures some characteristic of the user for authentication purposes. This can be based on fingerprints, palm prints, retinal patterns, voice recognition, facial geometry, or other physical features that are unique to an individual.

The widespread use of public-key cryptography requires a means to manage and distribute public keys. The collection of hardware, software, personnel, policies, and procedures that are needed to create, manage, store, distribute, and revoke public keys is known as the *public-key infrastructure* (PKI). The principal role of PKI is to establish digital identities that can be trusted. Once they are established, these identities can be used in conjunction with cryptographic mechanisms for security services, such as authentication, authorization, or validation of a digital signature.

The *IP Security (IPSec) architecture* is designed to provide high-quality, interoperable cryptographic-based security for IP packets since they are inherently not secure. This architecture can provide secure communications across a LAN, private and public wide area networks, and the Internet. The two fundamental pieces of IPSec are the *Authentication Header* and the *Encapsulating Security Payload* protocols that implement the security services and support for key management. These protocols may be applied alone or together to offer exactly the mix of security services that a user wants.

A *virtual private network* (VPN) is a mechanism for *simulating* a private network over a public network such as the Internet. It is *virtual* because it depends on the use of virtual or *temporary* secure connections. The two fundamental security features of a VPN are to keep intruders out of a private computer network and to encrypt all information leaving a LAN so that unauthorized users are unable to read or modify it. A VPN can reduce telecommunication expenses by using Internet connectivity, which tends to be much lower in cost relative to the use of leased communication lines. The main concepts for VPNs are IPSec, encryption, packet tunneling, and firewalls.

PROBLEMS

12.1. Write a several-page security policy for a 500-person company that designs, manufactures, and sells electronic equipment. Consider the factors described in Sec. 12.2. A search of the Web using the term "security policy" may yield some helpful resources.

12.2. List and describe in a few sentences at least 12 factors that need to be considered when establishing a security policy for a large university. Helpful resources, including security policies of universities, can be found on the Web.

12.3. Using an alphabet permutation cipher with a fixed period $d = 5$ which permutes the sequence $j = 1\ 2\ 3\ 4\ 5$ into $f(j) = 2\ 4\ 5\ 3\ 1$, show that the message "Why do I have so many homework problems now" becomes

HDOYWHVEAIOANMSHMEOYOKPRWOLEBRSOWNM

12.4. Decrypt the following message which was encrypted using the shifted alphabet cipher $f(b) = (b + 4) \bmod 26$:

XLMWTVSFPIQKEZIQIELIEHEGLI

12.5. Let $Y = 11001001111010101011100110000101$ be the 32-bit input block to the permutation matrix P given in Table 12.4. Show that rearranging Y according to P yields

$$P(Y) = 00110001110010011110100111100101$$

12.6. The basic unit for processing in the AES (Advanced Encryption Standard) algorithm is the byte. For convenience byte values are denoted using hexadecimal notation with each of two groups of 4 bits denoted by a single character, as shown in Table 12.5. For example, the element {01100011} can be represented by {63}. Using Table 12.5, find the binary equivalent of the following words:
(a) 32 43 $f6$ $a8$ 88 $5a$ 30 $8d$ 31 31 98 $a2$ $e0$ 37 07 34
(b) $2b$ $7e$ 15 16 28 ae $d2$ $a6$ ab $f7$ 15 88 09 cf $4f$ $3c$

12.7. Write a program to solve for x when $x = b \bmod n$. Solve the following expressions for x using this program:
(a) 13 mod 11
(b) 87 mod 9
(c) 2594 mod 48
(d) 2^7 mod 21

TABLE 12.4
Permutation function for Problem 12.5

Original bit position	Permutation function P			
1–4	16	7	20	21
5–8	29	12	28	17
9–12	1	15	23	26
13–16	5	18	31	10
17–20	2	8	24	14
21–24	32	27	3	9
25–28	19	13	30	6
29–32	22	11	4	25

TABLE 12.5

Hexadecimal representation of bit patterns for Problem 12.6

Bit pattern	Character	Bit pattern	Character
0000	0	1000	8
0001	1	1001	9
0010	2	1010	a
0011	3	1011	b
0100	4	1100	c
0101	5	1101	d
0110	6	1110	e
0111	7	1111	f

12.8. First solve the expression 3^7 mod 5 using ordinary arithmetic followed by mod 5 reduction in the end. Next solve 3^7 mod 5 using modular arithmetic. Compare the number sizes used within the computation steps in the two methods.

12.9. Solve the following congruences for X in the range $[0, n-1]$:
  (a) $3X$ mod $7 = 1$
  (b) $5X$ mod $17 = 1$
  (c) $3X$ mod $7 = 2$
  (d) $5X$ mod $8 = 3$

12.10. Find all the solutions to the equation $6X$ mod $10 = 4$ in the range $[0, 9]$.

12.11. As a simplified exercise for the RSA algorithm, choose $p = 47$ and $q = 61$. Then $n = pq = 2867$ and $\phi(n) = 2760$. Select a secret key $d = 167$, which is relatively prime to $\phi(n)$.
  (a) Calculate the multiplicative inverse of d mod $\phi(n)$ to derive the public key $e = 1223$.
  (b) To encipher a message, first divide it into a series of blocks such that the value of each block does not exceed $n-1$. One way to do this is to substitute the following two-digit numbers for each letter in the alphabet: blank $= 00$, $A = 01$, $B = 02, \ldots, Y = 25$, $Z = 26$. Using this code, write the message "RSA ALGORITHM" in blocks of 4 bits: $b_1b_2b_3b_4 \ \ b_5b_6b_7b_8 \cdots b_{25}b_{26}b_{27}b_{28}$.
  (c) Encipher each 4-bit block found in part (b) by raising it to the power e, dividing by n, and taking the remainder as the ciphertext. Show that the ciphertext becomes

$$2756\ 2001\ 0542\ 0669\ 2347\ 0408\ 1815$$

12.12. Using web-based resources, describe the capabilities of two different commercially available data encryption devices.

12.13. Using web resources, list at least five characteristics for each of several different types of commercially available firewalls and write a one-page summary of the features of one typical firewall.

12.14. Using web resources, list the characteristics of several different types of commercially available smart cards and write a one-page summary of the features of one typical smart card.

12.15. Using web resources or the literature (such as Ref. 25), compare the advantages and limitations of at least three biometric devices for authentication purposes. For example, the technologies might be based on fingerprints, palm prints, retinal patterns, or voice recognition.

12.16. What are some advantages and limitations of using biometric devices instead of smart cards for authentication purposes?

12.17. Using web resources, write a half-page summary of the digital certificate services offered by a certification authority.

12.18. Using web resources, describe the products for secure e-mail and secure e-commerce for use in home offices or small businesses that a company such as VeriSign offers (www.verisign.com).

REFERENCES

1. R. K. Nichols, D. J. Ryan, and J. J. C. H. Ryan, *Defending Your Digital Assets,* McGraw-Hill, New York, 2000.
2. J. E. Canavan, *The Fundamentals of Network Security,* Artech House, Boston, 2001.
3. S. Kent, "On the trail of intrusions into information systems," *IEEE Spectrum,* vol. 37, pp. 52–56, Dec. 2000.
4. U. Black, *Internet Security Protocols: Protecting IP Traffic,* Prentice-Hall, Upper Saddle River, NJ, 2001.
5. W. Ford and M. S. Baum, *Secure Electronic Commerce,* Prentice-Hall, Upper Saddle River, NJ, 2nd ed., 2001.
6. B. Schneier, *Secrets and Lies: Digital Security in a Networked World,* Wiley, New York, 2000.
7. M. J. Moyer, J. R. Rao, and P. Rohatgi, "A survey of security issues in multicast communications," *IEEE Network,* vol. 13, pp. 12–23, Nov./Dec. 1999.
8. P. Cox and T. Sheldon, *Windows 2000 Security Handbook,* McGraw-Hill/Osborne, New York, 2001.
9. W. Stallings, *Cryptography and Network Security,* Prentice-Hall, Upper Saddle River, NJ, 1999.
10. B. Schneier, *Applied Cryptography,* Wiley, New York, 2nd ed., 1996.
11. R. K. Nichols, *ICSA Guide to Cryptography,* McGraw-Hill, New York, 1999.
12. S. Burnett and S. Paine, *RSA Security's Official Guide to Cryptography,* McGraw-Hill/Osborne, New York, 2001.
13. FIPS 46-3, *Data Encryption Standard (DES),* National Institute of Standards and Technology (NIST), Oct. 25, 1999. This document specifies the DES and the Triple DES algorithms.
14. *Advanced Encryption Standard (AES),* National Institute of Standards and Technology (NIST), Draft, Feb. 28, 2001.
15. (*a*) J. Daemen and V. Rijmen, "The Block Cipher *Rijndael,*" *Smart Card Research and Applications,* J.-J. Quisquater and B. Schneier, eds., Springer-Verlag, New York, 2000, pp. 288–296.
    (*b*) J. Daemen and V. Rijmen, "Rijndael, the advanced encryption standard," *Dr. Dobb's Journal,* vol. 26, pp. 137–139, Mar. 2001.
16. R. L. Rivest, A. Shamir, and L. Adleman, "On digital signatures and public key encryption," *Commun. ACM,* vol. 21, pp. 120–126, Feb. 1978.
17. D. M. Burton, *Elementary Number Theory,* McGraw-Hill, New York, 5th ed., 2002.
18. J. H. Silverman, *Friendly Introduction to Number Theory,* Prentice-Hall, Upper Saddle River, NJ, 2nd ed., 2001.
19. RFC 1321, R. Rivest, *The MD5 Message Digest Algorithm,* The Internet Society, Apr. 1992.
20. FIPS Publication 180-1, *Secure Hash Standard (SHS),* NIST, Apr. 17, 1995.
21. M. Goncalves, *Firewalls,* McGraw-Hill, New York, 2000.
22. G. Held and K. Hundley, *Cisco Security Architectures,* McGraw-Hill, New York, 1999.
23. M. Hendry, *Smart Card Security and Applications,* Artech House, Boston, 2nd ed., 2001.
24. M. Hashem, "Standards for biometric identification," *IEEE Commun. Mag.,* vol. 39, pp. 48–50, Jan. 2001.
25. P. J. Phillips, A. Martin, C. L. Wilson, and M. Przybocki, "An introduction to evaluating biometric systems," *Computer,* vol. 33, pp. 56–63, Feb. 2000.
26. ISO 7816, *Identification Cards,* International Standards Organization (ISO), 1999.
27. R. Perlman, "An overview of PKI trust models," *IEEE Network,* vol. 13, pp. 38–43, Nov./Dec. 1999.
28. E. Nash, D. Brink, W. Duane, and C. Joseph, *PKI: Implementing and Managing E-Security,* McGraw-Hill/Osborne, New York, 2001.

29. ITU-T Recommendation X.509, *The Directory: Public-Key and Attribute Certificate Framework,* 2001.

30. P. Zimmermann, *The Official PGP User's Guide,* MIT Press, Cambridge, MA, 1995.

31. RFC 2440, J. Callas, L. Donnerhacke, H. Finney, and R. Thayer, *OpenPGP Message Format,* The Internet Society, Nov. 1998.

32. Network Associates, Inc. (http://www.nai.com and http://www.pgp.com).

33. C. Davis, *IPSec: Securing VPNs,* McGraw-Hill/Osborne, New York, 2001.

34. RFC 2408, D. Maughan, M. Schertler, M. Schneider, and J. Turner, *Internet Security Association and Key Management Protocol (ISAKMP),* The Internet Society, Nov. 1998.

35. RFC 2402, S. Kent and R. Atkinson, *IP Authentication Header,* The Internet Society, Nov. 1998.

36. RFC 2406, S. Kent and R. Atkinson, *IP Encapsulating Security Protocol (ESP),* The Internet Society, Nov. 1998.

37. D. L. Clark, *IT Manager's Guide to Virtual Private Networks,* McGraw-Hill, New York, 1999.

38. S. Brown, *Implementing Virtual Private Networks,* McGraw-Hill, New York, 1999.

39. T. Braun, M. Guenter, and I. Khalil, "Management of quality of service enabled VPNs," *IEEE Commun. Mag.,* vol. 39, pp. 90–98, May 2001.

ACRONYMS

AAL	ATM adaptation layer
ABR	Available bit rate
AC	Access control
ACK	Acknowledgment
ADS	Active Directory Service
AES	Advanced Encryption Standard
AH	Authentication Header
AM	Amplitude modulation
ANSI	American National Standards Institute
AP	Access point
API	Application Program Interface
ARP	Address Resolution Protocol
ARPA	Advanced Research Projects Agency
ARQ	Automatic repeat request
ASIC	Application-specific integrated circuit
ASK	Amplitude-shift keying
ATM	Asynchronous transfer mode
AUI	Attachment unit interface
BER	Bit error rate
BPSK	Binary PSK
BSA	Basic service area
BSS	Basic service set
BUS	Broadcast and unknown server
CA	Certification authority
CAC	Channel access code

CBR	Constant bit rate
CCK	Complementary code keying
CDDI	Copper Distributed Data Interface
CDMA	Code Division Multiple Access
CDV	Cell delay variation
CER	Cell error rate
CLP	Cell load priority
CLR	Cell loss ratio
CoS	Class of service
CPU	Central processing unit
CRC	Cyclic redundancy check
CSMA	Carrier sense multiple access
CSMA/CA	CSMA with collision avoidance
CSMA/CD	CSMA with collision detection
CTD	Cell transfer delay
CTR	Classic token ring
CTS	Clear-to-send (frames)
DAC	Device access code
DBPSK	Differential binary phase-shift keying
DCE	Distributed computing environment
DCF	Distributed coordination function
DES	Digital Encryption Standard
DFM	Device Fault Manager
DHCP	Dynamic Host Configuration Protocol

DIFS	Distributed coordination function IFS
DNS	Domain name system
DQPSK	Differential QPSK
DSAP	Destination service access point
DSSS	Direct sequence spread spectrum
DTE	Data terminal equipment
DTR	Dedicated token ring
DTU	Data transfer unit
DWDM	Dense WDM
ED	End delimiter
EDI	Electronic data interchange
EGP	Exterior Gateway Protocol
EIA	Electronic Industries Association
ELANs	Emulated LANs
EMI	Electromagnetic interference
ESP	Encapsulating Security Payload
ESS	Extended service set
FCS	Frame check sequence
FDDI	Fiber Distributed Data Interface
FDM	Frequency division multiplexing
FEC	Forward error correction
FHSS	Frequency-hopping spread spectrum
FIFO	First-in first-out
FM	Frequency modulation
FOIRL	Fiber optical inter-repeater link
FS	Frame status
FSK	Frequency-shift keying
FTP	File Transfer Protocol
GFSK	Gaussian-filtered frequency-shift keying
GMII	Gigabit medium-independent interface
GUI	Graphical user interface
HDLC	High-level Data Link Control (protocol)
HEC	Header error check
HMAC	Hash message authentication checksum
HSRP	Hot Standby Router Protocol
HSTRA	High-Speed Token Ring Alliance
HTTP	HyperText Transfer Protocol
IAC	Inquiry access code
IBSS	Independent basic service set
ICMP	Internet Control Message Protocol
ICSA	International Computer Security Association
ICV	Integrity check value
IEEE	Institute of Electrical and Electronic Engineers
IETF	Internet Engineering Task Force
IFG	Interframe gap
IFS	Interframe space
IGRP	Interior Gateway Routing Protocol
IP	Internet Protocol
IPG	Interpacket gap
IPSec	IP Security
IPX	Internet Packet Exchange
ISI	Intersymbol interference
ISM	Industrial, scientific, and medical (bands)
ISO	International Standards Organization
ISP	Internet service provider
IT	Information technology
ITU	International Telecommunications Union
JBOD	Just a bunch of disks
LAN	Local area network
LANE	LAN emulation
LEC	LAN emulation client
LES	LAN emulation server
LLC	Logical link control
LRC	Longitudinal redundancy check
MAC	Medium access control
MAC	Message authentication checksum
MAN	Metropolitan area network
MAU	Medium access unit

MDI	Medium-dependent interface
MIB	Management information base
MID	Multiplexing identification
MII	Medium-independent interface
MIS	Management information systems
MLT	Multilevel transmission
MSDU	MAC service data unit
NAK	Negative acknowledgment
NAP	Network access point
NAU	Network access unit
NFS	Network file system
NIC	Network interface card
NIST	National Institute of Standards & Technology
NMS	Network management system
NNI	Network-to-network interface
NNM	Network Node Manger
NRZ	Nonreturn-to-zero (code)
NSP	Network service provider
OFC	Open fiber control
OFDM	Orthogonal frequency division multiplexing
OOK	On-off-keying
ORB	Object Request Broker
OSI	Open System Interconnection
OSPF	Open Shortest Path First (protocol)
OTDR	Optical time domain reflectometer
PAM	Pulse amplitude modulation
PAN	Personal area network
PAR	Positive acknowledgment retransmit
PCF	Point coordination function
PCM	Pulse code modulation
PCS	Personal communication system
PDA	Personal digital assistant
PDU	Protocol data unit
PGP	Pretty Good Privacy (protocol)
PHY	Physical layer
PIM	Protocol-independent multicast (sublayer)
PIN	Personal identification number
PKC	Public-key certificate
PKI	Public-key infrastructure
PLCP	Physical layer convergence procedure
PLS	Physical signaling (sublayer)
PM	Phase modulation
PMA	Physical medium attachment (sublayer)
PMD	Physical medium dependent (sublayer)
PMI	Physical medium-independent (sublayer)
POF	Plastic optical fibers
PPDU	PLCP protocol data unit
PPM	Pulse position modulation
PSDU	PLCP service data unit
PSK	Phase-shift keying
PVC	Permanent virtual circuit
QAM	Quadrature amplitude modulation
QoS	Quality of service
QPSK	Quadrature phase-shift keying
RAID	Redundant array of inexpensive disks
RAM	Random-access memory
RARP	Reverse Address Resolution Protocol
RFC	Request for Comment
RIF	Routing information field
RIP	Routing Information Protocol
RMON	Remote monitoring
ROM	Read-only memory
RPC	Remote procedure call
RSA	Rivest, Shamir, and Adleman (algorithm)
SA	Security association
SAN	Storage area network

SAP	Service access point
SAR	Segmentation and reassembly
SCR	Sustained cell rate
SCSI	Small Computer Systems Interface
SD	Start delimiter
SDU	Service data unit
SFD	Start frame delimiter
SHA	Secure Hash Algorithm
SIFS	Short interframe space
SMON	Switch monitoring
SMT	Station management
SMTP	Simple Mail Transfer Protocol
SNA	Systems Network Architecture
SNMP	Simple Network Management Protocol
SNR	Signal-to-noise ratio
SOHO	Small office/home office
SONET	Synchronous Optical Network
SPI	Security parameter index
SQL	Standard query language
SRT	Source routing transparent
SSAP	Source service access point
STP	Shielded twisted-pair (wires)
SVC	Switched virtual circuit
SWAP	Shared Wireless Access Protocol
TAG	Technical Advisory Group
TCP	Transmission Control Protocol
TDM	Time division multiplexing
TDR	Time domain reflectometer

TELNET	Terminal networking
TFTP	Trivial File Transfer Protocol
TIA	Telecommunication Industries Association
TKP	Token-Passing Access Protocol
UBR	Unspecified bit rate
UDP	User Datagram Protocol
UNI	User-to-network interface
UNII	Unlicensed national information infrastructure
USB	Universal Serial Bus
UTP	Unshielded twisted-pair (wires)
VBR	Variable bit rate
VC	Virtual circuit
VCI	Virtual channel identifier; virtual circuit identifier
VCN	Virtual circuit network
VLAN	Virtual LAN
VoIP	Voice-over-IP
VP	Virtual path
VPI	Virtual path identifier
VPN	Virtual private network
VRC	Virtual redundancy check
WAIS	Wide area information service
WAN	Wide area network
WDM	Wavelength division multiplexing
WEP	Wired Equivalent Privacy
WLAN	Wireless LAN
WLANA	Wireless LAN Association
WWW	World Wide Web

INDEX